AIRBORNE OPERATIONS

Field Manual
No. 90-26

FM 90-26
Headquarters
Department of the Army
Washington, DC, 18 December 1990

AIRBORNE OPERATIONS

CONTENTS

Page

Preface vii

CHAPTER 1. INTRODUCTION

1-1.	Preparation for War	1-2
1-2.	The Soldier	1-2
1-3.	The Leader	1-2
1-4.	The Unit	1-2
1-5.	Unit Training Program	1-3
1-6.	Capabilities of Airborne Forces	1-3
1-7.	Missions of Airborne Forces	1-4
1-8.	Fundamentals of Airborne Operations	1-5
1-9.	Characteristics of Airborne Operations	1-5
1-10.	Limitations of Airborne Forces	1-6
1-11.	Phases of Airborne Operations	1-6
1-12.	Battlefield Operating Systems and Airborne Operations	1-7

CHAPTER 2. AIRBORNE PLANNING

Section I. FUNDAMENTALS

2-1.	Planning Responsibilities	2-1
2-2.	Key Personnel Responsibilities	2-2

Distribution Restriction: Approved for public release; distribution is unlimited

i

FM 90-26

Page

Section II. PREPARATION OF PLANS AND ORDERS

2-3. Commander's Estimate of the Situation 2-3
2-4. Reverse Planning Process 2-3
2-5. Planning Considerations 2-7

CHAPTER 3. GROUND TACTICAL PLAN

Section I. PLANNING

3-1. Estimate of the Situation 3-1
3-2. Development of the Ground Tactical Plan 3-4
3-3. Selection of Assault Objectives and Airhead Line 3-4
3-4. Reconnaissance and Security Forces 3-7
3-5. Boundaries and Task Organization 3-8
3-6. Designation of Reserve 3-11

Section II. EXECUTION

3-7. Conduct of the Assault 3-12
3-8. Development of the Airhead 3-14
3-9. Buildup of Combat Power 3-14

CHAPTER 4. LANDING PLAN

Section I. PLANNING

4-1. Requirements 4-2
4-2. Considerations 4-3
4-3. Sequence of Delivery 4-4
4-4. Method of Delivery 4-5
4-5. Place of Delivery 4-10
4-6. Time of Delivery 4-14

Section II. ASSEMBLY AND REORGANIZATION

4-7. Cross Loading 4-15
4-8. Assembly Techniques 4-16
4-9. Assembly Aids 4-16
4-10. Assembly Plan 4-21
4-11. Unit Assembly 4-22
4-12. Multiple-Lateral Impact Points 4-24
4-13. Keys to Rapid Assembly 4-25
4-14. Activities in Assembly Areas 4-25
4-15. Departure from the Assembly Area 4-25
4-16. Reports 4-26
4-17. Security Measures 4-26
4-18. Reorganization 4-27
4-19. Briefbacks 4-28

Page

CHAPTER 5. AIR MOVEMENT PLAN

5-1. Joint Planning 5-1
5-2. Elements 5-1
5-3. Types of Movement 5-2
5-4. Aircraft Requirements 5-2
5-5. Load Planning Considerations 5-3
5-6. Load Planning Sequence 5-6
5-7. Load Planning of Vehicles 5-6
5-8. Air Movement Planning Worksheet 5-8
5-9. Basic Planning Guide Form 5-8
5-10. Unit Aircraft Utilization Plan 5-10
5-11. Aircraft Loading Tables 5-10
5-12. Development of Aircraft Loads 5-10
5-13. Air Movement Table 5-12
5-14. Manifests 5-13
5-15. Automated Airload Planning System 5-13

CHAPTER 6. MARSHALING

Section I. THE MARSHALING PLAN

6-1. Preparation Before Marshaling 6-1
6-2. Movement to the Marshaling Area 6-2
6-3. Passive Defense Measures 6-3
6-4. Dispersal Procedures 6-3
6-5. Selection of Departure Airfields 6-4
6-6. Selection and Operation of Marshaling Camps 6-4
6-7. Facility Requirements 6-5
6-8. Staff and Support Agency Responsibilities 6-10

Section II. OUTLOAD

6-9. Outload Plan 6-12
6-10. Outload Procedures 6-14

CHAPTER 7. TACTICAL OPERATIONS

Section I. GROUND TACTICAL OPERATION

7-1. Raids 7-1
7-2. Recovery Operations 7-4
7-3. Withdrawal/Evacuation of Units 7-6
7-4. Linkup 7-7
7-5. Exfiltration 7-8
7-6. Survival Operation 7-9
7-7. Breakout from Encirclement 7-9
7-8. Relief 7-10

FM 90-26

Page

Section II. AIRFIELD SEIZURE

7-9. Requirements 7-10
7-10. Sequence of Operations.. 7-13
7-11. Security Force Operations.. 7-14
7-12. Noncombatant Evacuation Operations 7-14

Section III. SUPPORTING OPERATIONS

7-13. Remote Marshaling Base 7-17
7-14. Intermediate Staging Base.. 7-18
7-15. Forward Operating Base 7-19

CHAPTER 8. COMBAT SUPPORT

Section I. COMMAND AND SUPPORT RELATIONSHIPS

8-1. Elements 8-1
8-2. Decentralization.. 8-1

Section II. FIRE SUPPORT

8-3. Unique Aspects... 8-2
8-4. Missions 8-3
8-5. Principles 8-4
8-6. Planning 8-5
8-7. Artillery Employment 8-6

Section III. NAVAL GUNFIRE

8-8. Air and Naval Gunfire Liaison Company.. 8-7
8-9. ANGLICO Organization.. 8-7
8-10. Tactical Missions 8-8
8-11. Coordination and Control Measures 8-9

Section IV. AIR FORCE SUPPORT

8-12. Types of Missions 8-9
8-13. Organization of Tactical Air Support 8-10
8-14. Planning Tactical Air Support 8-11
8-15. Command and Control 8-11
8-16. Air Traffic Control 8-12

Section V. ARMY AVIATION OPERATIONS

8-17. Helicopter Tactical Missions 8-12
8-18. Deployment 8-13

Section VI. AIR DEFENSE

8-19. Air Defense Artillery Elements.. 8-14
8-20. Early Warning.. 8-15

FM 90-26

Page

Section VII. ENGINEER SUPPORT

8-21. Engineer Employment 8-16
8-22. Tactical Missions 8-16

Section VIII. FORWARD AVIATION COMBAT ENGINEERING

8-23. Capabilities 8-17
8-24. Responsibilities 8-18
8-25. Planning 8-18
8-26. Site Selection 8-18
8-27. Expedient Surfacing 8-19
8-28. Repair of Captured Facilities 8-19
8-29. Engineer Packages 8-19

Section IX. INTELLIGENCE AND ELECTRONIC WARFARE SUPPORT

8-30. Interrogation Support 8-22
8-31. Counterintelligence Support 8-22
8-32. Electronic Warfare/Signal Intelligence Assets 8-23
8-33. Remote Sensors 8-24
8-34. Ground Surveillance Radars 8-25
8-35. Employment 8-26

Section X. SIGNAL SUPPORT

8-36. Joint Airborne Communications Center/Command Post 8-26
8-37. Aircraft Communications 8-26
8-38. Radar Beacons 8-28

Section XI. MILITARY POLICE SUPPORT

8-39. Military Police (Airborne) Structure 8-32
8-40. Military Police Operations 8-33

Section XII. NUCLEAR, BIOLOGICAL, AND CHEMICAL PLANNING

8-41. Command and Staff Responsibilities 8-33
8-42. Chemical Staff 8-34
8-43. Unit Protective Measures 8-34
8-44. Defense Against Chemical Attack 8-36
8-45. Mission-Oriented Protection Posture 8-36
8-46. Decontamination 8-39

CHAPTER 9. COMBAT SERVICE SUPPORT

Section I. LOGISTICAL PLANS AND PREPARATIONS

9-1. Logistical Structure 9-1
9-2. Logistical Planning Responsibilities 9-2
9-3. Logistical Planning Considerations 9-3
9-4. Phases of Supply 9-5
9-5. Classes of Supply 9-6

v

Page

9-6.	Distribution of Supply.	9-8
9-7.	Resupply by Air	9-9
9-8.	Maintenance	9-9
9-9.	Transportation	9-12
9-10.	Field Services	9-12

Section II. PERSONNEL PLANS AND PREPARATION

9-11.	Personnel Strength Accounting	9-13
9-12.	Personnel Replacement Operations	9-13
9-13.	Casualty Reporting	9-14
9-14.	Health Service Support	9-14
9-15.	Prisoners of War and Captured Materiel	9-17
9-16.	Other Personnel Service Support.	9-19
9-17.	Civil Affairs	9-20

CHAPTER 10. COMMUNICATIONS

10-1.	Fundamentals for Using Signal Facilities	10-2
10-2.	Considerations	10-3
10-3.	Communication Plans	10-4
10-4.	Army Nets	10-6
10-5.	Techniques	10-17
10-6.	Airspace Control	10-18
10-7.	Electronic Warfare Planning	10-18

APPENDIX A. JOINT AIRBORNE ADVANCE PARTY ... A-1

APPENDIX B. DROP ZONE SUPPORT TEAMS ... B-1

APPENDIX C. AIRLIFT PLANNING FACTORS ... C-1

APPENDIX D. AIRBORNE ELEMENTS OF THE TACTICAL AIR CONTROL SYSTEM ... D-1

APPENDIX E. BRIEFINGS, INSPECTIONS, AND REHEARSALS ... E-1

APPENDIX F. INTELLIGENCE PREPARATION OF THE BATTLEFIELD ... F-1

APPENDIX G. N-HOUR DEPLOYMENT SEQUENCE ... G-1

Glossary ... Glossary-1

References ... References-1

Index ... Index-1

PREFACE

This manual discusses the employment of airborne brigades, battalions, and regiments in airborne operations within the context of the AirLand Battle. It sets forth tactical and administrative support doctrine for the employment of Army forces in joint airborne operations. It discusses command and staff procedures, tactics, and techniques used in the planning and execution of parachute operations at brigade and lower echelons.

The discussions are written in general terms so they apply to brigade or smaller units taking part in joint airborne operations. For this reason, the term "airborne force" is used to refer to the Army component in the operation.

The principal tactics and techniques peculiar to airborne operations are of primary concern. Details of unit organization/capabilities, and guidance for employment of units in other than airborne operations are in other field manuals.

This publication implements the following international agreements: STANAG 3466/ASCC 44/18C, Responsibilities of Air Transport Units and User Units in the Loading and Unloading of Transport Aircraft in Tactical Air Transport Operations and STANAG 3570/ASCC 44/13G, Drop Zones and Extraction Zones–Criteria and Markings.

The proponent of this publication is US Army Infantry School. Send comments and recommendations on DA Form 2028 (Recommended Changes to Publications and Blank Forms) directly to the Commandant, United States Army Infantry School, ATTN: ATSH-ATD, Fort Benning, Georgia 31905-5410.

Unless this publication states otherwise, masculine nouns and pronouns do not refer exclusively to men.

CHAPTER 1

INTRODUCTION

Airborne forces of the US Army have often demonstrated their ability to conduct decisive, short notice, forced entry operations deep into enemy territory. They seize and maintain the initiative until follow-on forces are committed to the fight and then move to hit the enemy where he is the most vulnerable. The ability to rapidly deploy, land, and sustain a powerful ground combat force is vital to US interests and worldwide commitments.

From their origins early in World War II, the US Army's airborne forces have dramatically demonstrated their responsiveness and flexibility many times on DZs and battlefields all over the world. As the threat of regional conflict has grown, the XVIII Airborne Corps, the 82d Airborne Division, and the 75th Ranger Regiment have demonstrated that well-trained, determined airborne soldiers armed with modern light weapons and led by skilled officers and NCOs can dominate the close fight and impose their will upon the enemy—wherever he is.

During Operation Just Cause in 1989, the actions of the 75th Ranger Regiment and the 82d Airborne Division clearly demonstrated the advantages of US airborne forces. The operation was well supported by other US Army units, the US Air Force, and US Navy.

On 17 December 1989, the National Command Authority decided to commit specially trained airborne units to military action in Panama. The President established H-hour for 0100 on 20 December, just three days after the decision to intervene. The complex operation was centrally planned due to the need for thoroughly synchronized operations. The mission assigned to the airborne force was to quickly isolate, neutralize, and, if needed, destroy units of the Panamanian Defense Force by overwhelming combat power. These forces were then to link up with elements of the 7th Infantry Division (Light), the 5th Infantry Division (Mechanized), and the 193d Infantry Brigade.

Deploying by strategic airlift from multiple bases in the continental United States, paratroopers jumped into action on two principal DZs. Ranger task forces seized airfields at Rio Hato and Torrijos-Tocumen Airport. Another task force built around the 1st Brigade of the 82d Airborne Division followed the rangers. Their mission was to jump, assemble, and conduct immediate air assaults to eliminate PDF garrisons at Fort Cimarron, Tinajitas, and Panama Viejo These initial offensive operations were later followed by ground combat and stability operations. They were sustained by air lines of communication front the US and by CSS units already in Panama.

Largely through airborne operations, capable and aggressive combined arms task forces were brought to bear on short notice against u dispersed enemy. Thirty-two separate objectives were attacked at the same time, paralyzing the enemy. The resounding success of Operation Just Cause was due mostly to the parachute assault and rapid follow-on missions made possible by the airborne operation. Operation Just Cause demonstrated once again the capability, flexibility and value of airborne forces.

1-1. PREPARATION FOR WAR

Airborne and ranger units are organized and equipped to conduct parachute assaults to close with the enemy to kill him, to destroy his equipment, and to shatter his will to resist. This close personal fight requires combat-ready units composed of skilled soldiers and resourceful leaders. These units are the result of a tough, thorough, and demanding training program conducted by leaders who understand the effective employment of airborne forces, the combined arms team, and joint operations.

1-2. THE SOLDIER

Paratroopers must be experts in marksmanship, close combat, individual parachute techniques, and fieldcraft. They should be proficient with their assigned weapons and other weapons in the unit. They should also be familiar with foreign-made weapons that the enemy will use. In the close fight, paratroopers must be skilled in employing all weapons to include the rifle, the bayonet the AT4, grenades, mines, and bare hands. They must be confident in their ability to fight with these weapons They must be highly skilled in land navigation, camouflage, and tracking and stalking techniques. Paratroopers must be able to move undetected close to enemy soldiers. Stealth is required for reconnaissance, infiltration, and achieving surprise. Paratroopers must have the skill and the will to dominate the close fight.

1-3. THE LEADER

Infantry leaders must be the most capable soldiers in their unit and be tactically and technically proficient. The quality of the leadership determines the unit's success or failure in battle. Leaders must be proficient in land navigation and have an appreciation for terrain and parachute assault techniques. For a foot soldier, the terrain is both protector and ally. When properly exploited, it can increase the combat potential of the unit and support the achievement of surprise. All leaders must also be resourceful, tenacious, and decisive warriors. They are the combined arms integrators closest to the fight. They must be highly skilled in the employment of all the weapons and assets in the combined arms team. Leaders must be innovative and flexible when employing their units. They must have the mental agility to quickly grasp the situation and the initiative to take independent action, based on the situation and the commander's intent. Above all, they must personally lead their unit to success in close combat.

1-4. THE UNIT

The strength of airborne forces comes from the skill, courage, and discipline of the individual paratrooper. The paratrooper's abilities are enhanced by the teamwork and cohesion that develop in squads and platoons. This teamwork cohesion is essential to the survival and success of airborne forces in close combat. Cohesion enhances the paratrooper's will and determination to persevere, to accept the hardships, and to refuse to accept defeat. In the close fight, when the decision hangs in the balance, these are the factors that decide the victor. It is at the small-unit level (squad and platoon) that cohesion and teamwork provide the greatest benefits to the combat effectiveness of the unit. Paratroopers must have complete trust and confidence in their leaders. Leaders earn this trust and confidence by sharing the hardships and by displaying the leadership attributes described in FM 22-100. They must entrust the same confidence in their soldiers for this bonding to develop.

1-5. UNIT TRAINING PROGRAM

The unit training program must instill individual and collective skills and confidence, and must develop combat-ready units. It must consist of difficult, challenging training events that prepare soldiers, leaders, and units for the close fight. It must be conducted IAW FM 25-100, FM 25-101, and the MTP. The program must emphasize physical fitness, marksmanship skills, and parachute techniques. Paratroopers must be challenged to achieve expert proficiency in all of the combat critical skills. Night training, especially night live-fire exercises and parachute assaults, should be routine. The environment of the close fight should be simulated when possible. Training events that require subordinate leaders to use their initiative and take independent action are essential to prepare for decentralized operations that the unit normally conducts. Training to standard also develops cohesive, tenacious squads and platoons that can overcome all obstacles to ensure the safety of their unit and the accomplishment of the mission. The training program must continue after the unit begins conducting combat operations. The skills, teamwork, and cohesion must be sustained as replacements arrive in the unit. This is essential to maintain the combat effectiveness of the unit.

1-6. CAPABILITIES OF AIRBORNE FORCES

Airborne forces may be strategically, operationally, or tactically deployed on short notice to DZs anywhere in the world. They can be employed as a deterrent or combat force.

a. The USAF provides support to airborne operations that include:
- Airlift.
- Counterair.
- Close air support.
- Tactical air reconnaissance.
- Air interdiction.
- Special air warfare operations.
- Electronic warfare.
- Suppression of enemy air defense.

b. The strategic mobility of airborne forces permits rapid employment to meet contingence across the operational continuum anywhere in the world. Airborne forces provide a means by which a commander can decisively influence operations. The primary advantages of airborne operations are as follows:

- Quick response on short notice.
- Ability to bypass all land or sea obstacles.
- Surprise.
- Ability to mass rapidly on critical targets.

Airborne forces, when augmented with appropriate combat, CS, and CSS, can conduct sustained combat operations against any enemy.

1-7. MISSIONS OF AIRBORNE FORCES

Airborne forces execute parachute assaults to destroy the enemy and to seize and hold important objectives until linkup is accomplished. The parachute assault enhances the basic infantry combat mission: to close with the enemy by fire and maneuver, to destroy or capture him, and to repel his assaults by fire, close combat, and counterattack.

a. Missions for airborne forces can be strategic, operational, or tactical.

(1) *Strategic missions.* Simply alerting airborne forces for employment is a show of force that is politically significant in a strategic context. Airborne forces have strategic mobility. They can move from distant bases to strike at important targets deep in enemy-held territory with little warning. Strategic missions may require airborne forces to seize an airhead from which follow-on ground or air operations can be launched. Operation Just Cause was a strategic mission.

(2) *Operational missions.* Airborne forces can be employed anywhere in the theater of war. They attack deep to achieve operational-level objectives. For example, the seizure of objectives, such as airfields, bridges, or other key terrain deep in the enemy's rear area, is an operational mission. This is linked to the operational-level commander's concept and simplifies his accomplishment of assigned tasks. These airborne operations are usually short and require a linkup with other friendly forces or extraction of the airborne force. Operation Market Garden in the fall of 1944 is a good example of an operational mission.

(3) *Tactical missions.* Airborne forces assault in the rear or to the flank of the enemy, preferably where few fixed defenses exist and where well-organized enemy combat units are not initially present.

(a) Airborne units either assault their objectives and move to link up with friendly forces, or seize an objective and hold for the arrival of other friendly ground forces. They can also be used for rapid reinforcement of friendly ground units.

(b) Airborne forces can vary in size from an airborne company team to a division. Their size depends on the mission to be accomplished and the time, soldiers, and aircraft available. In January 1945, Company C and elements of Company F of the 6th Ranger Battalion executed a tactical operation to liberate American PWs from the Japanese at Cabantuen, Philippines. Usually only the assault echelon and its immediate follow-up are delivered into the objective area by parachute. Tactical airhead operations often involve the airlanding of heavy equipment, supplies, and supporting/reinforcing units to consolidate and exploit the initial lodgment.

b. Airborne forces can—

(1) Provide a show of force.

(2) Seize and hold important objectives until linkup or withdrawal.

(3) Seize an advance base to further deploy forces or to deny use of the base by the enemy.

(4) Conduct raids.

(5) Reinforce units beyond the immediate reach of land forces.

(6) Reinforce threatened areas or open flanks.

(7) Deny the enemy key terrain or routes.

(8) Delay, disrupt, and reduce enemy forces.

(9) Conduct economy-of-force operations to free heavier more tactically mobile units.

(10) Exploit the effects of chemical or nuclear weapons.

(11) Conduct operations in all four categories of low intensity conflict:
- Support for insurgency and counterinsurgency.
- Peacekeeping operations.
- Peacetime contingency operations.
- Combatting terrorism.

1-8. FUNDAMENTALS OF AIRBORNE OPERATIONS

The airborne commander and his staff must understand the fundamentals of airborne operations to plan and execute a successful airborne assault. These fundamentals are valid at every level:

a. Airborne forces require specially selected, trained, and highly disciplined soldiers and leaders.

b. Airborne operations must capitalize on surprise.

c. The ground tactical plan must drive all other plans through the reverse planning process.

d. Airborne operations require centralized, detailed planning and aggressive decentralized execution.

1-9. CHARACTERISTICS OF AIRBORNE OPERATIONS

Airborne operations are characterized by the following:

a. Joint operations.

b. A planned linkup with follow-on forces.

c. Complexity.

FM 90-26

d. Robust, flexible command and control that emphasizes mission-type orders.

e. Detailed, universally understood SOP.

f. Aggressive, rapid seizure of the assault objective.

1-10. LIMITATIONS OF AIRBORNE FORCES

The commander and planners must recognize the limitations of airborne forces and plan accordingly. They must consider the following:

a. An airborne force depends on USAF aircraft for long-range movement, fire support, and CSS. The availability and type of aircraft dictates the scope and duration of airborne operations.

b. Airborne forces are vulnerable to enemy attack while en route to the DZ. Although the USAF can conduct limited airdrops without air superiority, large operations require neutralization or suppression of enemy air defenses. This may require SEAD, radar jamming, and fighter aircraft in addition to transport and CAS sorties.

c. After the initial airdrop, the sustained combat power of airborne forces depends on resupply by air. Any interruption in the flow of resupply aircraft can cause a potential weakening of the airborne force. Enemy air defense fires against resupply aircraft and long-range artillery and mortar fires on the DZ can hamper the delivery, collection, or distribution of critical supplies.

d. Once on the ground, the airborne force has limited tactical mobility. That mobility depends on the number and type of vehicles and helicopters that can be brought into the objective area.

e. The airborne force has limited FA and ADA support until additional assets can be introduced into the objective area. Additional target acquisition assets are needed to provide accurate and timely targeting information.

f. Evacuation of casualties from the airhead is difficult. Until evacuation means are available, the brigade must be prepared to provide medical care through the attachment of divisional medical elements.

1-11. PHASES OF AIRBORNE OPERATIONS

An airborne operation is conducted in four closely related phases: marshaling, air movement, landing, and ground tactical.

a. **Marshaling Phase.** This phase begins with receipt of the warning order; it ends when the transport aircraft departs. During this phase, leaders–
- Plan joint tactics and support.
- Rehearse and conduct briefbacks.
- Assemble and prepare paratroopers, equipment, and supplies.
- Conduct briefings and prejump training.

- Move paratroopers, equipment, and supplies to the departure airfields and load them into aircraft.

b. **Air Movement Phase.** This phase begins with aircraft takeoff and ends with unit delivery to the DZ(s) or LZ(s).

c. **Landing Phase.** This phase begins when paratroopers and equipment exit the aircraft by parachute or are airlanded. The phase ends when all elements of the relevant echelon are delivered to the objective area.

d. **Ground Tactical Phase.** This phase begins with the landing of units and extends through the seizure and consolidation of the initial objective(s). It ends when the mission is completed or the airborne force is extracted or relieved. Subsequent operations can include an offensive operation, defense of key terrain, a linkup, a withdrawal, or any combination.

1-12. BATTLEFIELD OPERATING SYSTEMS AND AIRBORNE OPERATIONS

Airborne operations, like any combat operation, can be considered in terms of the battlefield operating systems. These systems must be considered for each of the four plans required for an airborne assault. (Table 1-1.)

BOS	GROUND TACTICAL PHASE	LANDING PHASE	AIR MOVEMENT PHASE	MARSHALING PHASE
INTELLIGENCE	A/I	A/I	A/I	A
MANEUVER	E	E	P	P
FIRE SUPPORT	E	E	P/E	P
AIR DEFENSE	E	E	E	P/E
MOBILITY/ COUNTER- MOBILITY/ SURVIVABILITY	E	P/E	P/E	P/E
COMBAT SERVICE SUPPORT	P/E	I/E	I	A/P
COMMAND AND CONTROL	E	E	E	P/E

A - Assess and acquire
I - Integrate
P - Plan and prepare
E - Execute

Table 1-1. Integration of battlefield operating systems.

a. **Intelligence.** The commander must consider the type, number, and location of enemy air defense weapons, observation systems (visual, radar, and satellite), and warning systems. He must also consider the locations and capabilities of enemy reaction forces near the objective. Tactical air reconnaissance requires close joint cooperation, and aerial and satellite photographs and stereoscopic pictures can help offset the lack of terrain reconnaissance before an airborne assault. Commanders insert LRS teams at critical locations for gathering needed information.

(1) Airborne operations, more than any others, are affected by weather. The more territory an airborne operation covers, the greater the need for a long-range weather forecast system. Weather satellites may provide much of the needed information. Some intelligence requirements can only be obtained through HUMINT resources.

(2) The selection of DZs, assault objectives, and subsequent AOs depends on a thorough analysis to capitalize on strengths of the airborne force.

(3) Target acquisition is a vital aspect of the intelligence battlefield operating system. The search, detection, and location of targets are needed for maneuver and CS forces to prepare plans for engaging and destroying the enemy. These intelligence assets also assess target damage.

b. **Maneuver.** Forces must fit the task. The airborne brigade task force can be part of an airborne assault by a larger unit, or it can constitute the initial assault force, preparing the way for deployment of a follow-on force.

(1) Airborne battalions rarely conduct an airborne assault as an independent operation just to establish an airhead. The battalion is not large enough to adequately defend an airhead that includes the approach and departure routes for airdrop sorties needed to sustain the airborne force. However, airborne raids with withdrawal by air or other means are well within the capabilities of a well-trained battalion TF.

(2) The airborne force must capitalize on surprise. The commander must carefully select the time, place, and manner of delivery for the attack. Everyone concerned must maintain strict security.

(a) The force can maintain deception by masking operations as rehearsal deployments.

(b) The force must neutralize the effectiveness of enemy detection devices through destruction, jamming, or operator distraction. The following actions can help nullify detection devices:
- Airborne forces can fly at low altitudes, using terrain masking and cloud cover to neutralize the effect of these devices.
- Deception flights can divert the attention of radar operators.
- Airborne forces can change course during the approach to confuse the operators.
- Night operations increase the possibility of surprise, although they make assembly of airborne force elements and seizure of assault objectives more difficult.
- They can pre-position to a REMAB from which to conduct the airborne operation.

(3) Rapid seizure of objectives is critical to success; speed and surprise are often more critical than numbers. Often, decisive action with a small force can succeed early where a fully assembled force cannot succeed later.

(4) Planning for a large-scale airborne operation should include preparation for air movement of large ground units to permit prompt reinforcement of paratroopers after their initial landing. To capture a suitable airhead for airland elements, the unit conducting the airborne assault must be able to capture airfields or terrain suitable for landing air transports. They must also be able to prevent enemy direct fire and observed indirect fire on the LZ. The suppression of enemy air defense assets along the aircraft approach and departure routes can be critical to success. Airlanded elements can be committed only when these conditions are met.

c. **Fire Support.** The primary source of fire support for airborne assaults is the US Air Force. US Navy/Marine Corps air assets and NGF if available will also be used. FA and mortars will provide fire support for the airborne force within 15 minutes after the beginning of the assault.

(1) The USAF must maintain air superiority for the airborne force to succeed in its mission. The more temporary the air superiority, the shorter the time-distance factors and duration of the flight should be. To establish and maintain air superiority, the USAF can neutralize nearby enemy airfields and C^2 facilities.

(2) The commander must plan to neutralize or avoid all antiaircraft installations along the route selected for the flight. This can be a joint responsibility, depending on the availability and capability of fire support assets. For example, when airborne operations are conducted near the sea, NGF may provide much of the fire support to include JSEAD.

(3) The USAF must isolate the objective by attacking the enemy's ground and air forces. These attacks must begin late enough that the enemy does not identify the objective until it is too late to react effectively. Immediately before an operation, the USAF should consider incapacitating the enemy's fighter airfields and immobilizing enemy radar, communications facilities, and reserves near the projected airhead. An air attack on any enemy reserves moving toward the airhead can give the airborne unit extra time to seize the assault objectives, to reorganize, and to prepare for the defense.

(4) Airborne units require CAS initially until division and corps artillery can support them.

d. **Mobility, Countermobility, and Survivability.** Engineers provide–

- Mobility.
- Countermobility.
- Survivability.
- General engineering.
- Topographic support to airborne forces.

(1) The nature of airborne operations often requires engineers to fight as infantry more often than in other operations. Engineers must be well trained in this aspect of their mission.

(2) A primary mobility mission for engineers in support of airborne operations is airfield runway clearance and repair. After the initial assault,

airborne engineer units are prepared to improve or create landing areas for follow-on units, equipment, and supplies.

(3) Countermobility efforts are vital to the survival and success of the airborne force inside the airhead. Obstacles are created or reinforced to secure the airhead and to isolate it from reinforcing enemy forces.

(4) Survivability and fighting positions prepared from local materials are normal in airborne operations. Because airborne engineer units have limited earthmoving equipment, priority in preparing protective positions is normally given to key antiarmor and other weapon systems, C^2 facilities, and vital supplies.

e. **Air Defense.** The force must provide its own air defense. This is achieved by establishing an air defense umbrella that is closely integrated with the USAF. Usually, the enemy can respond fastest by air, so rapid establishment of air defense is critical. To reduce fratricide, airborne forces must closely coordinate and train with the USAF.

f. **Combat Service Support.** Airdrop of equipment and supplies is the main resupply method for airborne forces and requires extensive planning.

g. **Command and Control.** Unity of command takes precedence over all other C^2 considerations. (Both air and ground units must be under one overall commander.) The senior officer in the landing area commands the airhead until the arrival of the ground force commander. Establishment of the shortest possible chain of command is critical to success.

(1) Redundancy in all C^2 systems should be established early in the planning stages of an airborne operation and maintained throughout the operation.

(2) Airborne operations require CPs both on the ground and in the air. The airborne force headquarters is divided into a mobile forward echelon and a stationary rear echelon. They can operate from a REMAB, an intermediate staging base, or a forward operating base. Commanders of airborne forces should land with the first units so that clear battle directions can be given from the outset.

(3) A highly qualified and trained force is required to successfully plan and execute airborne operations. A mutual understanding of the peculiarities, capabilities, and limitations of both air and ground assets by all leaders involved is critical.

(4) Leaders must train systematically with emphasis on well-functioning joint air-ground communications. (See Appendix G for more detailed information.)

(5) An airborne operation is as rapid in its execution as it is time-consuming in its preparation. Commanders must develop contingency plans for possible follow-on operations. These CONPLANs should be modified based on the most current intelligence Proactive advanced planning can allow more rapid decision making and timely commitment of forces.

CHAPTER 2

AIRBORNE PLANNING

Detailed planning and forceful, competent leadership are the keys to victory. Thorough, flexible planning gives direction to units and leaders, and allows them to concentrate combat power at the decisive point on the battlefield. This chapter summarizes the procedures essential to planning a successful airborne operation.

Section I. FUNDAMENTALS

Airborne operations are characterized by their complexity and joint nature. A successful airborne Operation requires–

- Use of the commander's estimate and the military decision-making process.
- Centralized, detailed planning and decentralized execution of mission-type orders.
- Adherence to the principle of simplicity.
- Use of the reverse-planning process.

2-1. PLANNING RESPONSIBILITIES

The commander of a JTF initiates airborne operations with a planning directive to participating units. The directive is assimilated through normal command channels at corps and division-level, and pertinent information is issued to brigades. The directive must–

- Specify missions.
- Outline the command structure.
- Identify participating ground and air forces.
- List forces in support.
- Provide a schedule of events.
- State conditions under which the operation will begin, be delayed, be altered, or be terminated.

2-2. KEY PERSONNEL RESPONSIBILITIES

The responsibilities of key personnel include the following:

a. **Airborne Commander.** The airborne commander establishes mission-oriented command and control by ensuring that his concept is understood and by defining the responsibilities of key personnel. The airborne commander is responsible for–

(1) Accomplishing the ground mission.

(2) Loading aircraft with equipment and personnel.

(3) Assigning personnel to aircraft and preparing flight forms.

b. **Airlift Commander.** The airlift commander is responsible for–

(1) Allocating sufficient aircraft to support the ground tactical plan.

(2) Delivering assault elements to the correct DZ.

(3) Conducting resupply and evacuation missions.

c. **Joint Responsibilities.** The airborne and airlift commanders have joint responsibility for–

(1) Establishing control parties at departure air bases.

(2) Supervising the loading of equipment and soldiers.

(3) Conducting rehearsals.

(4) Coordinating and standardizing SOI and prearranged signals.

(5) Selecting DZs, LZs, and EZs.

(6) Establishing control parties at DZs, LZs, and EZs.

(7) Unloading of aircraft at the LZ.

(8) Preparing the aerial resupply and evacuation plan.

(9) Securing departure airfields.

(10) Preparing the air movement table.

(11) Supervising JAAP procedures.

(12) Coordinating the movement of soldiers and aircraft.

Section II. PREPARATION OF PLANS AND ORDERS

Commanders begin planning for airborne operations with a visualization of the ground tactical plan and work backwards through the landing plan, the air movement plan, and the marshaling plan. Planning is conducted in this order regardless of the type and duration of the mission or the size of the force. It continues until the operation is executed or cancelled.

2-3. COMMANDER'S ESTIMATE OF THE SITUATION

This process helps the commander determine how best to accomplish a mission. Airborne commanders and staffs follow five steps to solve problems and plan tactical operations:

STEP 1. Analyze the mission.

STEP 2. Analyze the situation and develop courses of action.

STEP 3. Analyze courses of action.

STEP 4. Compare courses of action.

STEP 5. Make a decision.

a. **Decision-Making Process.** The airborne commander, his staff, and his chain of command use the related processes of troop-leading procedure and command and staff actions to develop and execute decisions. (FM 101-5 discusses the military decision-making process in detail.) (Figure 2-1, page 2-4.)

b. **Intelligence Preparation of the Battlefield.** The IPB process is that portion of the intelligence cycle that integrates enemy doctrine with the weather and terrain, and relates these factors to the mission and the specific battlefield situation. The formal IPB process is performed at division, corps, and higher levels. (See Appendix F.) (FM 34-130 contains a complete discussion of IPB.)

2-4. REVERSE PLANNING PROCESS

The airborne commander and his staff develop, in this order, the ground tactical plan, the landing plan, the air movement plan, and the marshaling plan. The ground tactical plan drives the development of all other plans. (See Appendix F.) (Figure 2-2, page 2-5.)

a. **Ground Tactical Plan.** The ground tactical plan is the basis for the development of all other plans. The airborne commander and his staff give special consideration to the reassembly and reorganization of the assault forces and to the decentralized nature of initial operations in the objective area. The subordinate commander requires the ground tactical plan of his higher headquarters before he can begin planning. He needs to know the type, location, and size of objectives; the mission and intent of higher headquarters two levels up; and his task and purpose. The ground tactical plan is generated down the chain of command as a mutual effort and includes the following:

- Assault objectives and airhead line.
- Reconnaissance and security forces to include OPs.
- Boundaries.
- Task organization.
- Designation of reserve.
- Supply (accompanying, follow-up, routine).

(Chapter 3 provides details on the ground tactical plan.)

FM 90-26

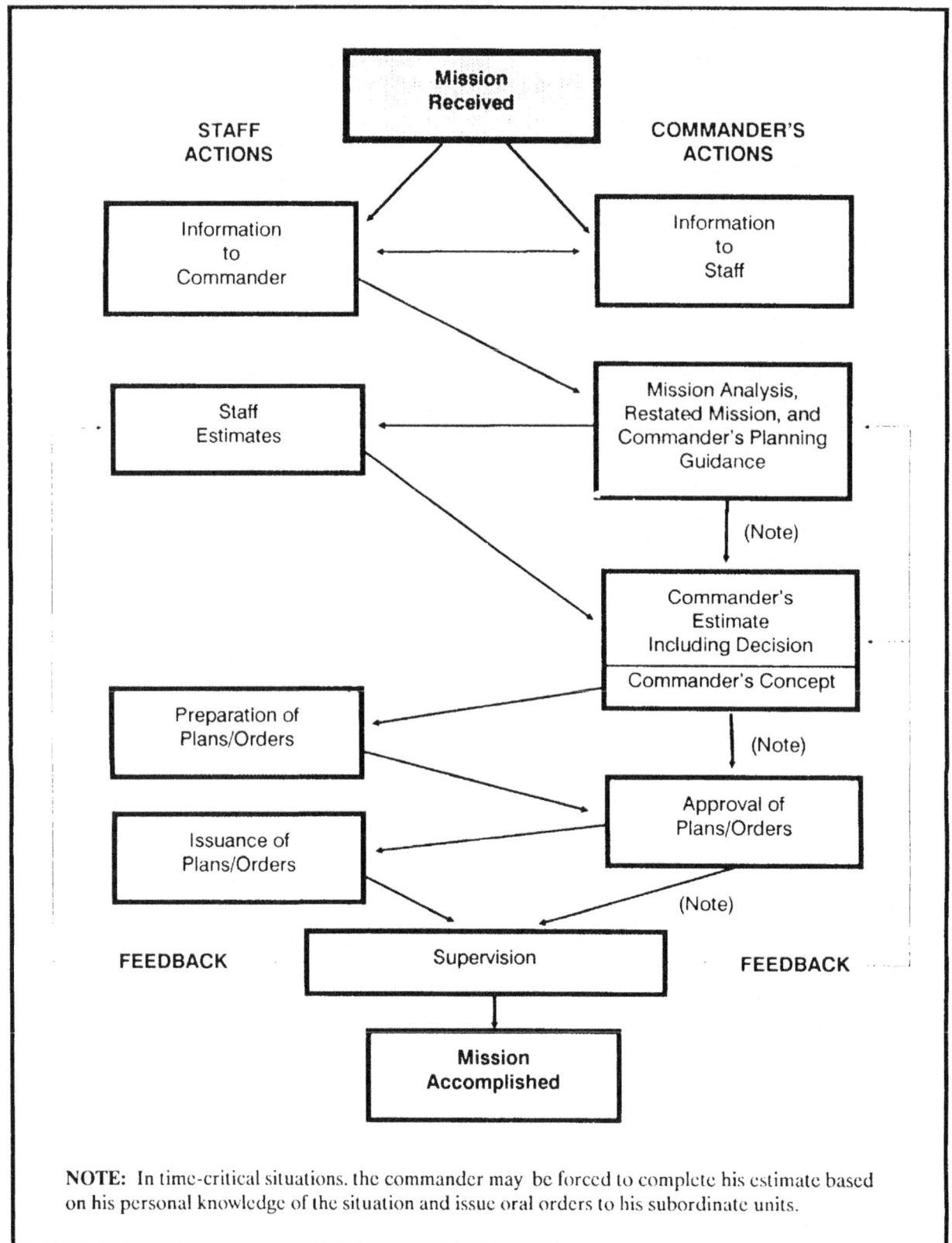

NOTE: In time-critical situations, the commander may be forced to complete his estimate based on his personal knowledge of the situation and issue oral orders to his subordinate units.

Figure 2-1. Decision-making process.

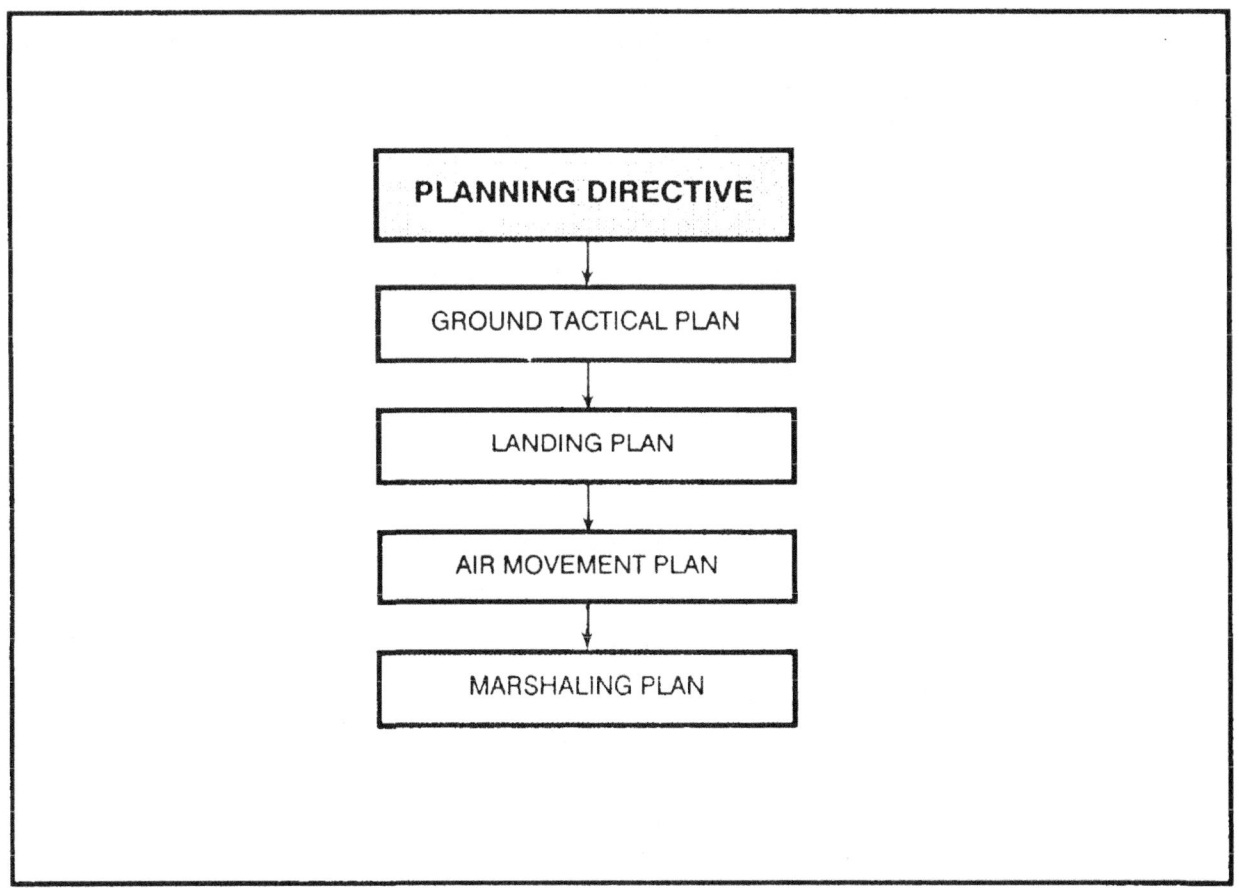

Figure 2-2. Reverse planning process.

b. **Landing Plan.** The landing plan is the airborne commander's plan that links the air movement plan to the ground tactical plan. It is published at brigade level and below. Before the airborne commander can prepare an overall landing plan, he must know where the subordinate commander wants to put his paratroopers. The landing plan is generated up the chain of command as a mutual effort. The landing plan includes the following:

- DZ/LZ/EZ locations and descriptions.
- Sequence of delivery.
- Method of delivery.
- Place of delivery.
- Time of delivery.
- Assembly plan.
- Type landing plan worksheet.

(Chapter 4 provides details on the landing plan.)

c. **Air Movement Plan.** The air movement plan provides the information required to move the airborne force from the departure airfields to the objective area. This plan is the third step in the reverse planning process and covers the period from when units load to when they exit the aircraft. The airborne commander designates the subordinate units sequence of air flow and allocates aircraft. This allows the subordinate commanders to conduct air movement planning. The air movement plan is generated up the chain of command as a mutual effort and includes the following:

- Departure airfields.
- Aircraft by serial.
- Parking diagram.
- Aircraft mission (air movement tables and flight routes).
- Unit providing the aircraft.

(Chapter 5 provides details on the air movement plan.)

d. **Marshaling Plan.** This plan is developed last in the reverse planning process and is based on the requirements of the other plans. It provides the needed information and procedures for units of the airborne force to prepare for combat, to move to departure airfields, and to load aircraft. The marshaling plan also provides detailed instructions for facilities and services needed during marshaling. It is generated down the chain of command and includes the following:

- Movement to the marshaling area.
- Passive defensive measures.
- Dispersal procedures.
- Departure airfields.
- Marshaling camp operations.
- Briefback schedule.
- Preparation for combat (inspection, supervision, rehearsal, and rest).
- Communications.

(Chapter 6 provides details on the marshaling plan.)

e. **Planning Assets.** The complexity of air-borne operations demands great attention to detail in the planning process. (Figure 2-3.) Planning is enhanced when subordinate commanders use–

(1) Small-scale air photos of the landing area.

(2) Large-scale photos of the landing area for selecting avenues of approach and planning ground operations.

(3) Air photo and interpretation reports covering enemy activities and ground and air installations within and adjacent to the projected airhead.

(4) Aerial reconnaissance reports.

(5) Overlays prepared with descriptions of obstacles and defensive works, navigational hindrances, and landing areas.

(6) Maps.

(7) Information concerning enemy capabilities, methods, and tactics.

(8) Special studies that apply to the airhead.

(9) Accurate, large-scale terrain models of the landing area.

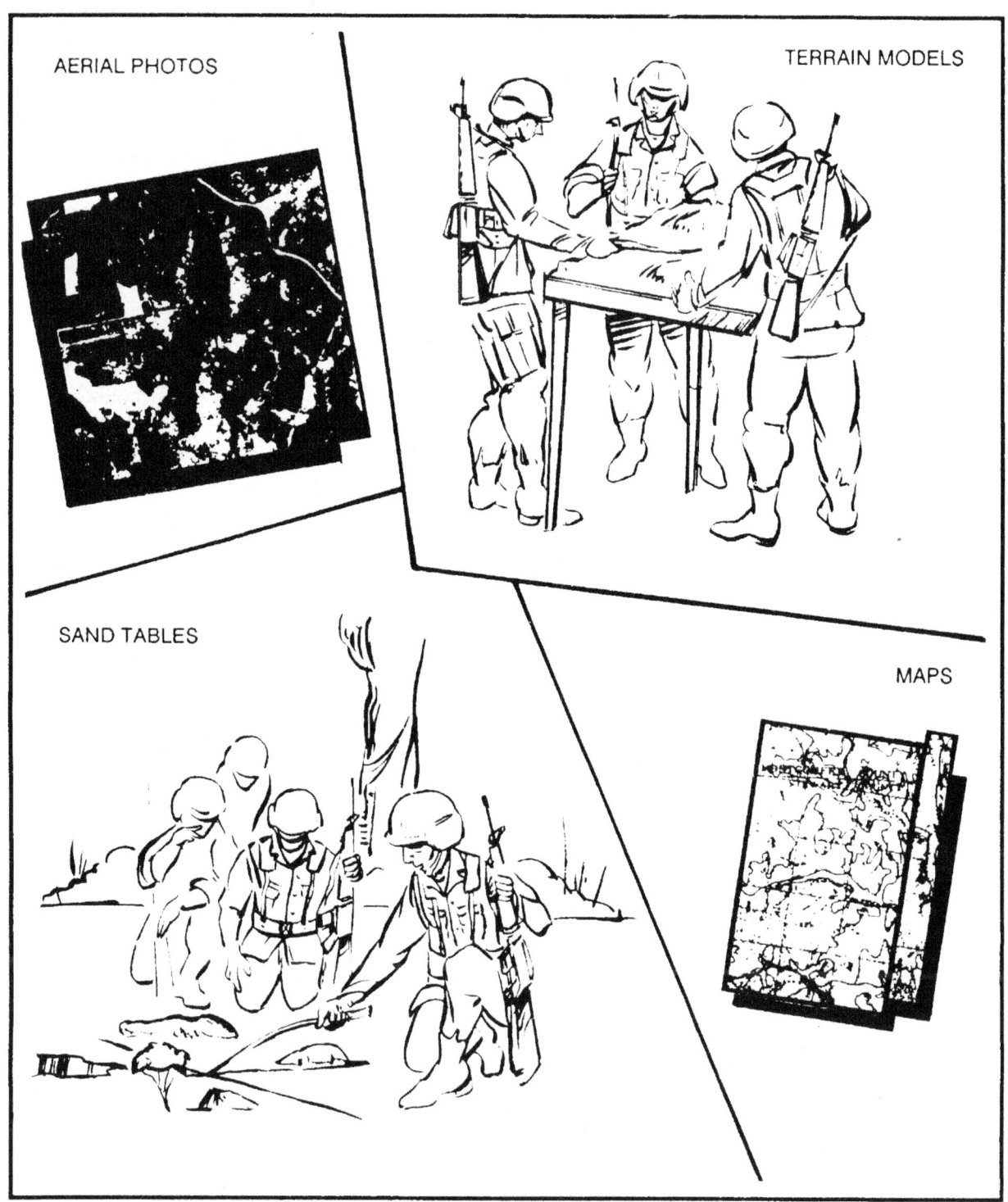

Figure 2-3. Planning assets.

2-5. PLANNING CONSIDERATIONS

The airborne commander considers the following additional factors in the development of his plans:

a. **Echelonment.** The airborne commander organizes Army combat elements within an airborne force into three echelons:

(1) *Assault echelon.* The assault echelon consists of those forces required to seize the assault objectives and the initial airhead, reserves, and supporting units.

(2) *Follow-on echelon* The follow-on echelon consists of forces required for subsequent operations. It enters the objective area by air or surface movement when required.

(3) Rear Echelon. The rear echelon consists of administrative and service elements that remain in the departure area. These elements may be brought forward to support in the airhead, as required.

b. **Concurrent Planning.** Commanders plan for all phases of an airborne operation at the same time since all phases are interrelated. This reduces the total planning time. A subordinate unit must maintain plans in draft until the next higher headquarters has finalized its plans.

c. **Coordination.** Commanders normally provide plans and orders down the chain of command. For airborne operations, however, higher headquarters often cannot complete their plans until subordinate units have conducted a briefback of their plans.

d. **Liaison.** Parallel echelons of the airlift and airborne units coordinate continuously from the time of the joint planning conference until the operation is executed or cancelled. Before the operation, complete coordination is essential down to the smallest detail.

(1) Commanders of US Army and USAF units exchange LOs to act as advisors and coordinators immediately upon receipt of orders to participate in an airborne operation. Army LOs must be familiar with all aspects of the airborne operation. They must attend briefings and conferences, and must be provided with adequate transportation and communications assets.

(2) Liaison officers are normally exchanged detween the airborne force and-

(a) Army units supporting the operation from outside the objective area.

(b) Airlift elements.

(c) Linkup forces.

(d) Special operations forces, especially AC-130 assets.

(3) The specific duties of liaison officers include the following:

(a) Represent their unit headquarters at the headquarters to which they are detailed.

(b) Act as advisors to the headquarters on matters pertaining to their own commands.

(c) Coordinate matters involving dual responsibility.

(d) Discuss the time, place, personnel required and material to be covered at joint staff meetings.

(c) Hold joint staff briefings.

(f) Examine parallel orders to ensure complete agreement of plans and arrangements.

(g) Assess and plan for the availability and procurement of equipment and facilities required from the higher headquarters

(h) Attend all joint conferences to become acquainted with the agreements reached by the commanders and with the operational plan.

(i) Prepare joint reports.

(j) Obtain copies of the marshaling plan and the parking diagram for their units.

(k) Know the location and capacity of all installations at the airfields and airlanding facilities that concern their units.

(1) Review the plans and arrangements for reserve aircraft if last-minute failures occur; prepare to assist the movement of paratroopers from aborting aircraft to reserve aircraft.

(m) Brief guides, who were furnished by the airborne unit, on airfield traffic procedures and locations of aircraft to be loaded. At dispersed locations, an airborne unit representative is located at the coordination facility to perform this function and to act as individual liaison.

(4) Commanders exchange Los on a continuous duty status at corps and division level. At brigade and lower echelons, the S3 LOs, the S3 air, or unit air movement officer can perform these duties. For operations of less than brigade size, commanders exchange LOs as needed at the discretion of the commanders concerned.

e. **Briefbacks.** Subordinate commanders must conduct brief backs on all aspects of their plan to the next higher commander. (Figure 2-4, page 2-10.) This ensures that unit plans are fully coordinated and in concert with the commander's intent. Commanders conduct briefbacks on a terrain model, a sand table, or a map. Planning for an airborne operation is a dynamic fast-changing process. A change in one plan has an impact on the other three. Plans remain in draft until every commander in the chain has conducted a briefback. All commanders must inform their subordinates of changes.

f. **Rehearsals.** Rehearsals are essential to the success of an airborne operation. They are conducted at every level and involve both air and ground components. They are performed on terrain similar to the objective and under the same conditions. Rehearsals may be conducted on a sand table, terrain model, mock-up, or map if time permits a full-scale rehearsal. Rehearsals are listed in order of priority as follows:

- Ground tactical plan.
- Landing plan with emphasis to assemble on the DZ.
- Air movement plan with emphasis on aircraft loading.

g. **Mission-Oriented Command and Control.** The purpose of command and control is to allow the airborne commander to generate and apply combat power at the decisive point on the battlefield hfo('z is a method of directing military operations in which subordinates are encouraged to act alone, consistent with the intent of senior commanders in executing assigned missions. (See FM 7-10, FM 7-20, and FM 7-30 for a detailed discussion of MOC^2.)

Figure 2-4. Conduct of a briefback.

h. **Dissemination.** Leaders must be able to make decisions to support the commander's intent. Plans and intelligence must be brissminated to the lowest level consistent with security requirements.

(1) *Security.* The staff follows security requirements in disseminating the intelligence required for subordinate units to develop their plans. Intelligence is provided on a need-to-know basis. As H-hour approaches, units are provided with more detailed intelligence.

(2) *Precombat briefing.* The commitment of an airborne unit is sudden and complete; there is no time for the commander to orient units immediately after landing. Plans and intelligence must be thoroughly briefed before the operation begins.

i. **Linkup With Special Operations Forces.** When the airborne force follows an SOF during a deployment, it requests a liaison before arrival in the operational area.

(1) During the planning phase, an SOF LO is assigned to the brigade along with all communications assets needed for immediate use with SOF assets at JSOF headquarters and at the objective area. The SOI and signal plan must standardize not only frequencies and call signs, but also address visual signals, and daylight and night operations.

(a) The SOCCE links up with the airborne commander through the SOF LO.

(b) The SOCCE coordinates with the S2/S3 sections and both elements provide the current situation, commander's intent, and future operations of their respective forces (within OPSEC limits).

(c) The SOCCE provides SOF locations through personal coordination, overlays, and other friendly order-of-battle data to the FSE and brigade operation section.

(d) The SOCCE requests appropriate restrictive fire support coordination measures and provides time windows when these measures are to be effective. The SOCCE must also ensure that FSE dissemination of these measures does not result in OPSEC violations.

(2) Rangers can be OPCON with terminating conditions. They normally conduct a relief in place with conventional forces.

(3) Communications capabilities are augmented to effect long-range communications and proper liaisons. Equipment compatibility, crypto use, information sharing, and security measures are considered when working with Army SOF, joint forces, and combined security forces.

CHAPTER 3

GROUND TACTICAL PLAN

The ground tactical plan is the base from which commanders develop all other plans. They must complete the ground tactical plan before finalizing the landing plan, the air movement plan, and the marshaling plan. It provides the commander's intent, his concept of the operation, fire support plan, and task organization of the units making the initial assault. Ground combat in airborne operations is conducted along conventional lines but under unusual conditions. Once these conditions are appreciated, the tactics and techniques of ground combat can be applied to airborne operations. (See FMs 7-20 and 7-30 for a detailed discussion of combat operations.)

Section I. PLANNING

Once the airborne force commander receives the initiating directive/WO, he begins planning. This dircctivc/WO includes the following:

- Missions for subordinate units.
- The higher commander's concept of the operation.
- Command structure for the operation.
- Time and duration of the operation.
- Intelligence and security requirements
- Allocation and distribution of airlift assets.
- Unit deployment list and sequence.
- Departure airfields, REMABs, and ISBs.
- Signal requirements and instructions.
- Linkup and withdrawal concept.

3-1. ESTIMATE OF THE SITUATION

The military decision-making process incorporating the estimate of the situation results in a course of action as in any other operation. Unit commanders and staff officers cannot afford to deviate from this accepted procedure for the development process. As a technique, the ground tactical plan will normally be developed as the basic operations order/plan as discussed in FM 7-20 and FM 7-30. This is the most critical phase of the airborne operation because all other plans are based on it. When conducting the estimate, the commander and staff consider the various aspects of airborne combat conditions with regard to METT-T.

a. **Mission.** The mission of an airborne infantry battalion or brigade is to close with the enemy by means of fire and maneuver to destroy or capture him, or to repel his assault by fire, close combat, and countcrattack. These missions usually require the seizure and defense of objectives and surrounding terrain. Forces rely strongly on the element of surprise. (See Appendix F for detailed information on the application of the IPB process as it relates to airborne operations.)

(1) In early linkup operations, the unit defends only the airhead and the required maneuver space.

(2) In linkup and independent operations, the tactical operation begins with an initial assault; it then passes to the defense of the established airhead until enough forces can be delivered to the objective area.

(3) On reinforcement or on linkup with other ground forces, the airborne units resume the offensive within the commander's concept of the operation or withdraw to prepare for subsequent operations.

b. **Enemy Forces.** Commanders analyze all available information to determine the enemy's situation. The following factors are considered:

(1) Enemy morale, leadership, and probable intentions.

(2) Enemy capabilities.

(3) Enemy tactics.

(4) Probable enemy reactions to an airborne assault.

(a) The enemy that can react the fastest poses the most immediate threat.

(b) The enemy that can cause the most damage or prevent the airborne force from accomplishing its mission poses the most significant threat.

(5) Enemy reserves and paramilitary organizations (gendarmeries, police, border guards, and militia) and their ability to mobilize and react. This is especially critical before deep attacks.

(6) Enemy capability to conduct guerrilla, partisan, or sabotage activities and the enemy's relationship to the local population.

c. **Terrain and Weather.** Within this category, the staff must consider and act on the following factors

(1) The availability of DZs, LZs. and EZs (division or corps staff provides a landing area study to subordinate elements before the preparation of the landing plan). However, the availability and selection of DZs should not influence the selection of assault objectives, the airhead line, or unit boundaries.

(2) Obstacles within the airhead line and out to the maximum effective range of direct- and indirect-fire weapons, with emphasis on those that can be prepared or reinforced with minimal engineer effort.

(3) Enemy avenues of approach, since the enemy will try to reach and destroy the airborne force before it can assemble and reorganize. This consideration weighs heavily in determining the location of assault objectives.

(4) Key terrain that can determine how the airborne force can best defend the area in depth.

(5) Friendly and enemy observation and fields of fire (particularly for indirect fires and antiarmor weapons).

(6) Cover and concealment (especially for assembly and reorganization).

(7) The staff must also consider the effects of climate and weather on the following:
- Flight formations.
- Trafficability.
- Visibility.
- Close air support.
- Logistics.
- Personnel and equipment.

d. **Troops Available.** Commanders consider all forces available to accomplish the mission. These include all assigned, attached, and supporting forces.

(1) *US ground forces.* Commanders evaluate the plans, missions, capabilities, and limitations of US ground forces. They consider whether artillery can support the airborne forces and whether the forces will perform a linkup or passage of lines.

(2) *Air Force.* Close air support can often make up for the lack of armor and heavy artillery. The airborne commander must consider the USAF ability to sustain the force and must bring knowledgeable airlift and tactical air planners together early.

(3) *Navy.* The airborne commander examines the availability and feasibility of NGF support and naval or USMC air support. Early arrangements for liaison and coordination must be made to support the operation.

e. **Time.** Time is critical in all operations. There are several time considerations that are unique to an airborne operation. Significant time may be required to mass the lift force (Air Force aircraft). The time between the initial assault and the deployment of the follow-on echelon must be considered. Supply and CSS planning is driven by the amount of time before linkup or withdrawal.

f. **Indigenous Population.** The airborne force commander must consider national and regional characteristics such as —
- Religion and customs.
- Politics and tribal affiliations,
- Support (or lack of it) for central and local governments or occupying powers.
- Loyalty to political or military leaders.
- Available labor.
- Support (or lack of it) for US forces.

3-2. DEVELOPMENT OF THE GROUND TACTICAL PLAN

The ground tactical plan incorporates considerations for those actions to be taken in the objective area; for example, during the assault and subsequent operations phases. This will be the first plan to be finalized. It must be keyed on accomplishment of the commander's concept of the operation.

a. The ground tactical plan is developed as any other tactical plan using the procedure as delineated in FM 7-20, Chapter 2. However, the initial goal of airborne operations is the establishment of an airhead and its subsequent defense.

b. The ground tactical plan's essential elements are developed in the following sequence: the airhead line and the assault objectives (selected concurrently); the security zone and R&S forces; boundaries and assault task organizations (selected concurrently); and reserves.

3-3. SELECTION OF ASSAULT OBJECTIVES AND AIRHEAD LINE

Based on an analysis of the situation, commanders select specific assault objectives. (Figure 3-1.) Although the airhead line is developed and the assault objectives determined concurrently, the assault objectives dictate the size and shape of the airhead.

a. This selection does not necessarily include those objectives that the force must seize to secure the airhead line. An appropriate assault objective is one which the force must control early in the assault to accomplish the mission, or they must control to enhance the security of the airborne unit during the establishment of the airhead.

(1) Objectives should allow for the accomplishment of mission-essential tasks while meeting the commander's intent. They can include key terrain within the airhead or terrain required for linkup. For example, the commander has directed the airborne force to secure a bridge for later use by linkup forces. The force must secure this bridge before the enemy can destroy or damage it; therefore, the commander designates the bridge as an assault objective.

(2) The airborne unit is vulnerable from the time it lands until follow-on forces can be delivered to the airhead. A mobile enemy unit attacking the airhead during these early moments can completely disrupt the operation. Therefore, the commander selects as assault objectives terrain that dominates places where high-speed enemy avenues of approach enter the airhead.

(3) Enemy positions that both threaten the mission and are located within the airhead can also be selected as assault objectives. However, commanders would not classify mobile forces as assault objectives.

(4) Assault objectives must be seized immediately to established the airhead and to provide security for follow-on forces coming into the airhead.

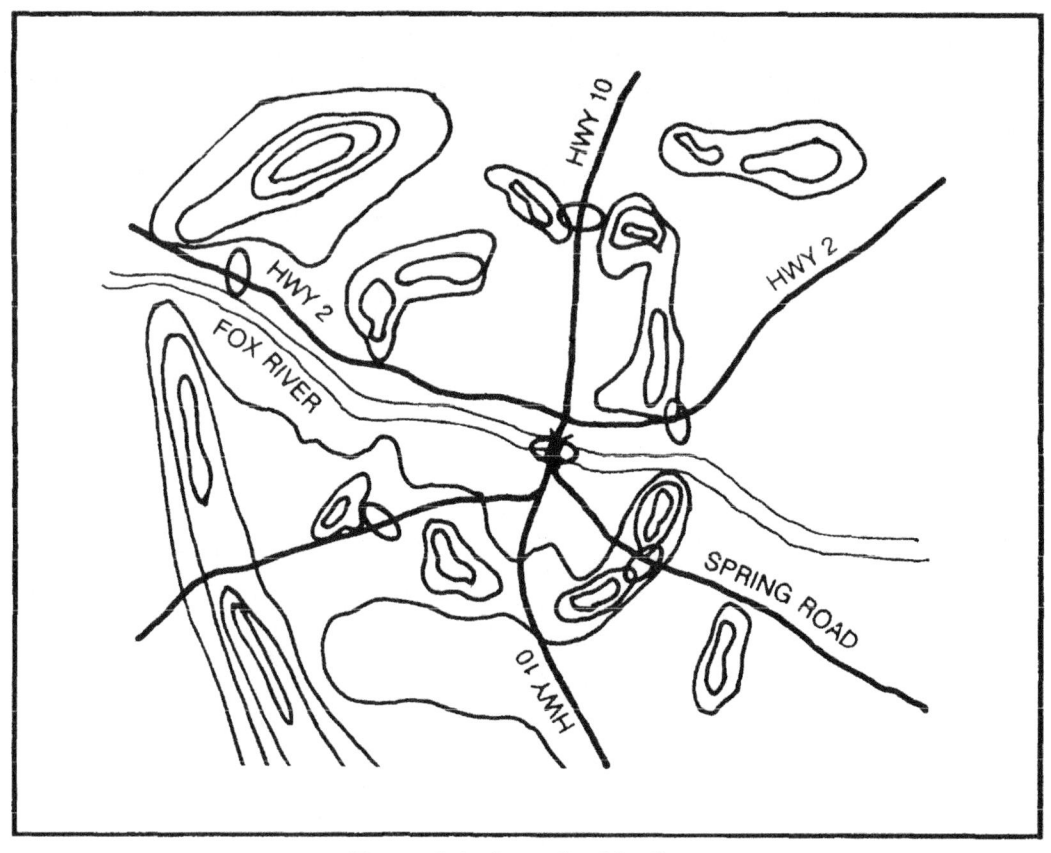

Figure 3-1. Assault objectives.

b. Other considerations impact on the development and final selection of assault objectives. Subordinate commanders decide the size, type, or disposition of the force to gain/maintain control.

- Division selects brigade assault objectives.
- Brigade selects battalion assault objectives.
- Battalion selects company assault objectives.

(1) Senior commanders choose as few assault objectives as possible since subordinate commanders must select additional objectives to establish a cohesive defense of their assigned sectors of the airhead.

(2) Assault objectives are ranked in order. A unit SOP may predesignate a numbering system for subordinate objectives. For example, all first brigade objectives begin with a "Q", or for OPSEC purposes, they may be randomly numbered or lettered. Priorities are chosen based on the most likely threat or on the needs of the friendly force.

(3) Assault objectives are secured before the defense is setup in the airhead line. The airhead is then cleared of organized enemy resistance and forces are positioned to secure the airhead line.

c. At the same time commanders select assault objectives, they consider the extent of the airhead. The airborne force seizes hostile or threatened territory. The airhead includes the entire area under control of the airborne force. It acts as a base for further operations and as a respite that allows the airborne force to build up its combat power. Once the force secures the airhead, they must clear any enemy force within it; then, they must defend it. The airhead line, which delineates the specific area to be seized, designates the airhead. Several principle factors determine the location, extent, and form of the airhead/airhead line.

(1) The actual trace of the airhead line reflects the control of key/critical terrain essential to the mission. (Figure 3-2.)

(2) The airhead line anchors on obstacles, and the airhead itself takes advantage of existing natural and man-made obstacles.

(3) The airhead contains enough DZs, LZs, and EZs to ensure interior rather than exterior lines of communication and to permit mass rather than piecemeal assault.

(4) The airhead must allow enough space for dispersion to reduce vulnerability to NBC weapons.

(5) The airhead must be large enough to provide for defense in depth, vet small enough for the unit to defend. Although this is largely METT-T dependent, a battalion can defend an airhead 3 to 5 kilometers in diameter. A brigade can occupy an airhead 5 to 8 kilometers in diameter.

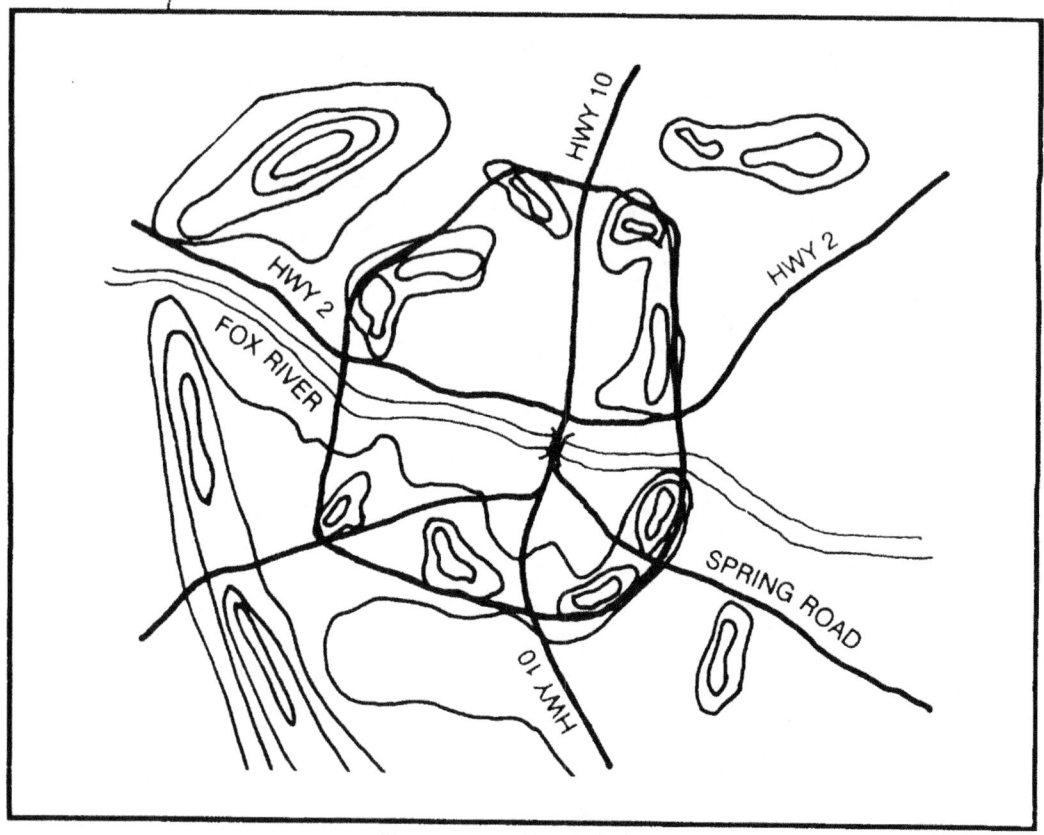

Figure 3-2. Airhead line.

3-4. RECONNAISSANCE AND SECURITY FORCES

Security in all directions is an overriding consideration early in any airborne operation, since an airhead is essentially a perimeter defense. In ground operations, there are several security echelons forward of the FEBA.

a. Security forces are landed early in the assault echelon. The reconnaissance and security line is established immediately 4 to 6 kilometers from the airhead line to afford security to the airborne force during its landing and reorganization, In the early stages of an airborne operation, the security force acts as a screening force. In later stages (when assault missions have been accomplished, when the airhead is relatively secure, and when more forces are available), it acts as a guard or covering force. Security forces come under brigade control except during short battalion missions such as raids, when they come under battalion control. The mission of the security force is as follows:

(1) To give the airhead early warning.

(2) To develop intelligence, including the location, direction, and speed of an enemy attack.

(3) To initially deny the enemy observation of and direct and observed indirect fire on the airhead.

(4) To deceive the enemy as to the actual location of the airhead.

(5) To delay and disrupt the enemy.

b. The need for and positioning of additional security forces is determined by the next subordinate commander. The security force includes scouts, AT weapons, engineers, Army aviation, and (sometimes) light armor. When possible, mobile forces are selected to facilitate rapid initial movement to positions and to facilitate withdrawal and adjustment. An aggressive R&S effort at lower echelons augments the security force. The following considerations apply to the selection of positions for the screening force:

(1) Locate them within radio communications and fire support range. However, this range can be extended, if necessary, with retransmission stations; split section indirect-fire operations; and attachment of vehicles mortars, or other assets to the security force.

(2) Locate them as roadblocks/obstacles, ambushes, patrols, or sensors (depending on the enemy) on dominant terrain. This allows long range observation and fields of fire out to the maximum range of supporting fires.

(3) Locate them to observe, control, and dominate enemy high speed avenues of approach.

(4) Locate them to deny enemy long-range observation and observed indirect fire into the airhead.

(5) Locate them far enough out to provide early warning.

(6) Locate them to provide routes of withdrawal to the airhead. Observation posts generally rely on their ability to hide as their main protection; they can allow the enemy to pass their position and not withdraw.

c. Designated forces under control of the airborne commander perform R&S missions beyond the security zone established by ground forces; emphasis is placed on likely enemy avenues of approach. The mission of these forces is to gain and maintain contact with enemy units reacting to the airborne assault. This force is mobile and is not used to defend a particular part of the airhead. It can include Army aviation, air cavalry, or light armor; it can be supported with fire from Air Force assets, NGF, or Army missile systems. The following considerations govern the employment of this force:

(1) These forces orient on enemy high-speed avenues of approach to develop intelligence, including the location, direction, and speed of the enemy's advance.

(2) Commanders of these forces consider known enemy locations, the number of high-speed approaches, and communications-relay abilities while orienting on enemy units.

(3) Usually employed beyond the airhead at a distance based on the tactical situation, these forces protect the main force from surprise attack. The airborne commander can extend their range if communications permit. Aviation assets can extend to 50 kilometers or more, although the commander must consider loiter time so the forces can provide continuous coverage. (FARPs can increase this distance.) Long-range surveillance teams may surveil enemy garrisons and major routes into the airhead.

(4) Reconnaissance forces must be mobile and task-organized for the mission from cavalry, armor, scout, LRS, and antiarmor units.

3-5. BOUNDARIES AND TASK ORGANIZATION

Commanders visualize the employment of subordinate units to organize them for combat commensurate with the brigade missions.

a. **Boundaries.** Commanders use boundaries to assign sectors of responsibility to major subordinate combat elements, who then clear the area of enemy forces. (Figure 3-3.) In selecting and designating assault boundaries for airborne operations, several points are considered:

(1) Each unit should be able to clear its assigned sector; therefore, commanders must consider boundaries concurrently with task organization. To assign boundaries, commanders subdivide the area into sectors with fairly equal tasks (not necessarily into equal sectors). This requires a careful analysis of the enemy, the tasks to be accomplished, and the terrain within the objective area.

(2) Commanders should avoid splitting (between two units) the responsibility for the defense of an avenue of approach or key terrain.

(3) Commanders should ensure there is adequate maneuver space in the sector, including key terrain features that control it.

(4) Commanders should avoid designating boundaries in such a way that a major terrain obstacle divides a unit sector; this presents problems for maneuvering forces.

(5) The boundaries should provide adequate room to permit the commander to maneuver forces on both sides of the assault objectives.

(6) The commanders must choose boundaries that are recognizable both on the map and on the ground. Roads should not be used as a boundary because they represent a high-speed avenue of approach and need to be covered with a clear understanding of responsibility. Instead, commanders can use rivers, streams, railroad tracks, the edge of a town, woods, the edge of a swamp, and so on.

(7) Ideally, each battalion sector should include at least one DZ and LZ to enable the battalion and its attachments to land within the assigned sector during the assault. This also facilitates resupply and evacuation of EPWs and casualties. Having an LZ and DZ reduces the problem of coordination with adjacent units. This does not mean that commanders must locate all battalion DZs in the battalion sector. Regardless of boundaries, units should drop on the DZs closest to their assault objectives.

(8) Commanders should establish boundaries that will serve during the assault and during later operations. These should be readily recognizable during limited visibility.

(9) Commanders should choose boundaries that do not require a unit to defend in more than one direction at once. Also, they should not expect a unit to secure objectives within the airhead at the same time they establish its defense.

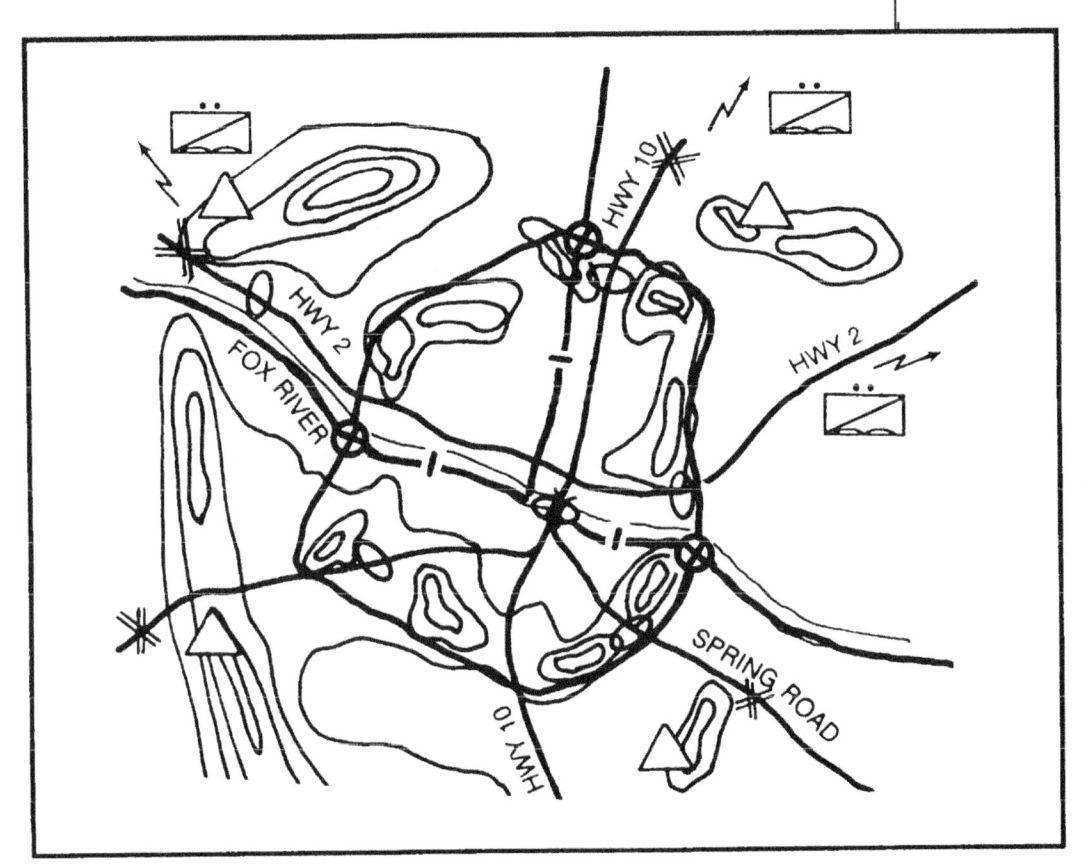

Figure 3-3. Boundaries.

(10) Boundaries should extend beyond the trace of the security force as far as necessary to coordinate fires. This also allows subordinate units to operate for-ward of the airhead with minimal coordination.

(11) Commanders should plan coordinating points at the intersection of the airhead line and security force ground trace boundaries.

b. **Task Organization.** Once commanders have determined the principal features of the ground assault plan (scheme of maneuver and fire support), they organize units to execute their assigned missions and they determine boundaries at the same time. To ensure unity of effort or to increase readiness for combat, part or all of the subordinate units of any command can be formed into one or more temporary tactical groupings (teams or task forces), each under a designated commander. No standard team organization can be prescribed in advance to meet all conditions. Infantry units usually form the nucleus tactical groupings of the team; infantry unit commanders lead the teams. These teams are tailored for initial assault by the attachment of required combat, CS, and CSS units. They are attached as soon as possible in the marshaling area. Many of the units detach as soon as centralized control can be regained and the parent unit headquarters can be established on the ground. Other units such as higher echelon assault CPs can be attached for the movement only.

(1) *Brigade.* Attachments for airborne infantry brigades usually include the following:

(a) An FA battalion.

(b) A combat engineer company.

(c) An MP platoon.

(d) A light armor company/platoon.

(c) An IEW support element, usually from the MI battalion.

(f) A forward area support team.

(g) An ADA battery.

(h) Other assets as determined necessary by the division commander based upon his estimate of the situation.

(2) *Battalion.* For control, the airborne infantry battalions are usually reinforced for the airborne assault and organized into task forces. This is especially true if battalions are to land in widely separated DZs or LZs. A battalion TF usually consists of an infantry battalion that is reinforced based on the brigade commander's estimate of the situation. Reinforcements can include more infantry, armor, antitank, engineer, dedicated artillery, and any other units or detachments needed in the initial attack. As in the brigade. attachments to infantry battalions are made early in the planning phase. They can be withdrawn as soon as the ground situation stabilizes.

(3) *Rifle units.* Rifle companies and platoons can be reinforced for the airborne assault according to the usual considerations governing a ground attack. Attachments are made before the move to, or on arrival in, the marshaling camp.

c. **Organization for Assault Landing.** After the task organization of soldiers for the assault landing is announced, units organize into assault, follow-on, and rear echelons.

(1) *Assault echelon.* The assault echelon is composed of those forces required to seize the assault objectives and the initial airhead, plus their reserves and supporting soldiers.

(2) *Follow-on echelon* The airborne force does not need the follow-on echelon in the objective area during the initial assault, but does need it for subsequent operations. When needed, the follow-on echelon enters the objective area as soon as practical by air, surface movement, or a combination of the two. It includes additional vehicles and equipment from assault echelon units, plus more combat, CS, and CSS units. The existence of any one of the following conditions requires an airborne unit to have a follow-on echelon:

- Shortage of aircraft.
- Aircraft that cannot land heavy items of equipment.
- Any enemy situation, terrain, or weather that makes it impossible to land certain soldiers or equipment in the assault echelon.

Airborne infantry units can be committed to an airborne assault without leaving a follow-on echelon that must be brought forward by means other than air; however. it is often desirable or necessary to leave certain personnel and equipment behind.

(3) *Rear echelon.* The rear echelon includes the part of an airborne unit that is not considered essential for initial combat operations. It also includes people left at its rear base to perform administrative and service support functions that cannot be done efficiently in the combat area. The rear echelon is normally small for a brigade or battalion. Higher headquarters usually controls the rear echelon for all units. The rear echelon can remain at the REMAB when the unit is to be relieved at an early date; or it can rejoin the unit when the brigade remains committed to sustained combat for a prolonged or indefinite period. Also, if the airborne force continues in the ground combat role after linkup, the rear echelon may be brought forward.

3-6. DESIGNATION OF RESERVE

The employment of the reserve element follows the normal employment of a reserve unit in a ground operation.

a. **The Battalion as the Division Reserve.** The division reserve can be held in the departure area ready to be committed by air when and where the situation dictates A battalion can be the division reserve. This usually happens in large-scale airborne operations when suitable airfields in the airhead are not available; however, it can cause delays in commitment–

- If signal communications fail.
- If the air move is very long.
- If flying weather is unfavorable.
- If time is added for coordination of air cover.

With the reserve element at the departure airfield, the reserve commander must continue planning for possible future commitment of his forces as far as maps, photos, and information of the situation permit.

b. **Brigade and Battalion Reserves.** These reserves enter the airhead as part of the assault echelon. They provide depth to the airhead by blocking penetrations, reinforcing committed units, and counterattacking. They consist of not more than a company at brigade level or a platoon at battalion level; however, their small size is dictated by tactical considerations and assigned missions. Commanders should organize, task, and position the reserve, ensuring that–

(1) The size of the reserve is compatible with likely missions.

(2) The reserve comes from the unit with the fewest priority tasks.

(3) The reserve is not assigned assault objectives or a sector of the airhead to defend.

(4) The reserve is near areas of likely employment such as near the main enemy avenues of approach to speed commitment.

(5) The reserve is mobile. (This can be achieved using organic vehicles – antiarmor company, support platoon, light armor, and so on.)

(6) The reserve is located in an AA (both initial and subsequent) or battle position, so that it does not interfere with units assigned assault objectives.

(7) The reserve is near an LOC in a covered and concealed location to provide ease of movement, to reinforce, or to block.

(8) The reserve is located within the sector of one unit, if possible.

(9) The reserve's location allows for dispersion of the force.

(10) The reserve commander prepares and rehearses commitment contingencies IAW guidance received from the commander designating the reserve.

Section II. EXECUTION

Execution of the GTP involves the initial seizure of DZs and LZs in and around the airfield or the actual seizure of an airfield. (See Chapter 7.)

3-7. CONDUCT OF THE ASSAULT

The initial assault emphasizes the coordinated action of small units to seize initial battalion objectives before the surprise advantage has worn off. As assault objectives are seized, the airborne force directs its efforts toward consolidating the airhead.

a. Tactical surprise and detailed planning should enable units to seize their assault objectives and to establish the airhead before the enemy has time to react in force. Missions of units are changed as required by the enemy defense of initial objectives. The enemy can be expected to quickly launch uncoordinated attacks along major avenues of approach using local forces. The degree of coordination and strength of these attacks increase progressively; the airborne force must develop correspondingly greater strength in its defensive positions. Preparation of early defense against armored attack is a major consideration.

b. Units assigned to perform R&S missions land in early serials so they can establish roadblocks; locate enemy forces; disrupt enemy communication facilities; and provide the commander with early warning, security, and information. Since ground reconnaissance by unit commanders is seldom possible before the airborne operation, it must begin as soon as the unit lands. The flow of information must be continuous. Information requirements do not vary from those employed by other ground units. However, the unit's method of arrival in the combat area makes immediate and thorough reconnaissance and transmission of information to higher headquarters necessary.

c. If the initial objectives are heavily defended, the bulk of the force is assigned the task of seizing these objectives. When initial objectives are lightly defended, the bulk of the force can be employed in clearing assigned sectors and preparing defensive positions in depth. Extensive patrolling is initiated early between adjacent defensive positions within the airhead line, and between the airhead and the R&S line. Army aircraft are well suited for support of this patrolling effort. Contact with any friendly guerrilla forces in the area is established as soon as possible.

d. Personnel are briefed on unit plans, adjacent and higher units' plans, and alternate plans. This helps units or personnel landing in unplanned areas to direct their efforts to accomplishing the mission. Misdelivered units or personnel establish contact with their respective headquarters as soon as practical.

c. Sufficient communications personnel and equipment must be moved into the airhead in advance of the CP they are to serve to ensure the timely installation of vital communications. As soon as communications and the tactical situation permit, commanders regain centralized C^2. Therefore, immediate establishment of the following is necessary for effective C^2:

(1) Command and fire control channels within the airborne forces.

(2) Communications with supporting air and naval forces.

(3) Communications with airlift forces concerned with buildup, air supply, and air evacuation.

(4) Communications with bases in friendly territory.

(5) Communications between widely separated airborne or ground forces, such as linkup forces, with a common or coordinated mission.

f. The commander influences the action by–
- Shifting or allocating fire support means.
- Moving forces.
- Modifying missions.
- Changing objectives and boundaries.
- Employing reserves.
- Moving to a place from which he can best exercise personal influence, especially during the initial assault.

g. When initial objectives have been secured, subordinate units seize additional objectives that facilitate the establishment of a coordinated brigade defense or the conduct of future operations. Defensive positions are organized, communications are supplemented, and reserves are reconstituted. These and other measures are taken to prepare the force to repel enemy counterattacks, to minimize the effects of attack by nuclear weapons, or to resume the offensive.

h. Reserves prepare and occupy blocking positions, pending commitment. Typical missions for reserves committed during the initial assault include taking over the missions of misdelivered units, dealing with unexpected opposition in seizing assault objectives, and securing the initial airhead.

3-8. DEVELOPMENT OF THE AIRHEAD

After the airborne forces make the initial assault landings and accomplish the initial ground missions, commanders must organize the airhead line.

a. **Size.** The airhead line extends far enough beyond the landing area to ensure uninterrupted landings of personnel, equipment, and supplies. It secures the requisite terrain features and maneuver space for such future offensive or defensive operations as the mission calls for.

b. **Occupation and Organization.** Units occupy and organize the airhead line to the extent demanded by the situation. Commanders adjust the disposition of units and installations to fit the terrain and the situation. Units take reconnaissance and security measures; this usually includes the reinforcement of the R&S line. The degree to which the airhead line is actually occupied and organized for defense is largely determined by the mission, enemy capabilities, and the defensive characteristics of the terrain.

c. **Buildup.** This proceeds concurrently with the seizure and organization of the airhead line. As more combat personnel arrive and commanders organize them by unit, frontline positions are reinforced, reserves are constituted, and preparations are mare for such offensive operations as the mission requires.

3-9. BUILDUP OF COMBAT POWER

The buildup of combat power is the introduction of the follow-on echelon into the airhead. This increase of friendly combat power yields a corresponding ability to conduct a defense of the airhead and to conduct a short term sustainment of those forces. The intent of the buildup is to provide a secure operating and logistic base for forces working to move the airhead away from the original point of attack. Usually, this distance is equal to the enemy's direct fire capability to harass and destroy incoming aircraft or landing craft (5 to 10 kilometers).

a. The composition of the follow-on echelon depends on the factors of METT-T. It can consist of heavy, light, long-range FA, and combat engineers as well as significant CS and CSS elements. Other forces required can include the following:

- Infantry Forces.
- Light/heavy task forces.

- Armored units task-organized with light forces already in the objective area.
- Field artillery.
- Engineers in addition to those in the assault echelon.
- Air defense artillery.
- CSS assets.

b. The time involved in defensive operations, if any, varies. It depends on the mission assigned, the composition and size of the force, the enemy reaction, and the type of operation contemplated. A well-prepared defense in short-duration missions in isolated objective areas may not be required. Security can be accomplished by completely or almost completely destroying or dispersing the enemy forces in the immediate objective area during the assault; then, airlifting the striking force before the execution of a coordinated enemy counterattack.

(1) *Defense of an airhead.* The airborne force usually defends an airhead by securing key terrain within the airhead and dominating likely avenues of approach. Units deny the enemy the areas between the occupied positions with a combination of patrols, mines, fire, and natural and man-made obstacles. Units aggressively reconnoiter between positions within the airhead, between the airhead and the RSL, and forward of the RSL. They increase emphasis on reconnaissance forward of the RSL during limited visibility. The airhead configuration allows the commander to shift forces, reserves, and supporting fires quickly to reinforce another sector of the airhead. Regardless of the form of defense chosen, the force prepares positions in depth within its capabilities.

(2) *Defense during withdrawal.* Should withdrawal from the initial positions be required, the final area to which the airborne force withdraws must contain adequate space for maneuver, for protection of critical installations, and for planned airlanding or air evacuation operations.

(3) *Defense against armor.* During the initial phases of an airborne operation, one of the main defenses against enemy armor is tactical air support. Aircraft attack enemy armor targets as they appear, as far as possible from the objective area, and continue to attack and observe them as long as they threaten the airborne force. Strongpoints defending the airhead use natural obstacles, plus mine fields, tank traps, demolitions, and man-made obstacles. Units emplace AT weapons in depth along avenues of approach favorable for armor. They cover all dangerous avenues of approach with planned fires. The Dragons and LAWs of the rifle companies, the TOWs of the battalion antiarmor company, and the AT weapons of division aviation units give the airborne force a substantial amount of antitank firepower. Some of the antitank weapons, organic to battalions that are holding sectors not under armored attack, can be moved to reinforce threatened sectors.

(4) *Defense against air assault.* All personnel must recognize that the enemy can conduct air assault operations and must defend against these attacks. Helicopters afford the enemy one of their best means of rapidly moving significant tactical forces to the airhead area.

(5) *Defense against airborne attack, guerrilla action, and infiltration.* The defense must include plans for countering enemy airborne attacks, guerrilla attacks, or infiltrated forces attacking the airhead area. The basic defense

against these attacks is an extensive patrol and warning system, an all-round defense, and designated reserve units ready to move out quickly to destroy the enemy force. Units must be especially alert during limited visibility to prevent the enemy from infiltrating. If the enemy can build up forces in the airhead interior, they can influence operations. During daylight, units must locate and destroy any enemy that have infiltrated the airhead.

CHAPTER 4

LANDING PLAN

The commander finalizes the landing plan after completing the ground tactical plan. The landing plan phases forces into the objective area at the correct time and place to execute the ground tactical plan. The execution of the landing plan is vital to the swift massing of combat power, protection of the force, and subsequent mission accomplishment. This was demonstrated by the 503d Parachute Regimental Combat Team in the airborne assault in support of the invasion of Corrigedor, Philippines on 16 February 1945.

February 16, 1945 was the beginning of one of the most unusual airborne operations in the Southwest Pacific area during World War II. Because of Corrigedor's fortifications, the joint commander was determined that more than just an amphibious assault was necessary. The plan called for an intense air and naval bombardment of the island, followed by an airborne assault to neutralize the fortifications and facilitate the amphibious landing.

The planning for the operation was extensive. The regimental and battalion commanders along with selected staff officers observed the island while riding as passengers in planes making preparatory air strikes. After the aerial reconnaissance, the Regimental Combat Team commander and his battalion commanders studied aerial photographs of the island. Because the island was 1 square mile in area, only two areas were suitable for a drop zone. The largest was only 150 by 275 yards and sloped down to an abrupt 500-foot drop to the sea. Because the RCT commander had confidence in the capabilities of his soldiers and a thorough knowledge of airborne techniques, he felt that the mission could be accomplished successfully.

Because sufficient aircraft were not available to lift the RCT at one time, the commander task-organized the regiment into battalion landing teams. There was a total of 51 aircraft available for the drop and about 3,000 men to be transported. This meant that the RCT had to be transported in three lifts. One battalion landing team would be dropped on the morning of D plus 1, one in the afternoon, and the third on the morning of D plus 2.

Because of the small DZs, the planes had to fly in trail formation (one behind the other), divided into two columns, one over each DZ. The planes in the left column would fly over DZA, drop eight paratroopers and an equipment bundle, circle to the left, join the tail of the column and, in a round-robin fashion, continue until all personnel and equipment had been dropped. The planes on the right would do the same thing over DZB, except they would turn to the right. An airborne command ship was used to control the drop and make corrections.

It took a little over an hour for the first battalion to be dropped. The operation was a success — the Japanese were totally surprised. The airborne force suppressed the defending Japanese and destroyed many gun and mortar emplacements, allowing the 3d Battalion, 34th Infantry to make the amphibious landings with few casualties. Later events revealed that the Japanese commander had been informed that he should devise a defensive plan to repulse an airborne assault of the island. After he made a reconnaissance he decided that such an attack was virtually impossible and did nothing.

The ability to rapidly assemble and conduct small-unit operations enabled the 503d RCT to accomplish its assigned mission. Extensive training, detailed planning, and thorough rehearsals contributed to the success of this combat operation. The regimental commander task-organized his force to accomplish the ground tactical plan while devising the simplest landing plan possible under the circumstances. He anticipated the development many years later of the ABCCC by using an aerial command ship to observe and control the drop.

Section I. PLANNING

The landing plan is the airborne commander's plan that links air movement into the ground tactical plan. The landing plan is published at the brigade level and below, but is informal and not published at the joint level. The landing plan is a tabulation of the sequence, method, and destination of paratroopers and materiel into the objective area. The landing plan has five elements:

- Sequence of delivery.
- Method of delivery.
- Place of delivery.
- Time of delivery.
- The assembly plan.

4-1. REQUIREMENTS

To develop the landing plan, commanders at each level need to know their commander's priorities the airlift tactics, the landing area study, the parent and subunit task organization and ground tactical plans, and the subunit landing plan. During the briefback of the ground tactical plan, the commander establishes airlift/delivery priorities and airlift tactics. He provides as much of this information as possible to subunits at the end of the ground tactical plan briefback.

a. **Commander's Priorities.** The commander must set the priorities for each assault objective to determine the delivery sequence for units that are to secure these objectives. This dots not necessarily match the sequence in which the units secure objectives. The commander must also know:

(1) The priorities for deliveries on each DZ (personnel drop, CDS, heavy drops, and LAPES).

(2) The DZ sequence.

(3) The priorities for delivering the remainder of the forces.

(4) The method of delivery for each unit and its equipment.

(5) The priorities for use of EZs.

(6) The location of the HEPI and the PPI.

b. **Airlift Tactics.** The Air Force element responsible for selecting airlift tactics develops them with the Army element to best support the ground tactical plan. These tactics include aircraft formations and the sequence of personnel drops, heavy drops, and LAPES. The Army element chooses this sequence and the time intervals between serials, which are groups of like aircraft (C-130s, C-141s) with the same delivery method (personnel drops, heavy drops, LAPES) going to the same DZ.

c. **Landing Area Study.** Division or corps staff, working with US Army Topographic Engineers and the Air Force, develops the landing area study and provides it to subunits. This study enables subunits to select the location, size, and orientation of DZs to best support their scheme of maneuver.

d. **Subunit Landing Plans.** Subordinate commanders should develop landing plans to support their own respective schemes of maneuver. Subunits then briefback their landing plans so that higher headquarters can finalize their plans. Units must also know the initial locations of CS and CSS elements. This information should become available as subunits briefback their ground tactical plan.

4-2. CONSIDERATIONS

Commanders should examine the following considerations when developing the landing plan.

a. **Basic Methods of Attacking an Objective.** There are three basic methods of attacking an objective.

(1) *Jumping or landing on top of the objective.* This method works best for attacking a small objective that is specially fortified against ground attack. However, an airborne landing into an area strongly defended against air attack requires surprise to succeed.

(2) *Jumping or landing near the objective.* This method works best for the capture of a lightly defended objective that must be seized intact such as a bridge. If the enemy has strong defenses against air attack, only surprise can enable the unit to achieve success with few casualties.

(3) *Jumping or landing at a distance from the objective.* This technique is the least often used of the techniques available. Airborne forces use this method for large complex objectives that must be seized by deliberate attack. The DZ is selected to emphasize security and preservation of the force. The plan is based on METT-T considerations and should capitalize on the principle of surprise.

b. **Basic Methods of Landing.** There are two basic landing methods.

(1) *Multiple drop zones.* The use of multiple DZs creates a number of small airheads in the objective area. This technique supports the principle of mass by placing the maximum number of paratroopers in the objective area in the minimum amount of time. Additionally, the commander can capitalize on the principle of surprise because the main effort is not easily determined by the enemy. This technique is normally used by division-size elements and larger.

(2) *Single drop zone.* Brigade and smaller-size airborne forces often establish an airhead by conducting the airborne assault onto a single drop zone. This technique allows the assaulting unit to assemble quickly and mass combat power against the enemy.

c. **Time-Space Factors.** Commanders schedule the delivery sequence and the time between serials to provide the least time and distance separation between each aircraft and serial. The airborne force assembles maximum combat power on the DZ as quickly as possible, using either of the following options:

(1) *Land all elements in the same area.* Aircraft approach the DZ in a deep, narrow formation and all soldiers jump into a small area.

(2) *Land all elements at the same time.* Aircraft in a wide formation approach various DZs situated close to each other and all soldiers jump at the same time or as near to it as possible.

d. **Landing Priorities.** Airborne units are cross loaded to land close to their assault objectives.

e. **Organization.** Airborne forces try to maintain tactical unity.

(1) Battalions or battalion TFs normally land intact on a single DZ. A brigade lands in mutually supporting DZs. Two or more battalions land successively on the same DZ or each can land on a separate DZ within a general brigade DZ area.

(2) The airborne force sends as many assault unit personnel and equipment as possible into the area in parachute serials. Commanders must consider the mobility of equipment after the landing. For example, the carriers or prime movers that are deliverable by parachute, but difficult to manhandle on the ground, can accompany the weapons in the assault clement. Paratroopers accompany their units' principal items of equipment.

4-3. SEQUENCE OF DELIVERY

The commander's priorities within the ground tactical plan determine the sequence of delivery. Neither aircraft allocations nor the availability of aircraft should influence these decisions. The commander determines final aircraft allocations after the landing plan briefbacks. JAAP serials may precede the main airlift column to drop combat control teams and Army LRSU. The CCT places and operates navigation aids on the drop and landing zones; the LRSU provides surveillance on NAI and reports to the ground force commander.

4-4. METHOD OF DELIVERY

This part of the landing plan addresses how the force with its needed supplies and equipment arrives in the objective area. The assault echelon comes in by parachute. The commander can use a number of other means to introduce additional personnel, equipment, and supplies into the objective area.

a. **Personnel Airdrop.** The airborne force delivers assault personnel by parachute drop. This method allows quick, nearly simultaneous delivery of the force. Planners choose any terrain free of obstacles that allows the assault force to land on or close to objectives. In some cases and with special equipment, it can deliver personnel into rough terrain. Special teams, such as the JAAP, can use HAHO or HALO techniques. These techniques allow for early delivery of the JAAP without compromising the objective's location.

b. **Equipment/Supply/Airdrop.** Airborne forces can airdrop supplies and equipment directly to units behind enemy lines or in other unreachable areas.

(1) *Advantages.*

(a) Prerigging and storing emergency items for contingencies considerably reduces shipping and handling time and increases responsiveness.

(b) Since the delivery aircraft does not land, there is no need for forward airfields/LZs or materiel handling equipment for offloading.

(c) This reduces flight time and exposure to hostile fire and increases aircraft survivability and availability.

(d) Ground forces can disperse more since they are not tied to an airfield or strip.

(2) *Disadvantages.*

(a) Airdrops require specially trained rigger personnel and appropriate aircraft.

(b) Bad weather or high winds can delay the airdrop or scatter the dropped cargo.

(c) Ground fire threatens vulnerable aircraft making their final approach, especially if mountains or high hills canalize the aircraft.

(d) Since the aircraft do not land, no opportunity for ground refueling exists. Planned aerial refueling can extend aircraft range and should be considered on long flight legs to increase objective area loiter time and mission flexibility.

(e) Bulky airdrop rigs for equipment prevent the aircraft from carrying as much cargo as when configured for airland.

(f) The possibility of loss or damage to equipment during the airdrop always exists.

(g) Ground forces must secure the DZ to prevent items from falling into enemy hands.

(h) Recovery of airdropped equipment is slow and manpower intensive.

(3) Types of *equipment delivery.* Free drop, high-velocity drop, low-velocity drop, HALO, and LAPES are different types of air deliveries. (See FM 100-27.)

(a) Free drop (less than 600 feet AGL). Free drop requires no parachute or retarding device. The airdrop crew can use energy-dissipating materiel around the load to lessen the shock when it hits the ground at a rate of 130 to 150 feet a second. Fortification or barrier material, clothing in bales, and other such items can be free dropped.

(b) High-velocity airdrop (400 to 600 feet AGL). Parachutes, which have enough drag to hold the load upright during the descent at 70 to 90 feet a second, stabilize loads for high-velocity airdrops. Army parachute riggers place airdrop cargo on emergy-dissipating material and rig it in an airdrop container. This method works well for subsistence, packaged POL products, ammunition, and other such items. The ground commander may usc the standard high-velocity delivery system, which is the container delivery system, to deliver accompanying and follow-on supplies; they can be delivered within an area 400 by 100 meters. A CDS is the most favored means of resupply; it is also the most accurate of all airdrop methods. Each pallet holds up to 2,200 pounds. A C-130 holds up to 16 of these containers, while a C-141B holds up to 40. Planners should calculate the CARP near AAs or resupply points. The ALO or Army DZ support team controls receipt of CDS. (Figure 4-1.)

Figure 4-1. Container delivery system.

(c) Low-velocity airdrop (1,100 feet or less AGL, depending on DZ size). Low-velocity airdrop requires cargo parachutes. Crews rig items on an airdrop platform or in an airdrop container. They put energy-dissipating material beneath the load to lessen the shock when it hits the ground. Cargo parachutes attached to the load reduce the rate of descent to no more than 28 feet a second. Fragile materiel, vehicles, and artillery can be low-velocity airdropped.

- Heavy drop. Airborne forces use this method most often to deliver vehicles, bulk cargo, and equipment. Airdrop aircraft deliver heavy-drop equipment just ahead of the main body or, if following personnel drops, at least 30 minutes after the last paratrooper exits. For night drops, the heavy drop precedes personnel drops.
- Door bundles and wedges. This procedure requires the use of either the A7A cargo sling or the A21 cargo bag. With these, aircraft personnel can drop unit loads of up to 500 pounds just before the first soldier's exit. Local SOPS dictate the number and type of door bundles that specific aircraft can drop.

(d) HALO. Airborne forces use HALO to airdrop supplies and equipment at high altitudes when aircraft must fly above the threat air defense umbrella. (Figure 4-2.) The rigged load is pulled from the aircraft by a stabilizing parachute and free falls to a low altitude where a cargo parachute opens to allow a low-velocity landing.

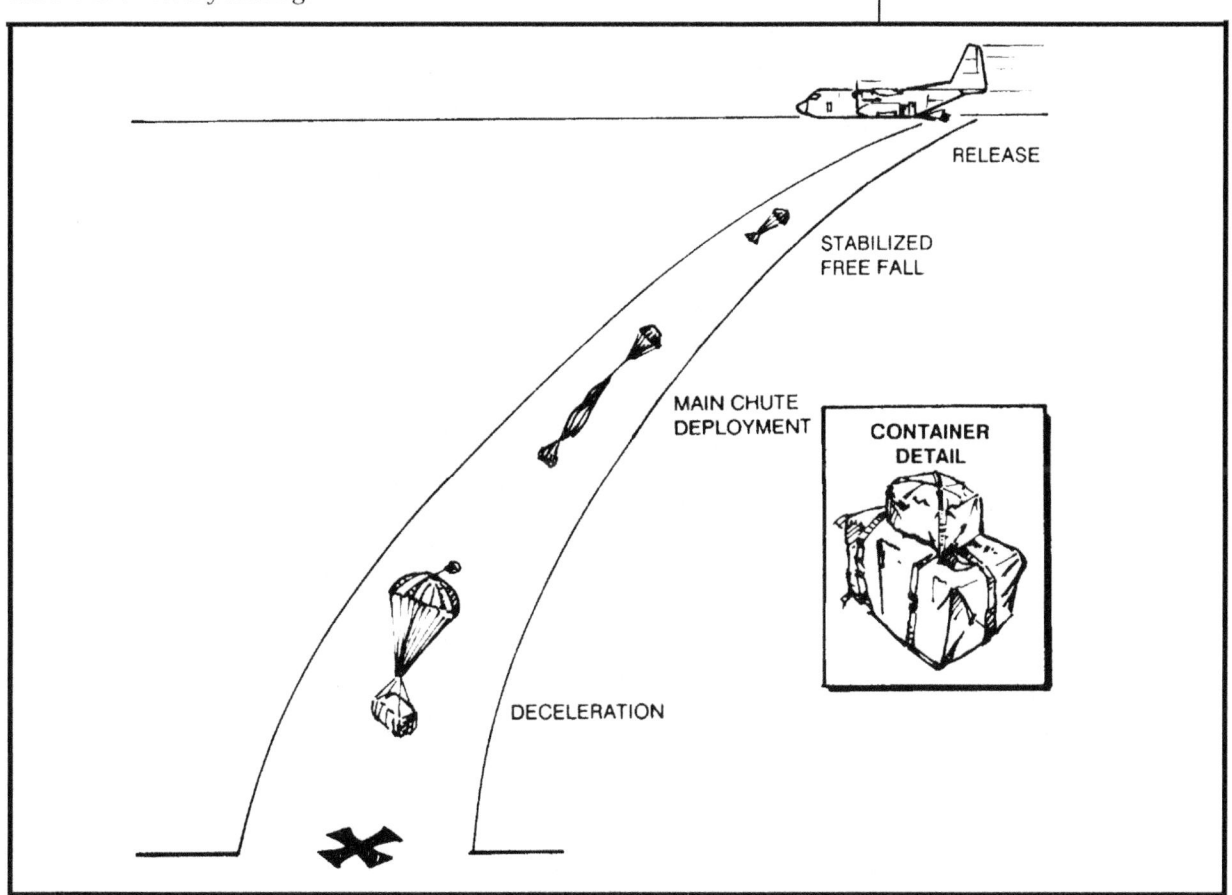

Figure 4-2. HALO supply delivery.

(c) Low-altitude parachute extraction system. The LAPES uses extraction parachutes to airdrop palletized loads and equipment from airlift aircraft flying about 5 to 10 feet above the ground. (Figure 4-3.) The extraction parachute that pulls the rigged load from the aircraft also helps to slow the platform and load as it slides across the EZ. Some airfields and EZs require special preparation for a LAPES delivery. (See Appendix A for detailed information on LAPES extraction zone requirements.)

- Airborne forces can usc the LAPES to deliver vehicles, artillery, ammunition, supplies, equipment, and water. It is a reliable way to rapidly introduce outsized or heavy loads (such as the M551 Sheridan) and bulk supplies (such as ammunition and fuel). It allows accurate delivery into small perimeters.
- Adverse weather conditions, such as excessive surface or altitude winds or low ceilings, inhibit airdrop, but they do not preclude the use of the LAPES. Airdrops by the LAPES can be accurately delivered on plateaus, mountains, cratered airfields, or assault LZs, and among other obstacles.
- The LAPES reduces aircraft radar signature; it allows the aircraft to avoid enemy air defense systems by flying low, and it negates having to defend against ground fire. once ground forces have cleared the EZ. aircraft can deliver LAPES airdrops in any sequence. Units must arrange the time, personnel, and equipment to derig and remove the delivered LAPES load from the EZ before that EZ can be used for another load. They can facilitate this by preparing multiple/parallel EZs.

Figure 4-3. Low-altitude parachute extraction system.

c. **Airland.** Airborne forces can accomplish certain phases of airborne operations, or even the entire operation, by using airland to deliver personnel and equipment to the objective area. (See FMs 7-20, 7-30, and 100-27.)

(1) *Advantages.* In some cases, airlanding rather than airdropping personnel and equipment may be advantageous because airlanding –

(a) Provides the most economical means of airlift.

(b) Delivers Army aviation elements, engineering equipment, artillery pieces, and other mission-essential items in one operation.

(c) Provides a readily available means of casualty evacuation.

(d) Allows units to maintain tactical integrity and to deploy rapidly after landing.

(c) Allows the use of units with little special training and equipment.

(f) Does not require extensive preparation and rigging of equipment.

(g) Offers a relatively reliable means of personnel and equipment delivery regardless of weather.

(h) Precludes equipment damage and personnel injuries units may experience in parachute operations.

(2) *Disadvantages.* In other cases, airlanding is not advantageous because it –

(a) Cannot be used for forced entry.

(b) Requires moderately level, unobstructed LZs with adequate soil trafficability.

(c) Requires more time for delivery of a given size force than airdrop, especially for small, restricted LZs.

(d) Generally requires improvement or new construction of airland facilities, which adds to the engineer workload.

(c) Requires some form of airlift control element support at offloading airfields. Mission intervals depend on airlift control element size, offloaded equipment availability, and airfield support capability.

(3) *Organization for movement.* The tactical integrity of participating units is a major consideration in an airland operation. Small units that are expected to engage in combat on landing, airland organizationally intact with weapons, ammunition, and personnel in the same aircraft, whenever possible. Joint planning stresses placing units as close as possible to objectives, consistent with the availability of LZs and the operational capability of the tactical aircraft employed. Because of aircraft vulnerability on the ground, units unload as quickly as possible.

(a) The airborne commander determines the makeup of each aircraft load and the sequence of delivery. The mission, the tactical situation, and the assigned forces influence this decision.

(b) Units should use existing facilities, such as roads and open areas, to reduce the time and effort required for new construction. They should consider layouts that facilitate future expansion and provide maximum

FM 90-26

deployment and flexibility. As the size and efficiency of an air facility improve, its value to the enemy as a target increases. To reduce this vulnerability, the facilities should be dispersed and simple.

4-5. PLACE OF DELIVERY

The selection of DZs/LZs/EZs is a joint responsibility. The airlift commander is responsible for the precise delivery of personnel and cargo to the DZ/LZ and for the selection of approaches to the DZ. Both joint and component commanders must base their decisions on knowledge of their respective problems and on the needs of the overall operation. The nature and location of landing areas are important considerations when preparing the scheme of maneuver. The general area in which they are to be established is necessarily governed by the mission. At higher echelons, commanders can assign landing areas in broad general terms. In lower units, leaders must describe their locations more specifically. Drop zones are selected only after a detailed analysis. Commanders should consider the following factors when making their selections.

a. **Ease of Identification.** The DZ should be easy to spot from the air. Airlift pilots and navigators prefer to rely on visual recognition of terrain features to accurately deliver personnel and equipment.

b. **Straight-Line Approach.** To ensure an accurate airdrop, the aircraft should make a straight-line approach to each DZ for at least 10 miles, or about four minutes at drop airspeed, before the start of the drop.

c. **Out of Range.** The commander should choose a DZ that allows the units to avoid enemy air defenses and strong ground defences and puts them outside the range of enemy suppressive fires. To get to the DZ, aircraft should not have to fly over or near enemy antiaircraft installations, which can detect aircraft at drop altitudes. They should fly over hostile territory or positions for the least possible time.

d. **Close To or On Top of Assault Objectives.** If the enemy situation permits, the commander should choose a DZ directly on top of assault objectives.

e. **Suitable Weather and Terrain.** The commander must consider the weather and terrain because these conditions affect the usability of a DZ.

(1) *Weather.* Commanders should consider seasonal weather conditions when selecting DZs. Adverse weather effects can be devastating. Ground fog, mist, haze, smoke, and low-hanging cloud conditions can interfere with the aircrew's observation of DZ visual signals and markings. However, they do offer excellent cover for blind or area DZs. Excessive winds also hamper operations.

(2) *Terrain.* Flat or rolling terrain is desirable; it should be relatively free, but not necessarily clear, of obstacles. Obstacles on a DZ will not prevent paratroopers from landing but will increase jump casualties. Sites in mountainous or hilly country with large valleys or level plateaus can be used for security reasons. Small valleys or pockets completely surrounded by hills

are difficult to locate and should be used only in rare cases. Commanders must avoid man-made obstacles more than 150 feet (46 meters) above the level of the DZ within a radius of 3 nautical miles. High ground or hills need not be considered a hazard unless the hills pose an escape problem that is beyond the aircraft's capability. High ground or hills more than 1,000 feet (305 meters) above the surface of the site should not be closer than 3 nautical miles to the DZ for night operations. The perimeter of the DZ should have one or more open approach sectors free of any obstacles that would prevent the aircrew's sighting of the DZ markings.

(a) Cover and concealment. Cover and concealment near the DZs/LZs area distinct advantage when the airborne forces assemble and when airland forces land.

(b) Road net. Having a DZ near a good road net expedites moving personnel, supplies, and equipment from that zone. If the landing area contains terrain that is to be developed into an airlanding facility, a road net is of particular value – not only for moving items from the facility but also for evacuating personnel and equipment.

(c) Key terrain. The DZ site selected should aid in the success of the mission by taking advantage of dominating terrain, covered routes of approach to the objective, and terrain favorable for defense against armored attack.

f. **Minimum Construction for DZs/LZs.** Because of limited engineer support in the airborne force, selected landing zones should have a minimum requirement for construction and maintenance. Unless more engineer support is requested and received, construction and maintenance restraints can limit the number of areas that can be used or developed.

g. **Mutual Support.** Commanders should select mutually supporting DZs/LZs that provide initial positions favorable to the attack.

h. **Configuration.** The division/brigade commander gives guidance on DZ size in OPLANs or OPORDs. Then each unit commander determines the exact shape, size, and capacity they need.

(1) *Shape.* The most desirable shapes for DZs arc rectangular or round; these permit a wider choice of aircraft approach directions. However, [hey also require precise navigation and timing to avoid collisions or drop interference

(2) *Size.* The DZ should be large enough to accommodate the airborne force employed; one DZ that allows the aircraft to drop all of its load in one pass is desirable. Repeated passes are dangerous because the initial pass can alert enemy antiaircraft and other emplacements, and they will be waiting for subsequent drops.

(a) There are certain situations, however, when multiple passes can be used. This occurs mainly when there is no significant air defense threat and orbits can be made over areas where enemy antiaircraft systems are not positioned. This applies especially to the seizure of islands where small DZs arc the rule. If there are enough aircraft available to deliver the force with less personnel on each aircraft, there is no real problem. However, if there are only enough aircraft to deliver the assault echelon in one lift with each aircraft carrying the maximum number of personnel, then the aircraft will have to make multiple passes over the DZ.

(b) A large DZ can permit several points of impact to be designated and used. Although it is desirable to saturate the objective area in the shortest possible time, there is a reasonable limit to the amount of personnel and heavy drop that can be stacked on a single drop zone. Therefore, it can be desirable to use multiple points of impact on a single DZ — provided the drop zone is large enough to permit this.

(3) Capacity. The DZ capacity is based on the expected number of units to be dropped and their dispersion pattern. (See Appendix A for criteria for determining DZ capacity.)

i. **Orientation.** Thoughtful orientation allows the quickest possible delivery of the airborne force into the objective area.

(1) Ideal DZs offset and parallel each serial. (Figures 4-4 and 4-5.) This allows aircraft to share a flight route until they approach the objective area; then they can split at an IP (RP) for simultaneous delivery on several DZs.

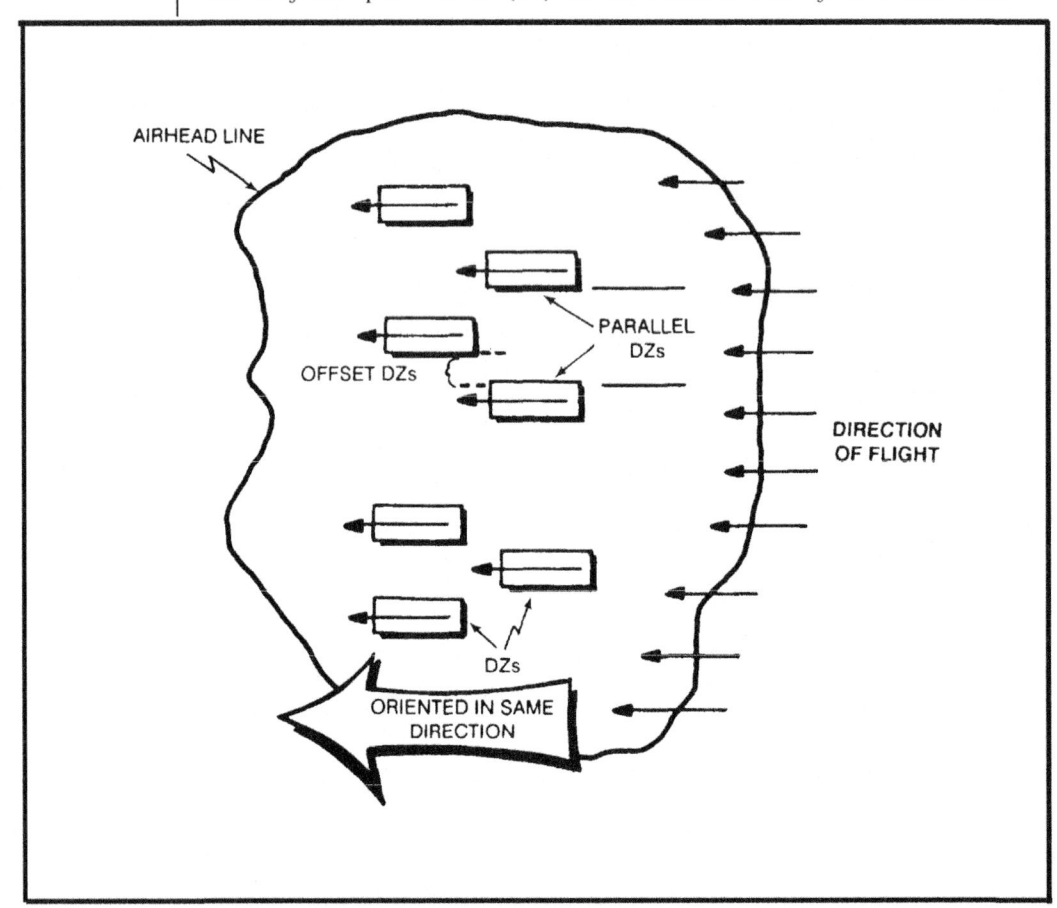

Figure 4-4. Ideal DZ situation.

```
┌─────────────────────────────────────────────┐
│           GOOD DZ SITUATION                 │
│         ╭─────────────────╮                 │
│        ╱   ┌──┐    ┌──┐   ╲                 │
│       │    └──┘    └──┘    │ ← AIRCRAFT     │
│       │    ┌──┐    ┌──┐    │   APPROACH     │
│       │    └──┘    └──┘    │ ←              │
│        ╲    ╲  DZs   ╱    ╱                 │
│         ╲   PARALLEL ON-LINE                │
│     ╱                                       │
│  AIRHEAD LINE                               │
└─────────────────────────────────────────────┘
```

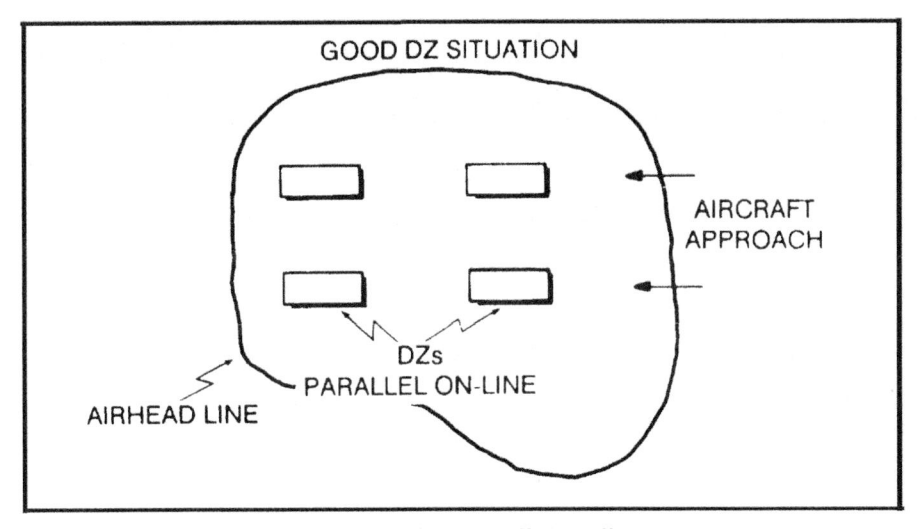

Figure 4-5. DZs parallel on-line.

(2) Another technique that can be employed is to make two drops on two DZs in line (thus eliminating a change of flight direction between the two drops). The DZs must be far enough apart to permit the navigators to compute the location of the second release point.

(3) Paratroopers are more likely to overshoot the DZ than to undershoot it. Therefore, selection of the trailing edge of the DZ should be at the objective to place personnel responsible for the primary assault objective at the front of the aircraft so that they exit last.

(4) If a fighter aircraft escort or rendezvous is required for the drop, they must be kept advised of the drop pattern, the direction of all turns to be flown around the DZ, and the areas to look for possible enemy activity.

(5) Drop zones that require intersecting air traffic patterns should be avoided whenever possible. They delay simultaneous delivery of the force because of the safety requirements to stagger delivery times and clear the air by at least a 5- or 10-minute formation separation time. They also require that JSEAD be accomplished for multiple routes instead of one. This may result in piecemeal delivery and an unnecessarily complicated plan, violating the principles of mass and simplicity.

j. **Alternate Drop Zones or Landing Zones. Commanders must select** alternate DZs/LZs to compensate for changes that may occur.

k. **Number of Drop Zones or Landing Zones.** The number of DZs to be used by the assault parachute element of an airborne infantry brigade depends on the number, size, and relative position of suitable sites; the brigade plan of maneuver; and the expected enemy situation. The battalions of a brigade can land successively on the same DZ, on separate battalion DZs, or on adjacent areas within a single large brigade DZ.

(1) *Single brigade drop zone.* The use of a single brigade DZ on which battalions land successively has these advantages:

(a) It permits greater flexibility in the plan of maneuver and the plan of supporting fires.

(b) It facilitates coordinating and controlling assault battalions.

(c) It applies the principle of mass.

(d) It makes logistical support easier.

(c) It decreases the area of vulnerability.

The usc of a single DZ also has disadvantages.

(a) It slows the buildup of combat power.

(b) It causes later airlift sorties to be vulnerable to enemy air as a result of the loss of surprise.

(c) It allows the enemy to focus his efforts.

(2) *Separate battalion drop zones.* The use of separate battalion DZs has these advantages:

(a) It increases readiness for action by deploying the brigade as it lands.

(b) It reduces confusion on the DZs during the landing and reorganizing.

(c) It tends to deceive the enemy as to the intention and strength of the landing force.

(d) It makes capture of the brigade objective easier when there is strong opposition on one drop zone.

(c) It increases the freedom of maneuver of the assault battalions.

The use of separate battalion DZs also has disadvantages.

(a) It makes C^2 more difficult.

(b) It reduces flexibility because units are dispersed.

(3) *Adjacent drop areas.* Landing battalions on adjacent areas within a single large brigade DZ has, although to a lesser degree, the same advantages and disadvantages of dropping on separate DZs.

4-6. TIME OF DELIVERY

No set rule can be prescribed for the timing of an airborne operation. It varies with each situation; however, the airborne force will try to conduct airborne assaults during limited visibility to protect the force and to surprise the enemy. The commander sets the specific time of delivery. However, for the landing plan, times are stated in terms of P-hour (when the first paratrooper exits the aircraft). The following considerations affect the timing of the operation.

a. **Support of the Main Effort.** The airborne assault can be a supporting attack. If so, the time of commitment of the airborne forces in relation to the main effort is usually directed by orders from higher headquarters. It is determined in advance IAW the mission, the situation, and the terrain. For example, the airborne force can be committed in advance of the main effort to give the airborne attack an increased element of surprise. It can be committed during the main effort to neutralize specific areas or to block the movement of enemy reserves. It can also be committed after the main effort to assist a breakthrough or to block an enemy withdrawal.

b. **Visibility.** The decision as to whether the airborne force is committed by night or day depends on the estimated degree of air superiority, the need for security from enemy ground observation, the relative advantage to be gained by surprise, and the experience of both airlift and airborne personnel.

(1) Night airborne operations offer the following advantages. They greatly increase the chance of surprise and survivability, and reduce the chance of attack by enemy aircraft during the air movement. They also reduce vulnerability to antiaircraft fire, conceal preparations for takeoff from the enemy, and reduce the effectiveness of the defender's fires.

(2) Night airborne operations offer the following disadvantages. In zero visibility, they require well-trained soldiers and aircrews to locate the DZ and assemble rapidly. They provide more air and land navigation problems and offer slower rates of assembly than daylight operations. Night operations also reduce the effectiveness of CAS.

(3) Daylight operations provide better visibility both from the air and ground, more accurate delivery, quicker assembly, and more effective friendly fires than night operations.

(4) However, daylight operations increase vulnerability to enemy air defense, ground fires, and air attack, and they result in loss of surprise.

c. **Intervals.** The time interval between delivery of the assault echelon (P-hour) and the follow-on echelon depends on the availability of aircraft, the capacity of departure airfields, the number of aircraft sorties that can be flown on D-day, the availability of DZs/LZs within the objective area, and the enemy situation. For example, if there are unlimited aircraft, ample departure airfields, numerous DZs/LZs within the objective area, and little or no enemy air defense, the commander could deliver the follow-on echelon immediately after the assault echelon Thus, the time interval could be so brief that it would be hard to determine which was the last aircraft of the assault echelon and which was the first aircraft of the follow-on echelon. Regardless of the timing selected, avoid setting a pattern.

Section II. ASSEMBLY AND REORGANIZATION

Success or failure of the mission can depend on how fast the airborne force can regain tactical integrity. The first goal of any airborne assault must be to deliver and assemble all available combat power as quickly as possible. The sooner soldiers assemble and reorganize as squads, platoons, and companies, the sooner they can derig their equipment and start fighting as cohesive units. How efficiently and rapidly this happens is a direct result of detailed planning, cross loading on the assault aircraft, and assembly on the DZ.

4-7. CROSS LOADING

Cross loading of key personnel and equipment is an important factor in rapid assembly. It must be given careful attention in training and on combat jumps.

a. **Personnel.** Separate key personnel in case any aircraft aborts or fails to reach the DZ. This prevents the loss of more than one key officer/NCO of any one unit.

b. **Heavy-Drop Loads.** Always plan for the possibility that one or more heavy-drop aircraft will abort before it gets to the DZ, or the equipment will streamer in and become unserviceable.

c. **Individual Equipment/Weapons.** Separate radios, mortars, AT weapons, ammunition bundles, and other critical equipment or supplies as much as possible. No like items of combat-essential equipment from the same unit should be on the same aircraft.

(1) The CWIE and the DMJP can and should be jumped at any position in the stick to support cross loading and assembly plans. The commander must make a risk assessment when he determines the location of paratroopers in the stick carrying this equipment.

(2) Risks to both the paratrooper and mission accomplishment are present. If the paratrooper falls inside the aircraft, the remainder of the soldiers may not be able to exit on that pass. Also, this equipment increases the risks of the paratrooper being towed outside the aircraft.

> **DANGER**
> DURING TRAINING, THE PARATROOPER WITH THE DMJP CAN ONLY JUMP FROM THE RIGHT DOOR OF THE AIRCRAFT. A DMJP AND M1950 WEAPONS CASE CANNOT BE JUMPED CONCURRENTLY BY THE SAME PARATROOPER. THE DMJP AND MISSILE SIZE REQUIRE THAT THE PARATROOPER MUST BE AT LEAST 66 INCHES TALL.

4-8. ASSEMBLY TECHNIQUES

Based on METT-T considerations, the ground force commander may elect to use one of the following techniques:

a. **Assembly on the Objective:** This technique may be used when speed is essential, the objective is lightly defended, or the enemy can be suppressed.

b. **Assembly on the DZ:** This technique maybe used when the DZ will not be used by follow-on forces, speed is not essential, and dismounted avenues of approach from the DZ to the objective are available.

c. **Assembly Adjacent to the DZ:** This technique may be employed when the DZ is to be used by follow-on forces or if the DZ is compromised during the airborne assault.

4-9. ASSEMBLY AIDS

To speed up assembly after landing, airborne units usc assembly aids to orient themselves on the ground and to locate their unit's AA. Assembly aids help identify personnel, equipment, and points or areas on the ground. Units can use visual, audible, electronic, natural, or individual aids; for reliability and ease of recognition, units combine these. Operators of assembly aids land as close as possible to their AA so they can mark the area. An Air Force CCT or LRSU places assembly aids if the situation permits. Partisans, special forces personnel, or high-performance aircraft can deliver assembly aids. Whenever possible, regardless of the method chosen to emplace the aids, commanders should provide backup operators, backup aids, and backup delivery means.

a. **Control Posts.** An assembly control post is established by a small party equipped with assembly aids, which moves after landing to a predesignated location to help assemble soldiers. (Figures 4-6 and 4-7.) Each DZ/LZ has a control post in or near the unit AA to coordinate and regulate assembly. No standard organization exists for control posts; their composition varies with the size of the parent unit, the number and type of assembly aids carried, the terrain, and the assigned mission.

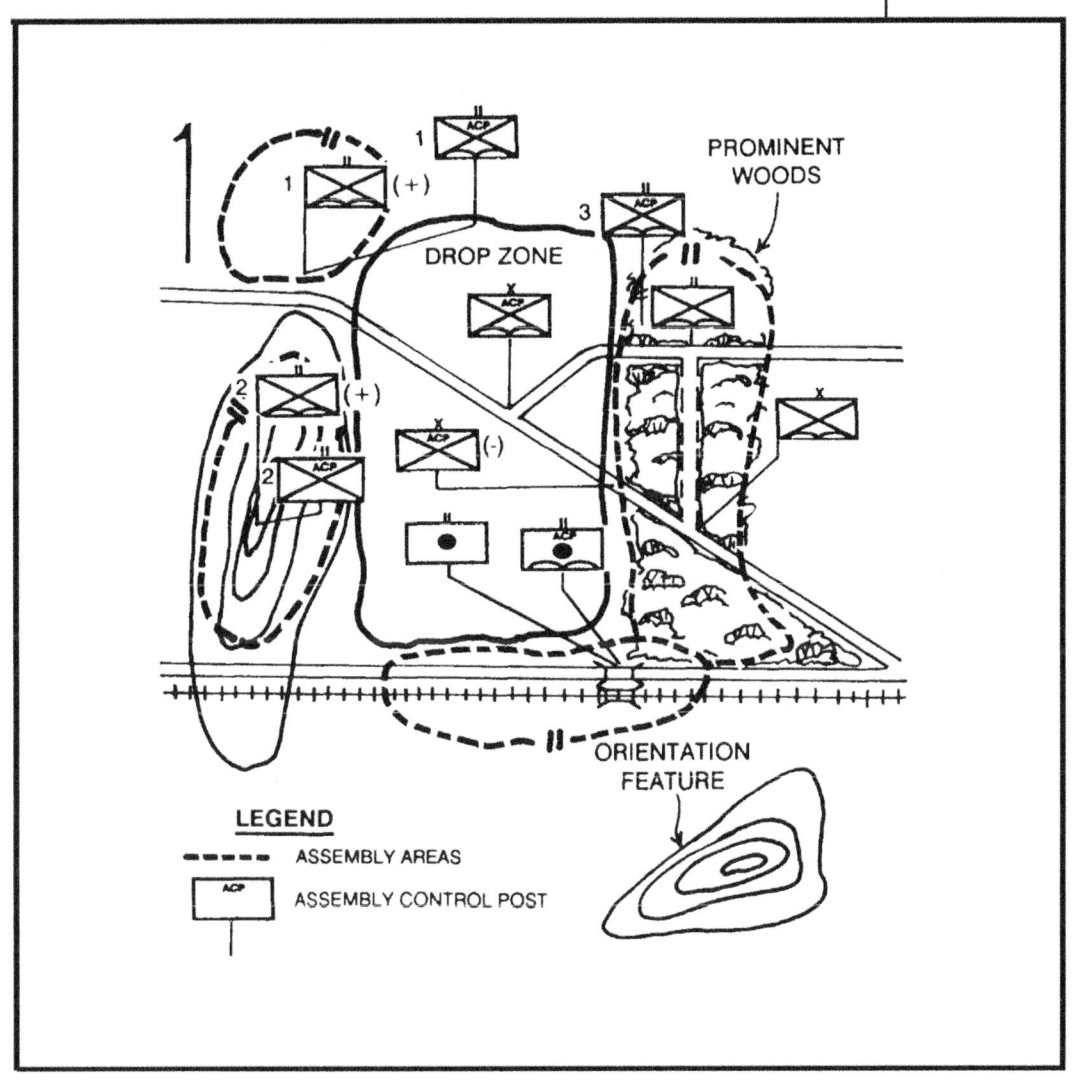

Figure 4-6. Control posts for brigade units landing on one DZ.

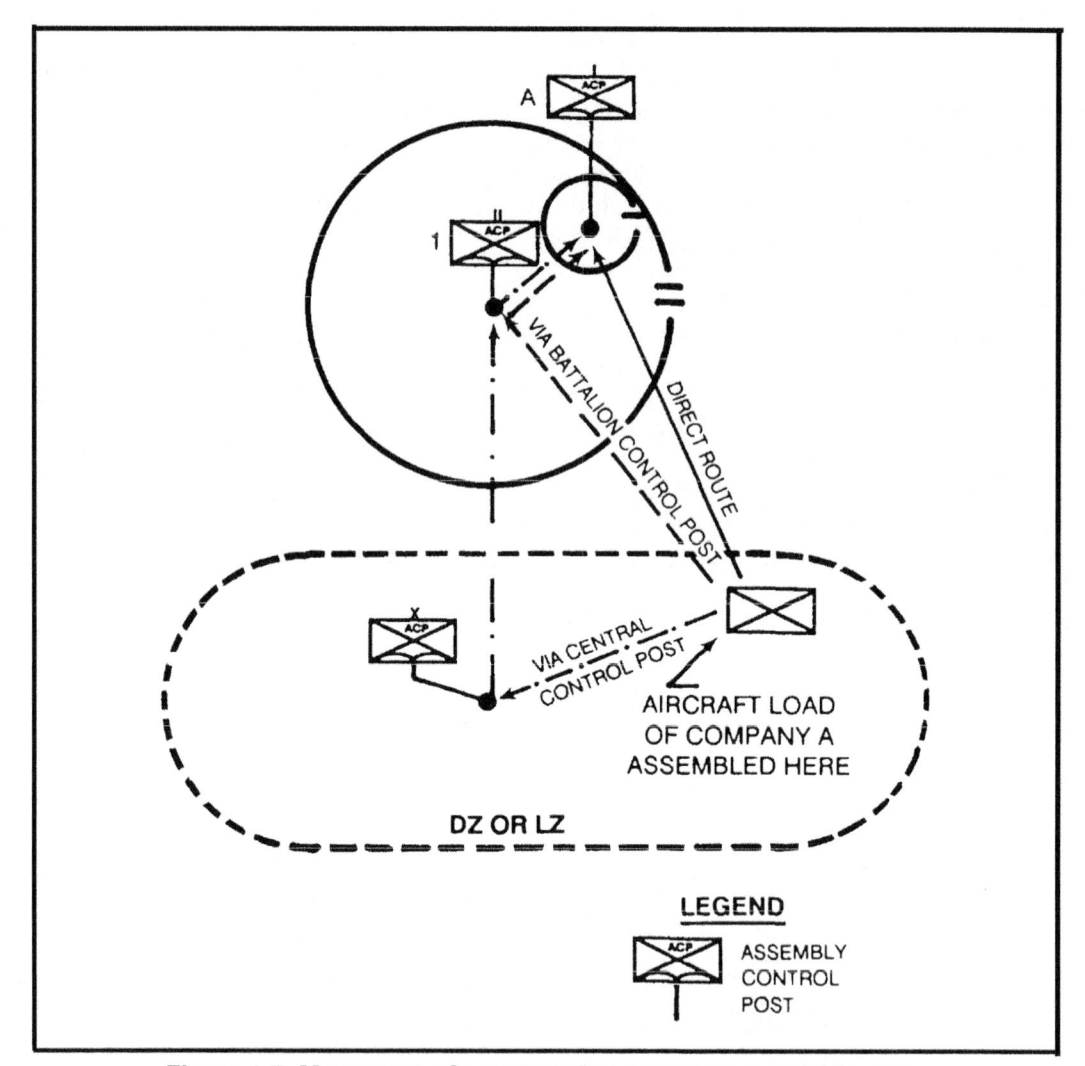

Figure 4-7. Movement of personnel to company assembly area.

b. Joint Airborne Advance Party. The JAAP has a variety of navigational and assembly aids. They usually land on the DZ/LZ from 15 minutes to 1 hour before the main elements arrive. The senior commander prescribes how the JAAP helps units assemble after landing.

c. Line-of-Flight or Clock System. Airborne soldiers observe the airdrop formation's line of flight. The line of flight parallels the parachute landing pattern; this helps each paratrooper establish his own landing position relative to those of the other members of their plane load. Leaders use the clock system to brief soldiers, calling the direction of flight 12 o'clock. (Figure 4-8,) After landing, soldiers assemble to the right of the DZ at 3 o'clock or to the left of the DZ at 9 o'clock. In AWADS conditions, commanders should avoid choosing this method of aid.

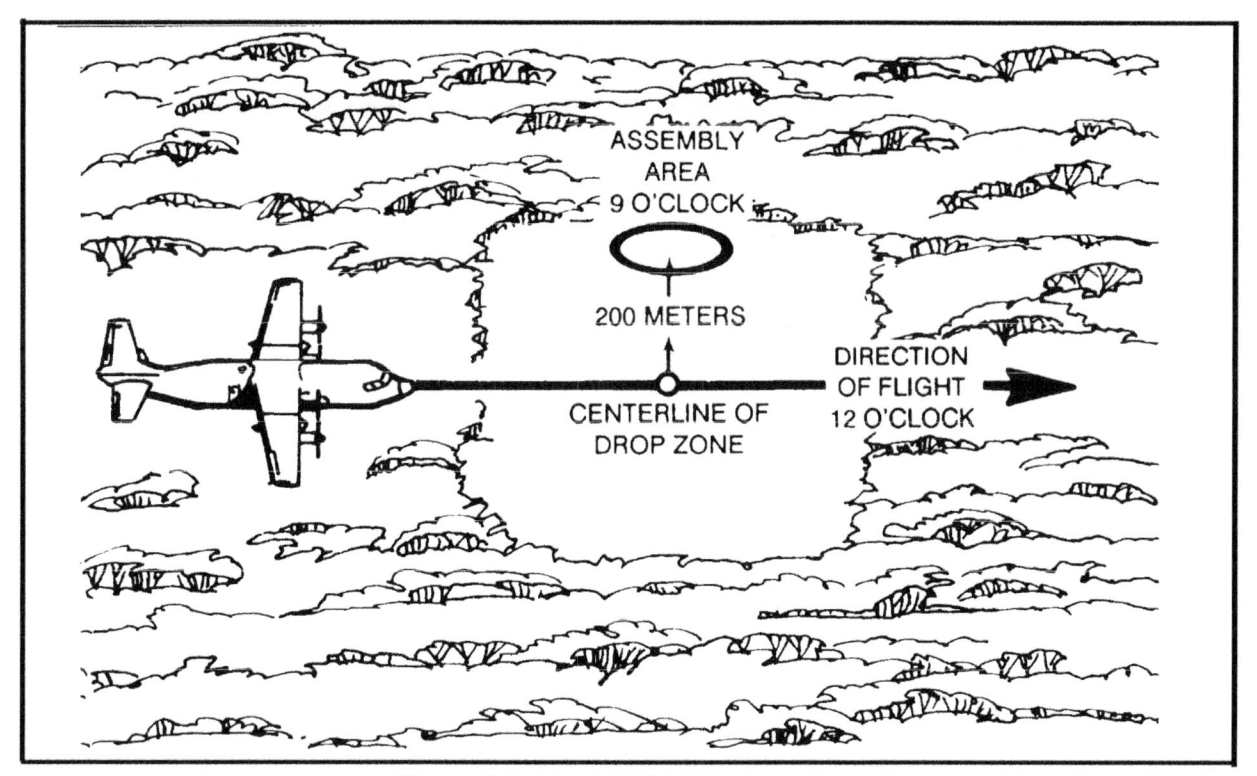

Figure 4-8. Line-of-flight/clock system.

d. **Natural Assembly Aids.** These aids include landmarks or easily recognizable terrain features that units can use as AAs or that personnel can orient their movement on. These features include hills; stream junctions; clumps of woods; or man-made objects like radio towers, bridges, buildings, crossroads, or railroads. Units cannot rely on natural features as the primary assembly aid. The assembly plan must be usable regardless of the DZ. Execution of contingency plans en route may require assembly on an alternate DZ; an emergency exit from the aircraft can place paratroopers on an unfamiliar DZ.

e. **Assembly Equipment.** Airborne units carry visual, audible, or electronic aids into combat to help them assemble. Planners assign different colors, sounds, and coded signals to each unit. The unit SOP standardizes assembly aids; however, units can adapt them to fit specific situations or environments. Terrain restrictions and battlefield noise do not restrict the use of the best assembly aids, which are also simple to use. Units usually use visual assembly aids.

(1) *Visual aids.* Visual aids include visible light sources, such as beacons, flashlights, strobe lights, or signal mirrors; panels; flags; balloons; infrared lights, such as metascopes, flashlights with filters, infrared weapons sights, or starlight scopes; pyrotechnics; and chemical lights. These aids are simple to use and afford positive identification of AAs. However, the enemy can see them as well as friendly personnel can. The Stiner aid has a cloth panel with a colored letter; that is, HHC = White "H". They are the same color for night use. (Figure 4-9, page 4-20.) It has pockets for 15-inch chemical lights; the

letter and pockets are on both sides. It is mounted on a sectional aluminum pole that fits into an M1950 weapons case.

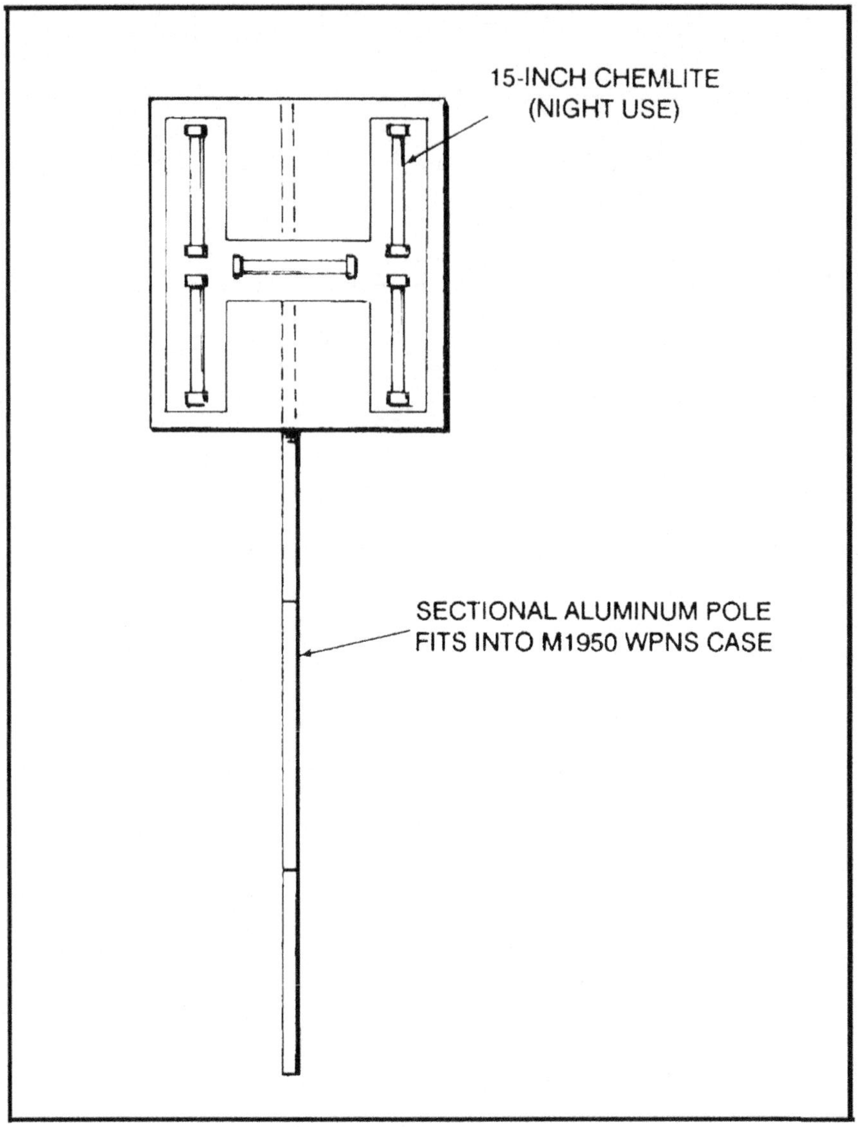

Figure 4-9. Stiner aid.

(2) *Audible aids.* Audible aids especially help small units assemble at night. They include tin crickets, sirens, cowbells, air horns, triangles, dinner bells, ratchets, drums, gongs, whistles, bugles, and voice signals; they can be used to identify individuals or AAs. Strong winds, gunfire, aircraft sounds, an elevation high above sea level, and other factors can limit their effectiveness. The normal sounds of the battlefield easily mask or confuse the sounds of audible assembly aids.

(3) *Electronic aids.* Units can use organic radios to effectively direct small units to AAs, using landmarks as references. They can also use radio homing devices. A homing device is a lightweight attachment to a standard field radio; it is an excellent aid for day or night assembly. With it, a RATELO can

pick up a coded signal beam from a transmitter at the AA. By following the beam, the RATELO homes in on the transmitter and leads the unit to the AA. The unit uses the AT-784/PRC antenna with the AN/PRC-77 to home in on the transmissions of another AN/PRC-77 or another FM radio on the same frequency. Signal crews can make an equipment homing assembly aid from a standard portable field radio or transmitter. The unit attaches the radio to the equipment and turns it to a designated frequency. They encase it in shock-absorbing material just before its extraction from the aircraft. This technique is especially useful for assembling crews on heavy-drop loads.

(4) *Field-expedient aids.* The unit uses any of numerous field-expedient assembly aids; only the unit members' imaginations limit the choices. For example, they can burn gasoline-soaked sand in cans or other containers; fashion a light gun or a one-direction light source by placing a flashlight in the receiver of an M203 grenade launcher; or lift a deployed main or reserve parachute so other unit members can see it.

f. **Identification Markings.** Positive, rapid identification of soldiers and equipment speed up a unit's assembly. The airborne unit standardizes personnel and equipment markings for all subunits.

(1) *Personnel markings.* Soldiers use individual assembly aids to help recognize individuals and assemble units. Individual aids include colored armbands or helmet bands, distinctive patches or designs on uniforms, or helmet bands of luminous tape. Sortie commanders and key leaders, jumpmasters, safeties, other jumpmaster personnel, medics, and bump personnel also use distinctive markings. Larger unit SOPs prescribe unit designations to prevent duplication and to allow unit-wide understanding.

(2) *Equipment markings.* Aerial equipment containers are identified by simple, distinctive markings. Distinctive unit markings are prescribed by larger unit (brigade or division) SOPs to prevent duplication and to assist in recognition by other units. Unit codes are placed on the bottom and all sides of each container; they should be visible for at least 50 meters. Various color parachute canopies, container colors, luminous tape and paints, smoke grenades, homing devices and lights can be used with the containers to facilitate identification on the ground and in the air. Lights, homing devices, and grenades attached to equipment can either be activated manually aboard the aircraft just before extraction, by improvised timer, or on the ground by the first individual to reach the equipment.

(3) *Assault aircraft markings.* A simple code symbol (using various designs, colors, and combinations of letters and numbers) can be painted on both sides of the fuselage of assault aircraft to identify the contents. This symbol is large enough to be readily seen, and it indicates not only the type of equipment contained in the aircraft but also the unit to which the equipment belongs.

4-10. ASSEMBLY PLAN

Because the assembly plan is a key to success, it must be as foolproof as possible. Assembly is more than accounting for personnel; the commander must also ensure the unit has regained tactical integrity, has organized tactically, and is prepared to fight as a combined arms team. The slower the force assembles, the more they risk failure. An airborne unit's assembly plan consists mainly of the following techniques:

a. Secure assault objectives.

b. Place all organic and attached weapon systems into action as quickly as possible.

c. Reestablish C2 such as radio nets or reporting to higher headquarters.

d. Assemble the force and account for casualties and stragglers.

4-11. UNIT ASSEMBLY

Commanders base the assembly of airborne units on a simple, flexible plan that adapts to any likely situation. They assemble the units speedily, silently, and without confusion.

a. **Drop Zone Assembly.** To speed assembly on the DZ, units should –

(1) Establish an assembly control point located near the DZ centerline. The assembly control point OIC or NCOIC accounts for all paratroopers as they report to the control point. He then gives them an azimuth and distance and sends them to the assembly area/assault objective. If the soldiers do not have a compass, they wait until someone with a compass reports in and they move out together.

(2) Locate the unit AA in a covered and concealed position off the DZ. The first group to arrive in the unit AA should erect an assembly aid ASAP to assist in directing the rest of the unit to the AA.

(3) Move out rapidly on the assigned mission once most of the unit has gone through the assembly control point and arrived in the AA. Leave a small element in the AA to handle stragglers.

b. **Troop Briefings.** Another key element of a good assembly is the thoroughness of unit briefings and individual soldier briefbacks.

(1) BRIEF soldiers–and rebrief them–on the assembly plan of his unit and on those of other units scheduled to share the same DZ.

(2) USE visual aids such as maps, aerial photos, terrain models, and sand tables.

(3) WARN soldiers to resist guiding on what appears to be a prominent terrain feature on a map. Once they are on the ground, the terrain feature probably cannot be seen. This is especially true if soldiers land on the wrong DZ or on the wrong part of a DZ.

(4) AVOID instructing soldiers to move out on a particular azimuth or to go in a precise direction unless they each have a compass.

(5) USE the clock directional system. Instruct soldiers to orient themselves and the general location of the AA by the direction of flight.

NOTE: Regardless of the actual azimuth, the direction of flight is always 12 o'clock.

c. **Factors Affecting Assembly.** When the assembly plan is prepared, the speed, altitude, and flight formation of airlift aircraft and their effect (along with wind) on dispersion of personnel and equipment in landing must be considered. The resultant landing pattern significantly affects assembly, as does the DZ length and width, the training level of the airborne soldiers and pilots, the enemy, and cross loading.

d. **Dispersion.** The extent of dispersion is the result of the airlift formation; type, speed, and altitude of the aircraft; number of serials; sequence of delivery weather conditions; and aircrew proficiency.

(1) The speed at which airplanes carrying paratroopers cross the DZ affects the length of the landing pattern. The greater the speed, the greater the distance that is covered between the exit of each paratrooper, thus increasing the length of the landing pattern. Planes cross the DZ as slowly as is safely possible, and paratroopers exit rapidly to reduce dispersion.

(2) As paratroopers descend, they drift with the prevailing wind, but usually not at a uniform rate for each soldier. They can pass through strata of varying wind direction and velocity that causes some dispersion within the unit. The higher the altitude, the greater the possibility of dispersion due to wind. Therefore the aircraft cross the DZ at minimum altitudes that are consistent with the safety of aircraft and paratroopers.

(3) In parachute landings, the width of the landing pattern of soldiers and equipment is the approximate width of the aircraft formation at the time of the drop. Therefore, the formation is kept as tight as possible to keep the soldiers and equipment together. If possible, a company or battalion is placed in the flight formation so that all plane loads of the unit land in a small pattern as close as practicable to the AA. (See FM 100-27 for basic patterns of aircraft formations.)

e. **Drop Zone Visibility.** Darkness, fog, haze, rain, brush, trees, and terrain affect DZ visibility on the ground, and hence impact on assembly. Assembly during darkness is complicated by poor visibility and difficulty in identifying or recognizing AAs, control posts, personnel, and equipment. The darkness contributes to confusion, to stragglers, and to the loss of equipment. An assembly during darkness takes longer and requires more elaborate assembly aids and larger control posts than a daylight assembly.

f. **State of Training.** One of the most important factors that affect rapid assembly is training. The degree of proficiency of the individuals in a unit has a much greater influence than the techniques they employ. Units must continuously practice parachute assaults and assemble as they would in combat. For specific missions, previous training is built on and tailored through detailed briefings, including maps, photos, and terrain models. When possible, rehearsals using assembly techniques planned for the assault are used. Thorough orientation, rigorous training, aggressive leadership, and individual initiative have the single greatest impact on assembly.

g. Enemy. Enemy action can have both a direct and indirect effect on assembly. Enemy action indirectly affects en route airlift capability to deliver the force to the correct DZ. It directly affects friendly assembly once on the ground.

(1) Every available device must be used to neutralize enemy air activity and antiaircraft fire.

(2) Enemy opposition during or immediately after landing is a critical consideration affecting assembly due to the unusual vulnerability of the airborne force between landing and completion of assembly. Every possible precaution is taken to ensure that the landing is unopposed or that provisions are made to deal with expected enemy resistance. This requires accurate intelligence, responsive (air alert) CAS, and effective OPSEC and deception.

4-12. MULTIPLE-LATERAL IMPACT POINTS

A slightly more complicated but more efficient method to facilitate rapid assembly of soldiers, CDS, and heavy-drop loads is the use of multiple-lateral impact points.

a. The theory and techniques of cross loading apply as much to this method of delivery as to any other. The Air Force drops the Army along a single track (line of flight) down the center of the DZ and uses just one soldier and one heavy-drop impact point. On special request, they fly multiple tracks across the DZ and use multiple impact points on the DZ. By efficient cross loading, selection of AAs, and careful selection of personnel and equipment impact points, soldiers, units, and equipment can be delivered closer to the AA than the single-track, single-impact point method. (Figure 4-10.)

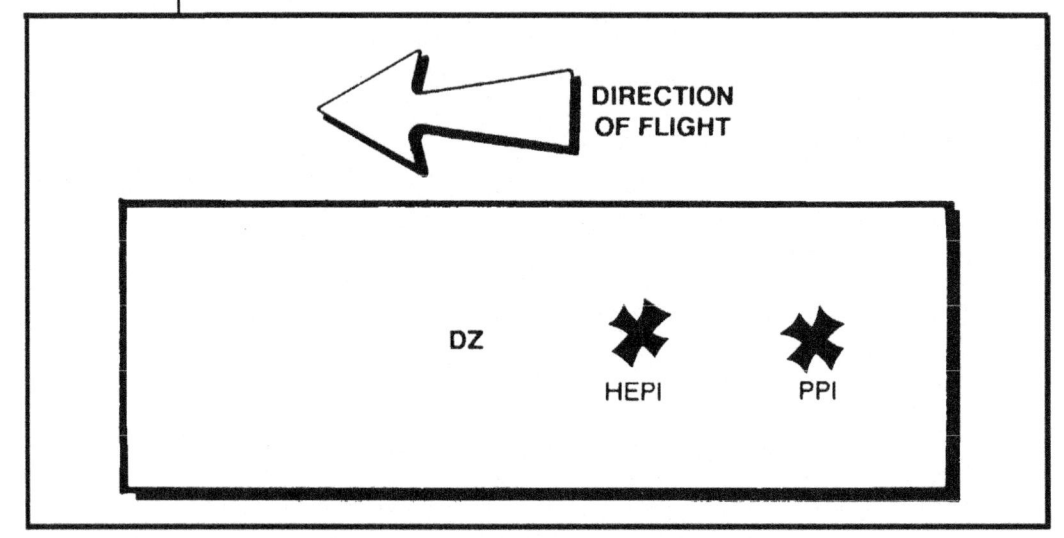

Figure 4-10. Single-track, single-impact point DZ

b. The DZ selected for multiple-lateral impact points must be wider than 700 meters. (Figure 4-11.) This is due to the requirement for all impact points to be at least 350 meters in from the surveyed edge of the DZ. Multiple, lateral impact points apply to all types of loads.

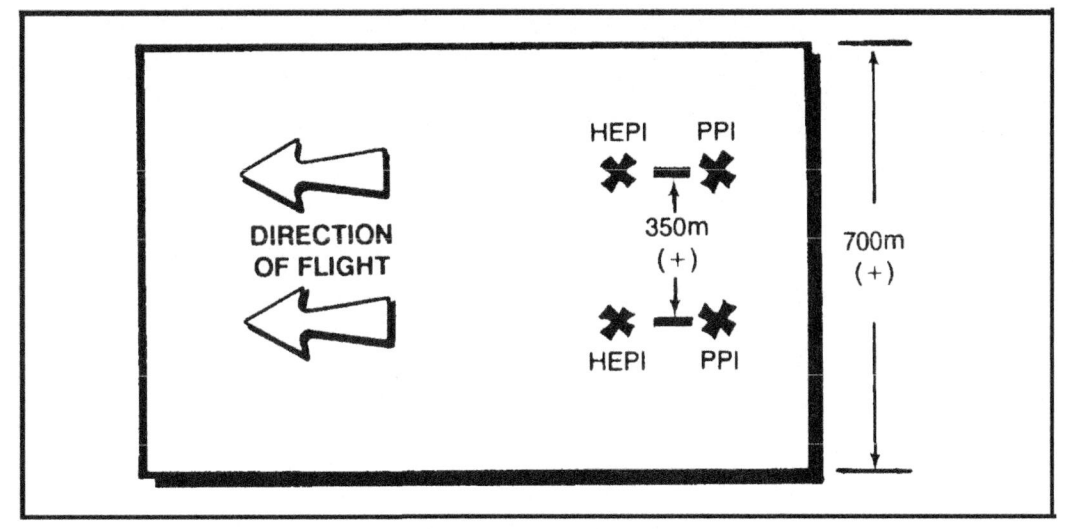

Figure 4-11. Multiple-lateral impact points.

4-13. KEYS TO RAPID ASSEMBLY

Certain simple guidelines can be followed to ensure rapid and relatively easy assembly. Rapid assembly results from well-thought-out and rehearsed cross loading, including heavy-drop loads, and a thorough, but simple plan that applies for any DZ. Use the clock system (not magnetic azimuth system nor north, south, east, west) for direction/route to the AA. Use AAs that are easy to find without complicated assembly aids, even if dropped on the wrong part of the DZ or on an unplanned DZ. Be prepared with both day and night assembly aids, especially for drops scheduled at dawn or dusk. Locate AAs as close as possible to where the soldier lands. To permit rapid assembly, never locate AAs at either end of the DZ (soldiers should not have to walk from one end to the other). Use special soldier/unit/equipment markings to speed assembly. Brief/briefback to all units what marking the same serial will use. Sand tables arc used extensively to brief/briefback each soldier. Rehearse the procedures as often as possible

4-14. ACTIVITIES IN ASSEMBLY AREAS

Not only do units assemble as quickly as they can, but they also get out of the AA as quickly as possible. They remain in the AA only long enough to establish CPs and communication, to organize into combat groupings, and to determine the status of assembly. They modify plans as needed to meet changes in the situation and issue orders to lower units.

4-15. DEPARTURE FROM THE ASSEMBLY AREA

Assault battalions proceed on their assigned mission when assembly is complete or on order of the brigade commander. Reorganization of a battalion is complete when all lower units are assembled and command and fire control communications channels are established. As a result of inaccurate landings, enemy action or excessive straggling, assault battalions may have to attack before assembly is complete. The brigade commander usually makes this decision. In the absence of other orders, the battalion commander decides when enough of his battalion has assembled to accomplish the mission. The time or conditions for assault units to move out on their assigned missions are ordinarily established in the plans of higher units.

4-16. REPORTS

Because of the dispersion of personnel and equipment in landing, the possibility of inaccurate landings, and the potential loss of aircraft during the air movement, commanders at all levels must learn the status of personnel and equipment in their units as soon as possible after landing. They need this information to determine the combat potential of the units before executing the ground tactical plan.

a. All units report their personnel and equipment status to the next higher unit at predetermined times or intervals until reorganization is complete. These status reports usually indicate the location of the unit; the number of soldiers assembled and the number of known casualties; the number and type of crew-served weapons, vehicles, radios, and other recovered key equipment; and any information available on missing soldiers and equipment. Units make abbreviated status reports on the DZ as soon they establish radio communications.

b. As soldiers arrive in company AAs, units make status reports by squad, platoon, and company. As commanders establish CPS in the AAs, they receive status reports from within the battalion by radio, messenger, or direct contact between commanders.

4-17. SECURITY MEASURES

Security during assembly includes protection of unit AAs and DZ/LZs. All units are responsible for their own security regardless of the security provisions of higher headquarters. Airborne units arc vulnerable to enemy ground attack from all directions during assembly. For this reason, and because of the size of DZs/LZs, the security requirements are great in comparison with the size of the airborne force.

a. In small-unit drops, jumpmasters or chalk leaders provide local protection as their plane loads assemble and recover equipment dropped in aerial delivery containers. Commanders of airlanded soldiers provide local protection while the equipment is unloaded. Soldiers move to company AAs in tactical formations suitable for security as well as speed and control.

b. The assault clement, after seizing assault objectives, has the mission of gaining and maintaining the security of the DZ. The assault clement protects the assembly of soldiers on the DZ; they accompany supplies and equipment not recovered by assault units and, in some cases, the later landing of other soldiers or unit air supply. The size of the security force for a DZ/LZ depends on the expected enemy. The security force can usc a series of small OPs or roadblocks and patrols. These security provisions arc usually quite simple because of the short time the AA is to be occupied. However, the planning is in minute detail, including mission, size, composition, and organization of each security element; location of OPS or roadblocks; routes of patrols;

communication; supporting fires; and boundaries. Security groups move out on their assigned missions promptly on arrival in the assembly area.

4-18. REORGANIZATION

The initial effort of all commanders and staff officers is the seizure of assault objectives followed by reassembling and regaining command and control. Smaller units with specific missions proceed without waiting for the parent units to assemble. Reorganization is faster and more precise in the daytime than at night.

a. **Planning.** Reorganization details are included in the landing plan. Reorganization occurs after initial assault objectives are secured. Factors to consider when planning reorganization include:

- Designation of unit AAs.
- Use of assembly aids.
- The assembly plan.
- Reports.
- Security measures.
- Establishment of command and fire control communications.
- Reconnaissance.
- Coordination and final preparations before the attack.
- Time or conditions for assault units to move out on their missions.
- Recovery of accompanying supplies.
- Assembly of stragglers.

b. **Considerations.** Planning considerations for reorganization of units following an assault landing include:

(1) Brigade commanders coordinate the reorganization plan of lower units. However, the actual reorganization takes place at battalion and separate unit levels.

(2) Battalions and separate units reorganize in a prearranged manner, making use of predesignated AAs, control posts, and assembly aids. The AAs are established on or just off the DZ. For reference, they are identified by prominent landmarks and marked by assembly aids carried by the soldiers. The first parachute units to land are charged with gaining and maintaining the security of the DZ. Other units move directly to their AAs. They carry all equipment needed for the assault.

(3) Units seize assault objectives and assemble as quickly as possible in the existing conditions.

(4) Designated personnel remain on the DZs/LZs to protect the area, assemble stragglers, care for casualties, and complete the removal of supplies.

(5) The reorganization is complete when units are assembled and communication is established.

4-19. BRIEFBACKS

As with the ground tactical plan, each echelon (fire team through brigade) must briefback his landing plan. The landing plan remains tentative until commanders complete briefbacks and coordinate changes.

a. **Landing Plan.** In the case of the landing plan, briefbacks ensure coordination of who is using what DZ/LZ/EZ and when, the preferred orientation of DZs, and who is landing in which sectors and when. The landing plans follow the commander's priorities, use the best airlift tactics, and support ground tactical plans. Assembly plans of one unit do not interfere with the assembly plans of other units.

b. **Assembly Plan.** One of the most critical parts of the landing plan is the assembly plan. Each leader must brief his soldiers, require a briefback, rebrief his soldiers, and require another briefback. Each soldier should know exactly what to do, how to do it, and when to do it to assemble quickly.

c. **Aircraft Requirements.** The briefback of the landing plan identifies aircraft requirements for each subunit. If there arc not enough aircraft available to lift the entire assault force at one time, commanders must decide the units that should be lifted first, and then allocate aircraft accordingly. In making this decision, they analyze the priorities dictated by the mission and the higher commander.

This chapter implements STANAG 3466/ASCC 44/18C

CHAPTER 5

AIR MOVEMENT PLAN

After development, briefback, and approval of the landing plan, planners begin to develop the air movement plan. This plan is the third step in planning an airborne operation and supports both the landing plan and the ground tactical plan. It provides the required information to move the airborne force from the departure airfields to the objective area. The plan includes the period from when units load until they exit the aircraft. The air movement annex to the OPORD contains the air movement plan.

5-1. JOINT PLANNING

Although the Air Force component commander is solely responsible for executing the air movement phase, the air movement plan is the product of joint Army/Air Force consulting and planning. The Army contributes its landing plan and the procedures for the control and disposition of personnel at the departure airfield(s). The Air Force controls takeoff times and, based on the Army's landing plan, coordinates timing between different departure airfields to ensure the proper arrival sequence at the DZ/LZ/EZ. The Air Force also designates rendezvous points and develops the flight route diagrams. The combination of METT-T and the orientation of DZs/LZs/EZs determine the orientation of the flight routes.

5-2. ELEMENTS

The air movement plan contains the information required to ensure the efficient loading and delivery of units to the objective area in the proper sequence, time, and place to support the ground tactical plan.

a. **Elements of Air Movement Table.** The air movement table forms the principal part of the air movement plan, including the following essential elements:

- Departure airfield for each serial.
- Number of aircraft for each serial.
- Chalk numbers for each aircraft, each serial, and each departure airfield; aircraft tail numbers correspond to aircraft chalk numbers.
- Unit identity of the airlift element.
- Name/rank of each USAF serial commander.
- Number and type aircraft.
- Employment method for each aircraft (PP/HD/CDS/LAPES).
- Army unit identity.
- Name/rank of each Army commander.

- Load times.
- Station times.
- Takeoff times.
- Designated primary and alternate DZs for each serial.
- P-hour for the lead aircraft of each serial (given in real time).
- Remarks such as special instructions, key equipment, and location of key members of the chain of command.

b. **Additional Elements.** Besides the air movement tables, the air movement plan contains the following information:

- Flight route diagram.
- Serial formation.
- Air traffic control.
- Concentration for movement.
- Allowable cabin/cargo loads.
- Airfield/FLS MOG (aircraft maneuver on ground space).
- Aircraft parking diagram.
- Army personnel and equipment rigging areas at the departure airfield.
- Army control procedures during preparation for loading.
- Emergency procedures including SERE/SAR planning.
- Weather considerations.
- JSEAD, counterair, and BAI considerations

5-3. TYPES OF MOVEMENT

The type of movement must be considered when determining how to load the aircraft. Is it *administrative* or *tactical?* Airborne units can conduct an administrative movement to an ISB or REMAB, and then transload into assault aircraft by using tactical loading. (Chapter 8 discusses transload operations.)

a. Administrative movements are nontactical. Soldiers and equipment are arranged to expedite their movement and to conserve time and energy. Economical use is made of aircraft cabin space, and planners make maximum use of ACL.

b. Tactical movements are when personnel and equipment are organized, loaded, and transported to accomplish the ground tactical plan. The proper use of aircraft ACL is important, but it does not override the commander's sequence of employment.

5-4. AIRCRAFT REQUIREMENTS

When the airborne unit deploys, planning guidance from higher headquarters indicates the type of aircraft available for the movement. Based on this information, the unit commander determines and requests the number of sorties by the type of aircraft required to complete the move. The air movement planner must ensure that each aircraft is used to its maximum capability. This is based on the information developed on unit requirements, ACLs, and available passenger seats. The methods of determining aircraft requirements are the weight method and the type-load method.

a. **Weight Method.** This method is based on the assumption that total weight, not volume, is the determining factor. Since aircraft sometimes run out of space before exceeding the ACL, this method is no longer widely used. It has been replaced by the type-load method. However, during recent operations, it was discovered that aircraft can actually exceed their ACL before running out of space. The long distances involved in reaching an objective area, the necessity of the aircraft to circle for extended periods before landing, and the large amounts of fuel needed to sustain the aircraft can result in the aircraft having to reduce its ACL. As a rule, the longer the deployment, the lower the ACL.

b. **Type-Load Method.** In any unit air movement, a number of the aircraft loads contain the same items of equipment and numbers of personnel. Identical type loads simplify the planning process and make the tasks of manifesting and rehearsing much easier. Used for calculating individual aircraft sortie requirements, the type-load method is the most common and widely accepted method of unit air movement planning. It requires consideration of load configuration and condition on arrival at a desired destination, rapid off-loading, aircraft limitations, security requirements en route, and the anticipated operational requirements. The type-load method, therefore, is more detailed and is used in planning unit movements.

5-5. LOAD PLANNING CONSIDERATIONS

When preparing the air movement plan, the S3 Air considers tactical integrity, cross loading, and self-sufficiency of each load.

a. **Tactical Integrity.** The S3 Air keeps units intact as much as possible. For parachute operations, this can mean placing units larger than squads on separate aircraft so they exit their respective aircraft over the same portion of the DZ. This facilitates rapid assembly by placing units close to their AAs on landing.

(1) The S3 Air keeps squads together on the same aircraft if possible; fire teams are never split.

(2) Fire support teams and their RATELOs should be on the same aircraft with the commander they support; they should jump so as to land next to him.

(3) Platoon leaders (and PSGs on different aircraft) should have their FOs and RATELOs and at least one machine gun crew and one Dragon gunner on the same aircraft.

(4) Each aircraft must have at least one unit NCO or commissioned officer for each unit with soldiers on board. Each aircraft has Army leadership present.

(5) Tactical integrity can be ensured by distributing the company commander, unit 1SG, and XO in the lead, middle, and trail aircraft, respectively.

b. **Cross Loading.** Cross loading distributes leaders, key weapons, and key equipment among the aircraft of the formation to preclude total loss of C^2 or unit effectiveness if an aircraft is lost. This is an important factor in rapid assembly and must be given careful attention in training and on combat jumps.

(1) Separate key personnel in case any aircraft aborts or fails to reach the DZ. This prevents the loss of more than one key officer/NCO of any one unit. Properly planned cross loading accomplishes the following:

(a) Soldiers from the same unit will land together in the same part of the DZ for faster assembly.

(b) Equipment/vehicle operators and weapon system crews will land in the same part of the DZ as their heavy-drop equipment so they can get to it, derig it, and get ready to fight quickly.

(c) If one or more aircraft abort either on the ground or en route to the DZ, some key leaders and equipment will still be delivered.

(2) When planning airborne force cross loading, remember – the fewer key people on the same aircraft, the better. If possible, separate the following personnel:

(a) The brigade commander and his battalion commanders.

(b) The battalion commanders and their company commanders.

(c) The commander, his XO, and his S3.

(d) The primary brigade and battalion staff officers and their assistants.

(e) The company commanders, XOs, and 1SGs from the same company.

(f) The platoon leaders and PSGs from the same platoon.

(3) Always plan for the possibility that one or more heavy-drop aircraft will abort before it gets to the DZ, or the equipment will streamer in and become unserviceable.

(a) Cross load heavy-drop equipment to have the least possible impact on the mission if it does not arrive in the DZ. Separate critical loads so if any aircraft aborts or fails to reach the DZ, no single unit loses more than one key officer/NCO or a significant proportion of the same type of combat-essential equipment.

(b) Coordinate closely with the Air Force so heavy-drop loads are loaded in the reverse order they should land.

(c) Do not include the same type of critical equipment from the same unit, or like equipment from different units in the same aircraft loads. This applies whether it is to be airdropped or airlanded.

(d) Cross load heavy-drop equipment in one of the following ways:
- Select HEPIs to support the ground tactical plan. Place loads so they land close to the location where they will bx used. Cross load the parachutists to first support the ground tactical plan; then coordinate their landings with those of the heavy-drop platforms. When using multiple HEPIs, coordinate the selected HEPI for each load with the Air Force mission commander.

- Do not load two or more like platforms from the same unit on the same aircraft because the aircraft are moving too fast to drop more than one platform in the same sector.

(e) Separate radios, mortars, antitank weapons, ammunition bundles, and other critical equipment or supplies as much as possible. No like items of combat-essential equipment from the same unit should be on the same aircraft.
- A weapons system should be loaded on the same aircraft as its crew. NOTE: Only one crew-served weapons squad/team should be on each aircraft.
- A RATELO should jump the same aircraft as the leader he supports, either just before or just after him. Another good technique is for the leader to jump the radio himself. In this way, he can still set up immediate communications even if he and his RATELO are separated on the DZ.
- The CWIE and the DMJP can and should be jumped at any position in the stick to support cross loading and assembly plans. The commander must make a risk assessment when he determines the location of parachutists in the stick carrying this equipment. Risks to both the parachutist and mission accomplishment are present. If the parachutist falls inside the aircraft, the remainder of the soldiers may not be able to exit on that pass. Also, this equipment increases the risks of the parachutist being towed outside the aircraft.

> **DANGER**
> DURING TRAINING, THE PARATROOPER WITH THE DMJP CAN ONLY JUMP FROM THE RIGHT DOOR OF THE AIRCRAFT. A DMJP AND M1950 WEAPONS CASE CANNOT BE JUMPED CONCURRENTLY BY THE SAME PARATROOPER. THE DMJP AND MISSILE SIZE REQUIRE THAT THE PARATROOPER BE AT LEAST 66-INCHES TALL.

- Individual crew-served weapons (such as machine guns, mortars, antitank weapons) and other critical equipment or supplies should be distributed on all aircraft.
- Communications equipment, ammunition, and other supply bundles must be cross loaded.

c. **Self-Sufficiency.** Each aircraft load should be self-sufficient so its personnel can operate effectively by themselves if any other aircraft misses the DZ, makes makes an emergency landing somewhere else, or aborts the mission.

(1) A single (complete) weapons system should have the complete crew for that system on the same aircraft along with enough ammunition to place the weapon into operation.

(2) For airland or heavy-equipment drop operations, trailers and weapons are manifested with their prime movers.

(3) Squads should stay together on the same aircraft; fire teams are never split. Squads/fire teams should jump both aircraft doors to reduce the amount of separation on the DZ.

5-6. LOAD PLANNING SEQUENCE

Planners scan best accomplish the movement of forces by air for an airborne assault by developing plans in an orderly sequence, such as —

a. Preparing vehicle load cards. (See paragraph 5-7.)

b. Preparing air movement planning worksheets for each unit (company through battalion). (See paragraph 5-8.)

c. Preparing basic planning guides (company and battalion) and forwarding them to higher headquarters (battalion and brigade). (See paragraph 5-9.)

d. Establishing priorities for entry into the objective area by echelon: assault, follow-on, and rear. Units establish priorities within each echelon to phase personnel and equipment into subsequent echelons if aircraft are not available.

e. Preparing a unit aircraft utilization plan to determine aircraft requirements and type loads. (See paragraph 5-10.)

f. Preparing air-loading tables to facilitate rapid deployment. (See paragraph 5-11.)

Units receive their missions and review previous plans. Then they–

a. Revise the plans based on the task organization dictated by the ground tactical plan.

b. Allocate available aircraft. If aircraft are not available, they phase low-priority items to the follow-on or rear echelon.

c. Prepare air loading tables and manifests.

d. Prepare the air movement table.

c. Prepare a DD Form 1387-2 for hazardous materials IAW TM 38-250.

5-7. LOAD PLANNING OF VEHICLES

Vehicle load plans arc based on SOP and mission tailoring. Then, they are updated according to aircraft availability and type.

a. Heavy-drop vehicles are first loaded with as much unit equipment as they will hold. The vehicle's load capacity should not be exceeded, and all cargo must be secured in the vehicle's cargo compartment. Vehicles arc measured and weighed after they have been loaded. (Guidance for weighing and marking of airdrop vehicles is in FM 55-9 and AR 220-10.) Some items, especially ammunition, cannot be rigged on the vehicle, but can be carried as ballast on the platform. (See the appropriate FM for rigging different vehicles for heavy-equipment drop.)

b. Vehicle load cards are made for each vehicle to be loaded aboard an aircraft. (Figure 5-1.) Each sketch includes such information as load data for the vehicle; length and width of the vehicle; and, when the vehicle carries cargo, the names and locations of the cargo in the vehicle.

VEHICLE LOAD CARD
(TB 55-46-1)

UNIT	BUMPER NO	DATE COMPILED
A/1-504	HQ	20 JUL 90

VEHICLE INFORMATION

TYPE	LENGTH	WIDTH	HEIGHT	EMPTY WT	CB/CG is ____ inches from
M998	180"	86"	72"	5400	

CARGO COMPARTMENT VIEW

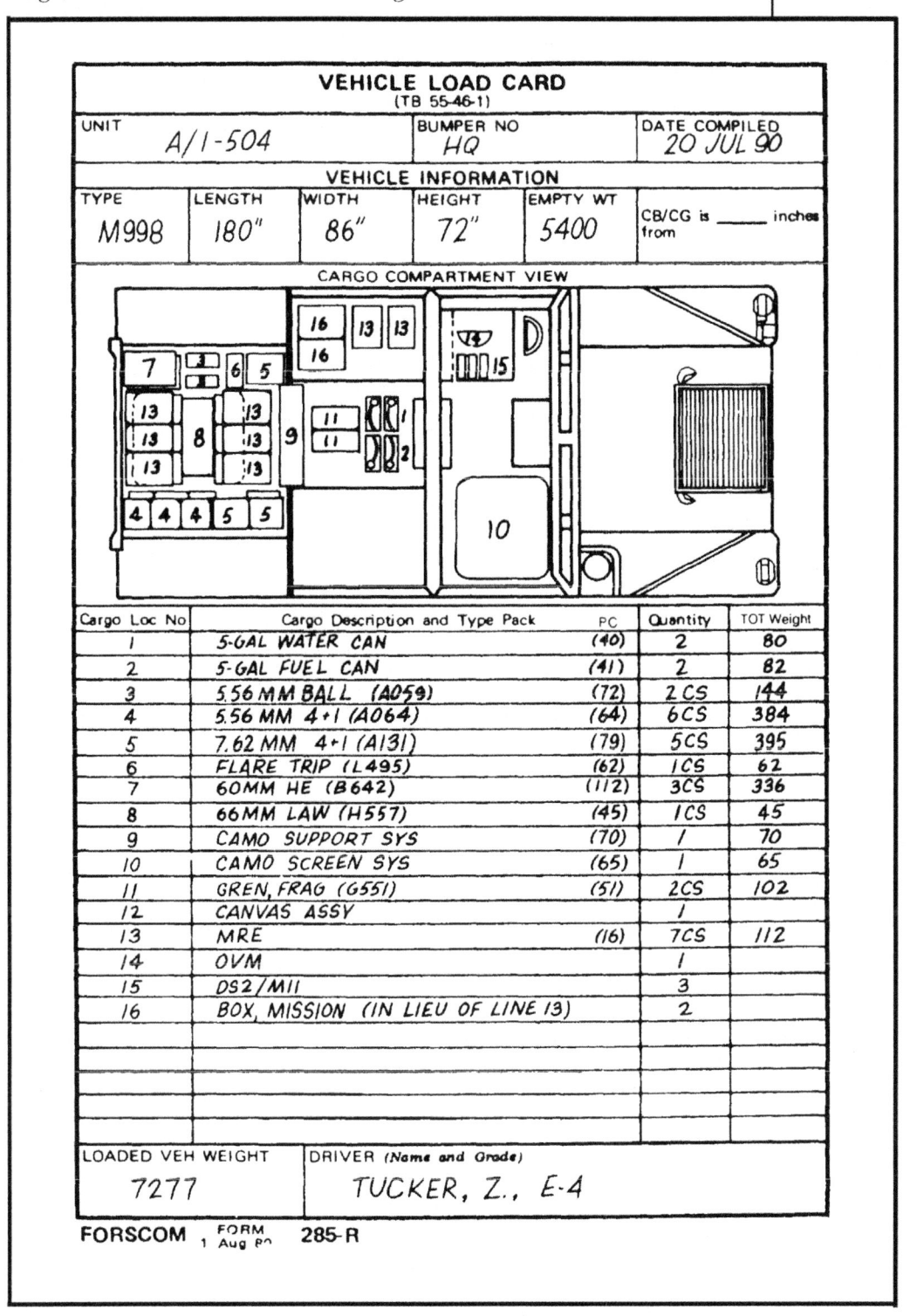

Cargo Loc No	Cargo Description and Type Pack	PC	Quantity	TOT Weight
1	5-GAL WATER CAN	(40)	2	80
2	5-GAL FUEL CAN	(41)	2	82
3	5.56 MM BALL (A059)	(72)	2 CS	144
4	5.56 MM 4+1 (A064)	(64)	6 CS	384
5	7.62 MM 4+1 (A131)	(79)	5 CS	395
6	FLARE TRIP (L495)	(62)	1 CS	62
7	60 MM HE (B642)	(112)	3 CS	336
8	66 MM LAW (H557)	(45)	1 CS	45
9	CAMO SUPPORT SYS	(70)	1	70
10	CAMO SCREEN SYS	(65)	1	65
11	GREN, FRAG (G551)	(51)	2 CS	102
12	CANVAS ASSY		1	
13	MRE	(16)	7 CS	112
14	OVM		1	
15	DS2/M11		3	
16	BOX, MISSION (IN LIEU OF LINE 13)		2	

LOADED VEH WEIGHT	DRIVER (Name and Grade)
7277	TUCKER, Z., E-4

FORSCOM FORM 285-R
1 Aug 80

Figure 5-1. Example of a completed vehicle load card.

FM 90-26

5-8. AIR MOVEMENT PLANNING WORKSHEET

The air movement planning worksheet is a consolidated list of a unit's equipment and personnel. (Figure 5-2.) It is not a formal DA form; it is an example of a locally made form. If necessary, any grid-type paper can be used in lieu of a printed form. The worksheet lists all the dimensions and cargo loads of vehicles. It must include all on-hand equipment and personnel, and the full amount authorized by the unit TOE. Items that are short are still included as equipment, and personnel shortages can be filled if alerted for deployment. This also prevents the need for constant revision of the worksheet. Basic loads of ammunition carried with the unit, which must be palletized or placed in door bundles, should also be included.

AIR MOVEMENT PLANNING WORK SHEET

UNIT	PERSONNEL Chalk No.	REMARKS	EQUIPMENT—VEHICLES Types	ID No.	Equipment	Length	Width	Height	Weight	Cargo	AIRCRAFT C-130	C-141	C-5A
HHC/1-504	0 0 2 8	A/L	M998	HQ6		187	96	74	6080				
HHC/1-504	0 0 2 8	A/L	M998	HQ2		187	96	74	5940				
HHC/1-504	0 0 2 8	A/L	M998	HQ9		187	96	74	5630				
HHC/1-504	0 0 2 9	A/L	M998	HQ3		187	96	74	5760				
HHC/1-504	0 0 2 9	A/L	M1008	HQ18		223	94	96	6590				
HHC/1-504	0 0 2 9	A/L	M1008	HQ21		223	94	96	6830				
HHC/1-504	0 0 3 0	A/L	M1008	HQ24		223	94	96	7020				
HHC/1-504	0 0 3 0	A/L	M35A2	HQ32		268	97	77	13,280				
HHC/1-504	0 0 3 2	A/L	M35A2	HQ35		268	97	77	14,320				
HHC/1-504	0 0 3 4	A/L	M35A2	HQ35		268	97	77	15,120				
HHC/1-504	0 0 3 6	A/L	M35A2	HQ37		268	97	77	14,870				
HHC/1-504	0 0 3 8	A/L	M35A2	HQ38		268	97	77	14,530				
HHC/1-504	0 0 4 0	A/L	M35A2	HQ40		268	97	77	14,560				
HHC/1-504	0 0 4 0	A/L	M105A2	HQ41		166	83	55	2670				
HHC/1-504	0 0 4 2	A/L	M35A2	HQ42		268	97	77	14,615				
HHC/1-504	0 0 4 2	A/L	M105A2	HQ43		166	83	55	3640				
HHC/1-504	0 0 4 6	A/L	M35A2	HQ44		268	97	77	14,670				
HHC/1-504	0 0 4 6	A/L	M149A1	HQ45		162	82	77	2540				
HHC/1-504	0 0 4 7	A/L	MOTOR CYCLE	HQ66	463L	66	27	34	386				

Figure 5-2. Example of air movement planning worksheet.

5-9. BASIC PLANNING GUIDE FORM

The basic planning guide form is a report prepared by ground units (o determine the aircraft required for an airborne operation. The example completed form shows the exact status of a unit's personnel, vehicles, equipment, and supplies. (Figure 5-3.)

a. **Preparation of the Form.** The example basic planning guide form is first prepared by commanders of lower units and consolidated by higher units that control and plan the operation. Thus, the ground forces commander has available for planning the exact status of the personnel and equipment of his entire force.

b. **Explanation of the Form.** The separate items of the form are completed as follows:

BASIC PLANNING GUIDE																	
HEADQUARTERS: 504 PIR							OPERATION: GIANT III						DATE: 20 AUG 90			
ORGANIZATION	PERSONNEL								VEHICLES, EQUIPMENT AND SUPPLIES									REMARKS
	ASSAULT ECHELON				FOLLOW UP		TOTAL REAR ECH	TOTAL INEF-FEC-TIVES	TYPE	ASSAULT ECHELON				FOLLOW UP		REAR ECHELON		
	AIRDROP		AIRLAND							AIRDROP		AIRLAND						
	TOTAL	WT	TOTAL	WT	TOTAL	WT				TOTAL	WT	TOTAL	WT	TOTAL	WT	TOTAL	WT	
1-504	620	155,000	0	0	0	0	58	0	M966	0	0	12	70,320					
									M35	0	0	9	119,520					
									M105			4	10,680					
									M998	0	0	0	0	36	189,360			
									M1008	0	0	4	26,360					
2-504	0	0	636	159,000	0	0	42	0	M966	0	0	12	70,320					
									M35	0	0	9	119,520					
									M105			4	10,680					
									M998					36	189,360			
									463L	0	0	12	24,000					CI IV
3-504	0	0	0	0	618	154,900	32	28	M966					12	70,320			
									M35					9	119,520			
									M105					4	10,680			
									M998					36	189,360			

Figure 5-3. Example of basic planning guide form.

(1) *Heading.* This information is completed by the preparing headquarters.

(2) *Organization.* The subordinate units of an organization are listed. The battalion commander lists each company in the battalion. The brigade commander lists each battalion and separate company or any attached units. The division lists each organic and attached unit in the division. Platoons and sections are not listed separately. Company planning guides represent consolidated figures. Attachments, such as medical specialists or FOs, are listed separately by organization to assist in identifying all units involved.

(3) *Personnel.* This item addresses any of the following:

(a) Assault echelon. The commander's advisors inform him as to the approximate number of planes or assault aircraft assigned to the unit. Advisors can inform the commander if the unit is to move by plane; if so, all personnel going on the move are listed under this column.

(b) Follow-on echelon. This echelon consists of personnel and equipment that are not airdropped or airlanded in the initial airlift, but join the parent organization as soon as possible or at a specified date during the operation.

(c) Rear echelon. This echelon consists of personnel who remain at the base camp or similar installation. They do not necessarily move with the overland detail but can be moved forward later.

(4) *Vehicles, equipment, and supplies.* The columns under this heading are used to show the distribution of materiel for the operation. The number of each type of vehicle, as well as heavy or bulky equipment and supplies, are listed herein.

(5) *Remarks.* In this item, additional information or notes concerning personnel or equipment (such as the contents of air delivery containers) are listed.

c. Collection of Forms. The S3 Air for the battalion collects the basic planning guide forms from the subordinate companies and consolidates them at battalion level. He submits them to US Army riggers, ALCE, and the DACG, depending on the type of movement required.

5-10. UNIT AIRCRAFT UTILIZATION PLAN

The unit aircraft utilization plan identifies equipment by aircraft load; this simplifies planning of identical types of loads. The goal is to have most aircraft loads the same. The first step is to weigh personnel and equipment by echelon. Then, add up the aircraft loads to determine how many aircraft are needed. If too few aircraft are available to meet the planned echelonment, this becomes readily apparent. At this point, priorities are applied and equipment and personnel are phased back to fit airlift constraints.

5-11. AIRCRAFT LOADING TABLES

The next step after completion of the unit aircraft utilization plan is to prepare the aircraft loading tables.

a. Loading Table Layout. Using DD Form 2131 or MAC Forms 342 or 559, depending on the type of aircraft employed, the placement of each vehicle and item of equipment is planned. Using templates (which can be obtained from ALCE) and the form for the appropriate aircraft, each type of load is laid out and lines are drawn around the template. The load must be within the aircraft's safe center of gravity limits; the ACL must not be exceeded.

b. Cross-Loading Plan. Before final completion of loading tables, cross loading must be accomplished IAW the landing and ground tactical plans.

c. Loading Table Approval. When all data have been entered on the appropriate form, the Air Force (the affiliated ALCE) approves the loads.

5-12. DEVELOPMENT OF AIRCRAFT LOADS

The development of aircraft loads is accomplished through reverse planning The planner must have a DZ mosaic or facsimile when developing the heavy equipment points of impact, personnel point of impact, and personnel manifests. Aircraft loads must support the assembly and ground tactical plans through effective cross loading.

a. Preparation of the Load. Using the mosaic, facsimile, or sketch, preparers mark the desired single or multiple HEPI for all equipment, and the PPI. The sketch is lined off in 70-meter (75-yard) increments from the PPI. This represents the normal one-second parachutist interval. These lines arc made perpendicular to the line of flight so that the name of the parachutist associated with a particular piece of equipment can be marked on the sketch. For planning purposes, heavy-drop equipment lands 400 yards apart on C-130 operations and 500 yards apart on C-141B operations. The name of the parachutist who must obtain his equipment is entered on the line nearest the equipment. Personnel not associated with a particular piece of equipment can be marked on the lines closest to their AA. The personnel manifest is then taken directly off the DZ schematic. The result is a manifest order that facilitates quick assembly.

b. **Allocation of Seats.** Once the commander has developed the cross-load plan, he notifies involved units how many and which seats they have on each aircraft. Platoons can be manifested in multiple aircraft to facilitate cross-loading, but personnel are placed in stick order on each aircraft to exit and land in the same general area on the DZ.

c. **Internal Adjustments.** Each company commander in turn cross-loads his part of the split platoon within his part of the stick to best support the assembly plan and ground tactical plan. (Figure 5-4.)

d. **Preparation of the Manifest.** Manifesting is accomplished in the reverse order of exit. (See paragraph 5-14.)

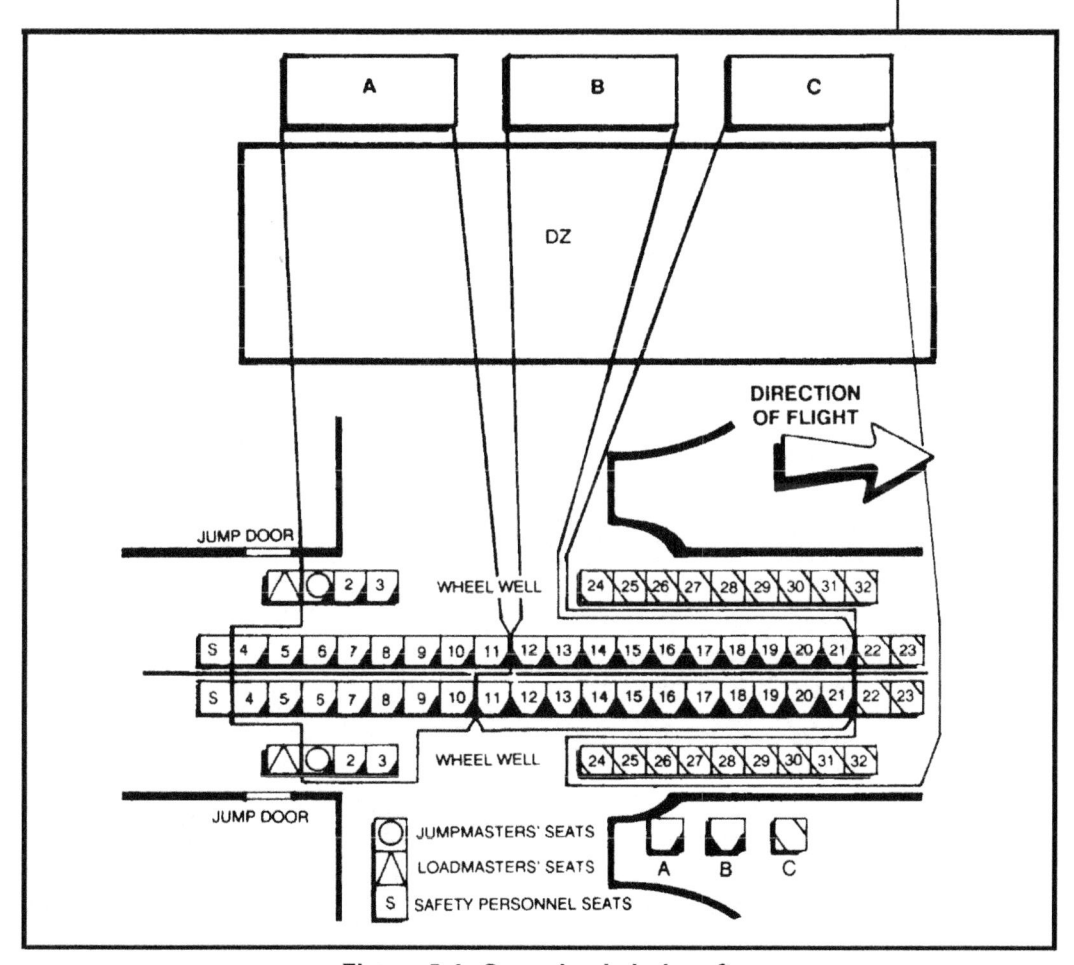

Figure 5-4. Cross-loaded aircraft.

5-13. AIR MOVEMENT TABLE

The air movement table assigns units to serials within the air columns. The location of units in successive serials is IAW priorities established for landing. Units maintain tactical integrity of Army and airlift units as far as practicable. All elements in a given serial land on the same DZ/LZ in the objective area; however, certain aircraft in a serial can continue on to drop R&S forces in their planned areas of employment. The air movement table form is prepared by the ground forces commander in coordination with the Air Force commander. This form, used as an annex to the OPORD, allocates aircraft to the ground units to be lifted. It designates the number and type of aircraft in each serial and specifics the departure area and the time of loading and takeoff. Exact format for the air movement table depends on the needs of the commander, which can be specified by unit SOP. There is no specific format, but the air movement table should provide the information herein.

a. **Heading.** When the air movement table is published as a part of the order, the following elements are included:
- Classification.
- Annex and operations order number.
- Headquarters.
- Place of issue.
- Date and time.
- Map reference.

b. **Serial Number.** Serial numbers are arranged consecutively in the order of flight. Factors to be considered in the assignment of units to serials arc the mission of the airborne unit, the size of the DZ/LZ, and the distribution (cross loading) of personnel, weapons, and equipment.

c. **Chalk Number.** The chalk number specifics the position of aircraft being loaded in each serial. Loads are numbered sequentially IAW serial numbering, such as Serial 1 contains Chalks 1 through 12; Serial 2 contains Chalks 13 through 24.

d. **Air Force Units.** This section includes Air Force information that is important to the ground force commander.

(1) *Airlift unit.* This is the designation of the airlift unit that is transporting or furnishing the aircraft for each serial.

(2) *Serial commander.* This is the senior Air Force officer in the serial.

(3) *Number and type of aircraft.* The exact number and type of aircraft that actually fly in the serial are shown in this column.

e. **Army Forces.** This section includes information directly related to the ground forces.

(1) *Aircraft required.* The number of airplanes required to transport the unit.

(2) *Employment.* Type of movement such as parachute, heavy equipment, CDS, LAPES, or airlanded.

(3) *Unit loaded.* The airborne unit being loaded.

(4) *Serial commander.* The senior airborne officer in the serial.

(5) *Departure airfield.* Name or code name of the departure airfield.

(6) *Load time.* The time established by the airlift and ground force commander to begin loading. Parachutists can require from 30 to 45 minutes to load, depending on the aircraft and any accompanying equipment (door bundles, wedges, and parachutes for in-flight rigging). Heavy-drop and CDS loads should take about two hours for loading.

(7) *Station time.* The time the passengers, equipment, and crew are loaded and ready for takeoff.

(8) *Takeoff.* The time the aircraft is scheduled to depart from the airfield.

(9) *Aircraft formations.* The type formation the aircraft will fly.

(10) *Objective.* The name or designation of the DZ, LZ, EZ, or airfield.

(11) *Time over target.* TOT is the time of arrival at the objective area.

(12) *Direction of flight over the objective area.*

f. **Other Items.** Other items that can be included in the air movement table (at the commander's discretion) are as follows:

- Number of personnel by serial/chalk.
- Initial and final manifest call times.
- Prejump training times.
- Type parachute.
- Weather decision.
- Weather delay.
- Time for movement to the departure airfield.
- Air Force station time.
- Remarks.

5-14. MANIFESTS

The flight manifest is an exact record of personnel by name, rank, SSAN, and duty position in each aircraft . It is also a brief description of the equipment, with the station number, as loaded in the aircraft. Load computations for personnel and equipment are also listed. A separate form is made for each aircraft. Copies are made for the DACG/DACO, pilot, ALCE, and AACG; a copy is retained by the jumpmaster or senior Army representative on the aircraft. The senior ground forces member or primary jumpmaster in each aircraft finalizes the form. The Air Force authorizes it, and the ground force representative signs it after verifying the personnel on the manifest.

5-15. AUTOMATED AIRLOAD PLANNING SYSTEM

The automated airload planning system is a computer-based automated system designed to simplify the outload plans for combat units.

a. **Files.** By computerizing the necessary loading characteristics, weight restrictions, and equipment configurations required to outload the airborne unit, this system automatically tells the commander the load configurations and number of aircraft required to move a specific force.

(1) *Air Force aircraft characteristics.* This file includes all data that affect the placement of equipment on a particular aircraft; it contains data on the C-130, C-141B, C-17, and C5A/B aircraft, which appropriate personnel update as changes occur.

(2) *Items and uniform.* This file contains size data on all the equipment in the unit that requires floor space. Commanders use the data for airland, airdrop, or LAPES. The file contains information about the aircraft center of balance, the psi of the tires, whether the item requires shoring or not, and whether the item is turnable or not. The unique feature of this file is that it considers inseparable items of equipment together; for example, a jeep and trailer or a HMMWV and 105-millimeter howitzer. This permits the program to load an item of equipment with its prime mover.

(3) *Force package and options.* This file contains 12 force packages and about 1,000 modular force package options.

b. **Commander Input.** The ALPS allows commanders to input force packages, options, items, prime movers and the towed pieces of equipment, and multiples of each. Once a force package or option is entered into the program, the force package or option can be changed for the specific run of the program to meet mission requirements.

CHAPTER 6

MARSHALING

After the air movement plan has been developed, briefed back refined (if necessary), and approved, the next plan to be developed is the marshaling plan; it supports the previous three plans. The tactical, landing, and air movement plans are used to determine the number of personnel and vehicles to be stationed at or moved through each airfield. The marshaling plan provides the necessary information and procedures by which units of the airborne force complete final preparations for combat, move to departure airfields, and load the aircraft. It also provides detailed instructions for facilities and services needed during marshaling. The procedures in this chapter assist airborne commanders and staffs in planning for marshaling and CSS.

Section I. THE MARSHALING PLAN

The marshaling plan appears as an appendix to the service support annex of the airborne force OPORD or as an annex to an administrative/logistics order. The S4 is the principal assistant to the commander for the marshaling plans of specific units. Marshaling begins when elements of the force are literally sealed in marshaling areas and it terminates at loading. The procedures are designed to facilitate a quick, orderly launching of an airborne assault under maximum security conditions in the minimum possible time.

6-1. PREPARATION BEFORE MARSHALING

Units complete the following preparations before marshaling – especially for airdrops. Last-minute marshaling activities include briefing personnel, inspecting, preparing airdrop containers, issuing rations and ammunition, and resting.

a. **N-Hour Sequence.** As soon as a unit is notified of an airborne operation, it begins the reverse planning necessary to have the first assault aircraft en route to the objective area in 18 hours. The N-hour sequence (see Appendix G) contains the troop-leading actions that must take place within a flexible schedule, ensuring that the unit is prepared and correctly equipped to conduct combat operations on arrival.

b. **Rehearsals.** Rehearsals are always conducted at every echelon of command. They identify potential weaknesses in execution and enhance understanding and synchronization Full-scale rehearsals are the goal, but time constraints may limit them. (For additional information, refer to FM 7-20.)

c. **Assembly, Inspection. and Maintenance.** As soon as practicable, units assemble the equipment and supplies that are to accompany them to the objective area. Inspections are held to determine the status of equipment. Maintenance is performed; parachutes, aerial delivery containers, and heavy-drop loads are prepared. Commanders and leaders brief soldiers, and rations and ammunition are issued. The soldiers should eat when time permits.

d. **Storage of Unneeded Items.** Individual clothing and equipment and unit equipment not needed in the objective area are packed in suitable containers and stored with the rear echelon or rear detachment.

6-2. MOVEMENT TO THE MARSHALING AREA

Unit marshaling areas should be located near departure airfields to limit movement, Higher headquarters can either control the movement to the marshaling area completely, or it can get a copy of the march table and use it to control the traffic out of the AA, along the route of march, and into the marshaling area. Advance parties assign soldiers to areas.

a. **Movement Resources and Requirements.** The S4 of the unit to be marshaled notifies higher headquarters on the number of organic vehicles that the unit can furnish to move its personnel and equipment to the marshaling areas. This information and the personnel list furnished by the S3 must be available early enough during planning to procure any other transportation required for the movement.

b. **Airfield Marshaling Areas.** When rnarshaling areas are on airfields, they are temporarily placed at the disposal of the airborne unit's higher headquarters. The air base commander's permission is obtained by the tactical units that must conduct activities outside of the camp area.

c. **Parachute Issue and Rigging.** Parachute issue and rigging may be conducted on the ramp, alongside the aircraft, or in-flight.

(1) Ramp side advantages are as follows:
- Reduces the parachute supply problem.
- Efficient use of personnel.
- Supply accountabaility.

(2) Ramp side disadvantages are as follows:
- Parachutists may require transportation to the aircraft.
- Parachutists are rigged for a greater period of time.

(3) Plane side advantages are as follows:
- Parachutists are not required to walk while rigged.
- Decentralized execution reduces rigging time.

(4) Plane side disadvantages are as follows:
- Parachutes must be transported to the aircraft.
- Rigging process may impede other activities.

(5) In-flight advantages are as follows:
- Prevents fatigue during long flights.
- Provides more time for rehearsals and inspections.

(6) In-flight disadvantages are as follows:
- Reduces the number of parachutists that an aircraft can carry.
- Requires loading of parachutes on the aircraft.

6-3. PASSIVE DEFENSE MEASURES

Uncommitted airborne forces pose a strategic or operational threat to the enemy. Concentration of forces during marshaling should be avoided to keep impending operations secret and to deny lucrative targets to the enemy. Dispersal techniques include the following:

a. **Move.** Units move rapidly under cover of darkness to dispersed marshaling areas near air facilities.

b. **Control.** Commanders control movement to loading sites so most personnel arrive after the equipment and supplies are loaded on the aircraft.

c. **Prepare.** Commanders prepare for loading before arrival at the loading site.

d. **Avoid.** Commanders avoid assembling more than 50 percent of a brigade at a single point at any time.

6-4. DISPERSAL PROCEDURES

The degree of dispersal is based on an intimate knowledge of the operation's problems and what is best for the overall operation. Regardless of the dispersed loading procedures, the airlift commander ensures that aircraft arrive over the objective area in the order required by the air movement plan. Depending on the situation, one of the following dispersed loading procedures is used:

a. **Movement to Departure Air Facilities.** Airborne personnel and equipment are moved to departure air facilities where airlift aircraft maybe dispersed.

b. **Movement to Intermediate Staging Base.** Before the mission, airlift aircraft fly to an ISB to pick up airborne personnel and equipment. Personnel and equipment are airlifted to dispersed departure airfields; the mission originates from these facilities.

c. **Combination of Procedures.** Airlift aircraft fly to ISBs for the equipment before the mission. The equipment is airlifted to the dispersed departure airfields and the mission originates from these facilities, or airlift aircraft stop en route at ISBs to pick up personnel. Crews load aircraft quickly, so the fewest possible aircraft are at the ISB at one time.

6-5. SELECTION OF DEPARTURE AIRFIELDS

Departure airfield selection is based on the proposed air movement and the capability of airfields to handle the traffic. Loading sites near departure airfields are designated after the selection of departure airfields. For any specific situation or operation, one or a combination of the following factors can determine the selection:

- Mission.
- Airfields (number required, location, and type).
- Runway length and weight-bearing capacity.
- Communications facilities.
- Navigational aids and airfield lighting.
- Location of participating units and marshaling areas.
- Radius of action required.
- Vulnerability to enemy action, including NBC.
- Other tactical air support available or required.
- Logistical support available, required, or both.
- Facilities for reception of personnel and cargo.
- Facilities for loading and unloading of personnel and cargo.
- Facilities for dispatch of personnel and cargo.

NOTE: While dispersion is necessary to avoid the effects of nuclear weapons, excessive dispersion increases control problems and can diminish the effectiveness of other supporting ground and air operations

6-6. SELECTION AND OPERATION OF MARSHALING CAMPS

The marshaling area is a scaled area with facilities for the final preparation of soldiers for combat Commanders select marshaling camps within the marshaling area based on the air movement plan and other considerations. Another way to avoid concentration of personnel is to time-phase the movement of soldiers from their home bases through the marshaling area to the departure airfield, minimizing the buildup of forces. After choosing the marshaling areas and departure airfields, choose loading sites near the airfields.

a. **Selection.** The following factors are considered when selecting marshaling areas.

- Distance to airfield(s).
- Time available.
- Existing facilities.
- Availability of personnel and materials for construction.
- Availability/access of maneuver and training areas.
- Communications requirements.
- Briefing facilities.
- Location of participating units.
- Security/vulnerability to enemy action.
- Logistical support available or required.

b. **Assignment.** In the marshaling plan, the S4 (in coordination with the S3) assigns units to marshaling areas near the departure airfields the units will use. Every effort should be made to locate the areas as closely as possible to departure airfields to reduce movement time between them; it also reduces the requirement for vehicles.

c. **Operation.** The airborne forces' higher commander is responsible for the operation and maintenance of the marshaling areas.

(1) Operating detachments and necessary equipment are provided for each camp. These detachments furnish signal communications, transportation, medical, and postal services. They also operate mess facilities and utilities.

(2) Personnel from the units being marshaled or from follow-on units of the airborne force can assist in the operation of the camps if it does not interfere with their preparations for the airborne operation. Equipment from these units cannot be used because it must be packed and loaded for movement to the objective area.

(3) Small stocks of supplies and equipment of all services are maintained at each camp to fill last-minute shortages of the units being marshaled. Service maintenance support is furnished as required.

(4) The number of personnel required to support operation and maintenance of marshaling areas varies. Based on past experience, about 10 percent of the number of personnel being marshaled is required for supporting services.

6-7. FACILITY REQUIREMENTS

Commanders can use this information as a guide to the selection and modification of existing facilities for brigade TF use. Figure 6-1 (page 6-6) shows a typical marshaling area layout for a brigade-size unit that needs about 100 acres.

a. **Task Force Camp.** The brigade or battalion (task-organized for the mission) and a MACG occupy a brigade TF camp. If no facilities exist, support elements must construct the camps.

b. **Camp Specifications.** The brigade TF camp should be near a departure airfield and large enough to support the brigade, its attachments, and supporting personnel, The MACG supports the marshaling requirements of the brigade camp. Each brigade camp has a site for rigging the brigade's equipment for air delivery (airland, airdrop, and LAPES).

c. **Camp Security.** The camp itself should be surrounded by security fencing or, at least, triple-strand concertina. It should have a posted security zone outside the perimeter that is at least 50 meters wide and cleared of brush and trees. If available, lights should be used to illuminate the security zone. Gates to the camp should be two lanes wide to accommodate heavy traffic.

FM 90-26

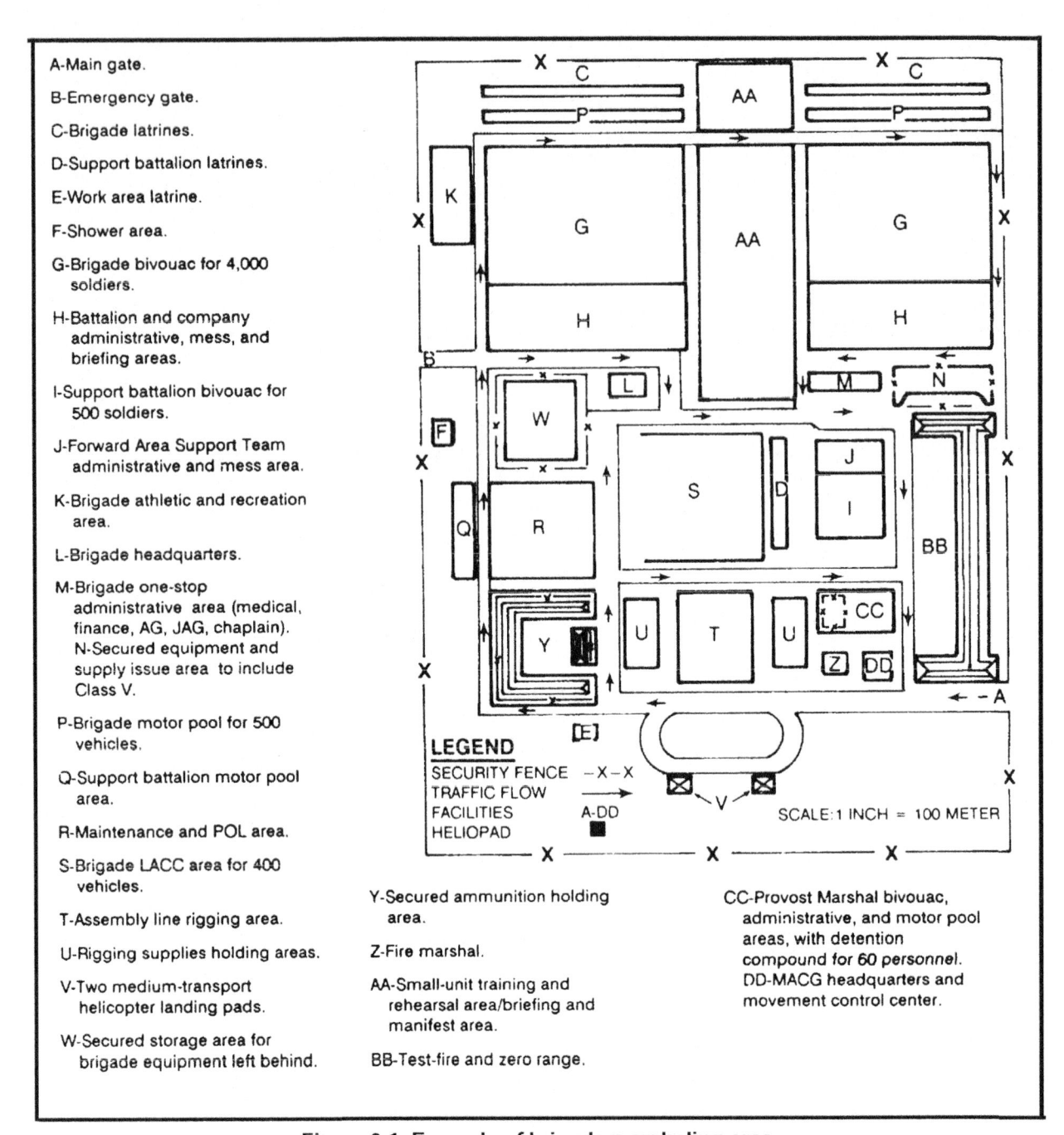

A-Main gate.
B-Emergency gate.
C-Brigade latrines.
D-Support battalion latrines.
E-Work area latrine.
F-Shower area.
G-Brigade bivouac for 4,000 soldiers.
H-Battalion and company administrative, mess, and briefing areas.
I-Support battalion bivouac for 500 soldiers.
J-Forward Area Support Team administrative and mess area.
K-Brigade athletic and recreation area.
L-Brigade headquarters.
M-Brigade one-stop administrative area (medical, finance, AG, JAG, chaplain).
N-Secured equipment and supply issue area to include Class V.
P-Brigade motor pool for 500 vehicles.
Q-Support battalion motor pool area.
R-Maintenance and POL area.
S-Brigade LACC area for 400 vehicles.
T-Assembly line rigging area.
U-Rigging supplies holding areas.
V-Two medium-transport helicopter landing pads.
W-Secured storage area for brigade equipment left behind.
Y-Secured ammunition holding area.
Z-Fire marshal.
AA-Small-unit training and rehearsal area/briefing and manifest area.
BB-Test-fire and zero range.
CC-Provost Marshal bivouac, administrative, and motor pool areas, with detention compound for 60 personnel.
DD-MACG headquarters and movement control center.

LEGEND
SECURITY FENCE —X—X—
TRAFFIC FLOW
FACILITIES A-DD
HELIOPAD
SCALE: 1 INCH = 100 METER

Figure 6-1. Example of brigade marshaling area.

d. **Billeting.** Quarters, unit headquarters, messes, supply rooms, and latrines should be constructed and allocated to maintain unit integrity.

(1) *Bivouac site.* If billets are not available, a bivouac site can be prepared with tents laid out in company streets. (See FM 101-10-1/2 and CTA 50-909.)

(2) *Mess facilities.* FM 101-10-1/2 provides the guidelines for determining mess hall size.

(3) *Latrine areas.* There should be enough latrines to serve at least 4 percent of the male soldiers and 6 percent of the expected female soldiers. Latrines should be built at least 100 yards downwind from food service facilities to prevent contamination of food and water. They need to be 30 yards from the end of the unit area, but within a reasonable distance for easy access.

(4) *Shower facilities.* Enough shower facilities should be provided to support the size force in the marshaling area.

e. **Rigging.** The airborne force requires facilities for rigging heavy-drop equipment, CDS, and LAPES platform loads. Although equipment can be rigged outdoors, it should be rigged in a large building, such as a hangar, where it is protected from weather. The following facilities are needed to out-load:

(1) *Loading area control center.* The LACC is provided for the initial preparation of vehicles for heavy drop, LAPES, or airland. It should have a 10-foot by 20-foot area for each vehicle and a 20-foot-wide area between rows for maintenance. A large area must be provided on either side of the LACC for maneuverability within the LACC for maintenance or other vehicles. Figure 6-2 shows an example LACC for heavy-drop rigging.

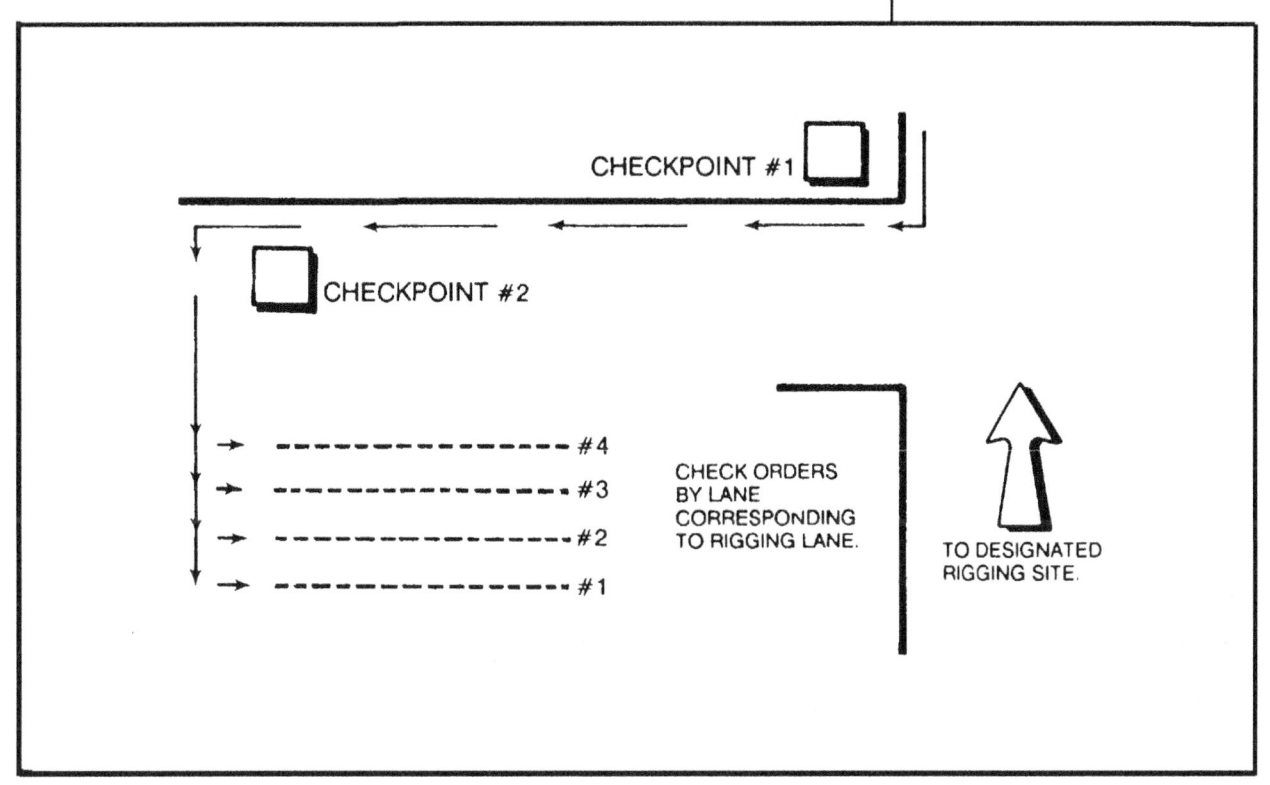

Figure 6-2. Heavy-drop LACC.

FM 90-26

(2) *Rigging sites.* The rigging site shown in Figure 6-3 accommodates the rigging and outloading of about 50 platforms in a 24-hour period, depending on the availability of trained personnel, equipment, and supplies. The rigging site uses an assembly line rigging technique. Riggers can operate as many lanes as required (with augmentation and as available space allows), although four are provided in this example.

(a) Lanes. Each lane has five rigging stations, one for each of the following:
- Vehicle preparation.
- Platform preparation and load positioning.
- Lashing installation.
- Parachutes and extraction system.
- Joint Army/Air Force load inspection.

(b) Personnel. Each rigging site requires about 240 support personnel and 60 riggers (two shifts), Support personnel typically include:
- One OIC for each rigging site.
- Two warrant officers (MOS 921A) for each rigging site.
- Twenty-five support personnel for each rigging lane.
- Twenty support personnel for each platform outload at a rigging site.
- Each site requires 30 riggers, plus 1 for each rigging station, 2 for each joint airlift inspection station, and 1 for each outload station.
- One ammunition specialist (MOS 55B) for each rigging site.

(c) Equipment. The following items of equipment are usually required to load equipment on platforms and to load platforms on vehicles for transportation to the departure airfield:
- Four 14-ton air-transportable cranes.
- One 40-ton crane
- Two 5-ton wreckers
- Ten 10-ton M172 semitrailers and tractors.
- One 6,000-pound, rough-terrain forklift.
- One 10,000-pound rough- terrain forklift
- Five tractors and trailers for hauling air items
- Trailers with ammunition for ballast.

(d) Rigging areas. A 75- by 110-meter area (roughly) is required for the rigging area itself. The ground surface should be clear, level, and compact. Each assembly line is about 25 feet wide by 110 feet long; it has at least a 30-foot gap between lanes to allow for vehicular movement Each line requires a foundation of 2-inch by 10- or 12-inch planks by 25-feet-long planks; it is laid side by side every 5 feet to support the roller conveyors (if a hardstand is not available). Space is reserved at the beginning of each lane to pack ammunit ion and other supplies onto vehicles and at the end of each lane to operate the loading equipment.

(c) Holding areas. Holding areas for rigging supplies are provided on either side of the rigging site for delivering and unloading rigging supplies. (Figure 6-4.) Enough space must be provided to drive through and park the trucks delivering materials to this site.

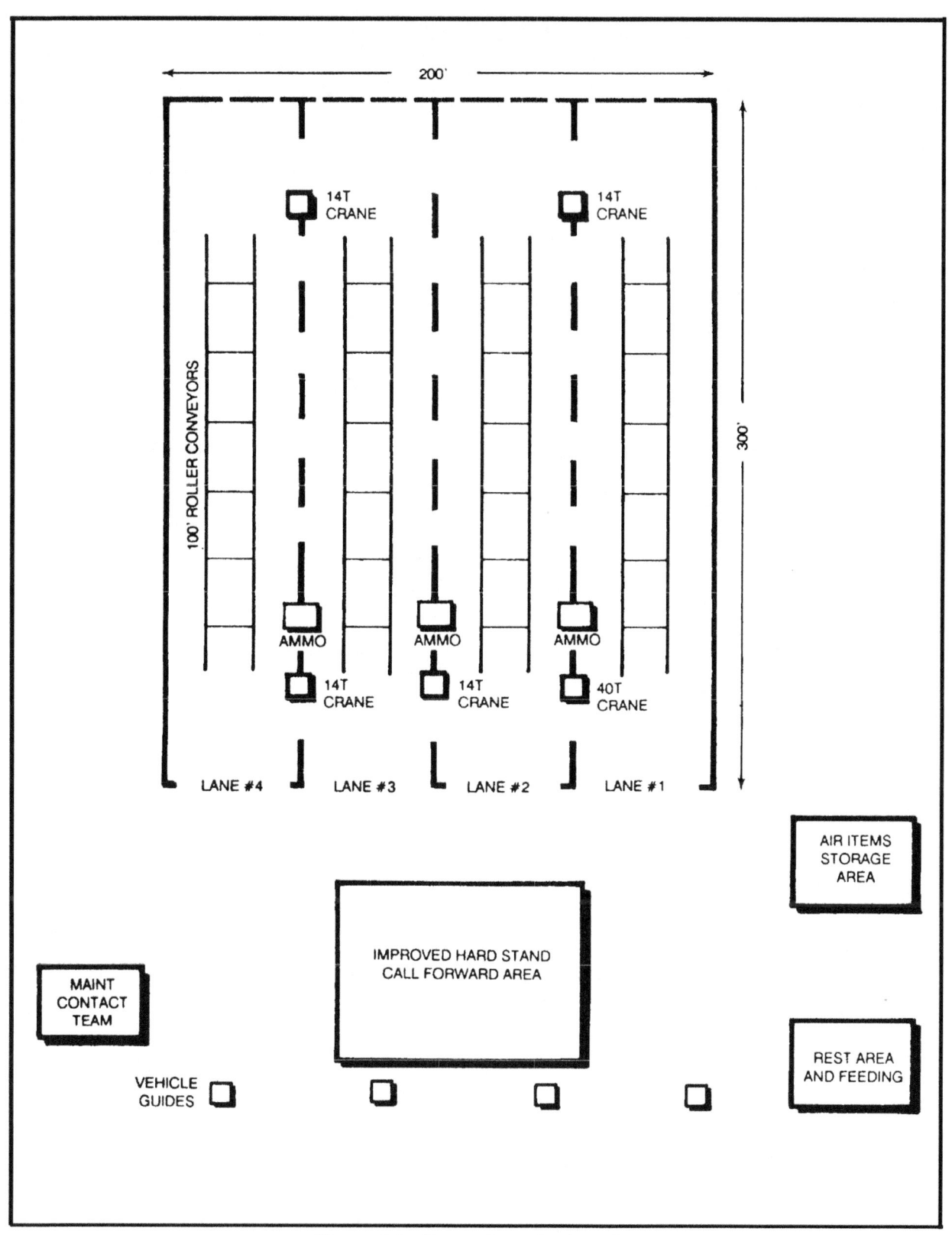

Figure 6-3. Heavy-drop rigging site.

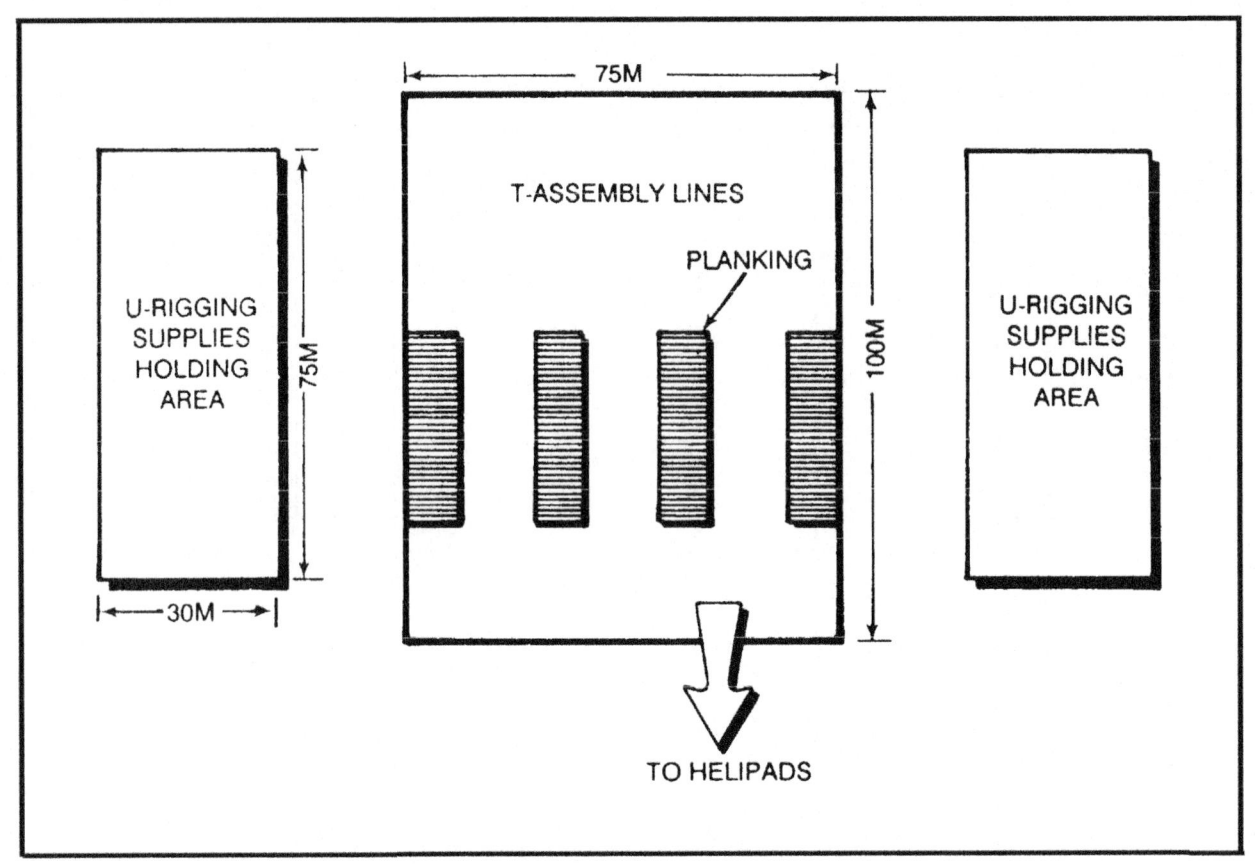

Figure 6-4. Holding areas

6-8. STAFF AND SUPPORT AGENCY RESPONSIBILITIES

The staff of the unit to be marshaled advises the MACG, through a liaison officer or by personal contact, of the requirements for the deploying unit at the marshaling areas. Support units provide their services until the assault force departs and the marshaling areas close.

a. **Staff Members and Duties.** Staff members of the marshaling unit perform specific duties as follows:

(1) The S1 requisitions replacements, requests recreational facilities, and coordinates medical support.

(2) The S2 coordinates security and deception measures to ensure secrecy.

(3) The S3 submits the personnel roster and outlines training, briefing, and rehearsal requirements.

(4) The S4 identifies the deploying unit's requirements for supply, maintenance, transportation, and storage facilities.

(5) The staff makes all arrangements far enough in advance of the marshaling period to enable support personnel to procure the facilities and install them where necessary.

b. **Support Agencies.** When the divisional airborne brigade deploys and the marshaling areas close, the division support command acts as the provisional logistical unit at the home station. The theater commander responsible for the AO provides the provisional logistical support unit for the ISB. If a support unit cannot pre-position at the ISB, a support unit from the home station command is included in the advance party. Marshaling control agencies assist the airborne and airlift force in the execution of the operation.

(1) *Marshaling area control group.* To enable the majority of the airborne force to concentrate on preparing for planned operations, support agencies are designated by division headquarters to provide most of the administrative and logistical support. These nonorganic units and certain organic units not participating in the airborne assault are organized into a provisional unit known as the MACG. The MACG commander is the principal logistical operator for the deploying force; he executes the logistical plan. Typical assistance provided by this unit includes:
- Transportation.
- All classes of supply.
- Communications.
- Campsite(s) construction, operation, and maintenance.
- Messing.
- Maintenance.
- Rigging.
- Recreation and other morale services.
- Local security personnel to augment the Air Force, when required.
- Health service support.

(2) *Airlift control element.* The ALCE coordinates and maintains operational control of all airlift aircraft while they are on the ground at the designated airfield. This includes aircraft and load-movement control and reporting, communications, loading and off-loading teams, aeromedical activities, and coordination with interested agencies, The ALCE's support function includes activities that relate to the airfield. Typical tasks for this Air Force unit include:

(a) Support and control exercises and contingency operations, as defined in MAC and TAC manuals and mission directives, on both a planned and a no-notice basis.

(b) Conduct around-the-clock operations to provide supervisory control and to ensure effective usc of the tactical airlift force on assigned missions.

(c) Direct, execute, and coordinate mission directives, plans, and orders assigned.

(d) Distribute completed loading manifests as required.

(c) Furnish copies of the aircraft parking plan to support units.

(f) Coordinate loading of aircraft.

(g) Coordinate disposition of Army equipment and personnel remaining behind or returning because of aborted sorties.

(h) Ensure that appropriate and adequate briefings for Army and AF personnel are conducted.

(i) Coordinate flight clearances.

(j) Coordinate configuration of aircraft.

(k) Schedule and coordinate proper AF coverage of assault LZs, DZs, and EZs.

(l) Schedule and publish air movement tables for supported units.

(m) Provide or arrange weather support for the mission.

(3) *Departure airfield control group.* The DACG ensures that Army units and their supplies and equipment are moved from the marshaling area and loaded IAW the air movement plan. Timing is critical at this point in the operation – strict control of both air and ground traffic must be maintained on and across active runways.

(4) *Arrival airfield control group.* The organization of the AACG is similar to the DACG. When personnel, supplies, and equipment are arriving on aircraft and need to be moved to marshaling camps or holding areas, the AACG is responsible for offloading them. Like the DACG, the AACG works closely with the ALCE unit at the arrival airfield.

Section II. OUTLOAD

Complex outload operations are more difficult because they are usually conducted at night under blackout conditions.

6-9. OUTLOAD PLAN

Since most or all of the airborne units' vehicles are rigged for air delivery, airborne units must rely on the supporting unit for transportation during outload. These requirements are closely related to and dictated by the loading plans developed for the operation.

a. **Contents of Loading Plan.** Loading preparations are included in the marshaling plan. Loading plans outline the procedures for moving personnel and heavy-drop loads from the alert holding area to plane side. They also outline the use of available materiels-handling equipment. The loading plans are closely coordinated with the supporting airlift units.

b. **Formulation of Loading Plan.** A loading plan is formulated at joint conferences. It contains information about the number of personnel and the amount of equipment to be airlifted, ACLs, and the general sequence of movement.

c. **Adherence to Loading Plan.** Strict adherence to the loading timetable is mandatory. The loading of equipment and supplies must be completed in time to permit postloading inspection, joint pretakeoff briefing, and personnel loading by the designated station time.

d. **Loading Responsibilities.** The general delineations of loading responsibilities in connection with the airborne operation are as follows:

(1) *Airlift commander.* He –

(a) Develops plans for specific loads and the sequence of movement in conjunction with the unit being moved.

(b) Establishes and disseminates instructions for documenting and manifesting all cargo and personnel.

(c) Provides instructions for loading and unloading aircraft and for cargo tie-down.

(d) Parks aircraft IAW the parking plan.

(e) Provides loading ramps, floor conveyors, tie-downs, load spreaders, and other auxiliary equipment such as operation ejection equipment.

(f) Prepares aircraft for ejection of cargo and for the safe exit of parachutists from aircraft in flight. Cargo to be ejected in flight is tied down by Air Force personnel.

(g) Ensures that an Air Force representative is present to provide technical assistance and to supervise the loading unit during the loading operations of each aircraft.

(h) Verifies documentation of personnel and equipment.

(i) Furnishes and operates materiels-handling equipment required in aircraft loading and unloading if the Army unit needs it.

(2) *Airborne commander.* He –

(a) Establishes the priority and sequence for movement of airborne personnel, equipment, and supplies.

(b) Prepares cargo for airdrop, airland, or extraction IAW applicable safety instructions.

(c) Marks each item of equipment to show its weight and cubage and, when appropriate, to show the center of gravity. Ensures hazardous cargo is properly annotated on DD Form 1387-2 IAW TM 38-250.

(d) Documents and manifests all loads of Army personnel, equipment, or both.

(e) Directs and monitors movement of ground traffic to the departure airfield or loading area, and accepts delivery at the destination.

(f) Delivers properly rigged supplies and equipment to the aircraft IAW the loading plan.

(g) Loads, ties down, and unloads accompanying supplies and equipment into and from the aircraft with technical assistance from a representative of the Air Force. Cargo to be ejected in flight is tied down and ejected by AF personnel. (Exception is made in the case of containers of supplies and equipment that are pushed from the jump exits by paratroopers immediately before their exit from the aircraft.)

(h) Ensures that Army personnel are seated aboard aircraft, are properly equipped, and have their safety belts fastened by station time.

(i) Briefs and supervises Army vehicle operators to ensure that the operators thoroughly comprehend airfield vehicular traffic procedures and pertinent safety precautions before they operate vehicles around aircraft.

(j) Provides vehicles and loading personnel to outload Army personnel and cargo from aborting aircraft and reload them on spare aircraft if time permits.

6-10. OUTLOAD PROCEDURES

A control system at arrival airfields is essential to prevent congestion and to facilitate orderly movement of cargo and personnel.

a. **Parking.** The main parking consideration is loading access. Dispersal must provide the most security possible with the least possible vulnerability and, at the same time, allow maneuvering room for loading the equipment.

(1) *Chalk number.* To facilitate identification of individual aircraft during loading, all aircraft are given a chalk number IAW the parking plan. The displayed chalk number should be readily discernible to personnel approaching the aircraft.

(2) *Parking plan.* The airlift force commander furnishes the airborne unit commander with an accurate parking plan to include airfield layout, location of aircraft by chalk number, location of standby aircraft, and access route(s).

b. **Controlling Traffic.** A traffic control system is essential to avoid congestion at loading and unloading sites. In outloading, any force control is accomplished by using a call-forward system in which loads are brought into the loading area as required. The following control system outline applies to airlanding facilities as well as airfields. (Figure 6-5, page 6-15.) The system provides a separate loading facility for personnel, heavy-drop loads, and aerial supply. The separation is essential to control loading and decrease the time required to load. The airfield control system is set up with the minimum required personnel and communications equipment, and with regard to the size of the forces being moved.

c. **Loading Procedures.** The actual outload is complex and requires close supervision to ensure all equipment and personnel are loaded on the correct aircraft as quickly and efficiently as possible.

(1) Initially, personnel and equipment are dispersed in marshaling areas distant from the loading airfields, but in close communication with control groups at the airfields.

(2) When called, the unit or equipment is moved by planeload to the call-forward area. The fewest possible planeload are maintained on hand in the call-forward area to ensure uninterrupted loading. Guides and military police are used as required.

(3) As aircraft arrive in the loading area, planeload are called forward; unit members load and tie equipment down with the technical assistance of Air Force personnel.

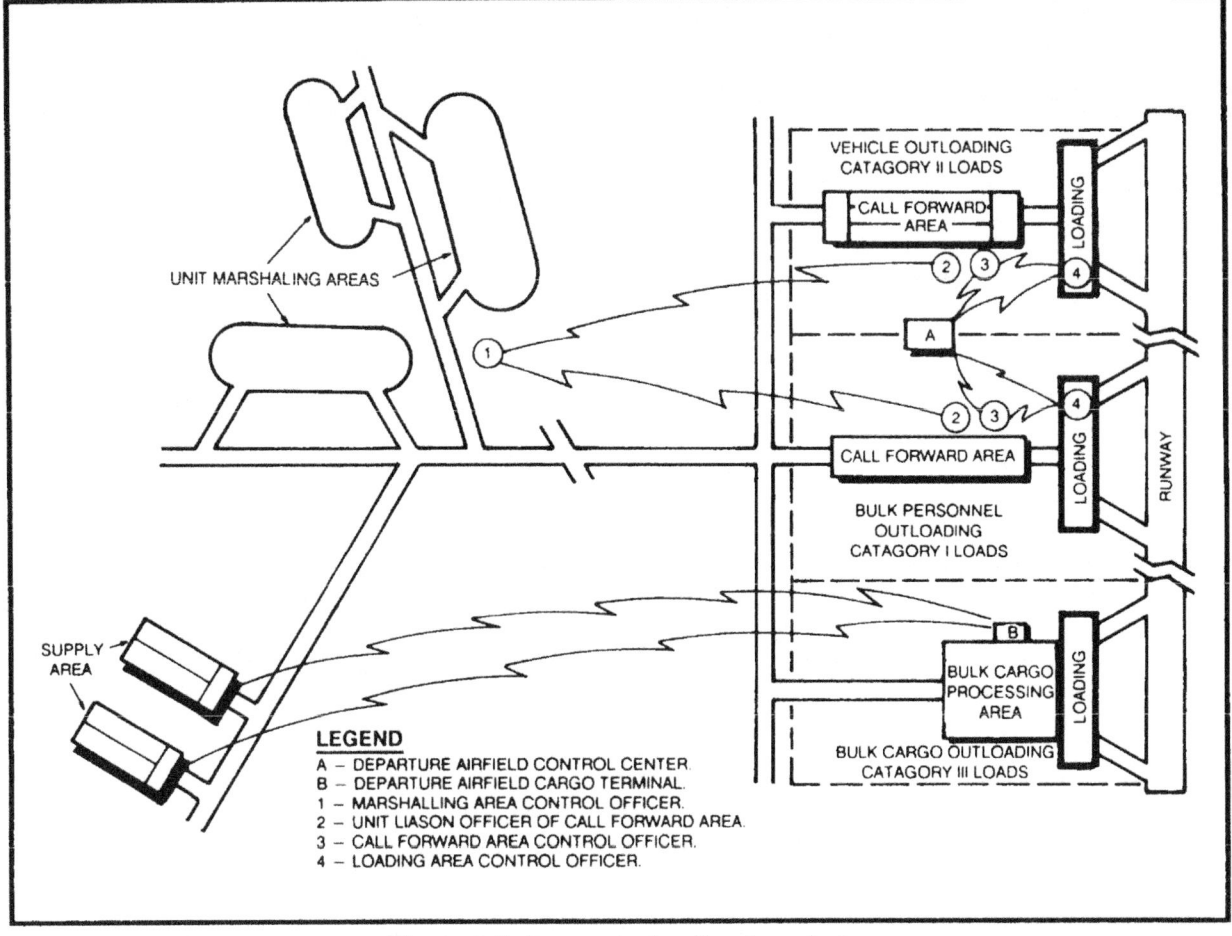

Figure 6-5. Concept of outload control.

(4) Control personnel maintain a log listing the departure of each aircraft. It contains the following information:
- Aircraft tail number.
- Summary of load or unit load number. (Manifests are correlated with this entry.)
- Time aircraft was available for loading.
- Station time.
- Takeoff time.
- Remarks.

d. **Unloading Procedures.** At arrival airfields, the control system is the reverse of that used at departure airfields. On arrival, crews unload aircraft and move the loads to dispersed holding areas where arriving elements build up to convenient size for further movements. Crews keep load categories separated to facilitate control and movement.

CHAPTER 7

TACTICAL OPERATIONS

The employment of airborne forces on the ground is similar to that of other infantry ground units. The entire range of these operations is movement to contact, deliberate attack, hasty attack defense, or withdrawals. FMs 7-8, 7-20, and 7-30 discuss doctrinal employment of airborne units. They also discuss tactics, techniques, and procedures for the conduct of tactical operations. This chapter only discusses the differences that result from variations in organization, equipment, and method of arrival in the combat area.

Section I. GROUND TACTICAL OPERATION

The ground tactical operation phase of an airborne operation can include raids, linkup, relief, withdrawal (either overland or by air), exfiltration, recovery, survival operations, or airfield seizure. Aspects of these operations, when conducted from the objective area, are in this section.

7-1. RAIDS

The organization, equipment, and capabilities of airborne units give them the ability to conduct airborne raids behind enemy lines. Dispersed and fluid-type warfare provide many opportunities for the conduct of airborne raids. Army, Air Force, or Navy aircraft can be used to transport the raiding force. (See FMs 7-20 and 7-85 for information on the planning, preparation, and execution of raids.)

a. **Mission.** The airborne force can conduct raids–

- To destroy enemy installations or positions.
- To capture or kill the enemy.
- To rescue friendly personnel.
- To harass or disrupt enemy operations.
- To seize critical equipment or similar intelligence objectives.

A planned withdrawal is executed on completion of the assigned mission.

b. **Objectives.** Types of objectives vary; commanders can find suitable objectives deep in enemy territory or close to the area of combat. When there is a choice, the objective that most nearly fulfills the following conditions probably gives the best chance for success:

- It can be successfully engaged with small forces.
- Once seized, it can be held and defended with available forces.
- It is difficult for the enemy to reinforce.
- It is easy to locate under poor visibility conditions.

c. **Similarities to Ground Raids.** Airborne raids are similar to ground raids, except the raiding force uses air transport to move to the objective area and can withdraw by air. Air transport permits the raiding force to bypass enemy positions and to overcome terrain barriers and distance factors. The objective of the airborne raid is more likely to be beyond the supporting distance of the parent unit than other types of raids.

d. **Coordination.** Commanders compile overall plans at higher command levels because of the coordination required with multiservice agencies. The raiding force is mainly concerned with the scheme of maneuver employed within the objective area. Higher headquarters coordinates the operation with other Army agencies, Air Force units, and Naval units that may be involved. The commander's initial estimate of the situation determines the time required for planning.

e. **Preparation.** This closely parallels the preparation required for an airborne assault with emphasis on the following aspects:

- Detailed intelligence.
- Deception and CI plans.
- Detailed withdrawal plans, including contingency plans.
- Force composition.

f. **Training.** Special training for each operation should be conducted except when raids must be mounted on short notice. The training should be immediately before the operation and teach the raiding force its duties and roles. Training should end with at least one joint rehearsal of the operation, including the withdrawal phase. This rehearsal should occur early to ensure that lessons learned can be incorporated into the OPLAN.

g. **Composition.** The nature of the mission may require attachment of specialized units or equipment to the airborne unit conducting the raid. The size of the force should be as small as possible and still accomplish the mission; usually, it is no larger than a battalion. The raiding force is reorganized into self-contained elements tailored to accomplish special tasks, including assault parties, security parties, and a reserve. However, the TOE structure is retained so the established chain of command can be used. To maintain flexibility, a reserve may be kept outside the objective area until needed.

h. **Time and Duration.** Airborne raids can be conducted at night, dawn, or twilight; in fog or mist; or during other low visibility conditions. These conditions facilitate surprise and the delivery of the raiding force to the objective with a minimum risk of detection. Executing a daylight raid usually requires greater use of support fires, including tactical air support, and the use of measures to limit enemy observation and intelligence.

i. **Conduct.** Immediately on landing, the elements of the raiding force independently begin their assigned tasks without further assembly.

(1) The actions of the raiding parties are decentralized; each operates as required by its own missions, but their actions are coordinated by the raid commander. In the attack of objectives, speed should be stressed.

(2) The force entering the objective area must be strong enough to defeat the enemy forces in the immediate AO and to accomplish the assigned mission. Therefore, the key to the success of the overall mission is to isolate the objective area; it prevents the enemy from moving strong tactical forces into it to defeat the raiding force. Isolating the battle area can be accomplished by stealth or force.

(a) Stealth. The raiding force can enter the objective area with such speed and stealth that enemy forces do not have time to locate them or time to react with sufficient combat power. Stealth operations are possible when the objective area is in a remote part of the enemy area or when the unit can quickly accomplish the mission.

(b) Force. If the mission cannot be accomplished before the enemy can locate the raiding force and move tactical forces to the area to attack, then force must be used. This requires extensive support from outside agencies to isolate the objective area, to keep the enemy from moving forces to the area, and to prevent the enemy from launching a major air attack into the area.

j. **Withdrawal.** The withdrawal is carefully planned because it is usually the most difficult part of the operation to execute. The raiding force can be withdrawn by air, land, or sea or a combination of these.

(1) The airborne withdrawal can be performed by assault or medium-transport aircraft, helicopter, or water-based aircraft; it can be preceded by overland withdrawal to pickup points. Space in the returning aircraft is restricted. All equipment and supplies should be evacuated if possible, but plans should stress the withdrawal of personnel rather than equipment. All equipment that cannot be withdrawn is destroyed.

(2) The commander must designate the required landing areas early in the planning phase. He should not change areas at the last minute.

(3) The raiding force can withdraw overland by exfiltration. (See paragraph 7-5.)

(4) Evacuation by sea is practicable wherever water approaches exist. Submarines, destroyers, and small boats can be used. Plans should provide for alternate beaches and possibly for NGF to cover the withdrawal.

k. **Requirements for Army Aircraft.** The characteristics of Army aircraft (mainly helicopters) make them ideal for use in raid operations. Habitual employment of the same Army aviation personnel during raid-type training lessens the need for extensive rehearsal before raid operations. Army aircraft are needed in the objective area for reconnaissance, movement, and evacuation of forces that remain in contact with the enemy.

l. **Communications.** A reliable communications system must be established within the objective area, and from the objective area to the headquarters outside the area that controls the overall operation.

m. **Command Structure.** The headquarters that controls the operation must have C^2 over all the units taking part in the operation; control of all elements by one commander is essential.

7-2. RECOVERY OPERATIONS

Recovery operations are specialized raids organized to liberate imprisoned or detained personnel or to return specific equipment to friendly control. These operations are normally performed by SOF, but may be performed by infantry units. They include recovering and extracting downed or hijacked aircrews and political or military leaders. Airborne forces use surprise and combat power to overwhelm resistance before detainees or prisoners can be harmed.

a. **Success of the Operation.** Success depends on–

- Speed and surprise.
- Violent action.
- Quickly identifying, securing, and safeguarding evacuees.
- Limited time on the objective.
- Rapid and orderly extraction.

b. **Planning.** The planning of personnel and equipment recovery operations is the same as for the raid. The difference is that the commander must plan for the extraction of recovered personnel and for the loading and extraction of sensitive equipment. Personnel and equipment recovery raids are often executed as contingency missions. They require the commander to plan and execute the recovery quickly. An ISB or REMAB should be considered for rehearsals and OPSEC.

c. **Augmentations.** This type of operation often requires augmentation by personnel with special skills. Examples are medical personnel, technical experts, mechanics, or crew members trained in repair and retrieval operations, and linguists or translators.

d. **Organization.** The recovery force is organized the same as for a raid. Special teams are sometimes needed to perform certain missions involved in the recovery. Reconnaissance teams can be inserted ahead of the force to reconnoiter the objective, to locate the detained or imprisoned personnel, and to provide guides.

(1) All planning and execution takes place as described for the raid. The emphasis must be on detailed, timely intelligence.

(2) Medical teams, to include a physician, must be available to care for the detainees; they should accompany the search team.

(3) Guide teams and escort teams are planned. Escorts should be planned on a 1:1 ratio for detainees.

(4) Teams must be trained in searching and clearing buildings and operations in a MOUT environment in general. (See FM 90-10-1 for detailed information on infantry operations in urban an area.)

e. **Execution.** The enemy must be assaulted when he least expects it. The force must ensure that friendly detainees are not harmed during the assault–either by friendly or enemy personnel. Evacuees can be categorized as follows:

- Category 1. All previously identified US nationals. No special security measures are required.
- Category 2. All other US nationals with credible proof (visa or passport), such as tourists, American expatriates, or US businessmen. No special security measures are required.
- Category 3. Those with questionable US citizenship and foreign nationals and their immediate families, such as those employed by the US government. Armed security guards are required.
- Category 4. Possible infiltrators, saboteurs, and unfriendly foreigners. These personnel are treated the same as EPWs.

Recovered personnel can be identified by total numbers or by name, if names are available to the recovering force. The evacuee's chain of command can assist in assembly and identification.

f. **Extraction.** The commander should plan for the extraction point to be close to the point of recovery. This prevents the detainees from moving cross-country or the raid force from transporting bulky equipment long distances. For small groups of detainees or small items of equipment, the extraction point can be farther away. Recovery operations can use any method, or combination of methods, of extraction. Close planning and coordination are required with Army, Air Force, or Navy aviation for evacuation of the target area.

g. **Operations After Recovery.** Once evacuees have been recovered to a secure location, they are processed for return to control of the appropriate authority. The recovery area is organized into five operational areas: command, reception, processing, comfort, and departure. All evacuees are registered and informed of their legal rights. They are screened for medical problems and intelligence information. Evacuees are updated on the host nation in a secure area. Their privacy is protected. Evacuees are later prepared for further transportation, if required.

7-3. WITHDRAWAL/EVACUATION OF UNITS

Evacuation/withdrawal of an airborne force can be preplanned or become necessary because of enemy action. The limitations of transport aircraft and the circular shape of the airhead introduce complicating factors not present in a normal ground withdrawal. (Figure 7-1.)

a. **Evacuation Sequence.** When the situation permits, the plan usually provides for evacuation in the following sequence: supplies, materiel, and soldiers.

b. **Withdrawal/Evacuation Factors.** The following factors must be considered when executing either a withdrawal or an evacuation.

(1) The operation requires sufficient aircraft and suitable LZs.

(2) Local air superiority or absence of enemy air interference is essential.

(3) The operation is sensitive to weather, primarily in the objective area, but also in the base area.

(4) Surprise and deception are essential to the operation's success. An alert and determined enemy can be expected to try maximum interference as soon as he detects evidence of a withdrawal.

(5) The withdrawal of the DLIC is the most critical phase of the withdrawal.

(6) The decision to withdraw by air must be made early to permit adequate planning and coordination.

(7) Priorities for evacuating soldiers, supplies, and materiel must be established; supplies and equipment that cannot be evacuated are destroyed (with the exception of Class VIII medical supplies).

c. Responsibilities and Procedures. The breakdown of withdrawal or evacuation responsibilities is as follows:

(1) *Airborne commander.* The overall commander directing the conduct of an airborne operation orders the withdrawal or evacuation of the force.

(2) *Ground force commander.* The ground force commander determines the priority of unit movement. He furnishes the airlift commander a list of units broken down by priority into aircraft loads, indicating departure points and destination. He establishes the DACG, which performs the following functions:

(a) Ensures that prescribed planeloads of personnel and equipment are available in the ready areas and are prepared to load.

(b) Calls prescribed paneloads forward from ready areas as aircraft arrive.

(c) Notifies the Air Force when aircraft are loaded.

In a planned withdrawal, the ground force commander provides trained teams to load and secure equipment; technical assistance is given by qualified airlift personnel. In a forced withdrawal, such teams are not available. Therefore, the ground force commander can request the airlift commander to land Army loading teams in the objective area.

(3) *Airlift commander.* The airlift commander controls air movement, establishing facilities within the objective area to coordinate the arrival and departure of aircraft.

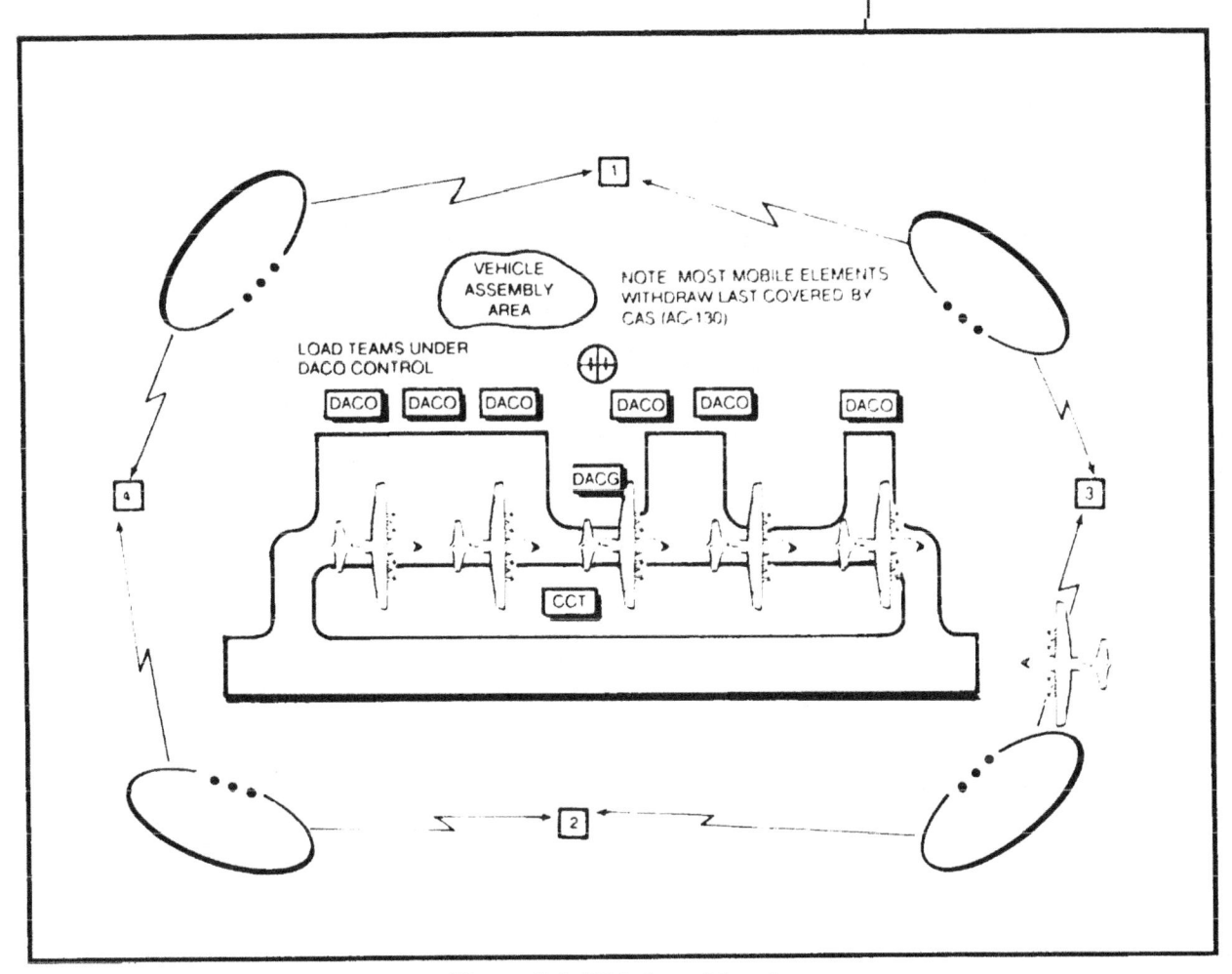

Figure 7-1. Withdrawal by air.

7-4. LINKUP

When the commander anticipates that an airborne force will engage in sustained combat after linking up with ground forces, planning should provide for this. Preservation of the force is vital since the airborne force will most likely be deployed behind enemy lines. (See FMs 7-20 and 7-30 for information on linkup operations.)

7-5. EXFILTRATION

If an airborne force cannot link up with ground forces or cannot be extracted by air, it must prepare to conduct an exfilttration by single companies, platoons, or squads to reach friendly lines.

a. **Situations.** Stealth and evasiveness are key elements of exfiltration Commanders favor this method of extraction when–

(1) The enemy has air superiority.

(2) The enemy can prohibit air or water extraction.

(3) The distance to friendly lines is short.

(4) The terrain provides cover and concealment (for movement on foot) and limits enemy mobile units.

(a) Soldiers and units can use multiple exfiltration routes if the enemy detects them. They can also use captured enemy vehicles and equipment to assist in the exfiltration.

(b) The exfiltration force can exfiltrate in one body or in small groups. Exfiltrating in small groups saves the time assembly can cost the unit.

(5) The exfiltrating force moves lightly equipped and unburdened with captured personnel or materiel.

(6) The exfiltration route passes through an area occupied by friendly locals or guerrilla forces who can assist the movement.

(7) Areas along exfiltration routes are uninhabited.

(8) The enemy force is dispersed or cannot concentrate against the exfiltrating force.

b. **Patrolling.** Units employ aggressive patrolling to detect enemy weak points.

c. **Size of Units.** Units should be small to avoid detection but large enough to protect themselves. Terrain (especially avenues of approach to friendly lines), enemy strength, and friendly strength (including fire support) determine the size of units. All elements should have communications equipment. They should move at night or during limited visibility over close terrain.

d. **Use of Vehicles.** Commanders can exfiltrate vehicles or can use them in a limited maneuver role. Before departure, units redistribute supplies. They also determine the disposition of dead and wounded personnel, and allocate vehicles for their transportation. Crews can destroy in place vehicles that are not mission capable or those to be left in the airhead, then join the main body as it exfiltrates.

e. **Approach of Friendly Lines.** Units should approach friendly lines in daylight. The units depart the airhead at a prescribed time interval while the covering force maintains security and simulates normal unit activity.

f. **Communications.** Units establish communications with friendly forward units and coordinate fire support, recognition signals, and passage of lines.

7-6. SURVIVAL OPERATIONS

A vital part of all premission planning is the development of en route plans and postmission plans for survival, evasion, resistance and escape operations, and for SAR operations. Such plans enhance survival of the force and the transport of aircrews. (See FM 20-150, FM 21-76, and AR 350-30.)

a. **Responsibilities of Airborne Commander.** The airborne commander is responsible for helping develop the plan in coordination with all supporting agencies Hc ensures that all members of the airborne force and supporting aircrews arc briefed on the plan.

b. **Development of Plans.** Each plan is unique because each situation has unique problems. The plan devised by the airborne commander must address these problems, while gaining from the individual abilities and training of the airborne soldiers and their supporting aircrews. The following considerations apply to SERE/SAR plans devised during airborne operations.

(1) Plans enhance survival of soldiers who can no longer accomplish their assigned missions. The group's senior combat arms officer must decide if any missions remain that the group can accomplish. If not, then he must try to evade and escape enemy capture if unable to link up and be extracted with the rest of the force. Because of the depth of penetration behind enemy lines, most successful plans can involve either air or water movement away from enemy-held territory.

(2) Dismounted forces can move a great distance (especially at night) over rugged terrain to reach an area where they can rendezvous with SAR aircraft or boats. Escape and evasion plans for airborne elements should include avoiding contact with the locals; however, the aid of friendly insurgent forces can be enlisted. The plan can also include the use of E&E networks that arc in place behind enemy lines; however, these nets must not be compromised by the volume of evaders.

7-7. BREAKOUT FROM ENCIRCLEMENT

A breakout from encirclement is conducted when units operating behind enemy lines are cut off from friendly forces and surrounded by superior forces. Given airborne unit missions, the chance of operating as an isolated force behind enemy lines is great. The breakout is characterized by determination of enemy weak points, deception, massing of combat power, and a direct attack for a violent and timely breakout. (FM 7-20 discusses the considerations for planning and the execution of breakout operations.)

7-8. RELIEF

Airborne personnel are capable of sustained action after their heavy equipment has been introduced into the airhead. They can be used in any role that might be assigned to an infantry unit. When ground or naval forces link up with airborne personnel who may face employment in another airborne operation, the controlling headquarters should relieve the airborne forces so they can be withdrawn to a rear base, reorganized, and readied for the next airborne operation. (Reliefs are discussed in FMs 7-20 and 7-30.)

Section II. AIRFIELD SEIZURE

An airfield seizure is executed to clear and control a designated airstrip. The purpose can be to allow follow-on airland forces to conduct transload operations or to establish a lodgment in order to continue combat operations from that location. Airfields can be seized and occupied by friendly forces for a definite or indefinite period.

7-9. REQUIREMENTS

Requirements for the seizure of an airfield, subsequent securing of the airhead, and the introduction of follow-on forces depend heavily on the factors of METT-T and the commander's concept of the operation.

a. **Planning Factors.** Certain factors must be considered when conducting the estimate for an airfield seizure.

(1) The key element is surprise. Assault of the airfield should be conducted at night to maximize surprise, security, and protection of the force. Timing is critical; the assault should be executed so that the follow-on assault echelon (airdrop or airland) can also be delivered under the cloak of darkness.

(2) Enemy air defenses near the airfield and along aircraft approach and departure routes must be suppressed.

(3) The size of the airfield must be sufficient for landing and takeoff of aircraft to be used after seizure. Minimum operating length determines how much of the airfield must be cleared.

(4) The configuration and condition of the airfield, including taxiways and parking, determines the maximum-on-ground capacity for aircraft at one time. This, combined with offload/transload time estimates, impacts directly on scheduling follow-on airflow into the airfield. Surface composition and condition and predicted weather conditions must allow the airfield to accept the required number of sorties without deteriorating the surface below minimum acceptable safety standards.

(5) The airfield location must facilitate follow-on operations. If transload operations must occur, the follow-on target must be within the range of the aircraft to be used. If not, then forward area rearm/refuel assets must be available and positioned to support the follow-on operation.

(6) The airfield must be defensible initially with assault forces against any immediate threat and with planned follow-on forces against larger, coordinated counterattacks.

b. **Airborne Force Task Organization.** The airborne force's task organization varies, depending on METT-T factors. However, airfield seizures require the designation of elements to clear runways, assault designated objectives, and screen areas valuable to the operation besides normal task-organization considerations. Supporting assets and attachments should be considered in organizing the force. As with any other airborne operation, the commander organizes his force into three echelons: assault, follow-on, and rear.

(1) The future of the army is fighting joint combined-arms operations with a mix of light and heavy forces. The original concept for the light division and the restructure of the airborne and air assault divisions envisioned that the needs for antiarmor and other CS would be provided by corps in the form of plugs. The concept of fighting pure is contrary to the concept of combined-arms warfare. Heavy units would be task-organized with light infantry and other forces into TFs to gain the complementary effect of the combined arms. The mix of the force would be determined by the threat. The insertion of light armored assets in the assault echelon would provide, in the early phases, an increased antiarmor capability.

(2) Reconnaissance and security teams can be deployed ahead of the main body. They can be used to determine enemy dispositions on the airfield and whether airfield runways are cleared or blocked. They can also look for enemy air defense assets near the airfield. These teams maintain radio contact with the airborne commander who is en route to the objective. They can be used in the selective destruction of enemy facilities by directing air strikes or by employing laser target designators to limit collateral damage to the airfield. Reconnaissance and security teams can also be used to sever land-line communications not vulnerable to friendly EW efforts or to provide early warning of the approach of enemy reaction forces. Reconnaissance and security teams can come from a LRSU, special operations forces, or battalion scout platoons. However, the commander must weigh the risk of team compromise and consequent loss of surprise against the value of intelligence obtained.

(3) Air Force CCTS are required to provide airspace management assistance as well as control of aircraft after landing (for example, parking locations and taxiing control). Combat control teams can be inserted ahead of the force as part of a JAAP; it can jump with the airborne assault or can airland with the first assault aircraft.

(4) TOW, scout, and MP vehicles, or other mobile weapons platforms, should be front-loaded in the airland assault echelon. These vehicles, relying on surprise and speed for security, must quickly move to blocking or screening positions. They also provide a mobile antiarmor capability.

(5) If engineer units are to accompany the assault force, they should be tasked to clear the runways of obstacles. Special consideration must be given

to the type and quantity of obstacles on the runway. This has a major impact on engineer assets required by the TF, the time for clearance, and the planned time of arrival of airland sorties. To assist the engineers, bulldozers and mine detectors (metallic and nonmetallic) can be dropped in the initial assault. To reduce injuries, the commander should outfit runway clearing elements with elbow and knee pads when they are parachuting onto a hard-surface runway. Selected personnel can be tasked to jump-start disabled vehicles or airfield support vehicles required to assist the offload. Engineer personnel must understand the amount of space required to land specific types of aircraft. (See Appendix C.)

(6) Civil affairs and PSYOP personnel help the commander control civilians and PWs.

(7) Depending on the threat, commanders can determine that certain objectives near the airfield and key terrain surrounding it (control towers, communications nodes, terminal guidance facilities) should be secured at the same time units are clearing the runways. This requirement increases the number of personnel designated to participate in the initial airborne assault. Should this be necessary, commanders can adjust aircraft loads. Those aircraft designated to drop personnel cannot transport as much airland cargo because the station near the jump doors must remain clear.

(8) A number of other assets can be available to assist insertion, C^2, and support.

(a) Airborne battlefield command and control center. The ABCCC's mobility and communications capabilities provide valuable C^2.

(b) C-130 Talon. This aircraft's sophisticated navigational equipment permits insertion even under the most adverse weather conditions.

(c) AC-130. The availability of AC-130s allows for continuous fire support from a mobile and accurate airborne platform. If air refueling is available, the AC-130 can stay on station and provide overhead support for extended periods. (For more information, see FM 7-20.)

(d) Unit-level communications. At this level leaders can augment communications by using hand-held radios for special elements and teams and by setting up special nets for the initial assault.

c. Airfield/Lodgment Actions. Several actions must take place to accomplish the seizure of an airfield and the subsequent establishment of the lodgment. These actions or considerations include:

(1) Quickly seize critical enemy C^2 facilities that will prevent the reinforcement of the enemy force defending the airfield complex. At the same time, the assaulting force must isolate the objective area to further reduce the possibility of reinforcement.

(2) Deploy and employ enough ground combat forces to prevent enemy penetration of the lodgment area (airhead, beachhead).

(3) Establish a coherent defense against air attack to ensure that the assaulting force is not interdicted or the airfield damaged or destroyed by air-delivered munitions.

(4) Ensure enough combat power (ADA, maneuver, FA, and so on) is employed to preserve the air and sea LOCs and to facilitate the delivery of follow-on forces by air, land, or sea.

(5) Seize the airfield quickly enough to facilitate a rapid buildup of forces to expand the airhead into a lodgment line. This ability is expressed in terms of airframes to perform over-the-horizon insertion of forces.

(6) Quickly establish an AACG. This group can be under the control of the battalion XO or S3 Air. It requires positive control to facilitate rapid offloading of aircraft. Aircraft execute either combat offloading of pallets or engine-running offloading of vehicles, equipment, and personnel. Personnel should prepare all vehicles and equipment for immediate offloading as soon as the aircraft stops. Dunnage and tie-downs remain on the aircraft to save time.

(7) Deny the enemy the use of airborne sensors and UAVs. All ADA measures, air superiority, and effective camouflage operations measures must be executed to contribute to this effort.

7-10. SEQUENCE OF OPERATIONS

The sequence of events during the assault, seizure and consolidation of the force on the captured airfield dictates the timing of the delivery of the follow-on echelon to the objective area.

a. Insertion of the CCT/JAAP Into the Objective Area. Insertion can be overt or covert based on the threat. Insertion of these teams depends on the ability to get them into the area undetected. If surprise is paramount, the airborne force may rely on other means to pinpoint the objective area and on other sources of intelligence and navigation.

b. Preassault Fires. Preassault fires maybe used when collateral damage can be controlled with no danger to the airfield. They are normally used to suppress or neutralize enemy air defense systems and installations (SEAD). Air Force assets may be used to jam enemy radar and communications during this period and before the parachute insertion.

c. Airborne Assault (by Assault Echelon A if the airborne force is so task-organized) to Isolate the Airfield and Establish the Airhead. The assault initially starts at P-hour to eliminate enemy resistance on the airfield and to secure the runway(s) from direct fire. The airfield complex is further isolated by the establishment of blocking positions to deny access to and from the airfield area. Simultaneously, key facilities are seized and or neutralized. Particular attention should be directed to limit collateral damage since these facilities may be necessary for sustained combat operations after the lodgment is established.

d. **Insertion of Assault Echelon B with Additional Combat, CS, and CSS Assets.** An RSL is established to provide early warning to the main body. It may consist of a series of infantry OPs and antiarmor ambush sites as well as a cavalry screen. Assets for this task are best formed from vehicle-mounted scouts or light armor assets. They should be task-organized with infantry to fight and delay the enemy as the main body prepares for a possible counterattack.

e. **Reserve.** A reserve should be constituted at every level to weight the main effort. A mounted reserve provides the greatest degree of flexibility. The reserve should be committed to exploit success, complete the mission, or to handle contingency missions. (For more information, see FM 7-20.)

f. **Clearance of the Runway(s).** The enemy may have pre-positioned vehicles or other obstructions on runways, taxiways, or parking aprons to deter and slow down the use of the airfield complex by attacking forces. Once the assault echelon has seized initial objectives, the runway clearance teams (engineers, infantry, and other designated personnel) begin clearing or repairing the runway(s), This clearance includes the removal of dunnage from heavy-drop platforms. It must be done immediately to facilitate the introduction of follow-on forces by airland delivery.

g. **Follow-on Echelon Deployment.** The follow-on echelon is deployed to the objective area once the initial assault objectives are secured and the airhead is established. This echelon may be deployed by paradrop or by air-land if the airfield facilities have been identified, repaired, and placed into an operational status.

7-11. SECURITY FORCE OPERATIONS

The battalion may be required to conduct security force operations in its area of responsibility, concurrent with offensive operations against the enemy. All actions, however, must be strictly within established rules of engagement and the law of land warfare. The objectives of security force operations are as follows:

- To isolate the insurgency from its civilian support (population and resource control).
- To prevent interference with friendly operations by the civilian population (population control).
- To secure military installations and lines of communication from insurgent attack.
- To solicit the active support of the civil population for the friendly cause. (For more specific information, see FM 7-20.)

7-12. NONCOMBATANT EVACUATION OPERATIONS

Political concerns dominate shows of force and demonstrations. Military forces conduct these operations within delicate legal and political constraints. The political will to employ actual force–should a demonstration of it fail–is vital to the succcss of these operations. Actual combat is not their goal. The force coordinates its operations with the country team or teams. Before commitment, the chain of command should certify that the force understands the national purpose, ROE, and inherent risks of the operation. Noncombatant evacuation operations relocate threatened civilian noncombatants from locations in a foreign or host nation. These operations normally involve US citizens whose lives are in danger. They may also include selected host nation natives and third country nationals.

a. Under ideal circumstances, there should be little or no opposition to an evacuation; however, commanders should anticipate possible hostilities. In the LIC environment, this type of operation usually involves swift insertion of a force and temporary occupation of an objective, followed by a planned, quick withdrawal. This mission is ideally suited to an airborne element. It involves only the force required for self-defense and the protection of the evacuees.

b. Military, political, or other emergencies in any country may require evacuation of designated personnel as the situation deteriorates. The Department of State initiates requests for military assistance; they also obtain necessary clearances from other governments. This assistance can include basing and overflight authorizations, and the use of facilities essential to performing the evacuation.

c. If the chief of the US diplomatic corp expects trouble, he should direct the early withdrawal of dependents and nonessential personnel by ordinary transport. If this has already occurred, only a minimum of personnel normally require emergency military evacuation. Thorough planning ensures that US, host nation, and international media understand the operation's intent. This enhances security and the dissemination of positive information.

d. The evacuation may take place in a benign environment, face a threat of violent opposition, or require combat action. The specific situation determines the type of evacuation required. The evacuation force commander has little influence over the local situation. He may not have the authority to preempt hostile actions by military measures; yet, he must be prepared to defend the evacuation effort and provide protection for his forces. Thus, the key factor in NEO planning is a correct appraisal of the political-military environment in which the force will operate.

e. An understanding of the role and status of host nation security forces is important. Host nation resources can provide essential assistance to the operation. These politically sensitive operations are often monitored or controlled at the highest level. Diplomatic and legal restraints limit military action to only those activities that permit the evacuation without hindrance. Care of the civilians and the maintenance of order at the evacuation site will be the ground forces commander's responsibility.

f. Airlift operations demand close cooperation among the airlift control element, the ground forces commander, and the diplomatic mission. Aircraft commanders supporting the evacuation should coordinate flight information with the appropriate sovereign airspace authorities to the maximum extent possible, However, positive airspace control may be difficult and airspace control systems may be inadequate. In cases where sovereign authorities are unable or unwilling to either approve or deny clearance, each aircraft commander must operate at their own discretion. They use caution proportionate to the circumstances to lessen risk. If no effective airspace control exists, the airlift commander should assume airspace control responsibilities and keep the diplomatic mission and ground forces advised on the progress of the airlift.

g. Commanders should remember that NEO can quickly turn into peacemaking or peacekeeping operations. They must plan for these contingencies.

h. Rescue and recovery operations are sophisticated actions that require precise execution, especially when conducted in hostile countries. They may be clandestine or overt. They may also include the rescue of US or friendly foreign nationals; and the location, identification, and recovery of sensitive equipment or items critical to US national security.

(1) Hostile forces can oppose rescue and recovery operations. On the other hand, these operations may remain unopposed if the potentially hostile force is unaware of them or unable or unwilling to interfere. Stealth, surprise, speed, and the threat of overwhelming US force are some of the means available to overcome opposition.

(2) Rescue and recovery operations require timely intelligence, detailed planning, deception, swift execution, and extraordinary security measures. They usually involve highly trained special units, but they may also receive support from the general purpose forces.

i. The US executes strikes and raids for specific purposes other than gaining or holding terrain. Strikes and raids can support rescue or recovery operations or destroy or seize equipment or facilities that demonstrate a threat to national collective security interests. They can also support counterdrug operations by destroying narcotics production or transshipment facilities or support a host government's actions in this regard, Strikes and raids are the most conventional of peacetime contingency operations The principles of combat operations apply directly. The unified CINC normally plans and executes them.

Section III. SUPPORTING OPERATIONS

Airborne units can deploy from a CONUS base directly to the objective area. A more common method would be for the airborne unit to first deploy to a REMAB or to an ISB before establishing a lodgment in the AO. In certain circumstances, the objective can be beyond the range of aircraft operating from a REMAB or ISB in friendly territory. Therefore, a forward operating base in hostile territory can be seized to facilitate or project further operations.

7-13. REMOTE MARSHALING BASE

The REMAB is a secure base to which the entire airborne unit (including organic and attached support elements) deploys and continues mission planning. (Figure 7-2.)

a. **Location.** The REMAB is within the geographical area encompassed by the command authority of the theater or JTF commander. This ensures that the CSS elements providing support to the airborne unit are operating within their normal area. It prevents or lessens out-of-sector support requirements for CSS elements. The REMAB should be in an area similar in terrain and climate to the objective area. Time spent at the REMAB lets the unit begin acclimatization.

b. **Planning and Coordination.** The REMAB also provides a secure location for the unit to conduct detailed planning and coordination with the controlling headquarters staff.

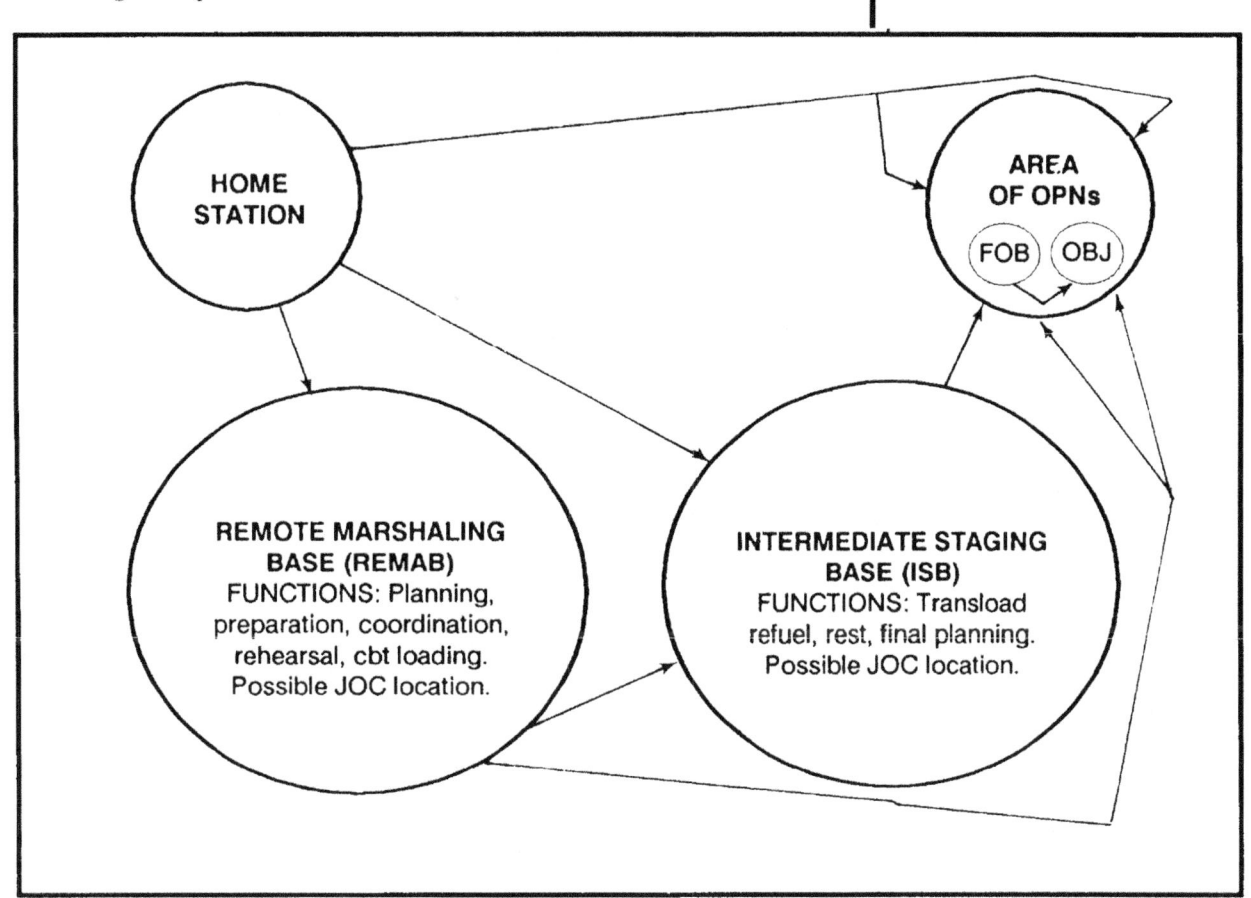

Figure 7-2. Base options for force projection.

c. **Command Preparation.** In the REMAB, the commander conducts rehearsals, refines and modifies plans, determines PIR, and coordinates with the proper intelligence source to receive that information.

d. **Additions to the Unit.** In the REMAB, individual specialists who augment the force are integrated into the unit if they have not already joined. Specially trained supporting units, such as aviation and communications elements, also join the force at the REMAB.

e. **Functions of a REMAB.** The REMAB must provide–

(1) Access to the controlling headquarters staff.

(2) Physical security of billeting, planning, maintenance, and communications areas.

(3) Mess, billeting, latrine, and shower facilities for the force and its supporting elements.

(4) Access to a C-141- or C-130-capable airfield, possibly with all-weather operations.

(5) Access to secure communications and processed intelligence.

(6) Access to rehearsal areas where sites can be built and live-fire rehearsals can be conducted.

(7) Access to the unit locations of major supporting elements such as naval landing craft or Army aviation units.

(8) An external security force and an active CI agency.

(9) Vehicle transport for personnel lift, equipment transfer, and administrative use.

(10) Access to maintenance support facilities.

(11) Medical support facilities to augment the airborne medical personnel.

(12) Covered areas for packing parachutes and rigging airdrop loads.

7-14. INTERMEDIATE STAGING BASE

Elements of the airborne force deploy to an ISB to make final plans, coordinate, and task-organize. The unit's organization and composition are finalized for movement to the objective area. Deployment to the ISB is common when terrain or distance precludes insertion to the objective area directly from the REMAB or CONUS. Contingency missions often involve the use of an ISB. Intermediate staging base operations are often employed when the mission requires transloading from strategic airlift assets to theater airlift assets.

a. **Facilities.** The ISB is not occupied for long periods; however, some facilities are needed to support the airborne force. These include the following:

- Materiels-handling equipment required for transloading.
- A location away from civilians or traffic routes.
- Security and CI elements.
- Secure communications.
- Fuel for aircraft and vehicles.
- Potable water supply.
- Austere airfield support facilities, possibly capable of all-weather operations.
- Areas for test firing weapons.
- Covered and concealed areas for assembly of the airborne force and rigging of parachutes and door bundles.
- Austere billets or rest areas.
- Austere messing arrangements.
- Medical treatment facility.

b. **Location.** The ISB location should provide adequate OPSEC to prevent compromise of the operation.

7-15. FORWARD OPERATING BASE

Objectives for airborne or airland assault operations maybe beyond the range of aircraft operating from an ISB or REMAB in friendly territory. Therefore, a base in hostile territory must be seized for the further projection of force or for the recovery of previously deployed forces.

a. Establishing an FOB requires seizure of an airfield or airstrip. The force conducting the follow-on operation can be a part of the force seizing the FOB or a new force introduced after the FOB is seized. In most operations, the FOB is retained only as long as necessary to support the follow-on mission. A planned withdrawal is executed on mission completion.

b. Before launching subsequent airborne or airland assaults, reorganization may be required. This is especially true if the subsequent assault force comes from the unit that seized the FOB. To lessen this requirement, the follow-on assault force can be the reserve for the initial mission, or it can be a completely new force that only refuels or transloads at the FOB. Transloading must be accomplished quickly. Loads must be prerigged and loaded to facilitate transloading. Control is established by the CCT and ADACG.

c. If the FOB is used to receive previously committed forces, planning considerations must include:

- Accountability procedures.
- Medical care and evacuation.
- Maintenance requirements.
- Resupply/refueling operations.

CHAPTER 8

COMBAT SUPPORT

The commander uses combat support elements to enhance the combat power of his subordinate maneuver units. He must know CS capabilities, assign them appropriate missions, and control their operations to apply superior combat power at the decisive time and place. Specific applications of the command and support relationships are discussed in this chapter and outlined in Table 8-1, (see page 8-2).

Section I. COMMAND AND SUPPORT RELATIONSHIPS

Regardless of the relationship of the CS element to the unit, the airborne commander is responsible for integration and synchronization of available CS to accomplish his mission.

8-1. ELEMENTS

Combat support elements provide significant amounts of more combat power. The leader of a CS element that is attached, OPCON, or DS serves as special staff officer to the commander besides functioning as the CS leader. During planning, preparation, and execution of the mission, the CS leader advises the commander and staff on the employment of the CS unit, then he follows the commander's directions.

8-2. DECENTRALIZATION

During the airborne assault, most CS units are initially attached to the elements of the assault echelon (battalion/company). As more assets enter the airhead, including the parent headquarters of these CS units, CS assets can be returned to parent-unit control for more effective employment.

UNIT	ATTACHED	OPCON	DS	GS
Under command/control of ...	ABN CDR	ABN CDR	PARENT UNIT	PARENT UNIT
Task-organized by...	ABN UNIT	PARENT UNIT	PARENT UNIT	PARENT UNIT
Receives mission, tasks, and priorities from...	ABN UNIT	ABN UNIT	ABN CDR	PARENT UNIT
Positioned by...	ABN UNIT	ABN UNIT	PARENT UNIT*	PARENT UNIT*
Maintains communications and liaison with...	ABN UNIT	ABN and PARENT UNIT	ABN and PARENT UNIT	PARENT UNIT
Receives CSS from...	ABN UNIT***	PARENT UNIT	PARENT UNIT**	PARENT UNIT

*With specific approval of the airborne commander if within his area of operations.

**Combat service support requirements beyond the capability of the parent unit are provided by the airborne unit after specific request coordination between the battalion, parent unit, and brigade headquarters. Attached elements may be unable to provide a CSS slice; therefore, CSS must be provided by a headquarters senior to the parent and supported unit.

***Attached element brings an appropriate slice of CSS equipment and personnel supplement the brigade/battalion's assets.

Table 8-1. Command and support relationships.

Section II. FIRE SUPPORT

Fire support planning for an airborne operation is initiated on receipt of the mission. Concurrent with the development of the concept of the operation, the commander plans for fire support so that it is provided throughout the operation.

8-3. UNIQUE ASPECTS

Fire support planning, coordination, and execution for airborne operations are more complex than in conventional ground operations; the differences are as follows:

a. The assault elements of the airborne force are quickly placed in direct contact with the enemy deep in hostile territory. Initial operations are decentralized and communications can be limited or nonexistent

b. Airborne unit vulnerability increases during the time between landing and assembly into a fighting force. This time varies based on unit size and METT-T factors. During this vulnerable period, reliable communications are essential to the coordination and execution of fire support missions.

c. Calls for fire are often sent under conditions where units are in critical need of fire support. Units lack firm knowledge of the situation, especially the location of friendly and enemy units. This can also come at a time when reliable ground communications have not been firmly established.

d. Initially, artillery support in the airhead is limited. This situation occurs at the same time as the arrival of the assault echelon, the main effort, or the operation's opening phase. Consequently, the bulk of fire support must come from air support, organic mortars, or NGF. Support can also be provided by long-range artillery of advancing friendly forces (if in range), long-range rocket/missile fire, and strategic air force bombs or bombers.

e. During the initial airborne assault and periodically thereafter, airspace over the DZ contains a high density of airdrop aircraft. This complicates fire support aspects of airspace management.

8-4. MISSIONS

Fire support assets can perform a variety of missions in support of the airborne assault. The following are examples of standard missions arranged by type of asset.

a. Tactical air support, mortars, and limited field artillery can be the only fire support available to the airborne force until the lodgment is established. It can provide any or all of the following types of support:

(1) Close air support.

(2) Column cover for the assault echelon, follow-up echelon, and resupply sorties.

(3) Suppression of enemy air defenses along the corridor selected for penetration and near the objective.

(4) Reconnaissance both before and during the operation.

(5) Counterair operations to gain and maintain air superiority along the corridor and in the objective area.

(6) Preassault fires of the airhead and other critical targets, and deception.

(7) Battlefield air interdiction of the objective area, including armed reconnaissance missions targeted against enemy forces that react to the airborne assault.

(8) Air defense of marshaling areas, resupply airfields, and the airhead.

b. Naval gun fire, when available and in range, is a reliable, accurate, high-volume source of fire support. It can provide any or all of the following types of support:

(1) Preassault fires of the objective and other critical targets.

(2) Suppression of enemy air defenses.

(3) Direct support and general support of forces in contact.

(4) Interdiction (land and sea).

c. Artillery of linkup forces within range can provide the following support:

- Interdiction fires.
- SEAD fires.
- Counterbattery fires.
- Direct support to maneuver units.

d. Army aviation assets can augment other fire support when the ISB/FSB is within range or when a secure airfield permits airland and buildup of Army aviation transported in USAF airlift aircraft. They can support–

(1) R&S forces.

(2) Interdiction of enemy reaction forces, especially mechanized forces with accurate, long-range antitank fires.

(3) Seizure of objectives with rocket fire and gunfire.

8-5. PRINCIPLES

Fire support planning and execution relies on careful, thorough planning based on fire support principles designed to support maneuver. (See FM 6-20-30 for a detailed discussion.)

a. **Unity of Control.** This principle is met through the establishment of a joint headquarters (such as JTF) to include a joint operations center, which is responsible for providing adequate fire support to the maneuver commander.

b. **Continuous Liaison.** Liaison, especially between Army and Air Force units, is necessary at all echelons down to battalion level. It must be supported with adequate communications to facilitate command and to control lateral dissemination of information and coordination. Joint agreements memorandums of understanding, joint SOPS, and joint SOIs all facilitate the use of this principle. Each assault battalion and brigade must have attached TACPs and naval gunfire LOS (if NGF is available).

c. **Centralized Coordination.** Due to the nature of the airhead (basically a perimeter defense) and the required continuous airflow into the airhead, fire support assets must be closely controlled to prevent fratricide and waste of assets.

(1) During the initial stages of an airborne operation and before adequate ground communications can be established, coordination and control of fire support are accomplished from an airborne platform (an ABCCC or JACC/CP). (Appendix D provides detailed information on operations of the ABCCC and AWACS.)

(2) On landing, each battalion or brigade/regimental headquarters establishes contact with the ABCCC (or JACC/CP) through the TACP or FSO. Fire support, such as CAS, beyond that available from organic or DS assets would be requested from the ABCCC. Prioritization and coordination of requests arc accomplished by the ground force commander's representative in the ABCCC. His responsibilities include the following:

- Prevent fratricide of ground personnel.
- Ensure that requests do not interfere with incoming serials, other aircraft, or naval operations.
- Determine the fire support means to be employed in coordination with appropriate battle staff members.
- Determine (in coordination with the battle staff) any added safety or control measures required; transmit them to the appropriate ground elements.

(3) For air missions, the battle staff establishes contact with the appropriate flight, provides essential information, and then hands the flight off to the appropriate TACP or FAC for mission execution. At that point, the mission is conducted the same way as conventional operations. If NGF or air support is available, it is essential that a naval gunfire LO be present in the ABCCC to perform a similar function.

(4) Once adequate C^2 facilities have been established in the airhead, fire support coordination responsibilities are passed from the airborne platform to the ground to be conducted as in conventional operations–there is no doctrinal time for this transfer. In some situations (for example, raids), this cannot occur; however, once a brigade main or tactical CP is on the ground, the transfer takes place.

d. **Application of Adequate Control Measures.** Fire support coordination measures, both permissive and restrictive, are employed to ensure the safety of friendly personnel, to synchronize all fire support means, and to permit maximum flexibility with minimum restrictions on the employment of fire support. The joint commander must also establish a common target and map grid system to permit transmission of target and friendly unit locations. This is critical if standard maps are not available. Provisions must also be made to identify friendly force locations through the employment of smoke, panels, beacons, or other devices. (Airspace control measures are discussed in Chapter 2. See FM 6-20-30 and FM 101-5-1 for a detailed description of fire support control measures.)

8-6. PLANNING

On receipt of the WO, the commander and his staff begin planning. They develop four basic plans (regardless of the type mission, force size, or duration of the operation) in a reverse planning sequence. The FSO responsibilities for each plan are as follows:

a. **Ground Tactical Plan.** The following fire support planning and coordination actions are the responsibility of the brigade/battalion FSO during ground movement.

(1) Support the scheme of maneuver. The goal is to place the maximum amount of indirect fire power on the ground as quickly as possible.

(2) Control indirect-fire systems. Initially, control is decentralized; an FO calls for fire directly to a fire support asset.

(3) Plan fires to block enemy avenues of approach (consider FASCAM delivered by air).

(4) Plan fires to eliminate enemy resistance (groups and series in the objective area).

(5) Plan fires to defend key terrain needed to link up with friendly forces.

(6) Plan fires to support security/reconnaissance forces in the objective area.

(7) Plan fires on top of, to the flanks, and beyond assault objectives.

(8) Plan close air support.

(9) Plan final protective fires.

(10) Recommend priority of fires.

(11) Select initial FA and mortar positions that can be quickly occupied from DZs/LZs.

(12) Select subsequent FA and mortar positions to provide combat outposts and security forces.

b. Landing Plan. Planning and coordination of fire support during the air movement and preassault fires are the JTF's responsibility; he plans SEAD fires along the flight route and in the objective area. Once on the ground, friendly positions are marked. The airborne FSO must ensure that preassault air strikes are planned against other enemy positions in the objective area. Preassault fires are planned as follows:

- On and around the LZ/DZ (alternate and false).
- On enemy air defense artillery.
- On enemy command, control, and communication.
- On enemy indirect-fire systems.
- Sequence and location of delivery for FA and mortars.

c. **Air Movement Plan.** Fire support during movement to the objective area is the responsibility of the airlift commander and staff. However, the airborne force commander must be closely involved because of the possibility of downed aircraft or a mission being diverted. Planning considerations include the following:

(1) Ensure fire support personnel and equipment are included on load plans and manifests.

(2) Plan targets on enemy ADA along flight routes and alternate flight routes (JTF level).

d. **Marshaling Plan.** The FSO starts planning on receipt of the mission and assignment of assets. All leaders and fire support personnel must take part in the planning process from the beginning. All fire support personnel and equipment are prepared and rehearsals are conducted. Then, the fire support plan is briefed to all other leaders and staff involved in the operation.

8-7. ARTILLERY EMPLOYMENT

The initial phase of the airborne operation is decentralized and flexible until the assault objectives are secured and the airhead is established. During the parachute assault, the FA battalion is attached to the airborne infantry brigade. As soon as practicable after organizing on the ground, normal command relationships are resumed; FA support is provided within thecontext of assigned tactical missions. After reorganizing, airborne artillery adheres to tactics and techniques applicable to other artillery units. (FM 6-20-30.)

Section III. NAVAL GUNFIRE

When operating on islands or near a coastline, NGF support maybe available to the airborne force. Naval guns can provide high-volume, long-range, accurate fires, which employ a variety of ammunition.

8-8. AIR AND NAVAL GUNFIRE LIAISON COMPANY

The ANGLICO provides ship-to-shore communications and fire control teams to adjust fire. In the absence of ANGLICO fire control teams, the FIST can call for and adjust fires through the ANGLICO team.

8-9. ANGLICO ORGANIZATION

Deployed ANGLICO forces comprise a command element, operational element (air/NGF teams), and support element.

a. The company is organized into groupings. (Table 8-2.) The headquarters/support section and divisional air/NGF section furnish command, control, administration, training, and logistics support for the company. They also provide fire support planning and liaison personnel to the airborne unit. Three brigade air/NGF platoons provide liaison and control for air and NGF to the assault companies, battalion, and brigade.

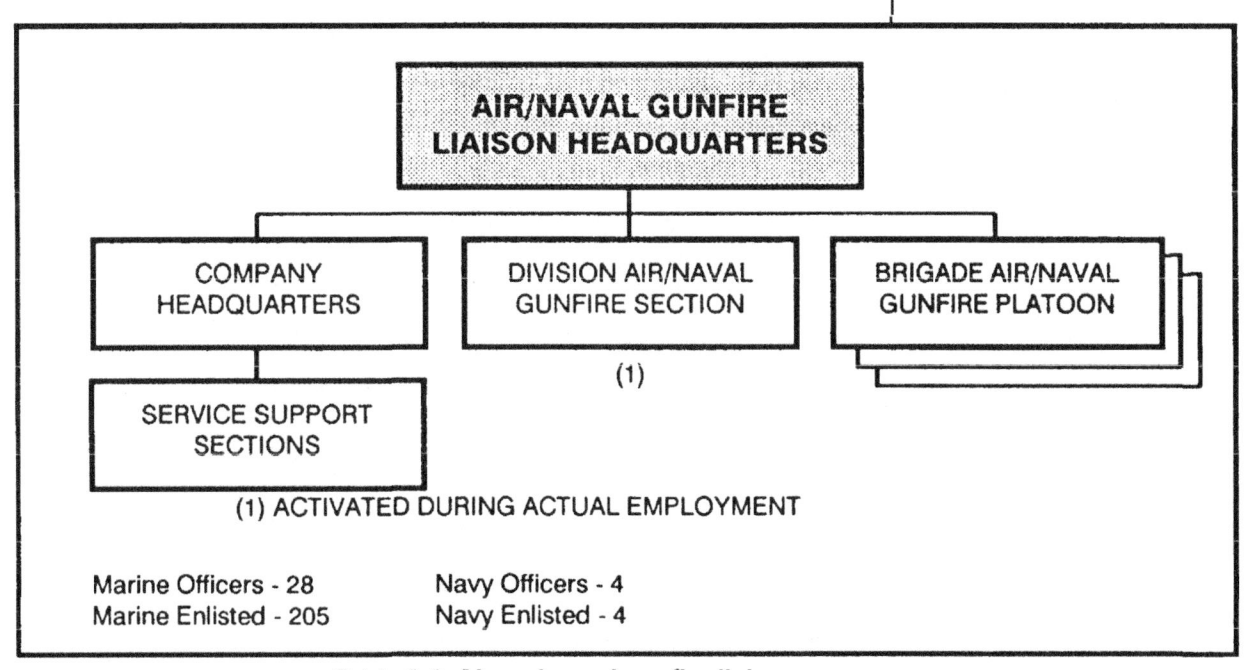

```
                AIR/NAVAL GUNFIRE
              LIAISON HEADQUARTERS
         ┌────────────┼────────────────────┐
   COMPANY      DIVISION AIR/NAVAL    BRIGADE AIR/NAVAL
 HEADQUARTERS    GUNFIRE SECTION      GUNFIRE PLATOON
      │                (1)
 SERVICE SUPPORT
    SECTIONS

         (1) ACTIVATED DURING ACTUAL EMPLOYMENT

 Marine Officers - 28      Navy Officers - 4
 Marine Enlisted - 205     Navy Enlisted - 4
```

Table 8-2. Air and naval gunfire liaison company.

b. Each brigade platoon is divided into a brigade team and two supporting arms liaison teams, which support two forward battalions. Each SALT has two firepower control teams, which support the forward companies of the battalions. (Table 8-3.)

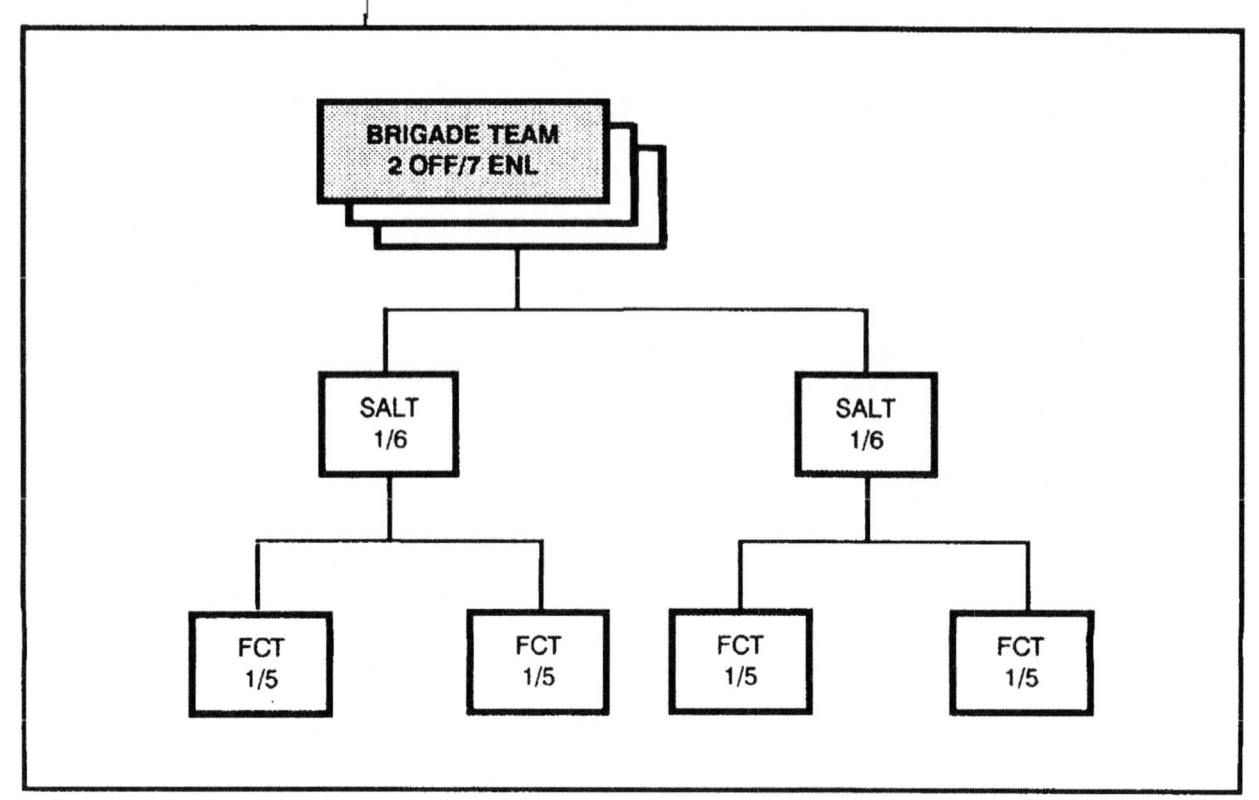

```
              BRIGADE TEAM
              2 OFF/7 ENL
                   |
         ┌─────────┴─────────┐
       SALT                SALT
       1/6                 1/6
        |                   |
    ┌───┴───┐           ┌───┴───┐
   FCT     FCT         FCT     FCT
   1/5     1/5         1/5     1/5
```

Table 8-3. Brigade air and naval gunfire team.

c. The ANGLICO assists the staff in matters concerning air and NGF. It coordinates requests for air and NGF support from the battalions of the brigade and represents the ABCCC, AC-130, and AWACS, if required.

d. The LO and FCTS operate in the ground spot net. They communicate with the ship by HF radio to request and adjust NGF. The FCT communicates with the LO, using VHF radios. The LO also can communicate with aircraft using UHF radios.

8-10. TACTICAL MISSIONS

Naval gunfire ships are assigned one of two tactical missions: direct support or general support.

a. **Direct Support.** A ship in DS of a specific unit delivers both planned and on-call fires. (On-call fires are to the ship what targets of opportunity are to artillery units.) A fire control party with the supported unit conducts and adjusts on-call fires; they can also be adjusted by an NGF air spotter.

b. **General Support.** General support missions are assigned to ships supporting units of brigade size or larger. The normal procedure is to have the fires of the GS ship adjusted by an aerial observer or to have the LO assign the fires of the ship to a battalion SALT for fire missions. On completion of the mission, the ship reverts to GS.

8-11. COORDINATION AND CONTROL MEASURES

Coordination and control measures that apply to NGF are the same as for FA except for the addition of the terms fire support area and fire support station.

a. **Fire Support Area.** The FSA is a sea area within which a ship can position or cruise while firing in support. It is labeled with the letters "FSA" and a Roman numeral–for example, FSA VII.

b. **Fire Support Station.** The FSS is a specified position at sea from which a ship must fire; it is very restrictive positioning guidance. It is labeled with the letters "FSS" and a Roman numeral-for example, FSS VII.

Section IV. AIR FORCE SUPPORT

A sound air support plan is an integral part of the ground combat plans. Reconnaissance, interdiction, and CAS are planned and ample communications for liaison and control are provided.

8-12. TYPES OF MISSIONS

All air combat missions are performed concurrently and are mutually supporting. They include CAS, interdiction, tactical surveillance and reconnaissance, tactical airlift, and specialized tasks.

a. **Counterair Operations.** The ultimate objective of counterair operations is to gain and maintain theater air supremacy. This has two purposes; it prevents enemy forces from effectively interfering with friendly areas and activities, and it precludes prohibitive interference with offensive air operations in the enemy area. This is accomplished by destroying or neutralizing the enemy's air offensive and defensive systems.

(1) *Offensive.* Offensive counterair operations are conducted to seek out and neutralize or destroy enemy air forces at a chosen time and place. They are essential to gain air supremacy and to provide a favorable situation for other missions. Typical targets include the following:

- Enemy aircraft.
- Airfields.
- Tactical missile complexes.
- Command and control facilities.
- POL and munitions storage facilities.
- Aircraft support equipment and their control systems.

(2) *Suppressive.* Suppression of enemy air defense is conducted to neutralize, destroy, or temporarily degrade enemy air defense systems in a specific area by physical attack, electronic warfare, or both.

(3) *Defensive.* Defensive counterair operations contribute to local air control by countering enemy offensive actions. An in-place and operational radar warning and control system, consisting of both ground and airborne elements, can be effectively used by theater forces. They integrate and control the employment of fighters, surface-to-air missiles, and antiaircraft artillery systems.

(4) *Tasks.* Counterair tasks that can be employed as a part of offensive and defensive counterair operations include air-to-surface attacks, fighter sweeps, and force protection (escort).

b. **Close Air Support.** The objectives of CAS are to support surface operations by attacking hostile targets close to friendly surface forces. Each air mission requires detailed integration with those forces.

c. **Air Interdiction.** The objectives of AI are to delay, disrupt, divert, or destroy an enemy's military potential before it can be brought to bear effectively against friendly ground forces. These combat operations are performed far enough away from friendly surface forces so that detailed integration of specific actions with the maneuver of friendly forces is not possible or required. AI attacks against land force targets that have a near-term effect on the scheme of maneuver of friendly forces, but are not close to friendly forces, are referred to as BAI.

d. **Tactical Surveillance and Reconnaissance.** The TSR operations are directed toward satisfying the requirements of joint force and component commanders engaged in surface and tactical air operations. These operations provide timely information, either visually observed or sensor recorded, from which intelligence is derived for all forces. Surveillance operations continuously collect information; reconnaissance operations are directed toward localized or specific targets.

e. **Tactical Airlift Operations.** Tactical airlift forces perform four primary tasks: deployment, employment, logistics support, and aeromedical evacuation. Deployment operations make possible the movement of entire units within an area of operations. When combat forces and their logistics support are moved by air into an objective area for combat, the airlift is termed an employment operation.

f. **Air Force Specialized Tasks.** Specialized tasks are those operations conducted in direct or indirect support of primary tactical air missions. These activities include, but are not limited to electronic combat, combat search and rescue, and air refueling operations.

8-13. ORGANIZATION OF TACTICAL AIR SUPPORT

Tactical air support can be provided through missions incidental to air activity throughout the combat zone. It can also be provided by air units in DS of or attached to a joint force, or under OPCON of a joint force commander. A single tactical air force supports an airborne operation. The tactical air force, or designated units, can be attached to or under OPCON of a joint airborne force. When the mission requires the basing of tactical air support units in the airhead, they are always attached to the joint airborne force.

8-14. PLANNING TACTICAL AIR SUPPORT

Adequate tactical air support of an airborne operation requires some integration of airborne forces and tactical air activity to support conventional ground operations.

a. The air support plan is based on the overall Air Force mission and the amount of available strategic, tactical, and airlift effort. The effect of forecasted weather en route and in the proposed AO must also be considered.

b. Offensive and defensive air operations must be continuously planned in support of an objective area. Immediate tactical air support must be continuously available (on air alert) in spite of an apparent absence of targets.

8-15. COMMAND AND CONTROL

With the beginning of air operations in the objective area, provision must be made for command and air control of these operations and for integration of the air and ground effort. A joint operations center, where the supporting tactical air force and the airborne force is represented, performs the planning, integration, direction, and supervision of the air effort IAW the needs of the airborne force.

a. **Preparatory Phase.** If a joint airborne force develops and includes tactical air elements, the joint force commander directs part or all of the preliminary air efforts while other preparations for the operation are completed. If the airborne force does not include tactical air elements, tactical air support before and during the mounting of an airborne operation is an Air Force responsibility. Therefore, requests from the joint airborne force commander involving both reconnaissance and fire missions are processed through normal JOC channels.

b. **Assault Phase.** Requirements during the assault phase are the same for all airborne operations. During the dropping or airlanding and assembly of assault elements, aircraft that are on air alert status over DZs/LZs defend against hostile surface or aerial reaction to the assault.

c. **Consolidation and Exploitation Phase.** Air control net facilities in excess of TACPS and ABCCC are meager until the airlanding of more supplies and reinforcements during this phase. In an operation that does not involve an immediate linkup after seizure of objectives, the airlanding of reinforcing or supporting elements provides for the rapid expansion and improvement of tactical air control nets to meet the needs of any anticipated emergency.

(1) Aircraft providing support subsequent to the assault phase can be based within the objective area, outside the objective area, or both. In view of the logistics demands of aircraft, air support is based within the objective area only when it cannot be effectively provided from outside. Limitations in the effective radius of aircraft are the determining factors. An existing airstrip or sufficiently adaptable terrain is one of these factors in the selection of an objective area.

(2) A single commander in the objective area has command over both ground and air elements. However, such command can be retained by an officer charged with broader responsibilities whose headquarters is outside the objective area.

8-16. AIR TRAFFIC CONTROL

Air traffic control in the airhead is initially an Air Force CCT responsibility. The CCT can be augmented with and later replaced by Army ATC units. Air traffic services provided to airborne units come from contingency corps assets. Liaison, beacon, and tower teams are the most frequently employed elements.

a. During alert, marshaling, and deployment, a liaison team is sent to the headquarters that is planning the operation; it serves as a part of the A^2C^2 section and provides advice on airspace management, especially in the airhead. The main concern in planning is the handoff between CCT and ATC parties, which takes place within 72 hours after the assault. CCT controls the airhead with the advice and assistance from ATC personnel until follow-on ATC elements arrive.

b. Beacon and tower teams deploy with the aviation or infantry brigade assault CP attached to the S3 section. These teams provide initial ATC in the airhead. The beacon team provides terminal guidance for Army aircraft from their ISB into the airfield. The tower team augments the CCT party and controls helicopter movement. The amount of control given up by CCT to the ATC teams depends on the size of the airflow.

c. Operational control of ATC assets usually passes to the senior aviation unit commander once he is established in the airhead. FARP and aviation assembly area operations include ATC elements and services, as specified by the senior aviation unit commander.

Section V. ARMY AVIATION OPERATIONS

Army aviation provides the force with unique capabilities. When properly used, it increases the force's combat power by providing the advantages of speed, range, mobility, flexibility, and increased firepower.

8-17. HELICOPTER TACTICAL MISSIONS

Army Aviation provides close support to units in contact and the capability for air assault operations in support of the ground tactical plan. (Table 8-4.) They serve as aerial CPS that enable the commander to make his presence felt on the battlefield and to influence the action at the decisive point in the battle. Army aviation assets can evacuate the wounded, provide aerial R&S, and transport radiological and chemical survey teams. Appropriate missions for these forces include the following:

- Exploitation of initial airborne assault.
- Armed aerial reconnaissance and counterreconnaissance.
- Limited CAS capability.

- Early warning of guerrilla, airborne, or other infiltration threats.
- Engagement and destruction of enemy ground forces by highly mobile maneuver tactics.
- Domination of unoccupied areas between highly dispersed friendly positions.
- Provision of immediately responsive air-to-ground fire support for either air or surface mobile task forces.
- Provision of tactical and logistics support for guerrilla and special forces.
- Provision of organized raid-type forces.
- Tactical cover and deception.
- Electronic warfare.

	UH-1H	OH-58C/D	CH-47D	UH-60	AH-1S	AH-64
Cruise speed (knots)	90	100/100	155	145	0-190	0-161
Endurance at cruise speed (hours and minutes)	2.1	2.0/2.2	2.5	2.3	22.4	2.2
Allowable cargo load	8	0	33-37	11-22	0	0
Litters/ambulatory	6	0/0	24	4/6	0	0
Maximum ferry range in nautical miles (normal)	180	200	310	330	475	280
Maximum ferry range in nautical miles (auxiliary)	330		1,179	1,114		1,089
Ferry speed	90		130	118		124

Table 8-4. Helicopter deployment capabilities.

Note: Table 8-4 should be used only as a guide for commanders because environmental conditions will affect capabilities.

8-18. DEPLOYMENT

When possible, organic and attached Army aircraft self-deploy to the objective area, arriving as soon as possible after the initial assault. Flights are closely controlled and regulated to avoid interference with airlift aircraft flights. Terminal guidance can be furnished by pathfinder teams, USAF combat control teams, or Army ATC teams in the airhead.

a. When the distance from the departure area to the objective area is beyond the range of Army aircraft, many deployment options exist. When the distance from the forward battle area is within their range capabilities, aircraft are serviced in the departure area and flown to forward areas within a planned schedule. They are reserviced in the forward area and depart over planned routes to the objective area. Forward arming and refueling points can be leapfrogged ahead if multiple legs are involved. A variation of this technique is the employmnet of Naval carrier-type vessels as a refueling base or for transport on one leg of the trip to the objective area. Selected utility and cargo helicopters can employ extended-range fuel tanks to assist in deployment. Also, USAF aircraft aircraft, such as the C-130, may refuel Army helicopters at remote, unimproved airfields using the wet-wing technique.

b. When none of these methods can be used because of the distance to the objective area, Army aircraft can be disassembled and transported in airlift aircraft. For light Army aircraft, no or partial disassembly for transport and reassembly for use in the objective area is possible. However, this can be time-consuming depending on the aircraft–the impact on tactical plans must be considered. For other aircraft, particularly large helicopters, the complexity of the reassembly process in the objective area prohibits their early employment.

NOTE: See FM 1-100 for a detailed discussion of combat aviation operations.

Section VI. AIR DEFENSE

Air defense of an airhead occurs in an environment that is unique in two respects: First, it is in an area that has a high density of friendly aircraft, Second, the quickest and potentially most deadly threat to the airhead can be enemy air. The principles and guidelines for employment of air defense weapons in support of airborne operations arc similar to those for other operations. The following major factors of ADA employment operations are unique.

- The phasing of units and air defense support into the airhead.
- Early warning procedures.
- Airspace control measures.

8-19. AIR DEFENSE ARTILLERY ELEMENTS

The airborne brigade is normally task-organized to include an ADA battery. This battery can be augmented with added assets, depending on the level of air threat expected.

a. During the initial phase of the operation, one battalion from the brigade will normally be inserted with one Stinger section, which will provide air defense as the battalion develops the airhead. Stingers are not jumped with the team members, but are palletized or door-bundled and dropped separately.

b. Once the entire brigade is on the ground, a main CP is established. The SHORAD battery commander normally locates his CP with the brigade CP. He assumes control of all platoons, and he coordinates defense of the airhead.

c. The SHORAD battery has three Vulcan platoons, a Stinger platoon, and, normally, two forward area alerting radars. Vulcans and FAARs are usually airlanded. FAARs should be moved into the airhead as soon as airframe availability permits since they provide essential early warning to the air defense and maneuver units.

d. The SHORAD battery commander ensures that early-warning information is disseminated to his Vulcan platoons and Stinger sections. This will normally be done over an early-warning net rather than the battery command net.

e. The air defense liaison team at the brigade CP is the SHORAD battery commander's representative to the brigade commander. The liaison team advises the brigade staff on the air defense status. They coordinate with the Air Force LO, the Army aviation officer, and the FA officer on all matters concerning airspace usage.

8-20. EARLY WARNING

Early-warning capability for the airhead can be provided by either the US Air Force or the Army.

a. Early warning will initially be provided by the Air Force in the initial assault or for short-term operations.

(1) An Air Force CRC will transmit early-warning information if the airhead is within range, or will retransmit by ABCCC if necessary.

(2) An Air Force CRP may also be deployed to the ISB to provide early warning. The CRP can employ the same communications as the CRC.

(3) If airland operations are scheduled, an Air Force vehicle-mounted FACP can be delivered to the airhead. (See Appendix D for more information.)

(4) The AWACS can send its early-warning messages to the ground commander's TACP, or the SHORAD CP. (Specific procedures for AWACS early warning of Army units in contingency operations are discussed in TRADOC Pam 34-4.)

b. The Army has two systems for early warning in the airhead.

(1) *Tactical defense alert radar.* The TDAR can be airdropped with the air defense unit, and then linked by wire or radio to all air defense units in the airhead. The TDAR has a 20-kilometer range, which provides a warning of air attack. The time of the warning varies, depending on air speed (fixed-wing can be one to two minutes in advance while rotary-wing may be up to ten minutes in advance). The TDAR can be mounted on a pedestal or in a HMMWV.

(2) *Forward area alerting radar.* The FAAR system is a complete, self-contained, acquisition radar system (AN/MPQ-49), which consists of a radar set (AN/TPQ-43 and TPX-50 IFF), the M561 Gamma Goat, and a trailer with a 5-kilowatt generator set. The system must be airlanded into the airhead. It requires about 30 minutes to emplace and can detect targets out to 20 kilometers.

Section VII. ENGINEER SUPPORT

Combat engineers are critical combat multipliers. The primary mission of airborne engineers is to increase the combat effectiveness of friendly soldiers, to facilitate their movement, and to hinder the enemy's movement. Many of the principle functions of the standard combat engineer battalion are carried on by airborne engineers but with different emphasis on the type and extent of work to be accomplished due to the limited transportation and heavy engineer equipment. Both corps and divisional engineer assets will be needed to support a divisional deployment. Airfield construction and repair packages, as well as airborne combat engineer battalions from the corps engineer brigade, will be task-organized to support divisional operations. This section focuses on forward aviation combat engineering as the primary engineer task in an airborne assault.

8-21. ENGINEER EMPLOYMENT

The task organization and subsequent C2 of engineer assets depends on the mission. An airborne combat engineer company is usually attached to a brigade for the airborne assault. The combat engineer company or its elements can be further attached to airborne battalions/companies based on the brigade's mission and ground tactical plan. After the engineer battalion lands, the combat engineer companies are brought under its control.

8-22. TACTICAL MISSIONS

During airborne operations, priority is established among the following engineer support missions:

a. **Mobility.** Engineers provide mobility support to ground and air units.

(1) Forward aviation combat engineering, including preparation or rehabilitation of airstrips/airfields, EZs, and LZs.

(2) Assistance in the assault of fortified positions.

(3) Removal of mines, booby traps, and obstacles.

(4) Construction and repair of roads.

(5) Assistance in stream crossing.

b. **Countermobility.** During the expansion and defense of the airhead before reinforcement by air or ground linkup, engineers provide the following countermobility support:

(1) Erection of obstacles, roadblocks, and mine fields to secure the airhead.

(2) Destruction of bridges, railroads, power plants, communications centers, and key installations, or the preparation of such installations for demolition as part of strategic interdiction operations.

c. **Survivability.** Based on the commander's concept of the operation, engineers plan and construct defensive positions for C^2 facilities, air transport facilities, antiarmor weapons, FA, and dismounted forces.

d. **Other Engineer Tasks.** Engineers can support the airborne force in other ways:

(1) Division and corps engineer terrain analysis detachments can analyze the terrain selected for DZs, LZs, and assault airfield sites.

(2) Army or corps topographic companies can produce quick response map overprints, map revisions, and photo maps to provide the deploying units with the most current information available.

(3) Engineer well-drilling detachments can be airlanded to provide water for sustained operations.

(4) Engineer bridge companies can be airlanded to provide medium or heavy bridging support.

Section VIII. FORWARD AVIATION COMBAT ENGINEERING

The combat engineer construction and maintenance effort in support of forward aviation operating facilities is a mobility functional area. Immediately available resources are used to accomplish FACE missions. Expedient techniques are used and extensive construction is limited to avoid enemy detection. The FACE projects that fall into this mobility function are discussed herein. (See FM 5-101 for detailed information on all facets of FACE operations.)

8-23. CAPABILITIES

The following are the capabilities of the combat engineer construction and maintenance effort:

a. **Construction of Landing Zones.** Landing zones are required during helicopter movement of personnel and logistics, refueling and rearming, medical evacuation, and reconstitution. Engineer support is rudimentary for each type. Locations are selected that have suitable soil conditions without strength improvement to carry helicopter loads. Loose objects, including powdery snow, are cleared from the rotor wash area; all trees must be cleared from the rotor zones.

b. **Construction of Low-Altitude Parachute Extraction System Zones.** LAPES zones require relatively flat, stump-free terrain with features similar to those for a C-130 landing strip as specified in TM 5-330. Since the fixed-wing transport aircraft (typically a C-130) does not land when discharging its cargo, the ground strength requirements are based on the equipment being discharged.

c. **Construction of Flight Landing Strips.** The flight landing strip allows landing and takeoff of specific fixed-wing aircraft (see criteria established by TM 5-330). It must be relatively flat with a surface that can support fully loaded, freed-wing aircraft. Proper site selection is based on minimal need for surface improvement and earthwork.

d. **Maintenance/Repair of Forward Aviation Facilities.** Maintenance includes all activities required to correct deficiencies resulting from normal damage and deterioration. Repair includes restoration of damage due to abnormal use, accidents, and hostile forces. As an economy measure, maximum use of existing facilities should be planned.

8-24. RESPONSIBILITIES

The ground force commander is responsible for the construction, repair, and maintenance of airlanding facilities in the airhead. The airlift commander furnishes the ground force commander his requirements and the recommended priorities in order of accomplishment. The ground force commander establishes final priorities after joint consideration of the ground force and airlift requirements. Any deviations are coordinated with the airlift commander.

a. Construction or rehabilitation of airlanding facilities and airfields is initiated early. Plans for the initial assault provide for the seizure of airfields or sites for airlanding facilities to support the tactical and logistics plans. Assault units are augmented to perform minimum initial construction.

b. The airborne and airlift commanders prepare plans to cope with the problem of disabled aircraft on landing facilities. Airborne personnel provide assistance in moving disabled aircraft that might interfere with subsequent operations.

8-25. PLANNING

A large number of widely dispersed, low-activity, airlanding facilities are used in preference to a few highly developed airfield complexes, both in the departure and in the objective areas.

a. The number and location of airlanding facilities and airfields vary with the–

- Size of the force to be employed and supported.
- Planned buildup, including the number and type of aircraft to be accommodated.
- Tactical and logistics plans.
- Terrain in the objective area with particular attention to airfields, highways and roads, open areas, soil characteristics, relief, and vegetation.
- Enemy capabilities.
- Engineer capabilities.
- Weather during the time of operations.

b. At least one assault airlanding facility is desirable in each brigade/battalion area. This does not include facilities for employment of organic and attached Army aviation, alternate facilities to offset losses from enemy action, or desired additional facilities.

8-26. SITE SELECTION

Certain technical principles should be considered when selecting sites for airlanding facilities. Maximum use should be made of all existing aviation facilities. The site selection should fulfill the mission and provide for future expansion. It should be on terrain with soil that can be quickly and easily compacted to the standards listed in TM 5-330. The amount of earthwork is minimized by choosing a location that takes advantage of all prevailing grades that fall within the required specifications.

a. Airstrips and EZs are constructed across long, gentle slopes for ease of drainage. The bottoms of valleys or other depressed areas are avoided. Locations that require extensive clearing of flightway obstructions to meet glide angle requirements are also avoided.

b. Approaches are oriented IAW the prevailing winds in the area. The orientation should ensure 80 percent wind coverage based on a maximum allowable beam wind of 13 mph. If dust is a problem, the runway should be located 10 degrees to the prevailing wind so that dust clouds blow diagonally off the runway.

8-27. EXPEDIENT SURFACING

Landing mats and membranes are used as expedients for FACE site surfacing. Landing mats are used when the strength or smoothness of landing surfaces is not adequate. Membrane surfacing is used where soil strength is adequate but can become too weak when wet. Membrane is placed under all landing mats in high-traffic areas, such as runways and taxiways, to provide a waterproof covering for the soil. It is also used for dust control in aircraft traffic areas where chemical dust palliatives are either less satisfactory or require more time and effort to use. (The types, specifications, and emplacement of matting material are described in TM 5-330. Placement techniques, anchoring, repair, and maintenance of surfacing membrane are discussed in TM 5-337.)

8-28. REPAIR OF CAPTURED FACILITIES

An appraisal of the damage to a captured aviation facility precedes the decision to rehabilitate it. Occasionally, the effort to restore a badly damaged site is greater than that required to construct a new one. The enemy usually uses one or more of the following destruction measures:

- Placing delayed-action bombs, mines, and booby traps.
- Demolishing drainage systems and pavements.
- Placing obstacles and debris on the landing surface
- Flooding surfaced areas.
- Blowing craters in runways and hardstands.

The first priority in restoring a captured airfield is to establish minimum facilities for immediate operation of friendly aircraft. This requires removing delayed-action bombs, mines, and booby traps from the traffic areas; clearing debris from the traffic areas; and repairing craters and landing surfaces. Adequate repair to the drainage system must be made promptly.

8-29. ENGINEER PACKAGES

A number of engineer support packages are available to the commander to meet his requirements for FACE tasks. The greater the requirement for construction, the larger the number of aircraft sorties needed. The teams discussed herein are typical and can be modified to fit the situation.

FM 90-26

a. **Airfield Seizure.** From an engineer perspective, airfield seizure involves three basic tasks: assessment, clearance, and repair.

(1) *Airfield assessment team.* This team consists of two or three qualified combat engineers who deploy into the airhead as early as possible. Once in the airhead, they assess runway/airfield damage and repair requirements and provide recommendations to the commander on use of undamaged portions of the airfield. They also determine what local construction materials and equipment are available, minimizing engineer impact on airlift sorties.

(2) *Runway clearance element.* This element is responsible for removing obstacles and demolitions from the runways in preparation for airland sorties and repair teams. It typically contains teams trained in detecting and neutralizing mines and booby traps, "hot wiring" secured vehicles, and an obstacle removal team that can be equipped with heavy equipment (bulldozers or scoop loaders) to remove runway obstructions too heavy to be manhandled. This equipment can also be used to jump-start inoperable equipment left on the runway as obstructions.

(3) *Light airfield repair team.* This (team repairs light damage to an airstrip due to bombing or erosion and sustains extensive airland operations. (Figure 8-1.)

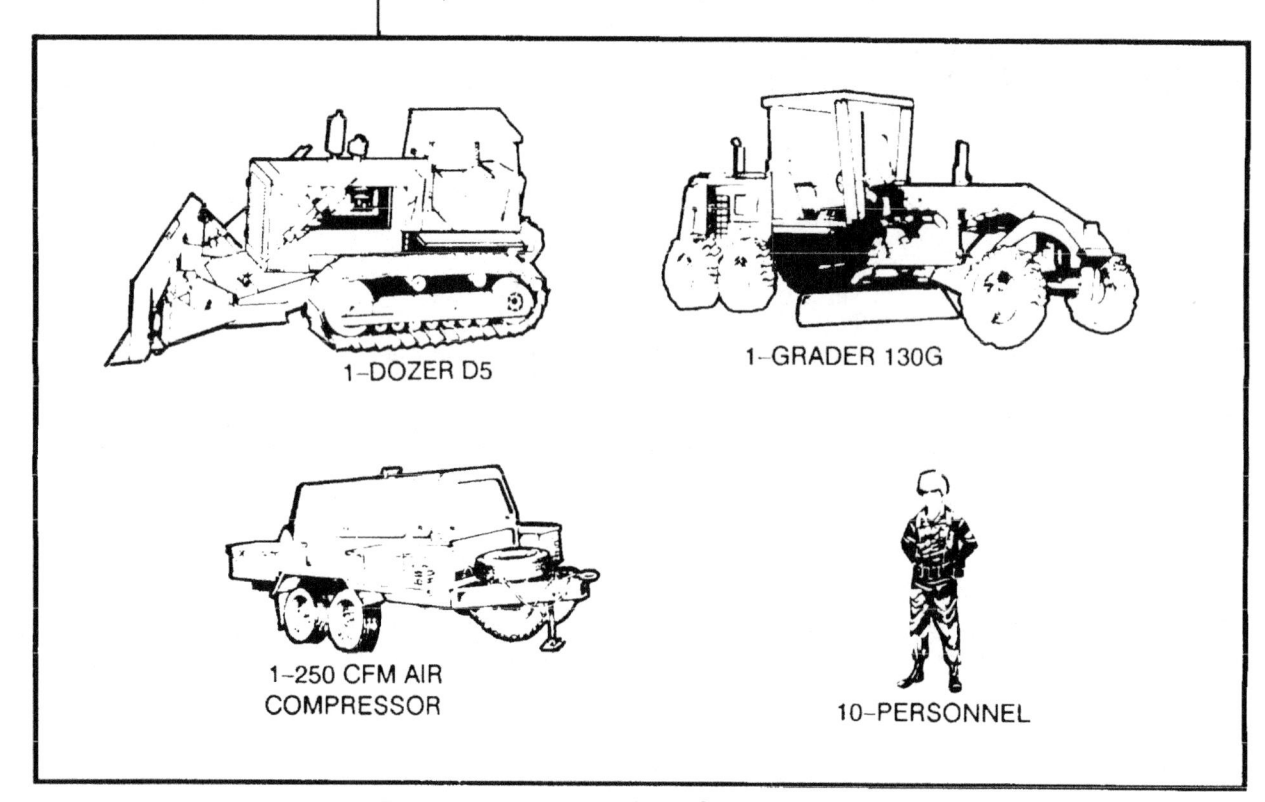

Figure 8-1. Typical light airfield repair team.

(4) *Heavy airfield repair team.* This team repairs extensive damage to an airfield. (Figure 8-2.) It can be provided by a construction platoon from the airborne light engineer company.

FM 90-26

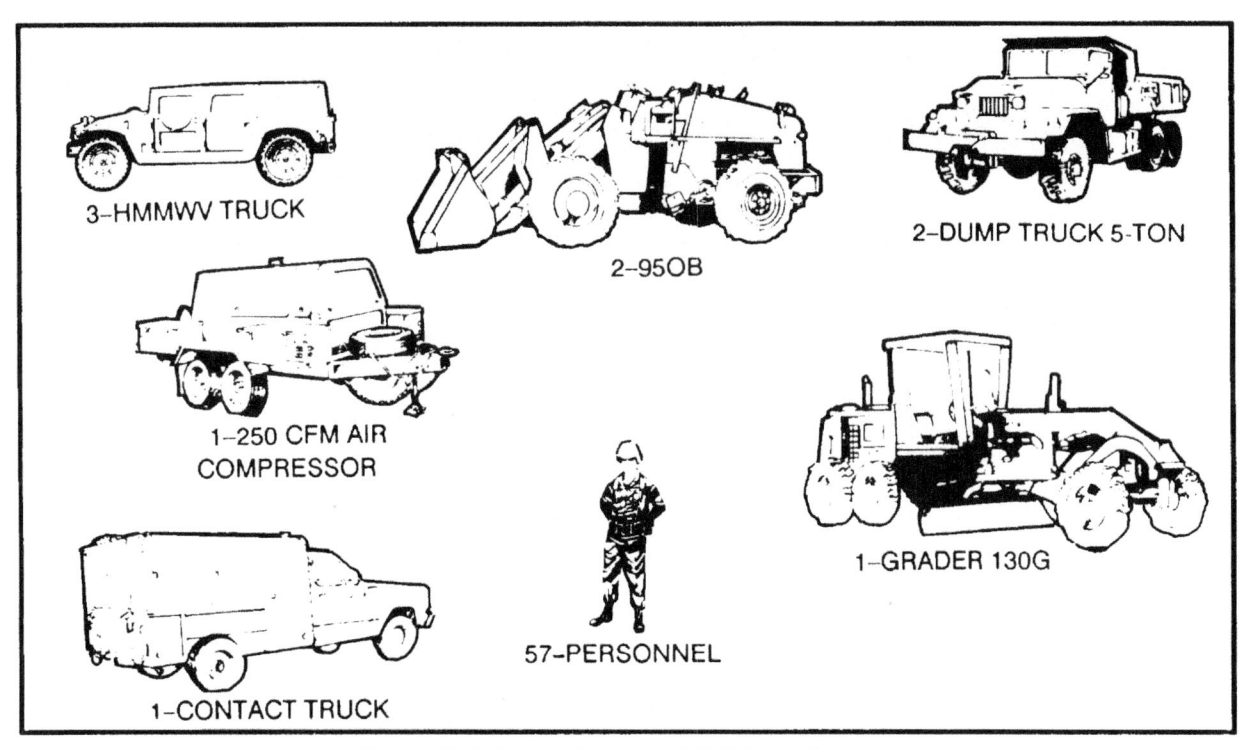

Figure 8-2. Typical heavy airfield repair team.

b. **Airfield Construction.** Tactical operations can occur where a facility does not exist for use in expanding the airhead and establishing the lodgment. In these instances, the airborne force must be tailored with enough engineer assets to build needed runway facilities within the allotted time. Airfield construction can be accomplished by an airborne combat engineer battalion (corps), an engineer combat support equipment company, or an airborne light equipment company with augmentation. The recommended equipment package is shown in Table 8-5.

EQUIPMENT	PERSONNEL
4– D5B Bulldozers	1– 21A Platoon Leader
2– 950B Scoop loaders	1– 62N4P Platoon Sergeant
3– 250 cfm Air compressors	1– 62E3P Construction Foreman
4– 5-Ton dump trucks	6– 62E2P Equipment Operators
6– 2 1/2-Ton dump trucks	3– 62E1P Equipment Operators
4– 15-Ton dump trucks	2– 62J1P General Machine Operators
1– Sheepsfoot railer	9– 62E1P Equipment Operators
1– 13 Wheel roller	1– 88M3P Section Sergeant
3– G13B Scrapers	11– 88M1P Vehicle Drivers
1– 613B Water distributor	1– 62B2P Construction Equip Mech/NCOIC
1– Fuel tanker (M939 w/2 pods)	7– 62B1P Consturction Equip Mechanics
1– Contact truck	2– 63B1P Wheeled Vehicle Mechanics
1– HMMWV	1– 31J1P Combat Signaler

Table 8-5. Typical light airfield construction package.

8-21

Section IX. INTELLIGENCE AND ELECTRONIC WARFARE SUPPORT

Airborne operations often take place well beyond the range of some intelligence assets, which otherwise could support the airborne force. During planning for airborne operations, corps, EAC, other services, and national systems are the primary sources of intelligence. During the operation, organic resources provide much of the intelligence needed with more support coming from higher levels. MI units provide the airborne force with teams for interrogation, EW, and signals intelligence collection as well as CI support. They also provide a key part of the C^2 system designed to quickly collect, analyze, and disseminate information to the airborne force.

8-30. INTERROGATION SUPPORT

Interrogators are specially trained linguists and intelligence analysts. Their job is to screen and interrogate EPWs, detainees, and refugees and to exploit captured enemy documents. Their mission is to collect and report all information that meets the priority intelligence and information requirements of the supported commands.

a. Interrogation operations conducted below division level stress rapid screening and brief tactical interrogations of EPWs, detainees, and refugees. Enemy documents found on EPWs are used to support the screening and interrogation efforts; these documents can provide substantive combat information or intelligence for the commander. All other equipment and documents are evacuated as soon as possible to the rear areas for exploitation.

b. Forward-deployed interrogation teams can be placed in DS of the maneuver brigade. The brigade can further allocate these DS interrogation teams to its subordinate maneuver battalions to accomplish specific missions for a specific period. Direct support interrogation teams are tasked by, and respond to, the brigade or battalion S2. These teams usually operate from the maneuver brigade's EPW collection point in the BSA. Each team has two interrogators, one vehicle, and one VHF FM radio.

8-31. COUNTERINTELLIGENCE SUPPORT

Contingency missions for the airborne division, and the manner in which its subordinate maneuver brigades are deployed, can dictate one or more CI teams (reinforced) to be placed in DS of brigade combat operations. The CI teams revert to MI battalion control for GS to the entire division once the division is deployed and operational.

a. Counterintelligence teams can identify and recommend countermeasures to the specific enemy HUMINT and surveillance and target acquisition means that pose a significant threat to airborne brigade operations. They help develop or refine friendly forces profiles and monitor and evaluate the most sensitive aspects of the brigades' OPSEC program and deception operations. More specifically, they assist the brigade's coordinating and special staff in the following:

(1) Identify the hostile collection and rear operations threat to the brigade and its subordinate maneuver battalions.

(2) Determine the EEFI that require protection.

(3) Identify brigade and battalion vulnerabilities to enemy RSTA, reconnaissance, and destruction activities.

(4) Maintaining intelligence, OPSEC, and deception data bases.

(5) Nominate enemy RSTA and reconnaissance assets or units for suppression, neutralization, destruction, or exploitation.

(6) Recommend OPSEC and deception measures to be employed, and monitor their effectiveness.

b. Individuals from supporting CI teams are located with EPW interrogators at the battalion/brigade EPW collection point. They perform CI screening and line-crosser operations from this location. These teams will operate in and out of the brigade's zone of operations and may cross boundaries to accomplish their mission.

8-32. ELECTRONIC WARFARE/SIGNAL INTELLIGENCE ASSETS

All ground-based EW/SIGINT systems available within the division MI battalion can support the airborne brigade/battalion. The division's airborne EW system, QUICKFIX IIB, also has a significant collection capability; it can operate within the airhead if airlanded via airlift aircraft. All these systems can support airborne unit operations once deployed into the airhead. Major Army EW/SIGINT systems available to airborne units are discussed herein. Additional assets are available from the corps MI assets (see FM 34-25).

a. **AN/ALQ-151(V)2, QUICKFIX IIB.** The AN/ALQ-151(V)2 subsystem is a division-level, special-purpose countermeasures system. This subsystem is part of the heliborne system (EH-60A). The EH-60A includes a modified UH-60A helicopter fitted with special avionics and EW mission equipment to include ESM and ECM equipment. The ESM equipment is used to detect a target signal of interest and to locate its transmitting antenna.

b. **AN/MSQ-103B, TEAMPACK (Lightweight).** The AN/MSQ-103B, TEAMPACK, is a division-level, special-purpose receiving set. It is mounted in a protective shelter on an M1028 CUCV. It is used to intercept, process, display, and record noncommunications signals. The set operates over a frequency range subdivided into six separate bands within the UHF/SHF ranges. The operator has a secure VHF radio for tasking and reporting. The operating range of the AN/MSQ-103B is line of sight out to 30 kilometers.

c. **AN/PRD-10, MANPACK.** The AN/PRD-10, MANPACK is a division-level, man-portable, vehicular radio receiver and DF processor system. It is configured using commercial, nondevelopmental item equipment, which is easily transported and maintained in the field. The AN/PRD-10 provides accurate intercept and line-of-bearing information.

d. **AN/TLQ-17A(V)1-Series, TRAFFICJAM.** The AN/TLQ-17A(V)1, TRAFFICJAM, is a division-level, transportable, electronic countermeasures set. This tactical mobile-jamming set is used against communications signals transmitting in the 1.5- to 80-MHz frequency range. The AN/TLQ-17A(V)1 can be used for surveillance or jamming against ground and airborne communications. It has both manual and automatic jamming capabilities for VHF and HF groundwave frequencies and can be operated in a mounted or dismounted configuration. The range is LOS dependent. A VHF secure voice radio provides communication.

e. **AN/TRQ-32(V)2, TEAMMATE.** The AN/TRQ-32(V)2, TEAMMATE, is a corps- and division-level radio receiving set. It is used to receive, record, and determine the direction of transmitted signals. Communications intercept is provided in the HF, VHF, and UHF ranges. Direction-finding LOB support is provided in the VHF range only. Up to four sets can be netted by way of FM data links for automated DF operations. The AN/TRQ-32(V)2, TEAMMATE, is housed in an S-457B/G shelter, which is mounted on an M1028 CUCV. The communications subsystem provides secure FM voice radio, nonsecure field telephone, and secure UHF data links.

8-33. REMOTE SENSORS

Remote sensors are a near all-weather, day/night surveillance system. They provide an added source of information for the battalion commander. These sensors can be used either alone or to complement or supplement other assets, such as GSRs. They provide information for the production of intelligence and timely, accurate target acquisition data. Sensors are emplaced in areas of expected enemy activity and monitored by teams in friendly forward areas. Movement of enemy forces within the sensor radius is detected and indications are transmitted to the monitoring team. These indications are then analyzed by the team, and the resulting information is reported to the battalion S2.

a. Ground surveillance system personnel from the division's MI battalion can be attached to, or placed in direct support of, the maneuver battalion. They can be further attached to the maneuver battalion's subordinate companies or the scout platoon. These sensors are used–

- To monitor roads, trails, and avenues of approach to the airhead.
- To monitor road junctions and bridges.
- To monitor possible AAs.
- To monitor DZs and LZs.
- To provide target data for immediate use.
- To extend OP capabilities.
- To monitor obstacles and barriers.
- To perform similar tasks designed to detect the movement of personnel or vehicles.

b. Sensors are hand emplaced in the target area by emplacement teams. The major advantages of hand emplacement include accurate determination of sensor location, better camouflage, and confirmed detection radius of each sensor. Disadvantages include threat to the emplacement team, the time required to install several strings, and the limited number of sensors that can be carried by the emplacement team. The emplacement team is transported by helicopter providing an accurate and quick response to the ground commander's request for support. This means of delivery provides access to areas normally inaccessible to ground elements, speeds emplacement, and increases the number of sensors that can be emplaced during a single mission.

c. Airborne units can employ the remotely monitored battlefield sensor system. In a tactical environment, REM BASS will provide the commander with a near all-weather, day and night target development capability in all types of terrain. Such a capability is necessary for the timely allocation of resources and combat power. With REMBASS, the commander has the capability for real-time detection of the enemy, and their exact location. REMBASS is integrated into the overall battlefield RSTA plans at each echelon (battalion and brigade).

(1) The REMBASS is a ground sensor system. It detects, classifies, and determines direction of movement of intruding personnel and vehicles. It uses monitored sensors emplaced along likely enemy avenues of approach. These sensors respond to seismic and acoustic disturbances, IR energy, and magnetic field changes to detect enemy activities.

(2) The three types of sensors (magnetic, seismic/acoustic, and infrared-passive) are normally employed in arrays of strings that complement one another. They are designed to function automatically, transmitting information when movement activates them. Each sensor has detection/classifying techniques suited to the physical disturbance (magnetic, seismic/acoustic, and infrared-passive). Each has a built-in, self-disabling and antitampering feature. Target data is transmitted by FM radio link to the monitor. The following information can be obtained:

- Target detection.
- Rate of movement.
- Length of column.
- Approximate number of targets.
- Type of targets (wheeled vehicles, armored vehicles, or dismounted forces).

(3) The REMBASS has transmission ranges of 15 kilometers, ground to ground and 100 kilometers, ground to air. Because of its flexibility and wide range of applications, various equipment combinations can be selected to suit any given mission.

8-34. GROUND SURVEILLANCE RADARS

Ground surveillance radars provide the maneuver battalion with a highly mobile, near all-weather, 24-hour capability for battlefield surveillance. Units can employ them on patrols and at OPS and can use them with remote sensors and NODs. Ground surveillance radars can be used near or forward of the units' FLOT, on their flanks, or in their rear areas. The S2, company commander, or scout platoon leader of the supported battalion selects general locations for the GSR; then GSR team leaders select the actual site.

a. Surveillance platoons organic to the division's MI battalion have two types of radar-AN/PPS-5 and AN/PPS-15-that provide the supported commander with timely and accurate combat information and target acquisition data. They can detect and locate moving objects when other assets cannot. They are best used for random, short periods of time to search small areas or on a schedule for random or specific targets.

b. The AN/PPS-5 radar detects and warns of enemy dismounted movement over 3,000 meters; AN/PPS-15 radar works between 1,500 and 3,000 meters.

Units can also use the AN/PPS-5 to search beyond engaged forces for indications of reinforcement, withdrawal, and enemy movements to outflank or bypass friendly forces in the engagement area.

c. The AN/PPS-15 radars provide the commander with highly mobile GSR support in operations where the heavier, less portable AN/PPS-5 radar is impractical.

8-35. EMPLOYMENT

The airborne force commander attaches intelligence and EW assets from the MI battalion to maneuver units for the airborne assault. The organization of the IEW unit varies based on the situation. Some assets return to higher echelon control as these levels of command establish CPs in the airhead. Other assets can remain attached (GSR, CI/IPW, and so on) to the battalion or brigade. (FM 34-80 provides a detailed discussion of employment, C^2, and information flow for IEW assets.)

Section X. SIGNAL SUPPORT

Victory on todays fast-moving, complex, lethal battlefield requires a reliable, secure, quick, and flexible communications system. This section discusses the key signal resources employed in airborne operations. Many sources provide signal support to the airborne force to include the joint communications support element in the joint headquarters, organic airborne signal units, and US Air Force or US Navy/Marine elements.

8-36. JOINT AIRBORNE COMMUNICATIONS CENTER/COMMAND POST

The joint communications support element provides modified C-130 and C-141 aircraft for the JTF commander to use en route to the theater or in orbit. The aircraft have roll-on/roll-off modules and provide SATCOM, UHF, VHF, HF, secure/nonsecure voice, and teletype to link the JTF commander with higher headquarters and component commanders. (Table 8-6.) After arriving in theater (for example, at an ISB or REMAB), crews can off-load the JACC/CP modules and place them into operation in a ground mode. The Defense Communications Agency provides more communications support through the Defense Communications System. Through DCS satellite relay support, the DCA connects the JTF commander in the JACC/CP to higher headquarters.

8-37. AIRCRAFT COMMUNICATIONS

Signal units organic to the airborne force usually provide support for installation of Army communications in Air Force aircraft. These units can install air-to-air or air-to-ground communications equipment and associated equipment based on mission requirements. Three communications systems options exist: a secure en route communications package that is UHF air-to-air; HF air-to-ground; and SATCOM air-to-ground and air-to-air.

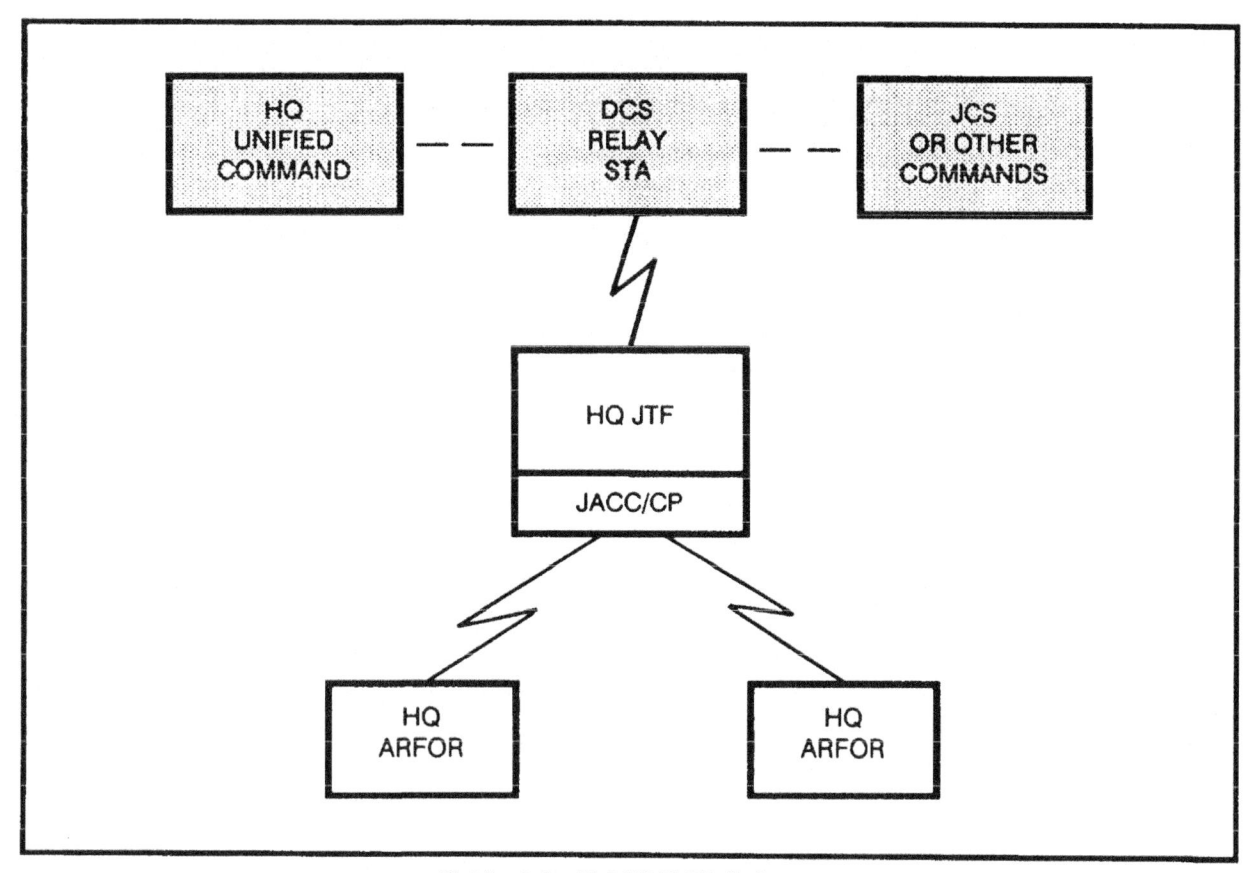

Table 8-6. JACCP/CCP linkage.

a. **Secure En Route Communications Package.** The SECOMP is used mainly for air to air between key ground force leaders on different airdrop aircraft. It has an AN/ARC-51BX radio that can transmit and receive voice between aircraft. The operator uses the intercom position to talk to the commander on the same aircraft when outside transmission is undesirable. The radio has KY-58 VINSON security. The operator can use a guard receiver to monitor a fixed-frequency guard channel. The frequency range is 225- to 399.95-MHz and the operator can preset up to 20 channels. About 10 minutes before the drop, the operator can set on LOS mode to net with JAAP SATCOM radios in the airhead, although this net is used only to deliver abort instructions or other last-minute information.

b. **High-Frequency Operations.** After coordination, the ground commander can use the second HF radio in the aircraft. He can secure this radio with the KY-65 PARKHILL device, using the DMDG with the secured radio for communications. The DMDG enables the commander to send and receive digital messages in electronic form.

c. **Satellite Communications Operations.** MC-130, AC-130, ABCCC, and JACC/PT aircraft (as well as HH-53, PAVE, low helicopters) have hard-mounted, hatch-mount, satellite antennas; they routinely employ SATCOM during operations. SATCOM is more reliable than HF for long-distance communications between airborne force elements, JTF headquarters, and any elements in the objective area. JCSE or organic signal units can provide SATCOM support. There are several SATCOM radios in the aircraft, but the main ones used are the URC-101 and AN/PSC-3, both of which operate in the 225- to 400-MHz range.

d. **Hatch-Mounted Antennas.** Sattelite communications and HF systems, which are employed on C-130, C-141, and C-5A aircraft, require hatch-mounted antennas. The most often used antenna is round, platter-shaped and, once mounted, sits parallel to the skin of the aircraft. Both UHF antennas can be used for SATCOM communications. Their radiation patterns slightly overlay. This provides useful information when the operator compares the flight route and aircraft location in reference to the satellite used. The operator can access both antennas, keeping one operational and one on standby.

8-38. RADAR BEACONS

The use of portable radar beacons in tactical operations improves radar-equipped TACAIR, bombers, and NFG support ships to provide night/adverse weather support to forces in the airhead. Commanders can use beacons in CAS, naval bombardment, AI, aerial delivery, and special operations.

a. **Close Air Support.** Radar beacons deployed with ground combat elements provide an accurate radar offset aim point for radar bombing of immediate or planned CAS targets. Commanders can use them to provide the direction to the target area while laser designators provide an exact aim point. Subordinate commanders request radar beacon CAS missions with standard air request procedures. The agency coordinating and directing CAS support ensures that the radar beacon and aircraft radar system are compatible, that the threat is permissive, and that radar beacons are the best delivery mode.

b. **Air Interdiction.** Planned AI attacks use previously emplaced radar beacons as radar-significant, offset, aim points. The positions, operational status, and codes of each radar beacon are published in the OPORD.

c. **Aerial Delivery.** Ground forces can deploy radar beacons for aerial delivery (airdrop) operations as agreed on between the CCT, or other terminal control personnel, and the mission controlling agency. Radar beacons provide airlift aircrews a positive means to locate, recognize, and align on a DZ, LZ, or EZ. Aircrews can make airborne radar approaches and airdrops under adverse weather/night conditions using the radar beacon as a terminal reference.

d. **Aircraft Position Updates.** Aircrews can use radar beacons placed along ingress routes to update their aircraft position. This reduces the need for navigation aids at or near the target and increases radar delivery accuracy.

e. **Naval Gunfire Operations.** The NGF radar beacons can be employed in any joint operation or to support other naval operations–for example, mine sweeping, patrolling, or coast-watching activities.

(1) *Navigation.* Accuracy of NGF depends on the ability of the ship to fix its position. Ships depend on visual reference points or landmarks to fix their position. When visibility is reduced, ships can use radar to determine their position relative to the known location.

(2) *First-round accuracy.* Radar beacons aid in the delivery of accurate NGF under all ceiling and visibility conditions. Navigation errors can be minimized, improving first-round accuracy.

f. **Operational Considerations.** When using radar beacons, units must consider the following:

(1) *Range.* Radar beacon employment range for an aircraft mission is limited by aircraft radar capability, offset data, and aircraft altitude. Targets should be within 15 NMs of the radar beacon location when the aircraft can ingress to the target at or above 10,000 feet AGL. When aircraft must ingress to the target at a low altitude (below 1,000 feet AGL): targets should be within 5 NMs of the beacon. Shipborn radar has the ability to "see" a full 360 degrees of horizon. However, because it sits lower than aircraft radar, target coverage for an NGF mission is limited by radar beacon signal transmission range.

(2) *Placement.* Placement of radar beacons depends on the following:

(a) Terrain and foliage attenuation. Since transmission of radar energy to and from the radar beacon is LOS limited, the beacon should be placed at the highest elevation available, while still providing for security of operations. Foliage attenuation greatly reduces acquisition ranges.

(b) Aircraft headings. Ideally, the axis of aircraft attack should be within 45 degrees of the beacon-to-target bearing, with the beacon placed beyond the target. Heading directly toward the beacon can degrade the accuracy of the system–some offset can be required. (Figure 8-3, see page 8-30.) Because of typical aircraft radar sweep limits, a heading variance of over 45 degrees can cause the beacon to disappear from the radar scope before delivery. If a run-in heading in excess of 45 degrees offset is dictated by other factors, degradation of delivery accuracy can occur. Overflight of friendly soldiers should be avoided to the extent threat and airspace permit. Placement of the beacon along the axis of the run-in heading is not a factor for gunship operations since the gunship usually orbits its target. For airlift aircraft, the beacon should be placed on the PI for airdrops, either side of the leading edge of the LZ for airland, and between the right release panels for extractions.

(c) Aircraft position updates. For aircraft position updates, the radar beacon should be located en route to the target and be within 10 NMs either side of the proposed ingress flight route.

(3) *Electromagnetic energy.* Radar beacons are vulnerable to enemy DF equipment. Operators should limit "on" times to prolong survivability. "On" times must be firmly established during premission coordination between supporting and supported units. Most beacons can be triggered by any pulse-type signals of sufficient power transmitted in the beacon-receiving frequency band. Like any radar system, the beacon is susceptible to radar jamming and accidental interrogation.

(4) *Weather.* Areas of heavy precipitation between the aircraft or NGF support ship and beacon can reduce the radar energy enough to prevent triggering the beacon. The trigger range and beacon detection range can be extended or reduced by atmospheric conditions, especially in the mid latitudes and tropics. Cold weather adversely affects most batteries; more time can be required for warming up the magnetron before use.

FM 90-26

(5) *Communication.* The controlling agency should relay mission data to the aircrew before takeoff or during ingress. When radio communications are impossible, alternate methods must be prearranged.

(6) *Air threat.* Radar beacons can be best employed in a permissive environment. This provides for higher flight profiles and better acquisition.

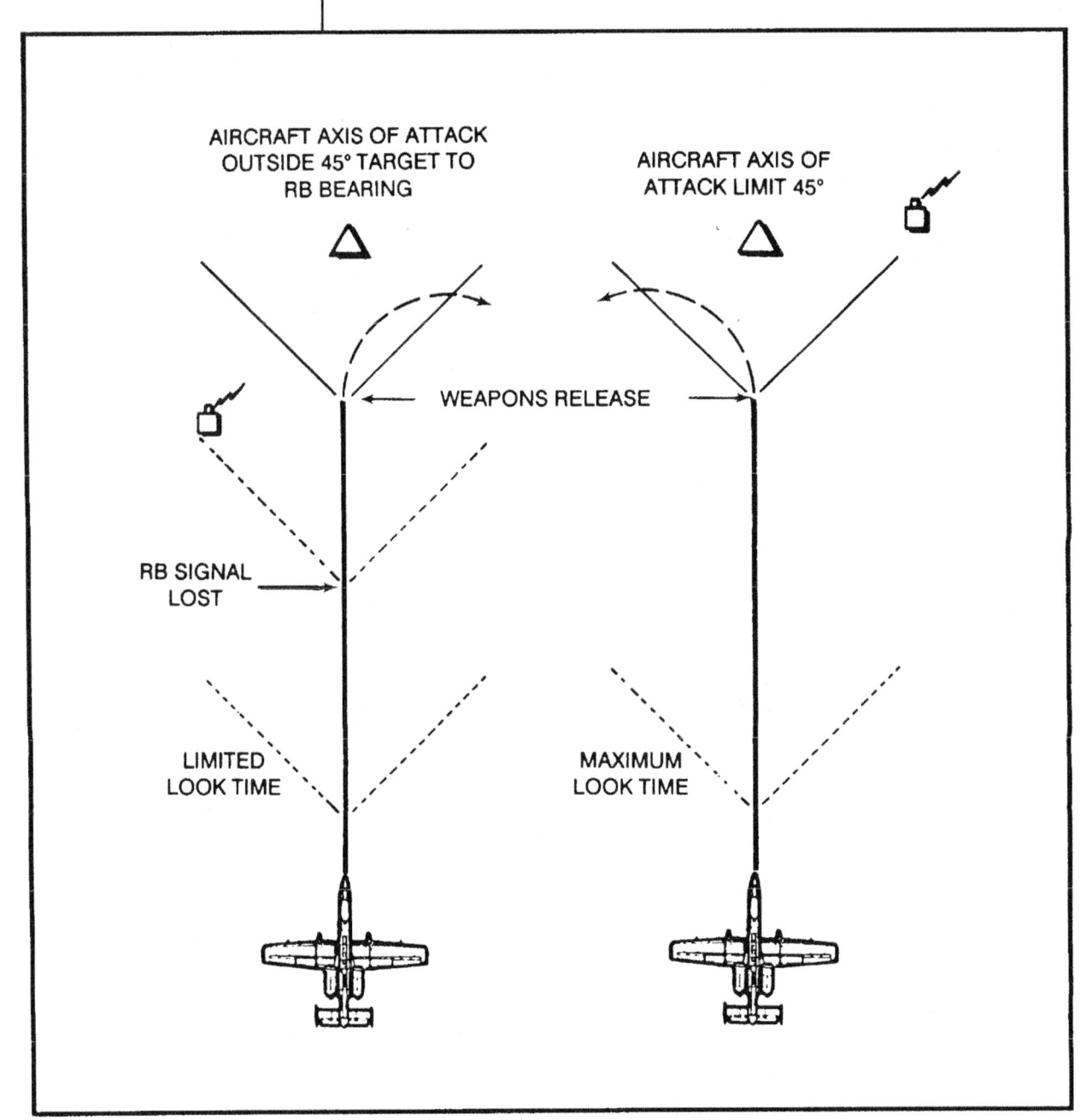

Figure 8-3. Effect of aircraft heading.

g. **Responsibilities.** Responsibilities for beacon employment during joint airborne operations are divided among a number of agencies.

(1) Before deployment, the Air Force TACC coordinates the allocation of Air Force radar beacon assets as required by the JFC and ensures that allocated aircraft are compatible with the deployed beacons. The JFC is responsible for frequency management.

(2) During execution of airborne operations, the ABCCC in its role as ASOC/TAC extension maintains operational control and a current status list of TAF RBs in its tactical area of responsibility. This includes the type, location, operational status, code, on/off status, and responsible ground unit or TACP. The ABCCC directs the employment of radar beacons in its area of responsibility and computes the required bombing data for planned and immediate missions. TACP computations can be used for actual missions when the ABCCC is unable to provide the data. The ABCCC can relay beacon bombing data to the AWACS or FACP for air interdiction and CAS missions. If AWACS is not available, the ABCCC controller can provide data to the flight.

(3) The AWACS, as an extension of the CRC, provides vector assistance to the beacon attack aircraft, as required. It passes radar beacon bombing data received from the ABCCC to the attack aircraft.

(4) The TACP employs beacons for CAS. They determine beacon location, target location, and bearing and range to the target. The TACP reports beacon status to the ABCCC.

(5) The airlift control center maintains close coordination with appropriate TACC for beacon use and directs the allocation of beacons for aerial delivery operations. The ALCC resolves conflicts between CCT radar beacon activity and associated ground or AF units before employment.

(6) The tactical airlift liaison officer coordinates the use of radar beacons for aerial delivery operations with appropriate units and agencies. He assists the airborne unit in forwarding specific aerial delivery mission beacon requirements to higher echelons.

(7) The CCT employs radar beacons to support aerial delivery operations in the airhead. They report beacon location, operational status, and code on/off status to the AATCC, TALO, ABCCC, and ALCC.

(8) During airhead operations, the airborne force commander forwards additional requirements for radar beacon coverage to the JFC and coordinates relocation of beacons with the ABCCC.

h. **Airdrop Procedures.** Radar beacons provide a positive means to locate, identify, and align on DZs, LZs, and EZs. While not a normal peacetime delivery method, with some restrictions aircrews can successfully perform airdrop missions using the beacon as a terminal reference. The navigator receives the beacon on the aircraft radar and provides headings for the pilots to fly to the release point. C-130 airdrops in IMC require either AWADS-equipped aircraft or a radar beacon. A C-141 requires an AN/TPN-27 (zone marker) or a radar beacon to perform IMC airdrops. Special restrictions must be complied with anytime the beacon is used to airdrop. All formation airdrops in IMC also require aircraft equipped with station-keeping equipment.

i. **AC-130 Gunship Procedures.** The primary concern in any AC-130 gunship operation with ground soldiers is the identification of friendly positions.

Beacon operations are ideal for this purpose, especially during adverse weather. Once in radio contact, ground personnel provide beacon offset range in meters and specify whether the bearing is in reference to magnetic or true north. When correcting fire, ground personnel call ordnance impacts in meters long/short, and meters left/right from the ordnance impact area to the target. They use bearing from the radar beacon to the target as the base line. If ground personnel are not at or near the radar beacon, they can elect to call the impacts in range and bearing from the target.

j. **Naval Gunfire Procedures.** Three fire control methods can be employed using a radar beacon. The NGF support ship selects the best method, considering ship position, target position, and whether the beacon position is accurately known.

(1) *Method Alpha.* This method can be used when the exact location of the radar beacon is known (OPORD or radar beacon team information). The beacon is used as a navigation aid to determine the ship's position.

(2) *Method Alpha modified.* This method can be used when the exact location of the radar beacon is unknown, and when combat grid charts are not available. The target location is given in polar coordinates from the beacon. The ship plots the beacon, the ship's relative positions, and target relative position to engage the target.

(3) *Method Bravo.* This method can be used whether or not the radar beacon location is known. Target location is expressed in polar coordinates from the radar beacon. The beacon location is the point of aim, and offsets are introduced into the NGF computer to lay the gun on target.

k. **Authentication.** Proper joint authentication procedures must be used during radar beacon missions. Because intraservice authentication tables differ, each air, land, and sea element must obtain the joint authenticator, AKAC-1553, through unit COMSEC custodians. This joint authenticator, which has been developed for crisis or contingency use only, is called the Dryad Numeral/Authentication System. This system is used for joint interoperability worldwide and is a portion of the intertheater COMSEC package.

Section XI. MILITARY POLICE SUPPORT

The MP have four battlefield missions: they ensure battlefield circulation control; they provide area security; they are charged with the EPW mission; and, at the discretion of the echelon commander, they provide law enforcement assistance. These missions are composed of a number of combat, CS, and CSS operations. The operations are performed independently or in any combination needed to accomplish assigned missions. The MP, in performing these operations, provide a full range of battlefield support.

8-39. MILITARY POLICE (AIRBORNE) STRUCTURE

Airborne MP companies (consisting of 99 soldiers each) have four 21-man platoons to support their divisions. The remaining platoon provides battlefield circulation control and area security near the division main CP.

8-40. MILITARY POLICE OPERATIONS

Airborne MP accompany their divisions during the assault phase to provide support to the division airheads and support areas. Military police generally provide DS to the maneuver brigades during the assault. After the assault is complete and the airhead established, the MP platoons revert to a GS role.

a. The nature of airborne operations makes the capture of EPWs likely. Thus, during the first stage of the assault phase, priority of MP support is given to EPW operations. After assembly on the DZ, MP collect EPWs captured during the assault. Combat elements are relieved of EPWs as far forward as possible. Enemy prisoners of war are collected at the airhead and held for later movement to a central collecting point. Also during the first stage of the assault, MP perform limited straggler control and undertake reconnaissance operations. They also provide security for critical supply storage points when possible.

b. When the airhead is established in the second stage of the assault, the priority of MP support normally shifts to BCC. Although vehicle support is limited in the airhead, BCC measures are needed due to the limited roadnets with the airhead. Battlefield coordination center measures ensure timely and efficient use of the roadways by vehicles needed to support the assault. Also, during the second phase of the assault, MP elements take on much of the EPW and security support requirements. They provide area security in the expanding areas created by the outward bound tactical forces, They also begin to move EPWs to the central collection point for later movement to a holding area.

c. As the airhead is expanded during the third stage of the assault, MP stress battlefield circulation control, area security, and EPW operations to support the division commander's tactical plan. When the operation enters the defense phase, MP support expands to include all MP missions, as dictated by the commander.

Section XII. NUCLEAR, BIOLOGICAL, AND CHEMICAL PLANNING

The airborne force will fight on the integrated battlefield the same as on the conventional battlefield. However, CSS and communications will be disrupted more and the airborne force may be isolated or its movement restricted by radiation or chemical contamination. Tactics used on the conventional battlefield are especially suitable to the integrated battlefield–full use of cover and concealment, overwatch, and suppression. However, in such an environment, the unit must be prepared to quickly implement protective measures to enhance its survivability. They must also provide timely information to higher headquarters to assist in the employment of and protection from nuclear and chemical weapons.

8-41. COMMAND AND STAFF RESPONSIBILITIES

The commander meets his responsibility for preparing individuals and units to operate in an NBC environment by the following:

- Reduce unit vulnerability through terrain shielding and increase protective measures, while positioning elements to accomplish the mission.
- Specify a level of protection, when faced with an NBC threat, that will reduce the risk of mass casualties.
- Receive and submit reports on enemy use of NBC weapons IAW procedures established by higher headquarters.
- Withstand an NBC attack with minimum interference to the assigned mission.

More specifically, the brigade/battalion commander in conjunction with his staff—

- Determines the presence of a chemical hazard (using observation, chemical alarms, or detection devices), warns personnel, and takes proper defensive action.
- Requires that tasks be performed while personnel are in MOPP.
- Determines the presence of a radiological hazard (using radiation detection equipment), warns personnel, and takes proper defensive action.
- Conducts monitoring and surveying to determine the extent and degree of contamination in a given area.
- Establishes priorities for the treatment and evacuation of casualties.
- Decontaminates personnel and equipment.
- Conducts area damage control operations to minimize the impact of NBC weapons.

8-42. CHEMICAL STAFF

The brigade/battalion commander relies primarily on his chemical staff to provide advice and recommendations on all aspects of NBC operations. The chemical staff consists of a chemical officer, a chemical operations NCO, and an NBC enlisted alternate. The chemical staff is normally assigned to the S3 section of the battalion staff. Specific responsibilities include the following:

- Prepare unit NBC defense SOP.
- Supervise NBC training and defense preparation.
- Ensure that NBC equipment is available and serviceable.
- Advise commanders and other staff officers on all aspects of operations in an NBC environment.
- Coordinate efforts of NBC defense assets within the company/battalion.

8-43. UNIT PROTECTIVE MEASURES

The following paragraphs provide guidance on measures which will reduce the brigade/battalion's vulnerability to NBC effects, and enhance its ability to detect, avoid, and measure NBC hazards.

a. **Unit Vulnerability.** A unit's vulnerability to an NBC attack is determined by its nearness to the enemy, its dispersion, its level of NBC training, and the degree of protection available to its personnel and equipment. When determining this vulnerability, it is assumed that the enemy can deliver his weapons on the most vulnerable location within the brigade/battalion area.

(1) To determine how vulnerable a brigade/battalion would be to an enemy-delivered weapon–

(a) Determine, from brigade, the yield of the weapon most likely to be used against the brigade/battalion.

(b) Determine the degree of exposure of brigade/battalion elements.

(c) Determine the radius of vulnerability. The Rv is the radius of a circle within which friendly soldiers will likely become casualties.

(d) Estimate the results of a potential enemy attack by drawing a circle showing the Rv on a transparent map scale, aligning the map scale to find the most vulnerable point, and making a visual estimate to determine coverage of the brigade/battalion.

(2) If coverage exceeds a level acceptable to the commander, the unit may decrease its vulnerability by digging positions or moving into existing protection, such as built-up areas. A centralized location maybe depopulated if the unit is in an assembly area. Units maybe separated laterally or in depth in a defensive situation. Distance between moving elements in the offense may be increased.

(3) While dispersion decreases the risk of destruction from nuclear attack, it may increase the possibility of defeat in detail and complicates the problem of control. The degree to which units can be dispersed depends on the mission of the brigade/battalion and on the risk the commander is willing to accept.

b. **Monitoring.** Radiological monitoring involves the use of radiac instruments to detect and measure residual radiation. Monitoring is performed while stationary. Its primary purposes are to allow warning of all personnel of the arrival or presence of a radiological haired and to provide a basis for prompt action by the commander to minimize the hazard. Monitoring is included in normal reconnaissance and intelligence activities of all units. Radiological monitoring at all levels is initiated on order of the commander, on order of higher headquarters, or as required by SOP or other standing instructions. Units discovering radiological contamination in an area report according to their SOP and mark the area with a radiological contamination marker. Company-size units ensure soldiers are trained to operate unit dose-rate meters.

(1) *Periodic monitoring.* Periodic monitoring is routinely conducted when operating on the integrated battlefield. It requires units to monitor a designated point in their area a minimum of once each hour.

(2) *Continuous monitoring.* All units initiate continuous monitoring when a fallout warning is received; when on an administrative or tactical move; when a nuclear burst is reported, seen, or heard; when radiation above 1 centigray a hour is detected by periodic monitoring; and on order of the commander.

c. **Surveying.** Surveying may be necessary if monitoring reports do not provide the information needed to evaluate the contaminated area.

d. **Operation Exposure Guide.** Battalion operations in a nuclear environment will be complicated by the necessity to control exposure of personnel to nuclear radiation. An OEG provides a method of determining the maximum radiation dose to which units maybe exposed. The OEG will be received from higher headquarters and stated in terms of degree of risk. The maximum dose is determined using the past accumulated dose or radiation history of the unit.

e. Defense Against Biological Attack. Defense against a biological attack is keyed on recognition of a biological threat by the enemy, preventive measures that can be taken by friendly units, and prompt evacuation of casualties.

(1) Recognition is accomplished by alerting unit personnel of indications that a biological agent may have been employed.

(2) Preventive measures can be taken by each unit to reduce casualties from biological attack. These include the following:

- Maintain personal hygiene and field sanitation.
- Avoid practices that produce extreme fatigue.
- Provide immunization for enemy biological agents.
- Provide instruction on the care of wounds.
- Use only approved sources of food and water.
- Ensure rodents and other pests are controlled.
- Quarantine contaminated areas.

(3) Casualties of biological attacks will be processed the same as an illness resulting from normally transmitted diseases. The patients are reported to an aid station by unit aidmen or evacuated from the airhead (on available aeromedical evacuation) to a hospital, as required.

8-44. DEFENSE AGAINST CHEMICAL ATTACK

Unit protective measures are governed by the nature of the threat, the mission, the situation, and the weather.

- Avoid crossing contaminated areas as much as possible consistent with the mission.
- Cross unavoidable contaminated terrain as quickly as possible, preferably in vehicles, at speeds and intervals that minimize contamination of following vehicles.
- Decontaminate after crossing.
- Plan heavy work-rate activities for the coolest part of the day, if the situation and mission permit.
- Thoroughly train each soldier in the use of individual and collective protective measures.

8-45. MISSION-ORIENTED PROTECTION POSTURE

Mission-oriented protection posture is a flexible system of protection used in chemical warfare to facilitate mission accomplishment. It requires soldiers to wear individual protective equipment consistent with the chemical threat, the work rate imposed by the mission, and the temperature. Individual protective clothing becomes standard combat dress when directed by the theater commander.

a. Mission-oriented protection posture gives the commander and staff a choice of chemical protection for their units ranging from no protection at all to full protective clothing and equipment (Table 8-7). Ideally, a balance between the need for chemical protection and the work rate required by the mission can be determined to minimize chemical and heat casualties.

PROTECTIVE EQUIPMENT				
MOPP LEVEL	OVERGARMENT	BOOTIES	MASK/HOOD	GLOVES
0	Carried	Carried	Carried	Carried
1 (Possible)	Worn, opened or closed, based on temperature	Carried	Carried	Carried
2 (Possible)	Same as MOPP1	Worn	Carried	Carried
3 (Likely)	Same as MOPP1	Worn	Worn, hood opened or closed, based on temperature	Carried
4 (Imminent)	Worn, closed	Worn	Worn	Carried

Table 8-7. MOPP levels.

b. All combat operations are conducted under the MOPP system. When there is a continuing immediate threat of chemical attack, the unit may be required to wear protective clothing and equipment for exxtended periods.

c. The flexibility of MOPP in providing for varying levels of individual protection is limited by heat exhaustion, fatigue, senses, and personal needs.

d. The staff, with primary staff responsibility in the S3 section, will be required to recommend appropriate MOPP for a particular mission. When the commander gives his planning guidance for a particular mission, he may specify variations on the MOPP levels and any such variations from the orders as published in the coordinating instructions of OPORDs and OPLANs. In determining what MOPP to recommned, the staff evaluates the following:

(1) The type of mission and its relative importance to the overall mission.

(a) What work rate does the mission involve?

(b) What will the temperature be during the mission?

(c) Can the mission given to subordinates be changed or modified to achieve similar results with an increase in protection or a decrease in risk?

(2) The chemical threat and the capability of the threat forces to employ chemical agents, and the probability that they will do so.

(3) The expected number of heat casualties versus chemical casualties.

(4) The support required to minimize casualties from all causes, and the estimated time to complete the mission.

(5) The effects of environmental factors such as temperature and windspeed. (High winds decrease the probability that the enemy will use chemical agents.)

e. Before the start of a mission, the commander specifies the MOPP level to be used. He may later direct that this level of protection be increased, decreased, or varied among individuals or elements within the unit according to his evaluation of the current situation and operational limitation. He must consider that as the temperature and work rate increase, the level of individual protection must be reduced and work-pacing options must be taken, or he must accept the possibility of more heat casualties. One option is to reduce the chemical protection according to the temperature and work rate. Other options arc contingent on the hazards of contamination present.

(1) In a contaminated area, the commander may do one of the following:

(a) Rotate jobs requiring a heavy work rate among subordinate units, elements, or individuals.

(b) Authorize longer and more frequent rest periods. Rest periods are necessary to allow enough cooling time for the dissipation of built-up body heat. Work/rest periods may be repeated as many times as necessary to complete a job.

(c) Provide adequate water supply so that personnel can increase their water intake by drinking small amounts frequently.

(d) Use vehicular transportation whenever possible.

(2) When there is no immediate hazard from chemical agents, a commander may rotate personnel to various combinations of reduced chemical protection to provide relief from buildup of body heat. The commander may also allow a small percentage of his soldiers to be out of their chemical protective clothing at one time. The number of personnel in reduced protection is determined based on his evaluation of the local situation. Reduced protection is permitted on a selective basis for personnel performing certain tasks that require manual dexterity, visual acuity, and voice communication. It may also be necessary after considering the long-term psychological effects on personnel wearing full chemical protective clothing and equipment for extended periods.

(3) When there is no danger from chemical contamination (verified by the use of the unit's chemical-agent detector kits) and soldiers are required to operate at moderate to heavy work rates, the commander may authorize them to progressively reduce their protection by–

- Opening the zipper of the hood (and possibly rolling it up) for ventilation.
- Removing the protective gloves.
- Removing the protective mask and hood.

- Opening the duty uniform or the chemical protective clothing for ventilation. (This will require loosening or removal of external LBE.)
- Removing some or all of the protective clothing.

(4) The commander can increase the work times significantly when a job requires a sustained effort for proper accomplishment or is an emergency. It must be noted, however, that soldiers who work for a long period will then require an extended rest to dissipate the built-up heat.

8-46. DECONTAMINATION

Chemical decontamination involves removing, neutralizing, absorbing, or weathering the chemical agent. Biological decontamination involves destroying or exposing the biological agent to sunlight. Radiological decontamination involves physically removing the radioactive material.

a. **Types of Decontamination.** There are three types of decontamination. See FM 3-5 for more information on all types of decontamination operations.

(1) Chemical contaminants on the skin are removed or neutralized by basic soldier skills.

(2) Hasty decontamination is done to remove gross amounts of NBC contaminants from weapons, combat vehicles, and each soldiers' clothing and equipment.

(3) Deliberate decontamination is conducted by specialized decontamination units so that soldiers do not have to wear complete NBC protective equipment.

b. **Priorities.** The battalion commander normally prescribes the priority of decontamination. He allocates necessary decontamination squads to ensure its accomplishment. The following are normal priorities:

(1) *Personnel.* Individuals or units are removed from contaminated areas, if possible, and are provided water for bathing. Fresh clothing and equipment are made available, and a means of disposing of contaminated clothing, equipment, and water is provided.

(2) *Food and water.* Ration containers are decontaminated with soap and water or other neutralizing agents, and rations are inspected by qualified medical personnel before consumption. Closed containers of water may be decontaminated by neutralizing agents, or uncontaminated water may be transported from another location.

(3) *Critical equipment.* Personnel and unit equipment vital to mission accomplishment are decontaminated or exchanged as required.

(4) *Terrain.* Small terrain areas may often be decontaminated by weathering, or by moving or turning the contaminated earth with spades or mechanical means.

CHAPTER 9

COMBAT SERVICE SUPPORT

Combat service support for airborne operations must be planned, organized, and executed to sustain a fast tempo in highly mobile and dispersed operations. Just as the airborne force is tailored for airdrop or airland combat operations, the logistical system is tailored to support and sustain the airhead or lodgment by airdrop, airland, overland, or sea, as resources are available. Doctrinal distances do not always apply to airborne operations. Therefore, the logistical planner must be prepared to adapt and innovate with the resources at hand. Thus, airborne operations logistics depend greatly on outside support.

Section I. LOGISTICAL PLANS AND PREPARATIONS

Logistical plans cover the four essential elements of logistics: supply, maintenance, transportation, and services. Brigades, battalions, and companies start their logistical plans as soon as they receive a WO or instructions to implement an OPLAN. The plan covers both support during combat and preassault preparation. The part of the plan covering the preassault phase includes supplying the unit, moving to the marshaling area, and conducting logistical operations in the target area. Brigade plans are more inclusive and detailed than battalion and company plans; battalions and companies are more concerned with the execution of scheduled logistical functions.

9-1. LOGISTICAL STRUCTURE

A DISCOM forward area support team in each brigade support area provides the brigade with CSS. The team is tailored to satisfy the requirements of the supported brigade and is formed around a forward support maintenance company and a forward medical company. The division support command forms three echelons to support the assault echelon, the follow-on elechon, and the rear echelon. Each is tailored to the mission.

a. **Assault Echelon.** This echelon consists of a portion or all of the FAST as determined by the commander's concept of the operation. It is normally attached to the supported brigade during marshaling. This attachment remains effective during the assault phase. The FAST is tailored for the mission and can include elements from a forward maintenance company, a forward medical company, and a forward supply company. It can also include a detachment from the quartermaster airdrop equipment support company that can assist in the recovery and evacuation of airdrop equipment from the DZ. The FAST may receive augmentation from corps based on mission needs.

b. **Follow-On Echelon.** Most of the DISCOM enters the AO in the follow-on echelon under control of the DISCOM. Normally deploying by airland assault, the CSS follow-on echelon includes the remainder of the DISCOM HHC (-), a detachment of the quartermaster airdrop equipment support company, the remainder of the maintenance battalion, and the supply and transportation battalion. Remaining DISCOM units stay at the departure airfield in the rear echelon.

c. **Rear Echelon.** This echelon remains at the departure airhead or ISB and consists of elements not immediately required in the airhead to support the airborne force. These elements include the remaining portions of the DISCOM MMC, maintenance battalion, quartermaster airdrop equipment support, and the finance and personnel service companies (corps unit). Depending on the duration and nature of the operation, the rear echelon may be called forward and deployed into the AO after the lodgment is established.

9-2. LOGISTICAL PLANNING RESPONSIBILITIES

Responsibility for planning various logistical aspects of the operation is shared by several agencies.

a. **Assault Force.** The airborne force (normally, a brigade or battalion TF) conducting combat operations has the following responsibilities:

(1) Concentrate, organize, and equip the airborne forces.

(2) Load soldiers and their accompanying supplies and equipment.

(3) Recover airdropped supplies and equipment, and provide CSS units to unload aircraft in the airhead.

(4) Move supplies from landing fields to airhead supply points by airhead supply units.

(5) Operate airhead supply points.

(6) Conduct logistical operations within the perimeter of the airhead with normal logistical agencies.

(7) Repair or construct the required airfields within the airhead until ground linkup.

(8) Consolidate, treat, and evacuate casualties from airhead airfields.

b. **Division Support Command, Rear Echelon, and COSCOM Units.** These units have the following responsibilities:

(1) Receive, procure, and deliver equipment and supplies to rear air bases for transportation to the airhead.

(2) Move airborne forces to the marshaling camps, and provide for accompanying equipment and supplies.

(3) Evacuate from rear air bases.

(4) Operate marshaling areas.

c. **Air Force Units and Installations.** These elements have the following responsibilities:

(1) Maintain aircraft.

(2) Receive unload, and temporarily store supplies at rear air bases.

(3) Load supplies for delivery to the airhead.

d. **Military Airlift Command.** These units have the following responsibilities:

(1) Conduct air movement of soldiers, equipment, and supplies to landing areas within an airhead.

(2) Assist in logistical organization for the receipt of supplies on airfields in the airhead.

(3) Evacuate casualties from airfields in the airhead.

(4) Construct, rehabilitate, and maintain airfields in the airhead after ground linkup.

(5) Supervise loading and lashing operations at the rear air bases for flying safety.

(6) Coordinate deployment of aeromedical evacuation liaison teams, and establish the tactical aeromedical evacuation system.

9-3. LOGISTICAL PLANNING CONSIDERATIONS

A number of factors and considerations affect logistical planning. Preliminary data needed to prepare the logistical plan includes an analysis of the AO, the ground tactical plan, the anticipated duration of the operation, and unit strength.

a. **Basic Decisions.** For the logistical plan to progress, planners make basic decisions as early as possible. This allows all responsible agencies to prepare and execute plans for procurement and assembly of aircraft, supplies, equipment, and personnel. They decide on the following:

(1) What forces will be involved, how they will be organized, and what their principal objectives will be.

(2) What the tentative strength and composition of logistical units in the airborne force will be.

(3) What amount/type of equipment should accompany the airborne force.

(4) What initial supplies will be taken.

(5) What level of supplies should be maintained in the airhead.

(6) What airfields will be used for the landing of soldiers and supplies.

(7) Where marshaling camps will be; what soldiers and materiel will be marshaled at each camp.

(8) How long it should take to organize airheads in the landing areas.

(9) How follow-on echelons of major airborne force units should be organized, and what method of movement should be planned for them.

(10) Where rear air bases to be used for supply purposes should be located.

(11) How available aircraft should be allocated for soldiers and supply.

(12) When (on what date) airborne forces should be ready for embarkation by aircraft.

(13) What capacity of the ISB should be maintained at advance air bases to facilitate supply.

(14) What evacuation policies should be set up.

b. **Detailed Plans.** Planners prepare detailed logistics based on the basic decisions. The following considerations also affect the plan:

(1) What facilities are required for staging soldiers at marshaling camps.

(2) How the desired quantities of supplies will be delivered to rear air bases at the proper time.

(3) How many, what size, and what type aircraft are available, and what their loading characteristics are.

(4) What materiels-handling equipment is available.

(5) What the distance is between rear air bases and landing areas.

(6) What the characteristics of the proposed airhead are, including road net, storage, and other facilities.

(7) How long the follow-on supply phase will go on before normal supply procedures are in effect, including time for construction, repair, or capture of airfields.

(8) How much or how many supplies, equipment, and materials will be available within the proposed airhead for possible exploitation.

(9) What is the climate, or what season.

(10) If units will have to designate transportation assets for the medical unit to transport casualties.

(11) If dedicated air MEDEVAC (fixed- or rotary-wing) are required and available,

(12) How casualty assets arc to be evacuated if no corps augmentation is available.

9-4. PHASES OF SUPPLY

There are three supply phases for airborne operations: accompanying supplies, follow-on supplies, and routine supplies.

a. **Accompanying Supplies.** These include supplies taken into the airhead by assault and follow-on units. Accompanying supplies are issued to units before marshaling for early preparation before air movement and for delivery in the assault. They are carried into the assault area and include the supplies airdropped with the deploying unit. Each unit receives and protects its own accompanying supplies, which include unit, force, and reserve supplies.

(1) *Unit supplies.* These supplies include each soldiers' combat loads, basic loads of ammunition and other supplies, and prescribed loads of other classes of supply. Rigging, loading, recovery, issue, and control of unit supplies are the responsibility of the airborne unit.

(2) *Force supplies.* These are bulk supplies retained at battalion or brigade that the backup unit provides. They include all classes of supply. The S4 of the deploying unit is responsible for controlling these supplies.

(3) *Reserve supplies.* These are additional supplies brought into the airhead under DISCOM control; they consist of the airborne force reserve of Class III, Class V, selected items of Classes II and IV, and Class IX.

b. **Follow-on Supplies.** Follow-on supplies include all classes of supply; they are air-delivered after the unit has made its initial assault to help the unit operate until normal supply procedures can be set up. They are usually

FM 90-26

prepackaged, rigged, and stored at the beginning of the operation for immediate distribution on request. COSCOM units will most likely provide assistance in the packaging of follow-on supplies. Quantities are based on the G4's estimate of the unit's daily requirements. Plans must be developed that permit flexibility in composition of daily requirements. The battalion S4 requests follow-on supplies for the battalion. Follow-on resupply is discontinued as soon as practicable.

(1) *Automatic follow-on supplies.* These are delivered on a preplanned schedule once a day, beginning at a time based on the ground tactical plan. The number of days of scheduled follow-on supply depends on the specific situation and should be enough for the airborne forces to continue their operations until routine supply is available. Automatic follow-on supplies are either airdropped to the unit or airlanded at a central supply point. Follow-on supply should not be scheduled for automatic delivery on the day the operation is to begin because units within the airhead should be fully occupied with seizing assault objectives, establishing the airhead, and recovering accompanying supplies.

(2) *On-call follow-on supplies.* These are held in the departure area in readiness for immediate delivery to units on specific request. They include more of the items supplied by automatic follow-on, major items of equipment, and supplies that arc not used at a predictable rate. The airborne force determines the quantities and types of supplies to be included in on-call supply. Depending on the situation, on-call supplies can be segregated and prepackaged into loads by type, such as 105-millimeter artillery ammunition, or can be maintained in bulk pending emergency requests for specific types and amounts. Emergency supplies must be delivered within 24 hours. Routine supplies arc delivered on a flexible schedule–24 to 72 hours after the request. Whenever any of the on-call follow-on supplies are used, the expended amounts are replaced.

c. **Routine Supplies.** These are requested and delivered by normal supply procedures. The DISCOM commander decides when routine supply deliveries should begin, depending on the tactical situation and supply status of the division.

9-5. CLASSES OF SUPPLY

The following paragraphs provide information about the classes of supply, the use of captured supplies and salvage, water supply, and special supplies and equipment

a. Supplies are divided into 10 major categories so that items can be readily identified to each particular class. Classes of supply are the same for all types of combat operations.

(1) *Class I.* This class includes meal, ready-to-cat, tray pack, and A-type meals. Airborne units use MREs as the basic load and for follow-on supply. Tray packs and A-type meals may be used later as the airhead develops and the lodgment becomes secure. Personnel strength reports determine Class I requirements, thereby eliminating complicated unit ration requests.

(2) *Class II.* This class includes clothing, individual equipment, tentage, hand tools, administrative and housekeeping supplies and equipment, and chemical decontaminants. It also includes supplies and some equipment (other than principal items) prescribed in authorization or allowance tables; it does not include repair parts. Accompanying supplies include some Class II items. Follow-on and routine supply include small stocks of individual clothing and equipment while on-call follow-on supply includes major items of equipment, as the situation dictates.

(3) *Class III.* This class includes POLs. Unit vehicles and equipment are usually delivered to the airhead with fuel tanks 3/4 full to allow for expansion during airlift. Forecasts for POL are used by units to program delivery of POL as part of the assault and follow-on supplies. Packaged POL and bulk POL supplies are used. Care must be taken to ensure that bulk aviation fuel is dispensed using fuel filters and separators. Plans for POL should include retrograde of containers for refill.

(4) *Class IV.* This class includes construction materials and all fortification/barrier materials. Units can only take a limited amount of Class IV supplies into the objective area. Careful choice of drop and assault LZs reduces the amount of Class IV supplies needed to support the operation by minimizing the requirement for construction equipment and material. Units exploit local resources.

(5) *Class V.* This class of supply includes all ammunition. Planners must consider that, during the assault phase, ammunition tonnage is greater than the combined weight of all other supplies. Units take a basic load only. The amounts are expressed in number of rounds for each weapon each day. Specified amounts of all types of ammunition for airborne forces weapons (enough for continuity of the combat operation) comprise follow-on supply. The amounts of ammunition needed depend on the type of operation and the strength of enemy opposition. Follow-on resupply should be cross loaded to offset loss of one type of item if aircraft are lost. Planners provide in advance for possible additions or deletions of certain types of ammunition. Expenditure rates are based only on staff estimates, which must take into consideration the following factors:

- Degree of opposition to be encountered during and after the landing.
- Number and type of weapons landed with airborne forces.
- Planned time of follow-on supply.
- Number and types of aircraft to be used.

(6) *Class VI.* This class includes personnel demand (Army and Air Force Exchange Service) items that are usually unavailable in the airhead for sale or issue to soldiers and other authorized individuals. It should not be confused with the ration supplement and sundries pack. (The sundries pack has items necessary to the health and comfort of soldiers such as essential toilet articles, tobacco, and confections. It is available in theaters of operation for issue through Class I channels, pending establishment of adequate service facilities.)

(7) *Class VII.* This class includes major end items. Certain items of this class can be retained for use in on-call resupply to replace those lost in combat or during airdrop. This is critical for certain items of equipment; especially, engineer items whose loss could significantly affect the operation.

(8) *Class VIII.* This class includes medical materiel, which is discussed with health services.

(9) *Class IX.* This includes repair parts such as kits, assemblies and subassemblies, and repairable and nonrepairable parts required for maintenance support of all equipment. Maintenance elements entering the airhead carry PLL, shop stocklisting, and designated items from the ASL.

(10) *Class X.* This includes materiel to support civil affairs and nonmilitary programs. Airborne operations usually require minimal Class X during the assault phase.

b. **Captured Supplies and Salvage.** Within limitations prescribed by the commander, units use captured or abandoned enemy materiel and supplies. The use of captured equipment/materiel eases the logistical burden in the airhead by reducing the number of airframes needed in the early stages of the operation. (See FMs 100-10 and 63-20 for information about restrictions on the use of captured equipment/materiel.) Logistical considerations require recovery of salvageable equipment; especially parachutes, air delivery containers, and heavy-drop platforms.

c. **Water.** Airborne forces carry filled canteens and water purification tablets. They carry enough full organic water containers for travel to the airhead and consumption while they are there. Planners must plan for resupply in the air flow to ensure soldiers have enough water in the airhead. Planners should also determine the location of possible water supply points. Water purification units are made available in the airhead as early as practicable.

d. **Special Supplies and Equipment.** Changing situations in airborne operations can make additions, deletions, and substitutions of standard equipment and units' prescribed loads necessary. Conditions often require the use of nonstandard items such as escape kits, recognition devices, currency, special individual medical supplies and equipment, and individual maps. Each unit arranges for these items and distributes them either before or during marshaling, according to security principles.

9-6. DISTRIBUTION OF SUPPLY

Supply and transport units can accompany the assault echelon to recover assault supplies transported under control of the airborne force and to establish necessary supply points. The airborne force can use supply point distribution, unit distribution, or both to handle supplies. Helicopters can deliver priority supplies.

a. Throughput distribution bypasses one or more intermediate supply echelons to avoid multiple handling. Commanders choose this method whenever possible to deliver supplies from the rear echelon to the using unit in the airhead.

b. In the unit distribution method, the issuing agency transports supplies to the receiving unit's area. They can use ground transportation from supply points near DZs or airfields, or they can airdrop supplies directly to the using unit.

c. With supply point distribution, the receiving unit picks up supplies from a distribution point and moves them in organic transportation. Distribution points for essential combat supplies are positioned close to the soldiers being served to benefit from the security provided by the combat elements. This also prevents infiltrating hostile forces from cutting the supplies off from the receiving unit, and shortens supply lines.

d. Supplies must be delivered to the airhead configured for easy handling. Limited MHE, CSS, and transportation assets available, as well as the tactical situation, affect supply distribution in the objective area. Multiple DZs must be selected including sites close to the forward battalions/companies. Some supplies should be packed into CDS bundles for expedient follow-on resupply.

9-7. RESUPPLY BY AIR

Army and Air Force assets are used for both airland and airdrop, although most Air Force deliveries are airdrop. Airland is better because special equipment or rigging is not required. When airdrop is necessary, the Army furnishes the airdrop equipment and rigs the loads. Airdrop rigging support for division airdrop resupply comes from division and corps airdrop units.

a. **Preplanned Resupply Requests.** Preplanned airdrop resupply can be automatic or on call. Automatic airdrop resupply can be arranged for a designated time and place to support specific operations. On-call airdrop resupply uses prerigged and pre-positioned supplies that are arranged for before an operation and delivered when requested by the supporting unit. To obtain a preplanned airdrop, units in the airhead request supplies and equipment from their DS unit in the FAST. (Figure 9-1, see page 9-10.)

b. **Immediate Airdrop Resupply Requests.** Immediate airdrop resupply missions result from unanticipated, urgent, or priority requirements. Immediate requests for resupply missions must be flown faster than preplanned missions. Unless the JFC has allocated airdrop assets for strip alert or has otherwise kept airlift in reserve, immediate airdrop resupply requests are filled by preempting, diverting, or canceling lower priority preplanned missions. (Figure 9-2, see page 9-11.)

9-8. MAINTENANCE

The problem of maintenance is usually magnified by the need for security for maintenance personnel in the assault during the initial combat and by the damage that may occur during the air delivery of equipment. (See FM 43-5 and AR 750-1 for detailed information on all maintenance resources found in airborne units, and their employment.)

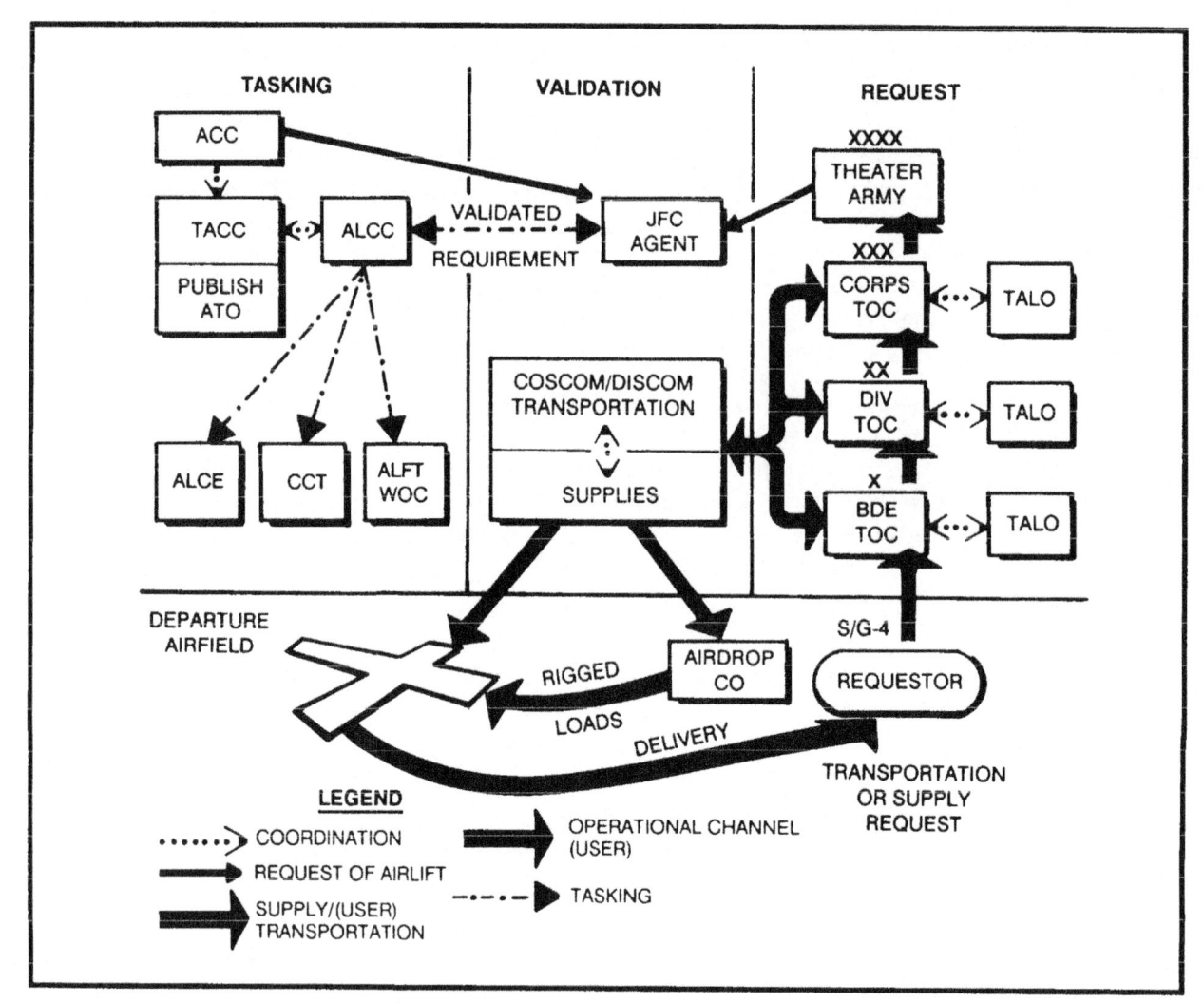

Figure 9-1. Preplanned resupply flow.

a. **Follow-On.** When deployed in the follow-on echelon, the maintenance battalion provides a forward support company to the FAST supporting each brigade. Habitual attachments are used to establish working relationships and develop SOPs. Maintenance responsibilities and procedures may vary through each phase of the operation.

b. **Marshaling and Deployment.** To reduce maintenance requirements in the airhead, intensive maintenance is performed before departure. Maintenance units support unit marshaling with unit and DS maintenance, as required. The maintenance battalion, augmented by MACG elements, provides maintenance contact teams to inspect and repair equipment during marshaling. Units report items requiring GS maintenance that cannot be repaired in time for the operation to the DMMC, which requisitions replacements for those items. The DMMC directs the maintenance battalion to use the operational readiness float to fill critical combat requirements. The maintenance battalion repairs all equipment that cannot be repaired at DS level in time for unit deployment and places it in the division's ORF.

Maintenance support units are positioned as needed to provide repair services.

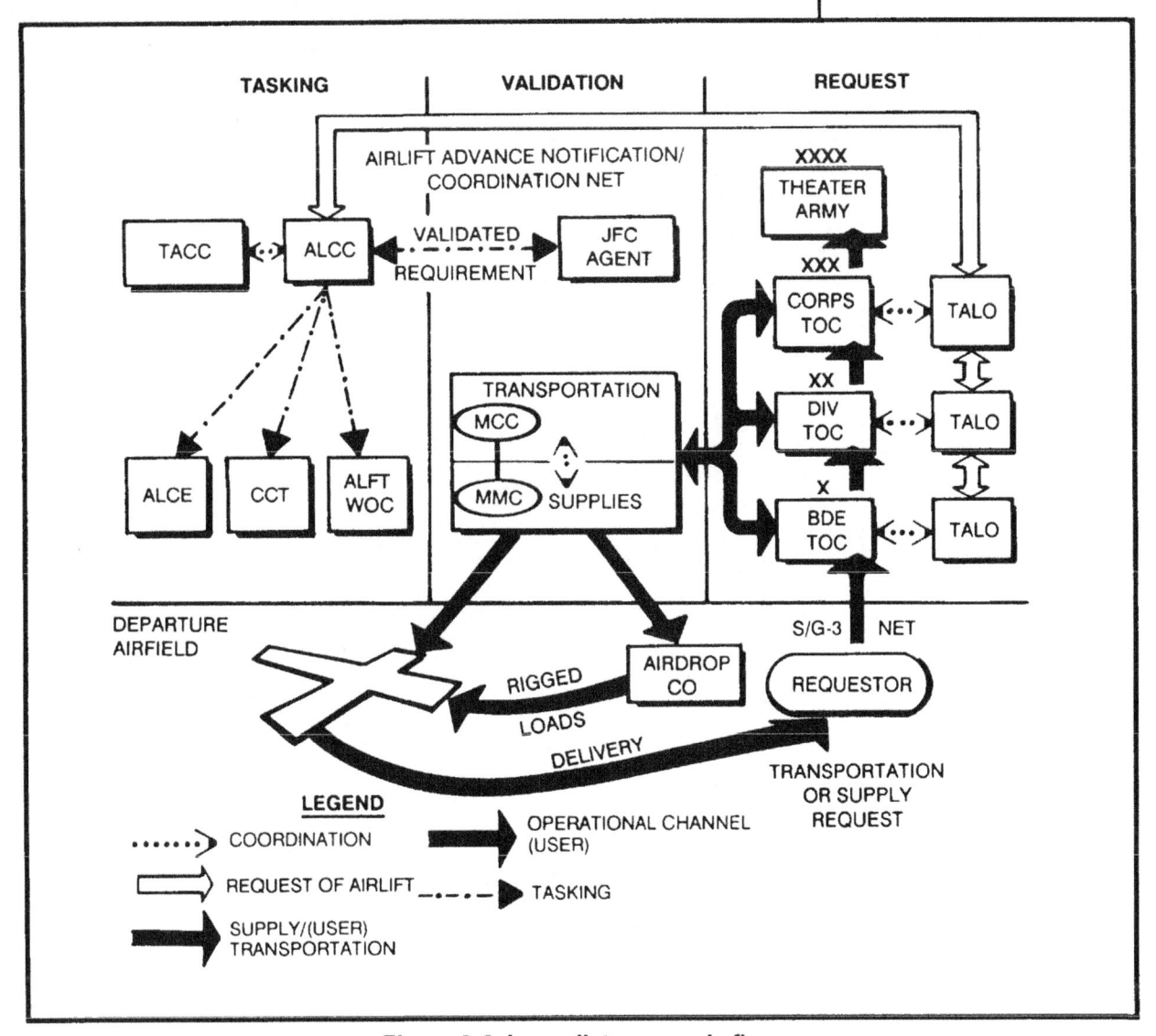

Figure 9-2. Immediate resupply flow.

c. Maintenance in the Objective Area. Maintenance during the initial assault and subsequent operations phase is usually performed by maintenance personnel organic to the battalions and separate companies. The complete forward support company plus other designated individuals and equipment from the maintenance battalion enter the objective area in the follow-on echelon. These personnel deploy as part of the FAST to provide DS of primary weapons systems and communications equipment. They carry the DS maintenance company's ASL. They use battle damage assessment and repair procedures for severely damaged or inoperable systems to maintain the maximum number of systems available for combat. Direct support maintenance support teams perform mission-essential maintenance; they perform other maintenance only as time permits. Priority for maintenance is usually given to weapon systems that require minimum effort to restore to mission-capable condition. Maintenance support teams are as far forward as practicable under the control and coordination of the FAST.

d. Expansion and Buildup of the Airhead. During this phase, the remaining DS maintenance elements are deployed. Direct support is provided to the brigade by the maintenance company in the BSA. Backup DS is provided by the remainder of the maintenance battalion in the DSA. The maintenance unit also provides backup DS to the forward maintenance elements. General support is provided to the division by nondivisional maintenance assets from the corps.

9-9. TRANSPORTATION

Transportation plans provide for the transport of soldiers and accompanying supplies to the marshaling area, transportation needed during marshaling, and the loading of unit transport with supplies and equipment for the assault.

a. In an airborne operation, transportation means in the airhead are limited. Captured enemy vehicles are used to supplement limited transportation resources; efficient use of organic transportation is essential. The assaulting battalions and brigades will have austere organic transportation assets and will not be capable of sustained combat operations without augmentation. Ground transportation for the brigade is provided largely by the division supply and transportation battalion. Requests for movement of supplies are processed through logistics channels from the requesting unit S4 through the FAST to the movement control officer on the DISCOM staff. The MCO controls and allocates vehicles from the S&T battalion. The MCO controls commitment of the transportation motor transport company vehicles for CSS within the division. Requirements that cannot be satisfied are forwarded to the division transportation officer. He can request the use of divisional aircraft or vehicles support from other units in the division from the G3 to satisfy these requiements These aircraft and vehicles may be provided by other divisional units, the COSCOM MMC, or the host nation when the tactical situation permits.

b. During an airborne operation, greater reliance is placed on Air Force transportation of supplies, personnel, and equipment than on ground transportation. Airhead transportation requirements can be reduced by delivering supplies and equipment directly to the battalion or company in Air Force aircraft. LAPES, CDS, and heavy-drop, properly used and delivered at the correct location, can reduce transportation requirements speed delivery, and reduce the vulnerability of ground transportation assets to enemy action. Air Force airlift missions are categorized as preplanned or immediate.

9-10. FIELD SERVICES

Field services provided by division personnel to the brigade and battalion during wartime operations include graves registration and salvage. A COSCOM service element provides these services when division personnel cannot. General support units operated by corps provide other field services such as laundry, bakery, textile renovation, and airdrop. Limited GRREG services are usually the only field service available in the airhead, although all can exist in the marshaling area. Staging bases in the rear provide airdrop support as a service.

a. **Graves Registration.** Airborne units have no graves registration capability and require augmentation to perform this function. Soldiers must learn how to identify and process remains and to establish and operate collection points. Units recover remains and evacuate them to designated locations IAW unit SOP.

(1) *Evacuation.* After identification, designated unit personnel evacuate remains to the collecting point in the BSA or the division collection point in the DSA using available transportation. After coordination with the Air Force, Army units move the remains to the airfield for aerial evacuation.

(2) *Burial.* Units perform hasty or mass burials only when the tactical situation prevents evacuation. The TF commander retains authority for mass burials. The training of graves registration personnel should include the procedures for marking and recording hasty burial sites.

b. **Airdrop Support.** Airdrop is a method of delivering supplies and equipment from aircraft to ground elements. The division relies on its organic quartermaster airdrop equipment support company and corps airdrop units for support. (See FM 10-400 for more information.)

Section II. PERSONNEL PLANS AND PREPARATION

Airborne operations pose all the personnel problems found in other types of operations. Many airborne unit administrative personnel remain at the rear base where administrative tasks are more efficiently performed. These factors usually require the airborne division to decentralize and delegate many of its personnel functions to brigades and battalions.

9-11. PERSONNEL STRENGTH ACCOUNTING

A record is kept of the personnel participating in the airborne assault and of those that remain in the departure area. After the assault landings have been made, the units of the airborne force submit strength reports as prescribed in the force SOP. They include the number of personnel from other units who have joined the reporting unit. Ideally, the air mission commander will notify the ground unit commander of personnel who do not exit the aircraft.

9-12. PERSONNEL REPLACEMENT OPERATIONS

Airborne operations should be launched with full-strength units. Replacements are retained at division level to fill initial combat losses, as required.

a. **Overstrength Replacements.** Personnel losses sustained during the initial stages (about the first three days) of the airborne operation are estimated and reported. These include loss estimates for the air movement and early ground phases. Shelf requisitions for overstrength replacements are based on the total loss estimate. These replacements should be received in time to be assigned to and train with subordinate units of the division. They do not participate in the initial airborne assault, but are held in the departure area and delivered to the objective area when required. Aircraft are allocated for the movement of overstrength replacements to the objective area.

b. **Unit Replacements.** It is desirable to have company- to battalion-size unit replacements briefed and available in the departure area for commitment as required. These units remain under the control of the next higher headquarters until released to the airborne commander.

c. **Other Replacements.** Replacements required besides overstrength replacements are requisitioned in the usual manner.

9-13. CASUALTY REPORTING

The first soldier having knowledge of casualties submits prompt, factual, and accurate casualty reports. This is done IAW appropriate regulations, through unit SOPS, and channels to headquarters DA for next-of-kin notification. The G1/AG and S1 prepare casualty-reporting plans, and furnish precombat instructions and procedures. Each echelon must prepare to make accurate and timely casualty reports. (See FMs 10-20 and 10-30 for a detailed discussion of casualty reporting at battalion and brigade level.)

9-14. HEALTH SERVICE SUPPORT

Limited numbers of tactical/strategic airframes or the limited duration of the mission (such as hostage rescue and withdrawal) makes comprehensive planning for austere operations necessary. Medical plans should include tailored medical packages to support the initial assault force, with follow-on support to arrive during the lodgment or subsequent operations phase. Health service support planners must be involved early in the planning process to ensure that timely and adequate medical support is provided to the deployed force. Planning considerations include, but are not limited to, the following:

- Medical threat.
- Casualty estimates.
- Anticipated areas of patient density.
- Anticipated casualty mix.
- Lines of patient drift.
- Field hygiene, sanitation, and other preventive medical considerations.
- Preplanned patient treatment stations, patient collecting points, and ambulance exchange points.
- Evacuation policy.
- Mode of evacuation.
- Augmentation for the provision of en route medical care on nonmedical vehicles.

- Augmentation for patient decontamination support.
- Mass casualty plans.

> **Note:** See FM 8-55 for a complete discussion of health service support planning factors.

a. **Health Service Support Planning.** The same principles of combat medical support that apply to other combat Army units also apply to airborne units. The mobility of airborne medical units must match that of the units they support. The medical units accompany soldiers at all times to provide prompt and efficient medical care and evacuation. Airborne and air assault divisions' medical support units are the only division-level medical elements that have emergency surgical capabilities.

(1) In short-duration operations, a very short-term evacuation policy is normal; usually less than 72 hours. When air evacuation is possible, necessary medical installations are near suitable airlanding facilities. When aircraft cannot land for purposes of evacuation, more medical facilities with an increased holding capacity will be required in the objective area.

(2) In long-duration operations, allowing for the establishment of medical facilities will permit a longer evacuation policy as the operation progresses. A firm policy for a long-duration operation cannot be established in advance; it is modified as circumstances permit or require.

(3) Evacuation and treatment elements of division-level health service support must enter the objective area early because unit-level health service support does not have a holding capability.

(4) Most of the division medical battalion is introduced into the airhead during the airland phase of the assault. One medical company is initially attached to the FAST to simplify operational control. The rest of the battalion is committed at a time and place that best supports the division as a whole and provides the best possible medical care. Medical battalion headquarters resumes control of subordinate companies supporting the brigade as early as possible to ensure effective use of the limited medical resources available in the airhead. Medical companies supporting brigades are scheduled for deployment early in the assault phase. They provide prompt relief for battalion aid stations temporarily performing an expanded treatment and holding mission. Unless the brigade mission requires offensive action over extended distances, the supporting medical company establishes a full-size clearing station near an LZ that is centrally located in the brigade sector.

(5) When a significant delay is anticipated between the deployment of medical companies and the scheduled arrival of Air Force aeromedical staging facilities in the airhead, the medical companies are reinforced by corps medical resources. These added resources provide the capability for holding patients and for helping to load them aboard evacuation aircraft.

(6) Medical company ambulance resources are reinforced to ensure the capability of simultaneous support to battalion aid stations and evacuation of patients from the clearing station to the LZ embarkation point. Elements of

the division medical battalion assigned to undeployed combat battalions are retained at departure airfields unless an extremely large patient work load develops in the airhead. One or more of the following methods can be used to evacuate from division clearing stations:

- Aeromedical evacuation from the airhead by the Air Force.
- Evacuation to airland corps medical units arriving in the airhead later in the operation.
- Evacuation through normal charnels after ground linkup.

(7) Medical elements of a division directed to link up with the airhead should be prepared to immediately supplement airhead medical support, to accept patient overloads, and to eliminate surgical backlogs in airhead clearing stations. The linkup division may require reinforcement to perform this relief mission.

(8) If corps medical resources are not readily available because of airframe shortage or limited response time, the division forward support medical company may have to assume some of the duties of the MASF. An aeromedical evacuation liaison team can be deployed with the medical company to interface with the AECC. The FSMC will assume the MASF duties of staging, manifesting, and locating the casualties.

b. **Phases of Employment.** Medical support planning is conducted for each phase of the airborne operation.

(1) Marshaling phase. Limited outload of divisional units from the CONUS base is accomplished by CSS within the division. Medical support for the outload of brigade-size or less airborne forces is accomplished with organic divisional medical assets. Medical support to a force greater than brigade-size must be provided by a fixed facility or corps-level medical units. Organic medical platoons within maneuver battalions and the lead medical company required during the deployment (assault) phase can provide only limited tailgate medical support to organic elements because personnel and equipment are preparing to deploy.

(2) Air movement and assault phase. Medical actions during this phase depend on the size of the deploying force. Unit members are cross loaded on multiple aircraft. This ensures that the loss of one aircraft does not keep other members of the unit from performing the mission. The fact that airborne operations usually occur at night to increase the elements of security and surprise adds further confusion on the DZ. The paratrooper must be able to perform independent actions (such as providing aid to himself and his buddy) because he maybe separated from the aidman during the initial assault.

(a) The medical platoon organic to the combat battalion provides immediate medical support on deployment. It has limited treatment capabilities and no holding capacity. After the initial parachute assault is completed, unit aidmen in the combat medic section link up with organic line companies and establish CCPs.

(b) As part of the DISCOM FAST, the FSMC provides division-level medical support to a two-battalion- to brigade-size element. The medical company can be tailored in size for the initial mission of the airborne assault (Alpha Echelon), with a follow-on complement (Bravo Echelon) to follow during airdrop or airland activities.

c. **Air Force Health Service Support.** The airborne unit collects and transports regulated patients to the Air Force MASF when it is established. It also provides patient staging in the airhead until the Air Force has facilities available. The Air Force, using the tactical aeromedical evacuation system, begins intratheater evacuation to supporting medical treatment units. The TAES is a highly mobile system designed to deploy/redeploy on short notice to any airfield, including the foremost assault airfields used to support combat ground forces. As a complete aeromedical evacuation subsystem, the TAES functions as a total system to provide interim medical care and expedite the evacuation of the sick and injured. In its deployed form, the TAES comprises three elements:

(1) The aeromedical evacuation liaison team coordinates with the MRO of the forward medical treatment units, the aeromedical evacuation control center, and the MASF to ensure a smooth and rapid flow of patients within the system.

(2) The AECC is the C^2 element for the subsystem, coordinating activities among the elements and ensuring tactical aircraft are made available to meet aeromedical evacuation requirements.

(3) The MASF provides short-term holding and supportive treatment for patients that are to be evacuated. The medical flight crews deployed in support of the TAES provide in-flight nursing care aboard the aircraft. In an emergency, personnel from the MASF can also provide in-flight nursing care.

The mission of the TAES is to evacuate patients between points of treatment within the combat zone, and from the combat zone to points outside. Using backhaul aircraft capability, TAES relieves combat commanders of patient care and protection. The MASF does not possess any aircraft or physicians. The aircraft are obtained from the ALCC and the physicians are at the origination and destination facilities. Therefore, it is vital that all patients be as stable as possible when they arrive at the MASF. Figure 9-3 (see page 9-18) shows request procedures for aeromedical evacuation via Air Force aircraft.

9-15. PRISONERS OF WAR AND CAPTURED MATERIEL

As with any combat operation, an airborne assault and the subsequent operations phase will produce PWS, captured materiel of the enemy, and damaged materiel both friendly and enemy. Plans must be made to handle these potential circumstances with limited physical battlefield clutter, to recover equipment for rehabilitation and reissue, and to process enemy PWs to minimize their effect on friendly operations.

a. **Prisoners of War.** Prisoners of war are captured and tagged with identifying information; then, they are evacuated from the objective area as directed by the airborne commander IAW instructions from higher headquarters. They are evacuated to designated facilities within the departure area. The Army processes, stages, and provides guards for the evacuation. Prisoner of war collection points are near airlanding facilities to ease air evacuation.

b. **Captured Materiel.** Captured materiel to be evacuated by air are designated, processed, and prepared for air movement by the Army IAW instructions from higher headquarters. An appropriate notation on the manifest informs the airlift unit of the classification, designation, and destination of materiel to be evacuated.

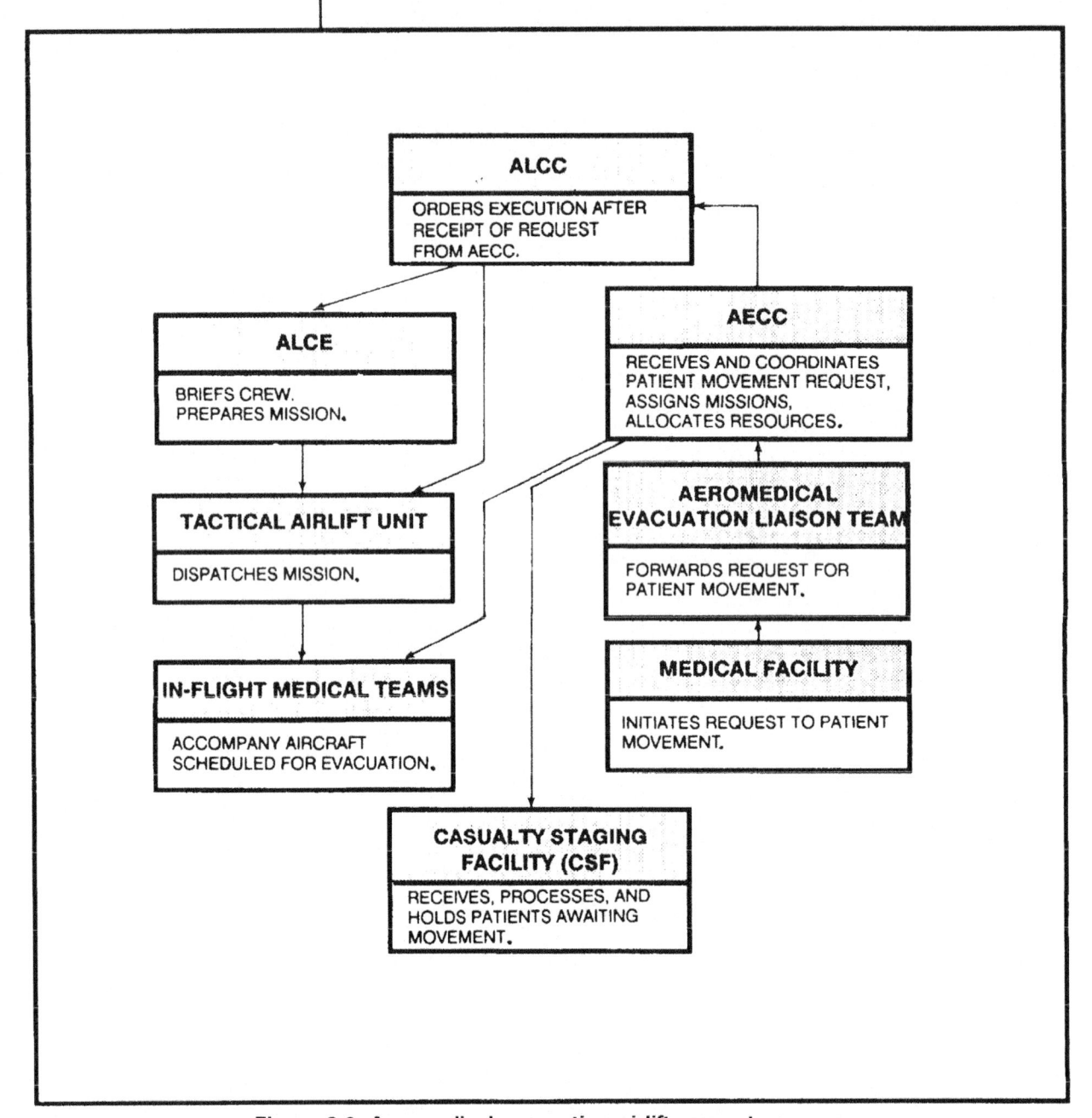

Figure 9-3. Aeromedical evacuation airlift request process.

9-16. OTHER PERSONNEL SERVICE SUPPORT

Other personnel support system functions include the following:

- Personnel actions.
- Personnel records.
- Administrative services.
- Chaplain activities.
- Legal services.
- Finance services.
- Morale support activities.
- Public affairs.
- Postal services.

(See FM 12-6 for more detailed information.)

a. **Personnel Actions.** Intense combat greatly reduces the processing of personnel actions. Therefore, actions that do not seriously affect morale receive a lower priority. Authority to process personnel actions is decentralized to the lowest organizational level consistent with effective management, but not so low that an unnecessary or unwanted administrative burden is placed on that level.

b. **Personnel Records.** Only the minimum individual personnel records required to support personnel services are kept within the theater. These records are maintained as far to the rear as possible, consistent with their use, and no further forward than division rear or separate brigade (regiment) rear. During contingency operations, personnel records are maintained in CONUS.

c. **Administrative Services.** The administrative services office of the G1 section provides only essential round-the-clock administrative services to the TOC and to the division main CP during combat operations.

d. **Chaplain Activities.** While the unit's religious program is under the authority of the unit commander, the chaplain is the commander's special staff officer responsible for implementing the program. He ensures personnel can freely exercise their religion. Unit chaplains perform and coordinate worship services, rites, sacraments, and religious observances. They give particular attention to providing religious services before deployment. The chaplain is also a personnel staff officer with direct access to the commander. (See FM 16-1 for more information.)

e. **Legal Services.** Legal services are provided to commanders and soldiers of the division by the Office of the Staff Judge Advocate. The judge advocate provides legal advice and assistance on all matters involving military, domestic, foreign, and international law and regulations. The staff judge advocate also supervises the administration of military justice, processes claims for and against the government, and furnishes legal assistance to authorized personnel. (See AR 210-1 and AR 210-10 for more information.)

f. **Financial Services.** Personnel deploying on an airborne operation will undergo processing for overseas replacement; any required pay documents will be completed at that time. Soldiers will be given the opportunity to buy invasion currency, if appropriate. Combat payments will also be offered, subject to the commander's approval. (See FM 14-7 for complete details of finance operations in a combat zone.)

g. **Morale Support Activities.** Morale, welfare, and recreation are the responsibility of the tactical force commander, but they depend on support from the rear support areas. The division G1 and brigade/battalion S1s are responsible for requesting external support from the corps/TAACOM.

h. **Public Affairs.** Commanders can expect a great deal of media interest in their activities as they prepare to deploy and conduct parachute operations. Deploying units should coordinate with the PAO to obtain information for briefings on soldier's responsibilities and rights when dealing with representatives from the media.

i. **Postal Services.** Outgoing mail is ordinarily suspended several days before the operation for security reasons. However, this fact need not be publicized. Because of the critical status of air transportation, incoming mail is usually suspended during the initial stage of airborne operations. Once the airhead is established, postal operations are located in the DSA and are composed primarily of mail-handling activities. Battalion mail clerks deliver outgoing mail to the postal section, and pick up incoming mail for delivery to soldiers assigned to their units. Unit mail clerks are responsible for the delivery of mail to each soldier. (See FM 12-6 for more information.)

9-17. CIVIL AFFAIRS

The G5/S5, if assigned, plans for civil affairs operations in the airhead. If the commander does not assign a G5/S5, the S1 assumes this role. During airborne operations, the airborne force cannot provide substantial care and assistance to the local populace beyond minimum needs. (See FM 41-10 for more information.) Civil affairs support includes civilian protection and control, labor, and equipment.

a. **Civilian Protection and Control.** Civil affairs takes population control measures, evacuates civilians from high-risk or sensitive areas, or relocates civilians from the airhead. This prevents congestion and provides space for military operations facilities.

b. **Civilian Labor.** Civil affairs identifies and locates civilians to work within the airhead. Civilian labor can handle supplies; construct airfields, field fortifications, and obstacles; and clear fields of fire. (See AR 210-10 for restrictions.)

c. **Civilian Equipment.** Civil affairs identifies and locates civilian equipment that can be used to support the airborne force. Key items include vehicles, construction equipment, and materiels-handling equipment.

CHAPTER 10

COMMUNICATIONS

Dynamic, effective leadership, more than any other element of combat power, decides victory. A reliable, durable, secure, quick, and flexible command and control system supports leaders. This system must communicate orders, coordinate support, and provide direction to the unit in spite of enemy actions, loss of command facilities, and loss of key leaders. The systems available to facilitate command and control of airborne operations have developed into detailed, universally understood operating procedures. These procedures are designed to enhance complex joint operations and to ensure that the airborne operaton capitalizes on surprise. This is achieved through centralized detailed planning that supports decentralized operations, emphasizing mission-type orders. The actions of the 82d Airborne Division during the invasion of Sicily in July 1943 demonstrate the need for a robust, flexible, command and control system and confirmed the key role mission-type orders play in airborne operations.

On 9 July 1943, the first of 226 planes loaded with 3,40.5 paratroopers and their equipment began taking off from departure airfields in northeastern Tunisia to take part in the invasion of Sicily. The force was composed of the 505th Parachute Infantry Regiment and the 3d Battalion of the 504th Parachute Infantry Regiment, along with other supporting units. The mission was to assist the 1st Infantry Division landing in Sicily, to capture the Parte Olivio airfield and to disrupt enemy communications and movement of reserves. This was the first time in military history that an airborne unit of this size had been given such a mission. It was also the largest night drop ever made.

During the flight across the Mediterranean, there was no interplane communication. A strong tail wind broke up the planned formations and blew some planes off course. As a result, many pilots missed their checkpoints and became lost. Some turned back but most continued on in the general direction of the island. Because the formations had been so badly broken up, planes approached Sicily from many directions. Once over land, the pilots found many of the planned DZs hidden by haze and dust from the preinvasion bombing. Many planes came under heavy antiaircraft fire and either turned away from their DZ or dropped their sticks of paratroopers early. Paratroopers and their equipment were spread over 60 miles of enemy-held territory-not dropped on the planned DZs.

Despite the scattered drop that forced drastic changes to the original plans, each soldier knew his mission When paratroopers realized they were not on their correct DZs, they immediately organzied into small groups led by whatever officers or NCOs were present. They began disrupting enemy communications, destroying enemy positions, halting enemy movement toward the landing beaches, and fighting their way to their orginal objectives. Later, Italian prisoners estimated the number of American paratroops to be between 20,000 and 30,000, a considerably larger number than the actual 3,405 paratroopers of the 82d Airborne Division.

During an interview after the war, General Kurt Student, commander of the German paratroops during the war, gave his assessment of the airborne operation in Sicily. He described it as effective even though the paratroopers were widely scattered. In his opinion, the amphibious landing could have been driven back to the sea if the soldiers of the 82d Airborne Division had not blocked the German reserves.

A comprehensive communications system has developed since the operation in Sicily. The system requires detailed planning and coordination to ensure effective control during airborne operations. This chapter outlines a communications system that allows the battalion or brigade commander to act within the operational concepts of AirLand Battle doctrine. (See FM 101-5, FM 7-20, and FM 7-30 for additional information and doctrine on C^2 for all levels of command.)

10-1. FUNDAMENTALS FOR USING SIGNAL FACILITIES

Several guiding fundamentals exist for using signal facilities in airborne operations C^2.

a. Airborne forces use all available means of communication with priority to command channels.

b. Airborne commanders have access to all signal facilities controlled by the USAF on a common-user basis.

c. Commanders exchange LOs with radios to maintain contact between headquarters and to ensure close real-time coordination.

d. Commanders coordinate with and thoroughly brief all personnel to include supporting combat aviation, airlift forces, higher headquarters, lateral units, and follow-on ground units. The briefings ensure proper use of a large number of channels in the integrated system.

e. Commanders ensure positive and continuous communication by establishing alternate or duplicate channels and routes of signal communication.

f. To ensure radio contact, commanders must make provisions for relaying or retransmitting messages.

g. Essential signal personnel must move in the first air serials; all subsequent signal units precede the echelon they serve.

h. Elements cross load communications personnel and identify them with their key leaders for relocation in the bump plan.

i. The joint commander establishes communications with the airborne and airlift commanders.

10-2. CONSIDERATIONS

Airborne operations require communications between all elements, which is not always easy. Communications inherent in airborne operations are discussed herein,

a. The use of special navigational aids and horning devices to lead the aircraft to the correct DZ,/LZ can cause communications problems. Highly specialized airborne force personnel (CCT/LRSU) equipped with navigational aids, homing devices, radar, and visual signals must be airdropped into the objective area in advance. Personnel can then set up their equipment to guide subsequent aircraft.

b. For proper control in the subsequent movement of personnel, supplies, and equipment into the objective area, units in the area must have long-range radio communication with the rear base. Units initially establish long-range radio communications from higher to lower headquarters. The higher headquarters can be on land, sea, or air many miles from the objective area. Often, they must maintain contact through a system of relays or retransmission sites.

c. Airlift forces bringing reserves or supplies require air-ground radio communications when–

- The operation is aborted.
- The weather prevents the planned resupply.
- The enemy gains control of the DZs/LZs/EZs.
- Undetected antiaircraft installations exist along the line of flight and preclude resupply.
- Reserves are needed at any one of several points other than the primary DZ/LZ.

d. Close air support plays a more important role in airborne operations than in normal operations. The airborne commander needs direct and positive radio communication with supporting CAS until sufficient fire support assets can be delivered to the airhead.

e. Key leaders jump with their tactical radios or use small handheld radios to quickly establish control once on the ground. Also, small radios can be carried in by soldiers or parachuted into the area in separate containers. The method of delivery and the need for ground mobility impose limitations on the size, weight, and amount of communications equipment for RATELOs. Larger vehicular-mounted sets can be brought in by heavy-drop platforms or airland aircraft.

> **NOTE:** Units plan for alternate means of communications to prevent loss of signal security. (See FM 24-1 for tactics and techniques.)

f. Commanders must resolve C^2 relationships, nets, frequency management, codes, navigation aids, and a myriad of other details before mission execution. The operation's joint nature creates the greatest potential for communication problems. Contingency plans, rehearsals, and joint SOIs aid the commanders in resolving problems. Airspace control and air defense communications deserve special attention for three fundamental reasons:

(1) DZs or LZs have a high volume of air traffic.

(2) Close air support initially provides the main means of fire support.

(3) The enemy might respond first by air, so Army air defense systems must quickly distinguish friend from foe to prevent fratricide.

10-3. COMMUNICATIONS PLANS

Commanders must prepare C^3 plans. These ensure integration and coordination of the signal facilities of each of the following airborne force components:

- Airlift units.
- US Naval, US Air Force, and artillery units that provide fire support.
- The command that retains control until it makes contact with advancing ground forces.
- The commander of advancing ground forces.
- Friendly advancing units with whom contact is expected in the airhead.

a. **Communications Plan.** Communications plans for airborne forces should include the following:

(1) Procurement of additional personnel for special communications facilities.

(2) Preparation of SOPs and SOIs.

(3) Headquarters communication to subordinate, adjacent, higher, and other concerned headquarters.

(4) Allocation of frequencies, channels, codes, and ciphers not included in the SOI.

(5) Instructions to subordinate signal officers concerning proposed signal responsibilities.

(6) Distribution of plans and orders for all units in the marshaling area.

(7) Signal intelligence and signal security.

(8) Use of joint and special cryptographic aids.

(9) Communications personnel and equipment to go into the airhead by teams with each serials.

(10) Communications equipment and supplies to be landed by aircraft and the sequence of their delivery. (This should include extra equipment to replace losses expected in the assault.)

(11) Signal unit elements that remain at the departure airfield to aid in the movement of communications supplies and equipment.

(12) Location of the rear echelon in the airhead or at the departure airfield/ISB and the communications personnel required.

(13) The installation and operation of communications channels used for air support requests.

(14) In addition to provisions for the standard ground communications system airborne communications plans must be provided for the following:

- JAAP units.
- Small-unit assembly in the forward area.
- Contact nets.
- Communication to and among base elements that remain in the departure area.

b. **Communications During Marshaling.** Communications during marshaling mainly concerns facilities provided by the MACG and the USAF. Airborne force communications personnel are mainly concerned with preparing for the operation.

(1) Facilities furnished by the MACG can include FM radio, HF radio, TACSAT, retransmission, wire, telephone, teletype, facsimile, and messenger sevice.

(2) Airborne and airlift unit communications centers maintain close liaison.

(3) For prompt relay of messages, signal personnel must maintain telephone, teletype, and auxiliary radio channels between the airborne headquarters in the rear area and the temporary headquarters in the departure area.

(4) Communications required to control the dispersed elements of the command in the several departure areas depend on–

(a) Length of time various elements are to be in the marshaling area.

(b) Communications facilities of the US Army and USAF units in the marshaling areas.

(c) Possibility of establishing a permanent rear echelon at the departure area.

(d) Requirements for communications with points of arrival and departure.

(e) Availability of personnel and equipment not destined for immediate tranfer into the airhead.

(5) Higher headquarters has the responsibility to establish an internal wire net within the marshaling area.

(6) Units must use existing facilities.

c. **Communications During Air Movement.** En route to the objective area, the airborne commander can use SECOMP to pass changes in the plan to other aircraft loads. In the absence of SECOMP, aircrews can relay messages. Aircraft key personnel or jumpmasters use internal PA systems to pass changes to onboard personnel. To pass key intelligence updates or to initiate contingency plans, selected aircraft have hatch-mounted SATCOM radios. These radios can receive transmissions from reconnaissance or JAAP teams in the objective area or from the rear CP at the marshaling camp or REMAB.

d. **Communications in the Objective Area.** The airborne force communications officer plans communications for the objective area. These plans include the following

(1) An assault net to operate early during the operation in the objective area.

(2) A transition from the assault net operations to the normal C^2 nets.

(3) Communications from the objective area are to–

- Airlift forces.
- Follow-on forces.
- Higher headquarters.
- Supporting tactical air elements.
- Departure airfield (if possible).
- Linkup forces (if applicable).

e. **Consolidation and Exploitation.** Communications during consolidation and exploitation of an airhead are the same as for other ground operations.

10-4. ARMY NETS

Army C^2 radio nets provide flexible communications for the initial assault phase of an airborne operation, for quick displacement of CPs, and for periods when commanders must maintain voice communication.

a. **Predeployment TACSAT/IHF Net.** Communications personnel from the deploying unit's higher headquarters install, operate, and maintain this net. Units use it for a variety of purposes, including intelligence updates and receipt of combat information from LRSUs or the JAAP. (Figure 10-1.) LRSUs or JAAPs operating in this net arrange predetermined contact times. They establish code words or procedures to indicate when the LRSU/JAAP net is operating under duress. The senior commander establishes contingency plans and procedures for when the LRSU/JAAP and headquarters miss their communications checks.

b. **Outload Net.** The deploying Army unit commander uses an outload net to monitor and control unit outload. (Figure 10-2.) The unit uses either small handheld radios or standard FM equipment, and should always use a secure net. FM equipment comes from a support unit employed until load time, so the deploying unit can load its own equipment. If the deploying unit uses handheld radios, it must coordinate frequencies to prevent interference with aviation operations.

FM 90-26

*1. IOM by supporting communications units.
**2. NCS.

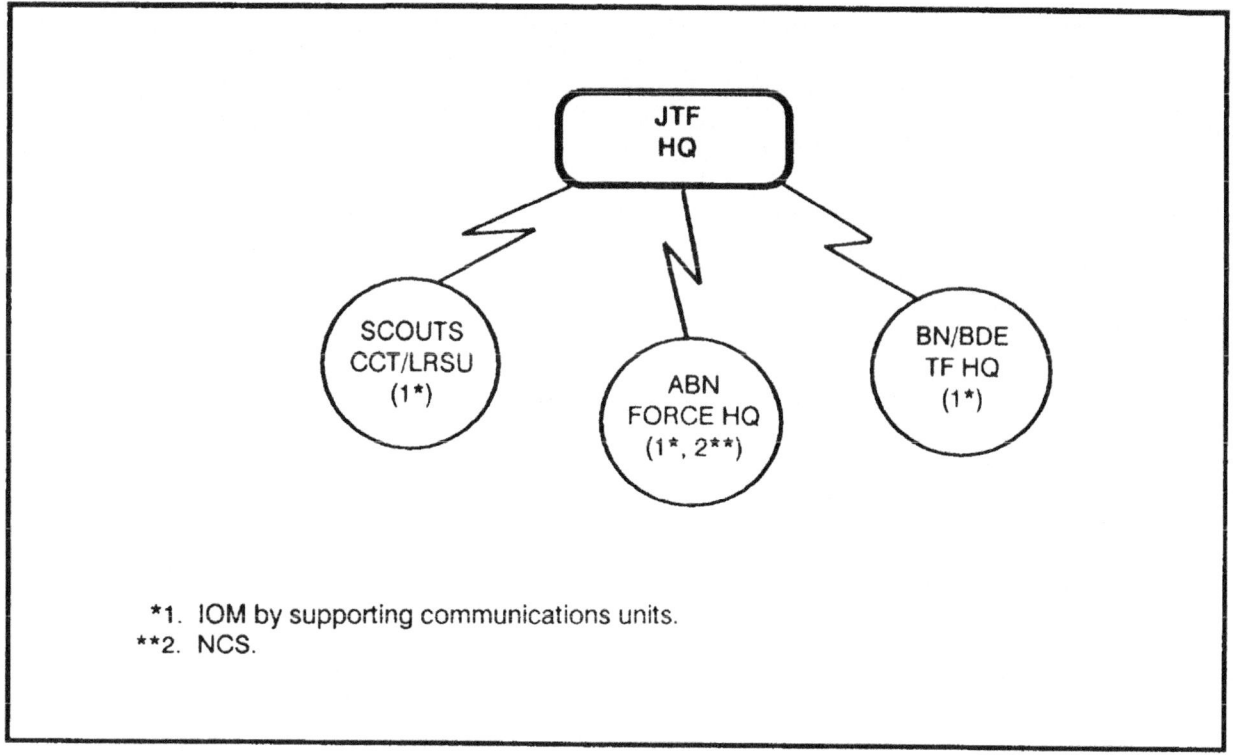

Figure 10-1. Predeployment TACSAT/IHF net.

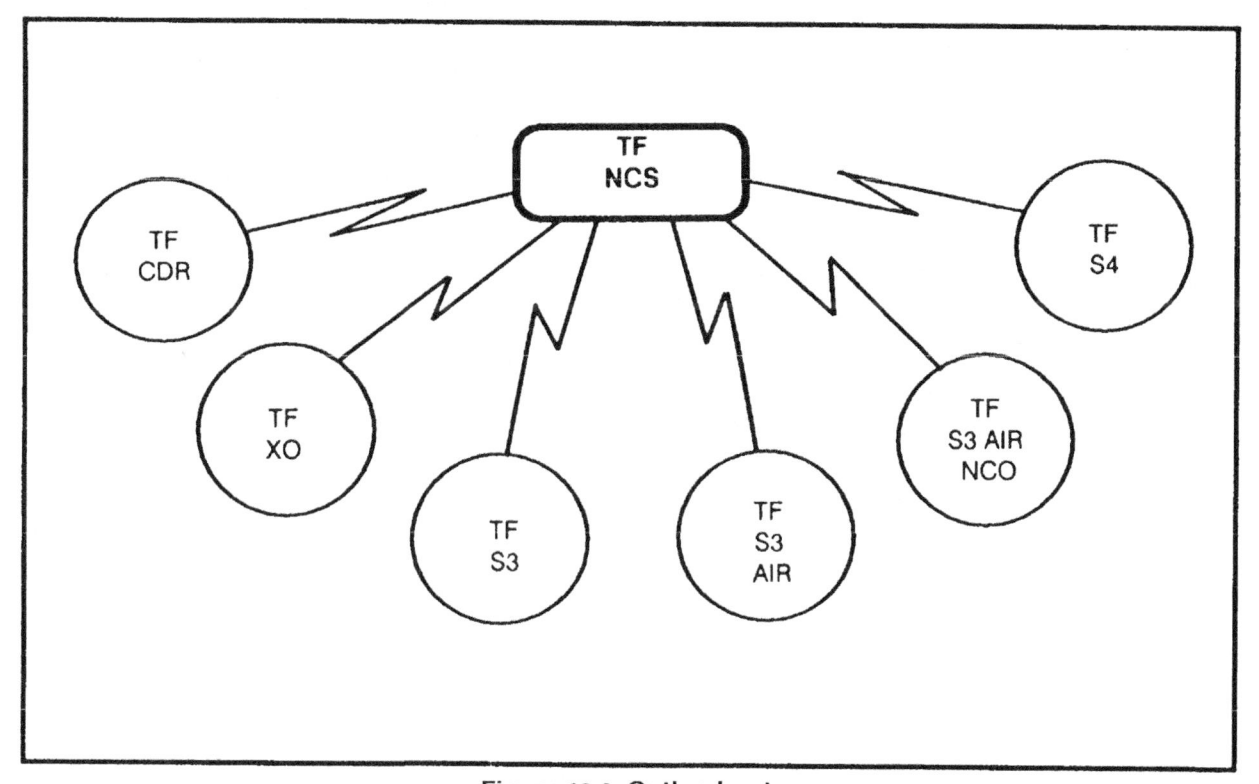

Figure 10-2. Outload net.

10-7

c. **En Route (LOS) VHF SECOMP Net.** The airborne commander uses this net to relay instructions and updates to subordinates in other aircraft. (Figure 10-3.) Supporting communications personnel install, operate, and maintain it. Although it is a secure net, the enemy may still detect transmissions Therefore, either US Army or USAF commanders can impose listening silence restrictions, mainly during penetration. The airborne commander's aircraft acts as the net control station.

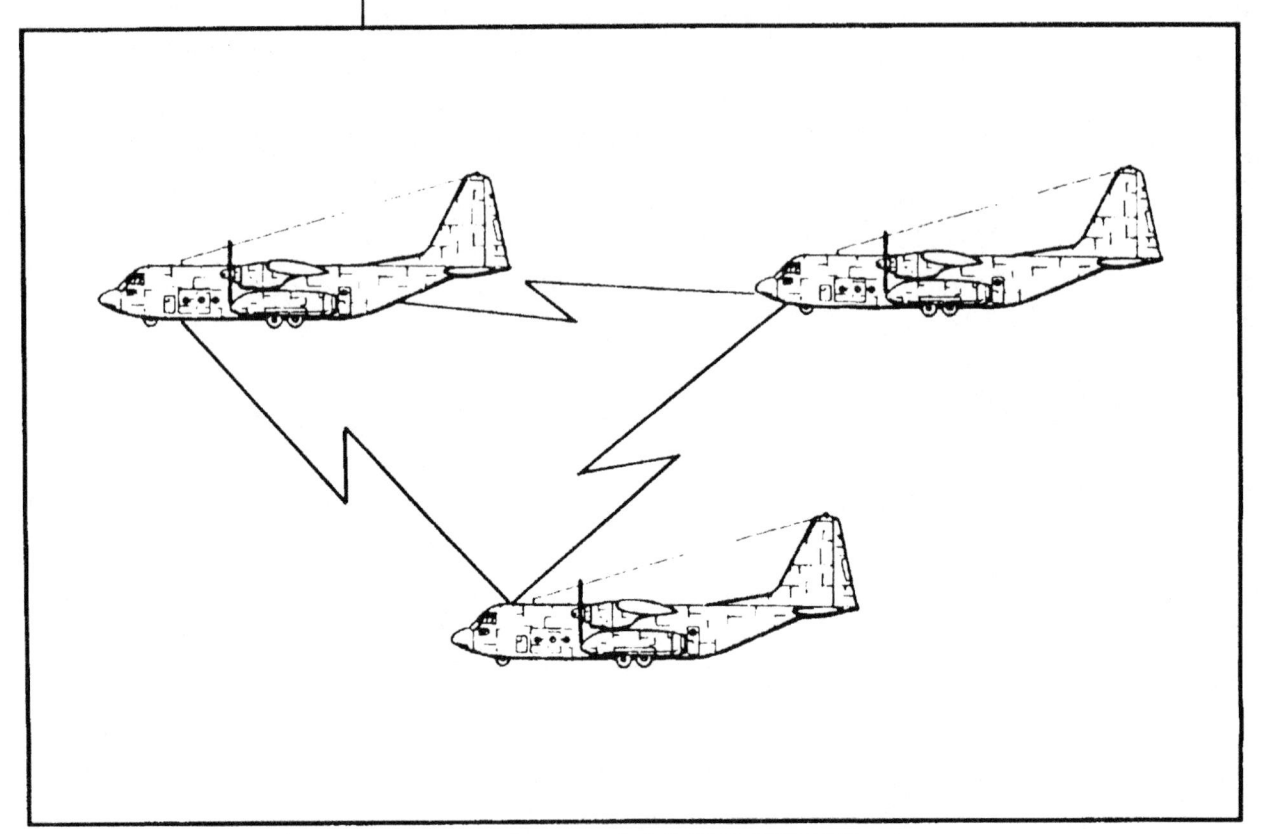

Figure 10-3. En route (LOS) VHF SECOMP net.

d. **En Route TACSAT Net.** Supporting communications units install, operate, and maintain this net; operators and equipment remain on the aircraft. (Figure 10-4.) The secure TACSAT net links the airborne force commander, airborne rear CP (which acts as NCS), ABCCC, and JAAP. This allows rapid adjustments and implementation of alternate plans that result from last-minute intelligence or combat information. Airborne elements can practice listening silence LRSU/JAAP and rear CP elements can employ blind transmissions to provide situation updates. To ensure that this net remains operational, at least two aircraft in the formation must have TACSAT capability. If ground aborts occur, the airborne commander can move to the second aircraft as part of the bump plan. If an air abort or communications malfunction occurs, the formation still has TACSAT communication with the objective area and the rear CP.

FM 90-26

*1. IOM by supporting communications units.
**2. NCS.

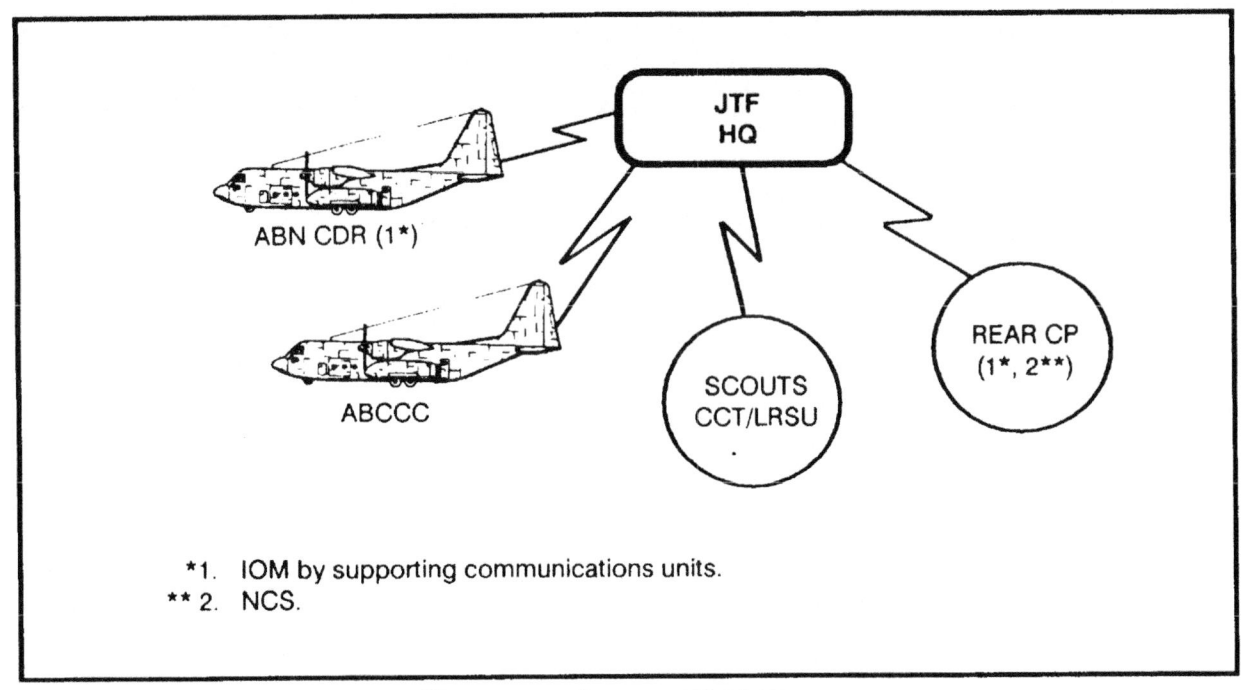

Figure 10-4. En route TACSAT net.

e. FM Nets. Brigade- and battalion-level TFs employ the following FM nets:

(1) *Brigade command net.* User stations install, operate, and maintain this FM-secure net. (Figure 10-5.) The brigade TOC serves as the NCS. This net can serve as the assault net for the initial phase of the airborne assault.

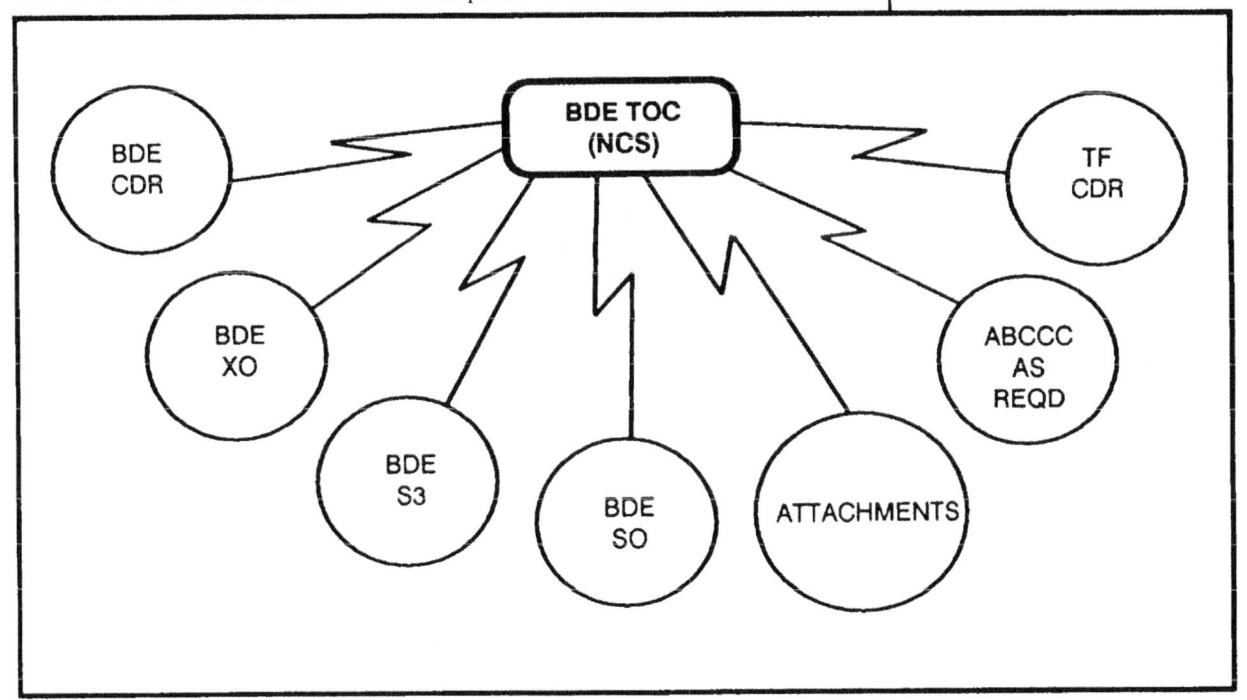

Figure 10-5. Brigade command net.

(2) *Brigade operations and intelligence net.* Units use this FM-secure net to pass routine and recurring intelligence reports. (Figure 10-6.)

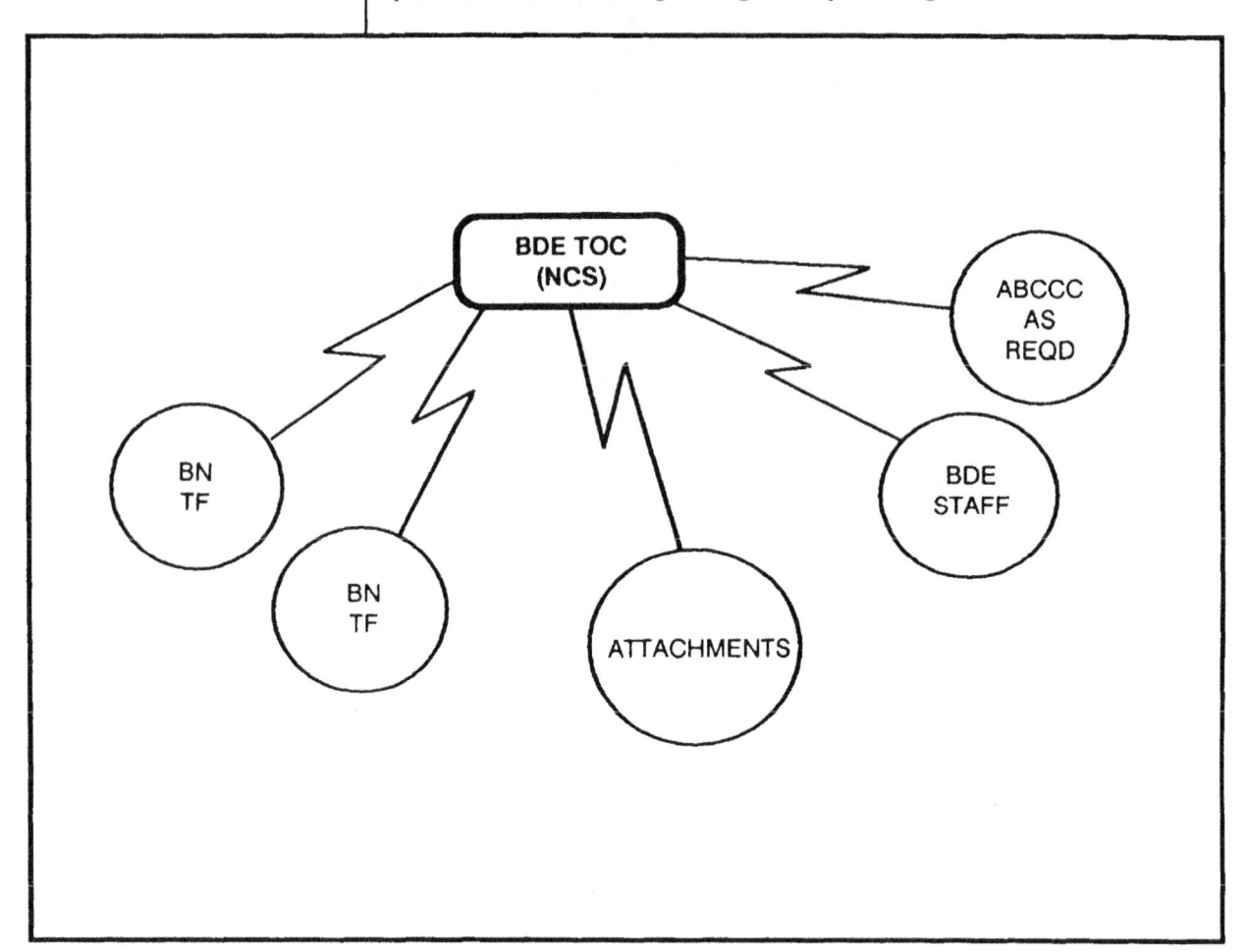

Figure 10-6. Brigade operations and intelligence net.

(3) *Brigade administrative and logistics FM net.* The Brigade S4 in the BSA serves as the NCS for this secure FM net. The net is used to coordinate CSS during ground operations. (Figure 10-7.)

(4) *Battalion task force command net.* Users install, operate, and maintain this FM-secure net, which serves as the assault net for the battalion. (Figure 10-8.) The TF TOC serves as the NCS.

(5) *Battalion task force operations and intelligence net.* Scouts, combat and reconnaissance patrols, and attached MI assets can use this FM-secure net as a reporting net. (Figure 10-9, page 10-12.) Assets for this net may have to be allocated from other noncommitted units to provide communications equipment to units.

(6) *Battalion task force administration and logistics net.* The unit S4 in the combat trains serves as the NCS for this secure FM voice net. (Figure 10-10, page 10-12.) The S4 uses it to coordinate CSS during ground operations.

FM 90-26

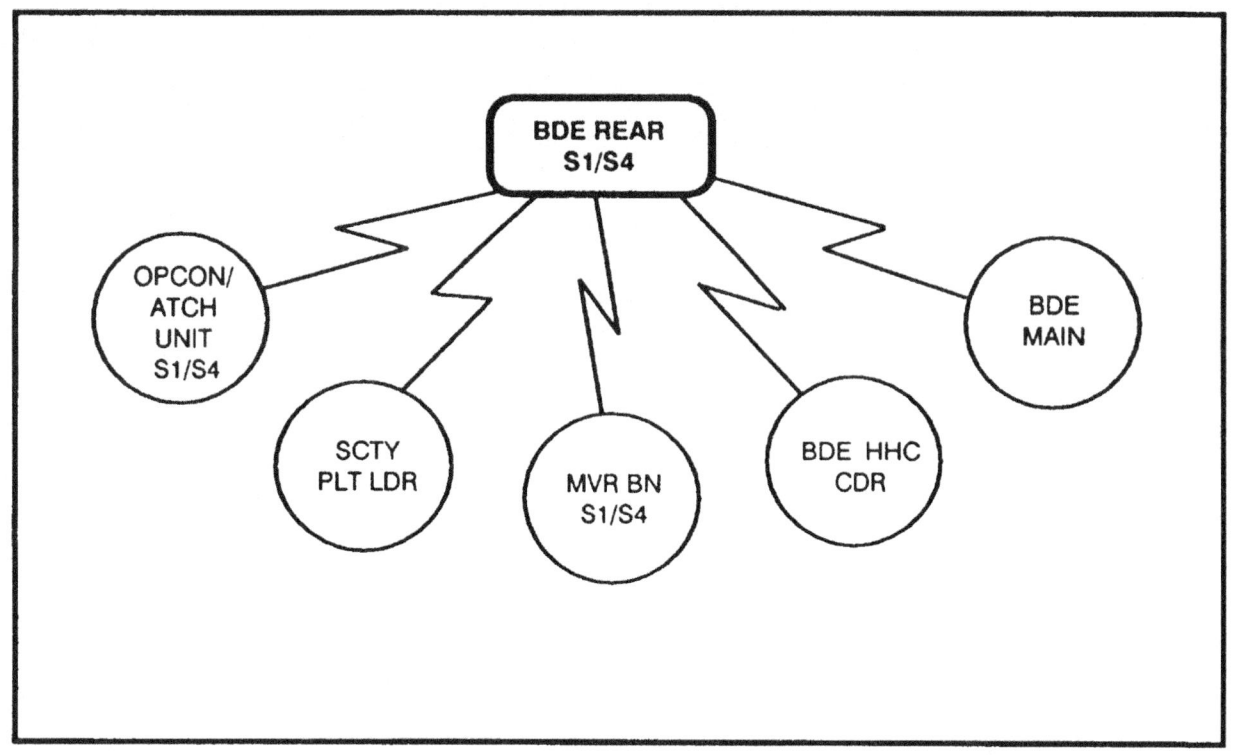

Figure 10-7. Brigade administration and logistics net.

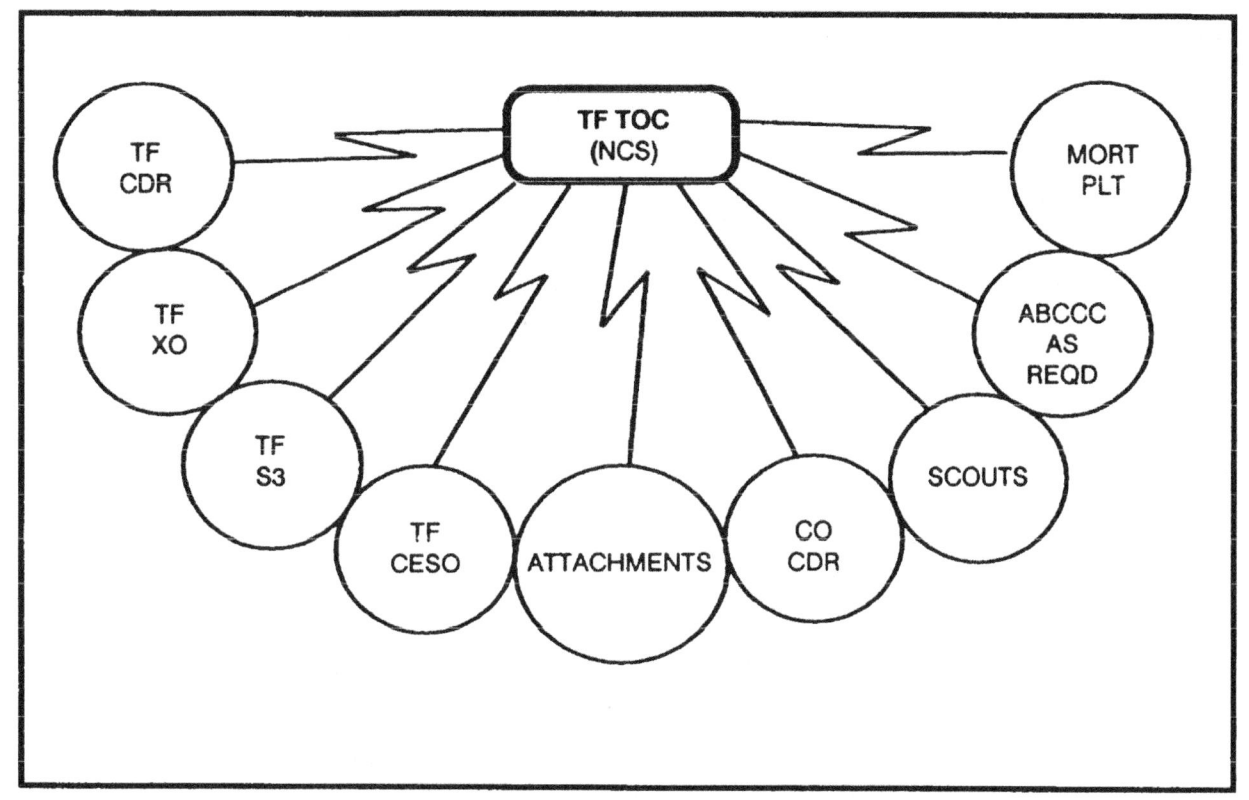

Figure 10-8. Battalion task force command net.

10-11

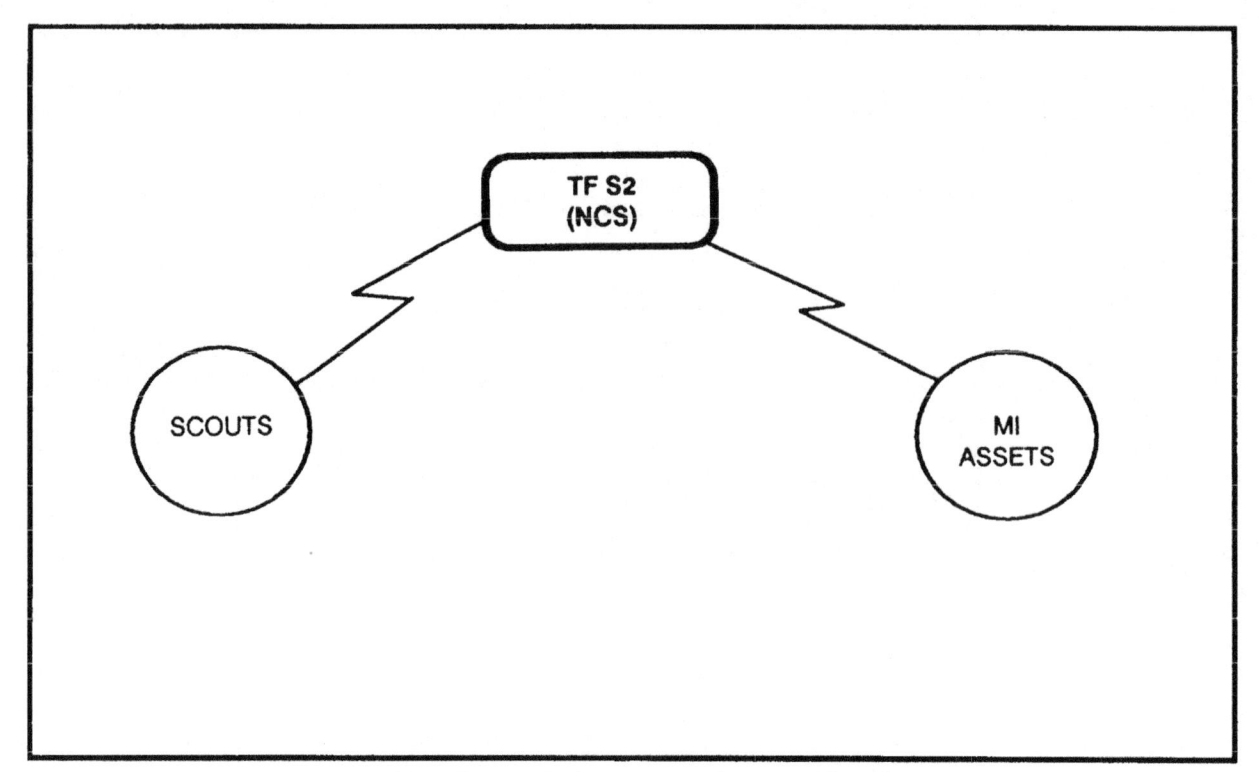

Figure 10-9. Battalion task force operations and intelligence net.

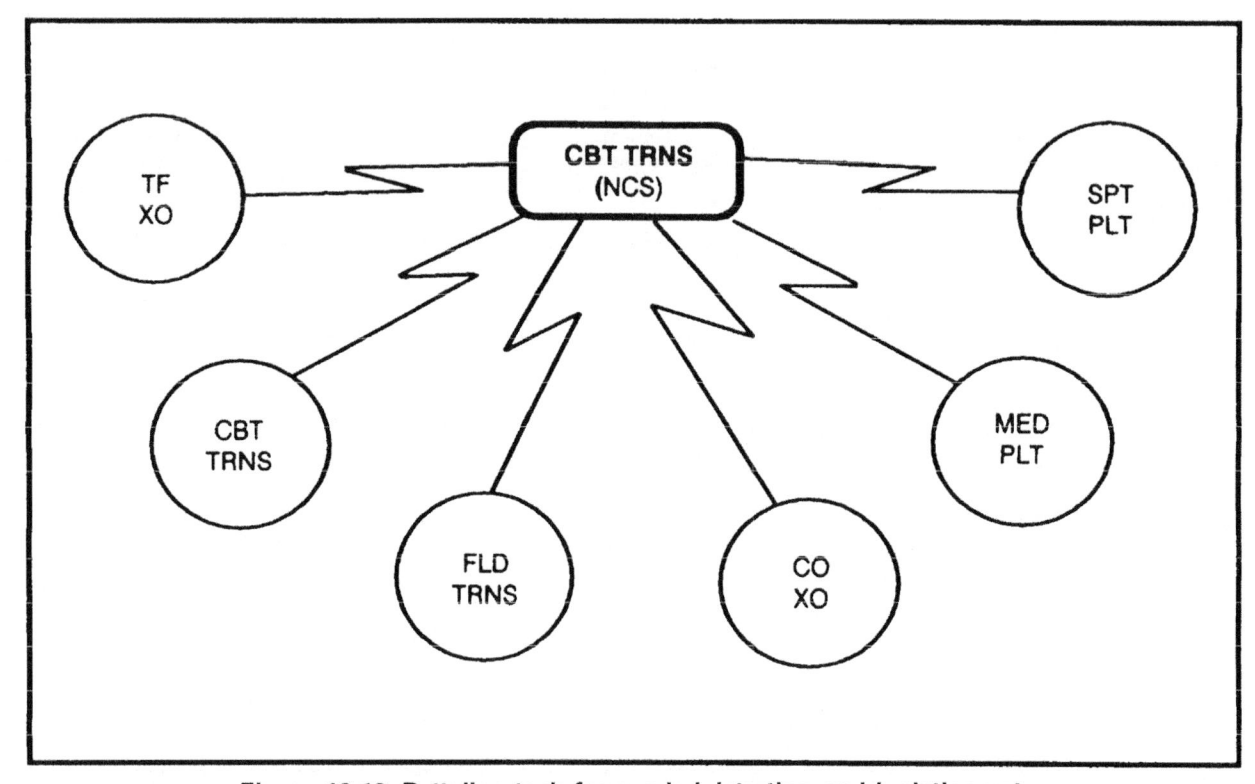

Figure 10-10. Battalion task force administration and logistics net.

f. **Special-Purpose Nets.** Units employ the following nets for special purposes connected with the conduct of airborne operations.

(1) *Airfield seizure net.* This secure net requires standard FM voice equipment normally handheld. (Figure 10-11.) Units use this net to command and control the airfield seizure operations during the airborne assault.

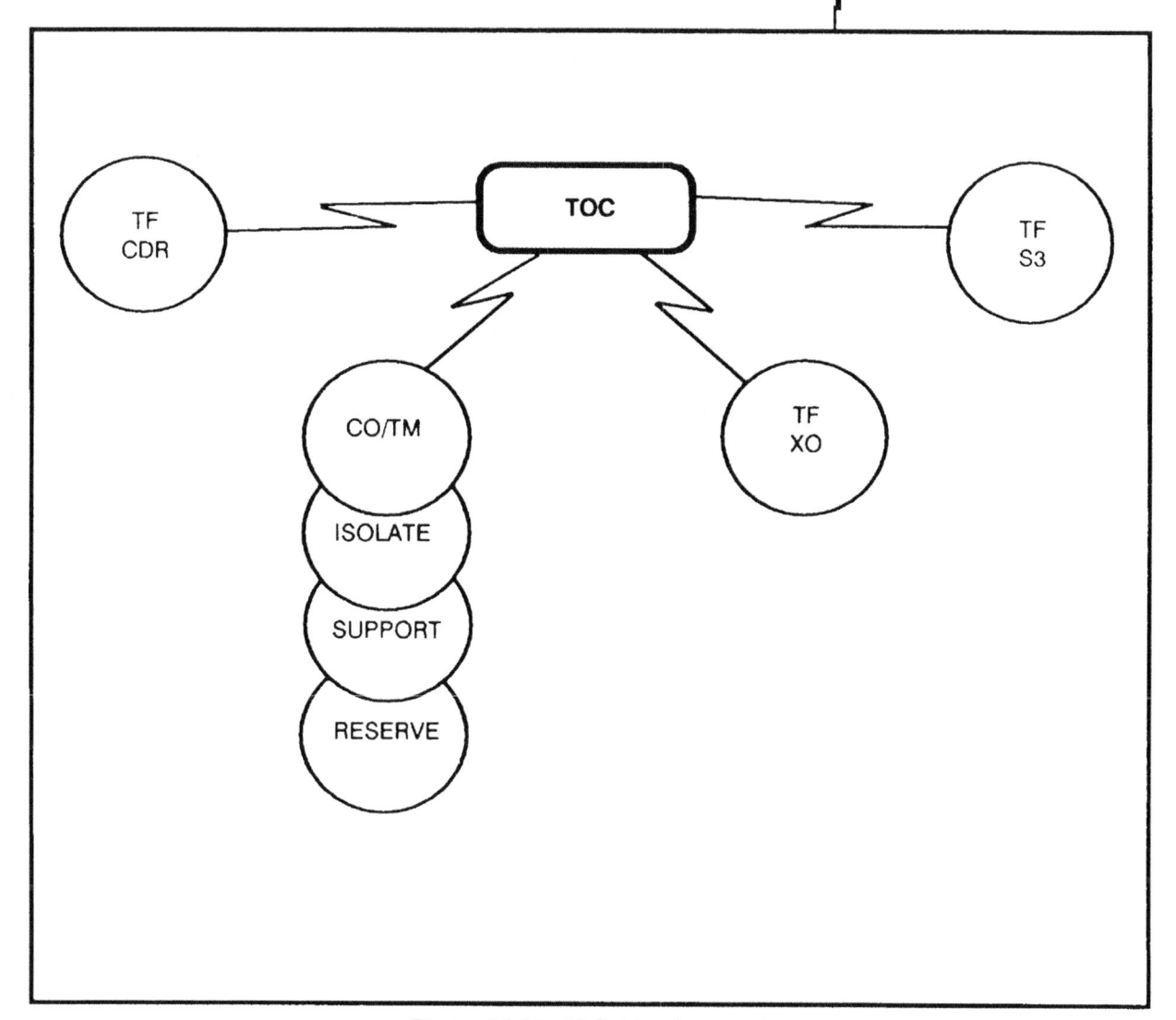

Figure 10-11. Airfield seizure net.

(2) *Airfield control net.* The TOC uses this FM voice net to control and coordinate airfield activities and airland sortie arrivals. (Figure 10-12, page 10-14.) The A^2C^2 element includes at least the S3 air officer, FSO, ADA officer, and TACP. Optional elements include aviation liaison personnel, Army ATC personnel, and ANGLICO personnel. Need and communications availability determine who participates in this net. When feasible, wire communications should supplement radio communications.

FM 90-26

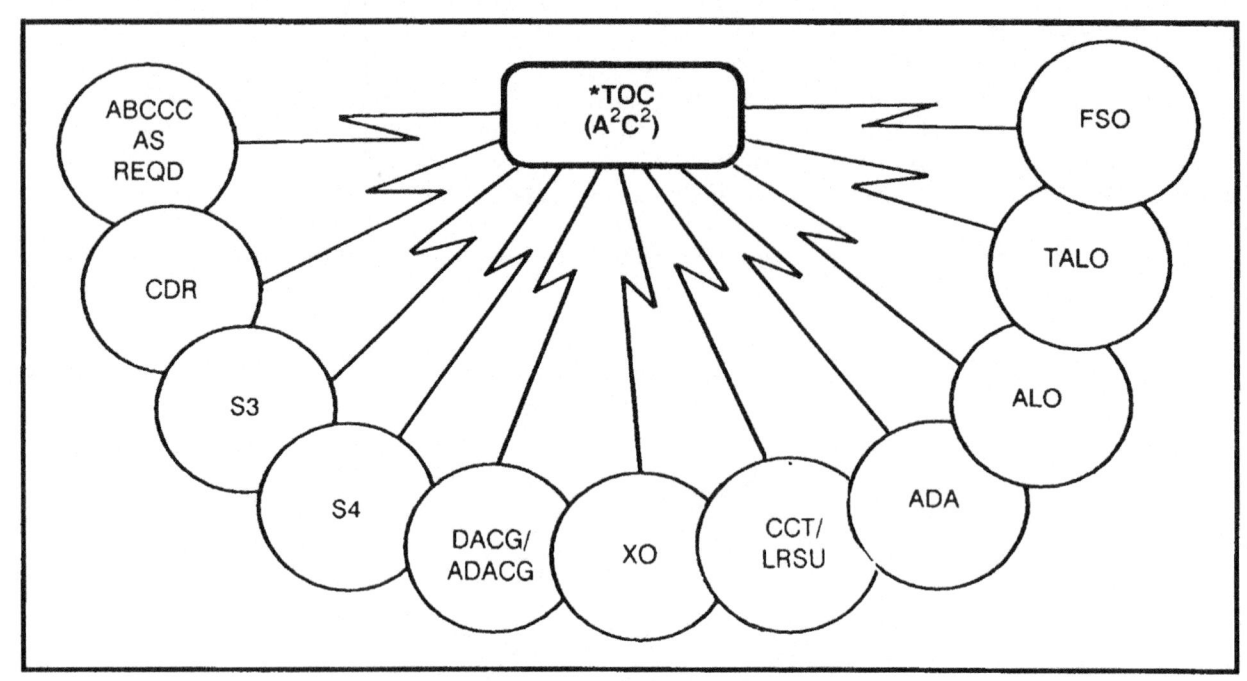

Figure 10-12. Airfield control and coordination net.

(3) *Air traffic control net.* This net actually includes two nets (UHF and VHF) for control of fixed- and rotary-wing communications. (Figure 10-13.) Collocated CCT/ATC elements act as the NCS for this net.

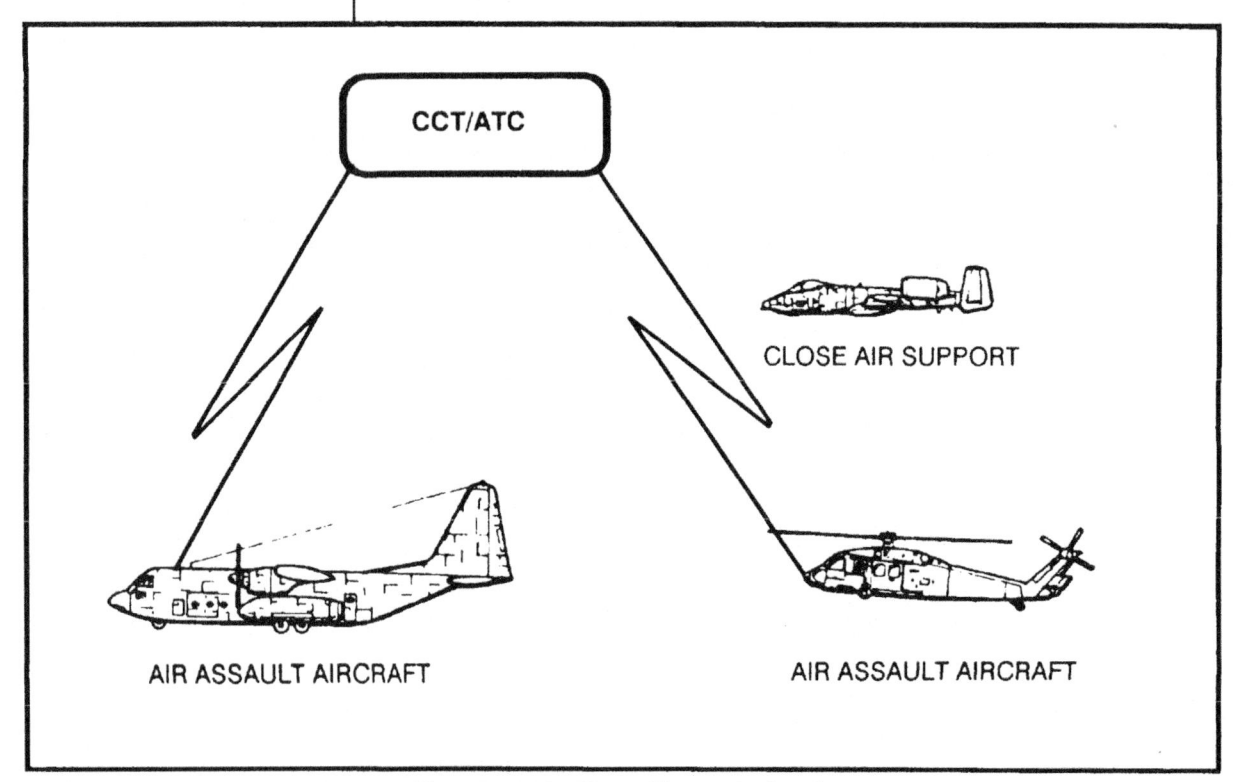

Figure 10-13. Air traffic control net.

10-14

(4) *JTF TACSAT VHF voice net.* This net interfaces TACSAT to FM. It allows the ground commander to talk to the JTF commander, the ISB, R&S forces, or other units via FM radio. (Figure 10-14.) This arrangement provides the advantages of TACSAT range and FM radio mobility. The JTF operations center serves as the NCS. Supporting communications units install, operate, and maintain this system. Planning for employment must include a TACSAT-to-FM interface frequency.

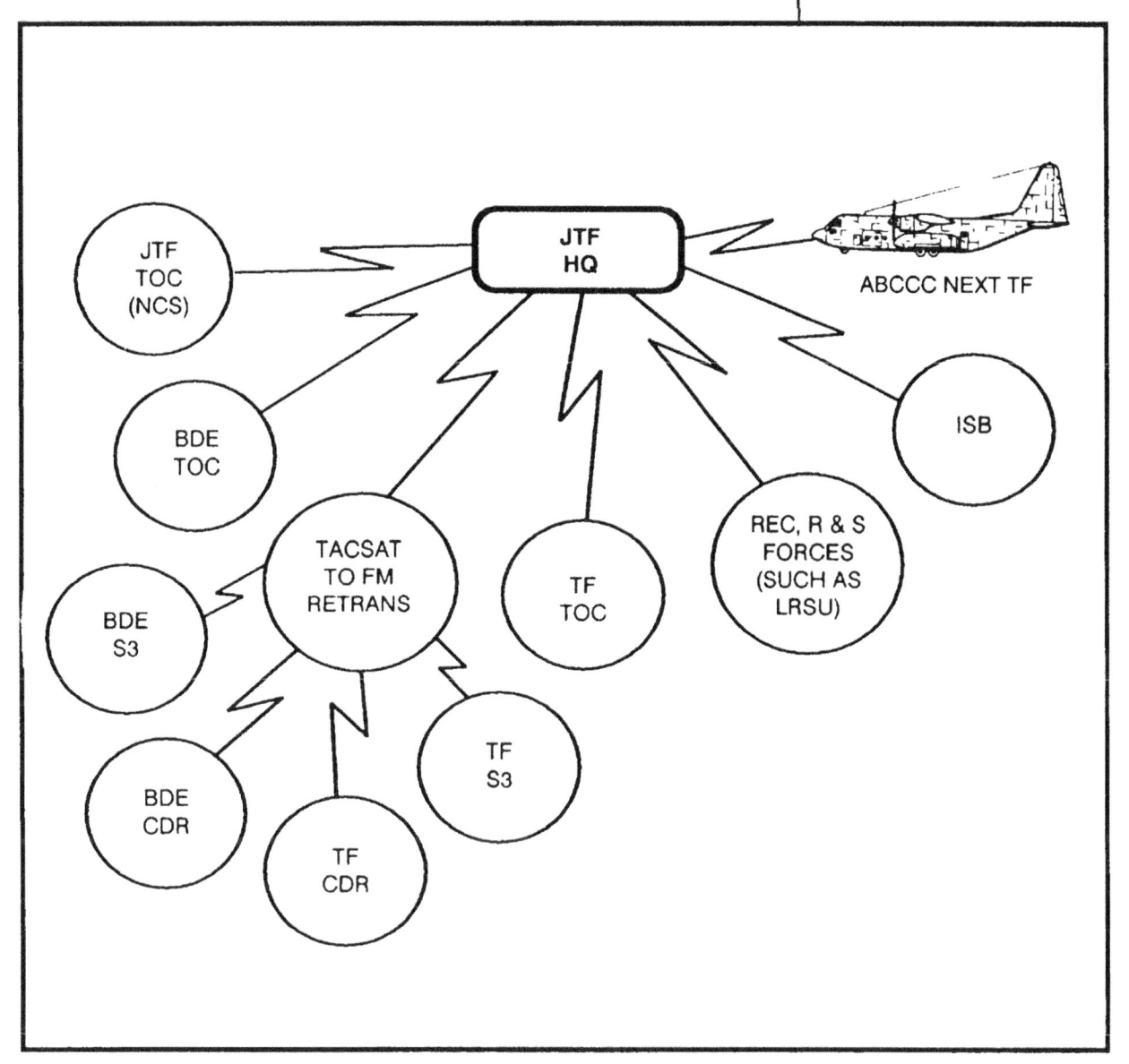

Figure 10-14. JTF TACSAT VHF voice net.

(5) *JTF TACSAT VHF data net.* This net provides facsimile support to elements of the JTF by rapidly transmitting plans, orders, and overlays. (Figure 10-15, page 10-16.) Supporting communications units install, operate, and maintain it. The JTF operations center functions as the NCS.

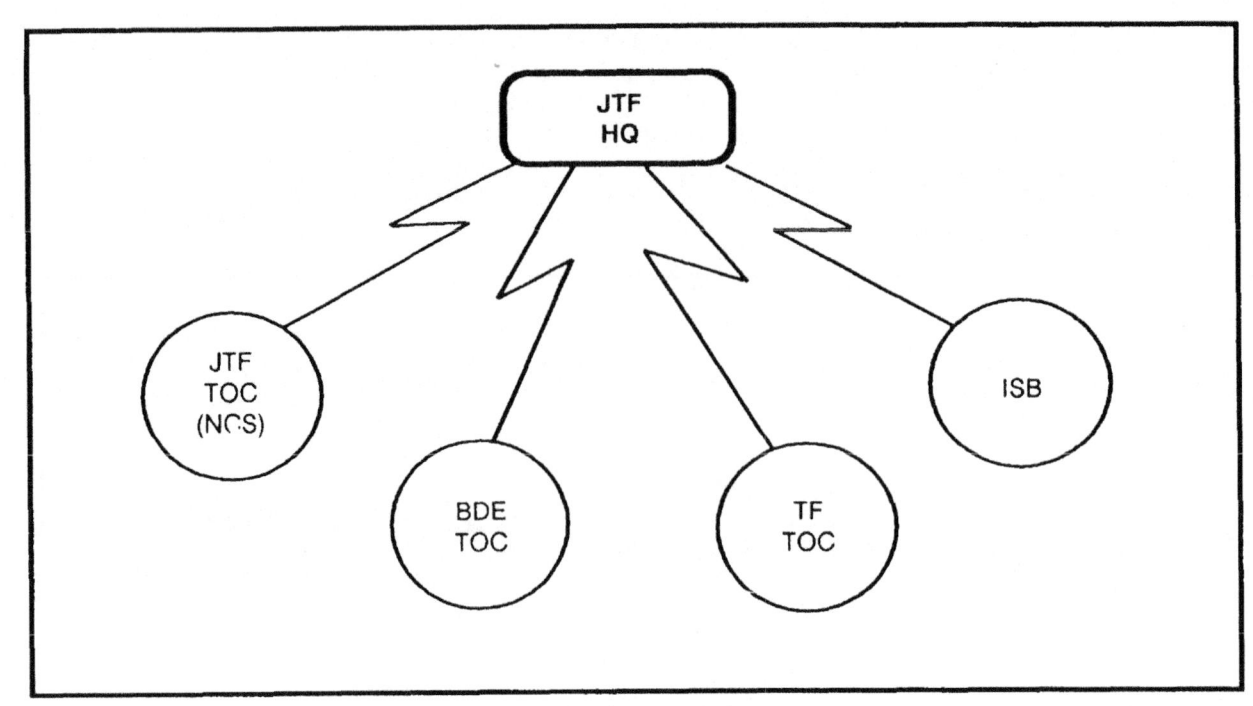

Figure 10-15. JTF TACSAT VHF data net.

(6) *Brigade radio teletypewriter net.* Units employ this RATT net to send hard-copy messages for long distances without reliance on SATCOM assets. (Figure 10-16.) Along with IHF radios, it serves as a SATCOM backup system.

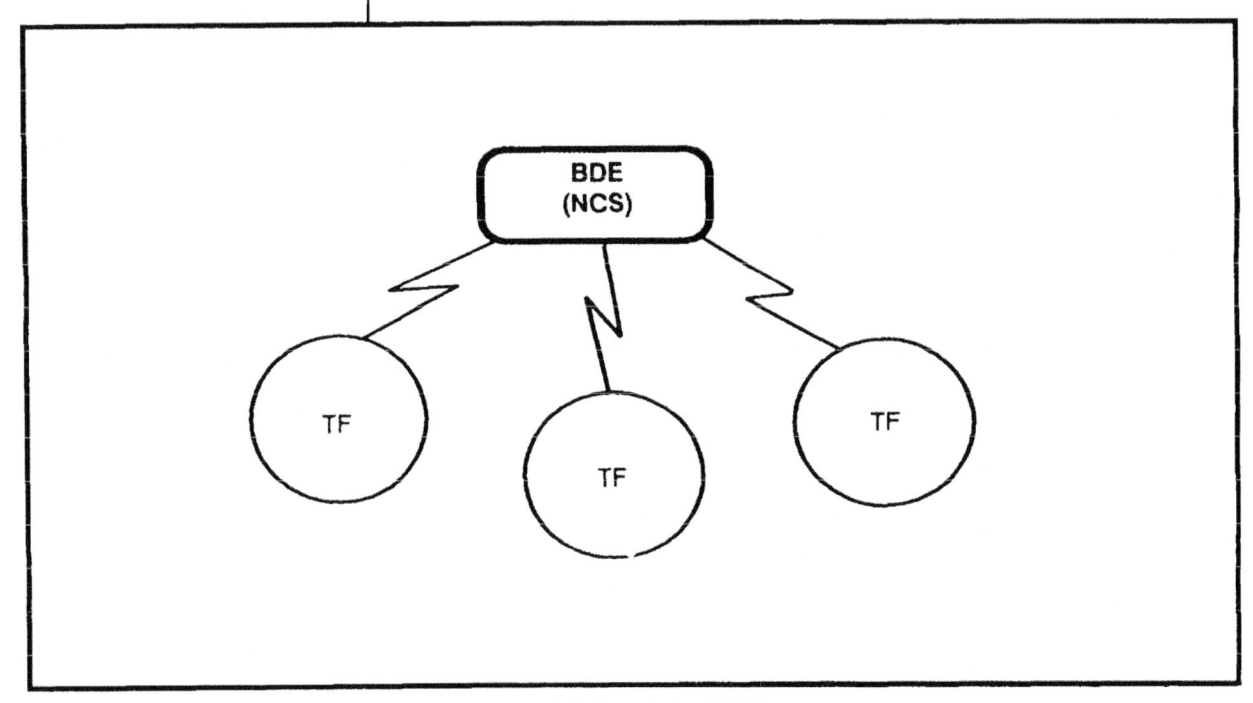

Figure 10-16. Brigade RATT net.

10-5. TECHNIQUES

The C^2 communications techniques depend on the communications equipment, which depends on the type, size, and mission of the unit.

a. **Initial Radio Communications.** Airborne units committed by parachute depend on lightweight, two-way radios; visual communications; and messengers. They can use TACSAT to send messages back to the rear echelon. The dispersion of landing forces and the quick action required for success on landing make communications difficult to establish and maintain.

b. **Reinforced Radio Communications.** Units can airdrop extra wire and radios and other communications equipment mounted on vehicles. The value of the vehicular-mounted radios in airborne operations lie in the unit's mobility-CPs and units are moving during the initial phase of an airborne operation. Units can also use longer-range vehicular-mounted radios to communicate with CAS and airlift aircraft; elements of the land, sea, or air LOC; and the rear support base. COMSEC is crucial, and units must train and rehearse regularly to maintain COMSEC.

c. **Wire Communications.** In the initial phases of the airborne operation, units seldom use wire communication because of the weight of materiel, the time needed for initial installation, distances involved, and the rapid initial movement off the DZ. As the situation stabilizes, units lay telephone wire between CPs and within units. Sometimes, units can use local communications systems that have been seized. To reduce the length of wire circuits, commanders locate CPs as near to subordinate units as conditions permit.

d. **Messengers.** Units use messengers often to carry documents, maps, photographs, and code books. Leaders must ensure messengers know their destinations and routes. Efficient messenger service requires intelligent, well-trained, resourceful personnel.

e. **Miscellaneous Communications.** Other forms of communications that can be used are panels, pyrotechnics, sound and visual signals, and code words.

(1) Units can use air-ground recognition panels extensively. Planned codes should always provide for-

- Unit identification.
- Location of friendly soldiers and installations.
- Target designation.
- A simple method of requesting supplies.

(2) Units can use pyrotechnics as a supplementary means for communicating with aircraft, adjusting artillery, designating targets, and marking bomb lines.

(3) Because airborne operations require precise timing and are normally executed in phases, units can develop code words for execution of tasks. When arranged in a desired sequence, this execution checklist performs two functions: units can use code words to report critical events or tasks when

they occur or are executed; and they can schedule reporting (due to events) to occur during the operation (enemy contact, mission abort, and so on). Units can use this technique to preserve radio listening silence. Tailoring execution checklists to unit requirements by certain elements aids memorization and prevents compromising the information.

10-6. AIRSPACE CONTROL

The joint force commander usually assigns overall responsibility for airspace control to the USAF component commander. The airspace control authority works through the Army Air Traffic Control Center and controls all aircraft operating in the designated airspace until completion of the airborne operation. This includes centralized control in the objective area as required by airlift/airborne concepts; it covers operations dispersed from air facilities over multiple routes with simultaneous operations at several DZs/LZs. USAF, Army aviation, and air defense units all participate in airborne operations by closely coordinating in their operations with the commander who controls the airspace. Brigade and battalion commanders must be prepared to manage this airspace with organic, assigned, and attached personnel and equipment until dedicated USAF personnel arrive and assume the responsibility. They may be reinforced with assets from corps and from the USAF to assist with this responsibility. (See FM 100-28, FM 100-42, and FM 100-103.)

10-7. ELECTRONIC WARFARE PLANNING

The need for air superiority in an airborne operation requires disrupting or destroying the enemy air force and air defenses so they cannot interfere with the operation. US Army and USAF EW assets aid in this process. The JTF commander or a designated component commander, has other dedicated assets. Commanders within a joint force have many resources that can satisfy their EW requirements. The information derived from all EW assets within the JTF must be available to its elements as quickly as possible.

a. **Staff Responsibilities.** All staff elements must coordinate to ensure a well-organized command and a successful operation. Commanders structure staffs to ensure the integrated application of intelligence, firepower, deception, OPSEC, logistics, and other staff functions. Rapid improvements in warfare technology require commanders to stress the integration of protective countermeasures such as EW.

(1) The intelligence staff offers recommendations to the command. The operations staff is responsible for operations to include applying ECM, firepower, deception, and OPSEC.

(2) The brigade or battalion commander is responsible for EW support within his command. He can assign this job to an existing staff element (S2), the signal officer, or a component element of the division that supports the assault force.

(3) Tactical units, brigade and below, request information from, or forward information directly to, subordinate tactical commands at the same time they forward it to higher commands.

b. **Support Requests.** The S3 coordinates EW support for the land battle. For conventional ground operations, he does this through the division G3. The G3 sets the priority for requests and forwards them to the appropriate agency based on the urgency of the request (planned or immediate) and on the assets available.

(1) *Predeployment.* Requests for EW support while planning for the airborne operation usually follow conventional lines. Units send requests through operations channels to the G3.

(2) *En Route.* Requests for EW support en route are the responsibility of the AMC. Immediate requests usually relate to adjustments needed to aid penetration of enemy airspace. These measures include counterair and JSEAD. The AMC commands and controls EW assets through an EW weapons controller located on the ABCCC. (Figure 10-17.)

(3) *Objective Area Support.* Once the airborne force seizes the airhead, they can relay requests for preplanned Air Force EW support back to ARFOR for tasking. Air Force channels (TACP) handle immediate requests similar to immediate CAS requests. The ABCCC, however, is the processing and tasking agency for these requests in its role as airborne TACC/ASOC.

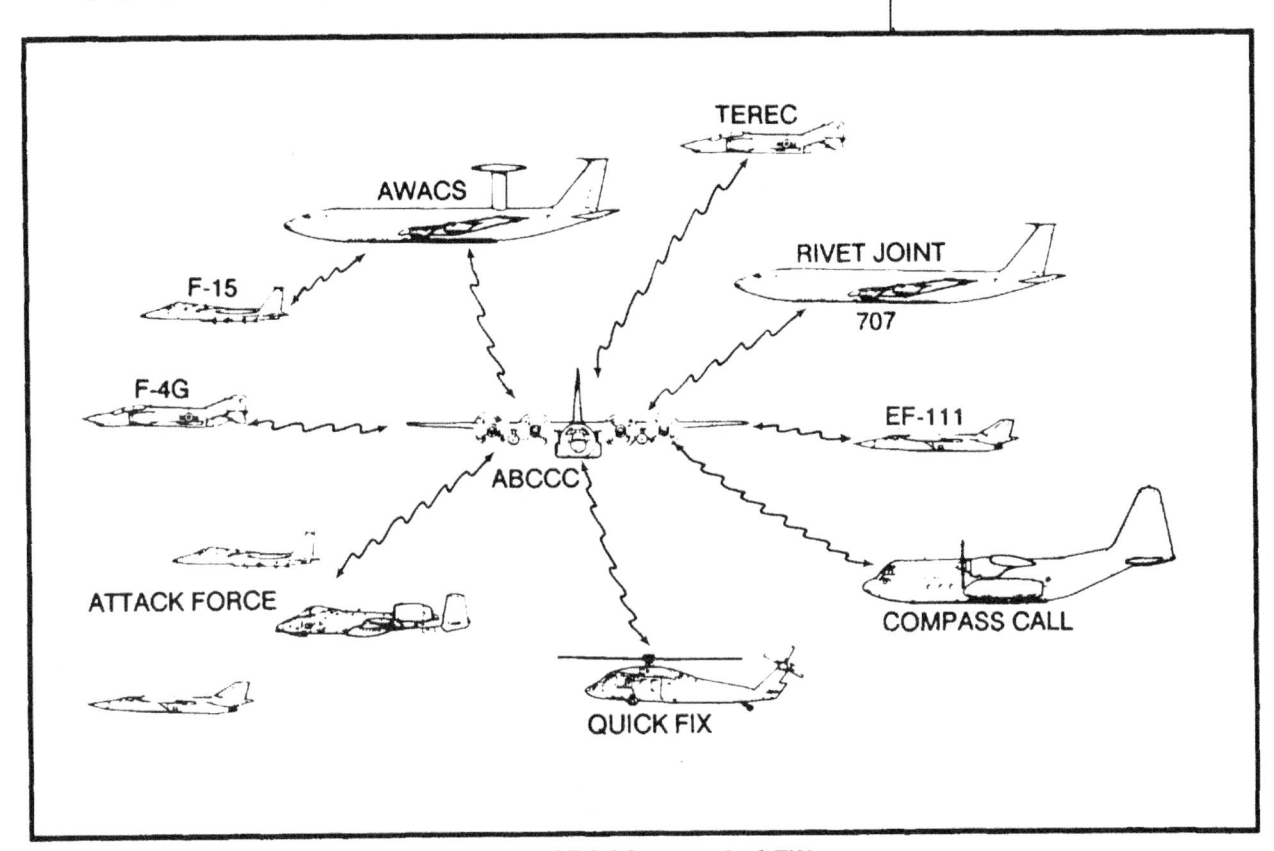

Figure 10-17. ABCCC control of EW assets.

This appendix implements STANAG 3570/ASCC 44/13G

APPENDIX A

JOINT AIRBORNE ADVANCE PARTY

Terminal guidance aids and control measures are used on the ground in the objective area to assist and guide incoming airlift aircraft to the designated DZs/LZs. Combat control teams comprised of Air Force personnel are organized, trained, and equipped to provide aircraft terminal guidance. Army teams from the LRSU, a divisional asset, are organized, trained, and equipped to deploy into the objective area and conduct R&S operations before the deployment of the airborne force. The combination of the CCT and LRS teams is known as the JAAP.

Section I. COMBAT CONTROL TEAM AND LONG-RANGE SURVEILLANCE UNIT

A-1. EMPLOYMENT

The CCT's mission is to locate, identify, and mark the DZ/LZ and to establish and operate navigational aids and ATC communications. This assists and guides airlift aircraft to the appropriate DZ/LZ. Long-range surveillance teams place under surveillance one or two NAI in the objective area. They observe and report to the ground force commander. One of the assigned NAI are usually the main body DZ/FLS.

A-2. DEPLOYMENT

The ground force commander develops plans to deploy the CCT and LRS teams during the planning stage of an airborne operation. Because of the risk of compromise in deploying teams into the objective area before the assault phase, the timing for employment and method of delivery is determined jointly by the airborne and airlift commanders. They consider the requirement for CCTs to be fully operational in minimum time after reaching the DZ/LZ. This allows navigational, identification, and directional aids to be available for the maximum number of aircraft. Early deployment of the LRS teams is also critical so that detailed and accurate information can be assembled and passed to the ground force commander.

a. The CCT and LRS teams can be delivered to the objective area by the following methods:

(1) Airdropped using static line or military free-fall parachuting techniques (HALO, HAHO) in advance of the airborne assault.

(2) Airlanded using STOL or rotary-wing aircraft in advance of the airborne assault.

(3) Airdropped or airlanded in the lead serial.

(4) Deployed over land by infiltration or other deceptive means.

(5) Deployed by submarine or small-surface craft.

(6) A combination of any of the above.

b. HALO is the preferred method of deployment for the JAAP. Insertion occurs about 24 hours before the insertion of the main airborne force.

c. The organization for deployment depends on the size of the CCT, the number of LRS teams, and the equipment to be deployed. Necessary airlift for the JAAP is from aircraft allocated to the Army airborne units.

d. The elements of the JAAP may operate independently in the objective area, or they may operate out of the same patrol base. They always remain in communication and conduct linkup immediately before the airborne assault to exchange information and report. Security of the JAAP is provided through stealth.

e. Unit integrity must be maintained if the JAAP is deployed with the main body. For airborne operations, they must be deployed with their equipment in a lead aircraft toward the front of the stick. In airland operations, allocate the JAAP and their equipment space in a lead aircraft to put required navigational and control facilities on the ground as soon as possible.

A-3. COMBAT CONTROL TEAM MISSION

The CCT's mission is to quickly establish assault zones (DZs/LZs) in austere and nonpermissive environments. The mission includes initially placing en route and terminal navigational aids; controlling air traffic; providing C^2 communications; and removing obstacles and unexploded ordnance with demolitions.

A-4. COMBAT CONTROL TEAM FUNCTIONS

For each tactical airlift mission involving the use of an assault DZ/LZ/EZ, a CCT performs the functions described below.

a. Formulates and issues ATC clearance, instructions, and advisories to effect safe, expeditious movement of air traffic in the assault zone area of responsibility.

b. Establishes an airport traffic area around each assault zone and controls all air traffic within this area under visual and instrument flight rules to include conventional approach control functions.

c. Relays advice and information to inbound aircraft about conditions in DZ/LZ/EZ areas that can have an impact on mission accomplishment. This includes any information deemed necessary to assist in guiding the inbound aircraft to the objective.

d. Develops terminal instrument procedures for assault zones.

e. Provides and operates navigational aids to support airlift operations that are not supported by a combat communications group or other agency.

f. Marks the assault zone. Army/Navy unconventional warfare forces employ a receiving unit on the ground to provide terminal guidance. A CCT is usually not required. Unconventional warfare forces use only the ground mark release system.

g. Removes obstacles and unexploded ordnance from assault zones.

h. Provides limited weather information and observation.

i. Establishes ground-to-air and point-to-point communications. For each mission, the CCT can establish any or all of the following communications nets:

(1) *UHF/AM.* Ground-to-air communications for the control of air traffic.

(2) *VHF/AM.* Ground-to-air communications for the control of air traffic.

(3) *VHF/FM.* Primary point-to-point communications with the CCT for intrateam C^2. It is also used as point-to-point communications between CCTs and other agencies within an objective area (such as LRS teams, FDC, medical personnel) or as an alternate ground-to-air communications capability with Army and allied aircraft.

(4) *HF/SSB, ground-to-air long-range communications net.* This net can be used to control air traffic.

(5) *HF/SSB, point-to-point.* This communications net is used by CCTs, ALCC, TALO, and ALCE for the C^2 of the airlift forces.

(6) *SATCOM, point-to-point.* This communications net is used for C^2, like the HF/SSB point-to-point net.

j. Enters the objective area by the most feasible means in a combat situation.

k. Selects or assists in selecting sites for assault zones and recovery zones.

l. Gathers current ground intelligence data in the objective area, and coordinates with intelligence representatives to ensure the timely exchange of data.

m. Coordinates with Army and Air Force medical personnel on casualty and patient staging points.

n. In the absence of an ALCE, performs limited ALCE duties when directed by the airlift commander.

o. Records statistical data concerning airland extraction and airdrop operations, including circular error and short field landing assessment.

p. Due to its unique qualifications, also functions in related tactical operations such as special missions, combat search and rescue, USAF special operations, and forward air guide duties.

A-5. COMBAT CONTROL TEAM ORGANIZATION

The Air Force assigns combat control teams to MAC. MAC numbered air forces task CCTs to support joint airborne operations and training exercises, surveys, and other higher headquarters requirements. Each team consists of Air Force parachutists trained and equipped for mobile operations. A standard team is composed of 2 officers and 24 enlisted men; however, a commander may tailor manning authorizations as required. If a tactical situation does not warrant the use of an entire team, it is task-organized into smaller elements for simultaneous operation of DZs, LZs, or EZs.

A-6. ARMY LONG-RANGE SURVEILLANCE TEAM MISSION

The Army LRS team in the airborne assault conducts R&S operations on one or two NAI in the objective area. The team also observes and reports on the status of the DZ/FLS. All reports are made to the ground force commander over long-range, man-portable communications systems.

A-7. ARMY LONG-RANGE SURVEILLANCE TEAM FUNCTIONS

On notification of impending deployment into an objective area, LRS teams can perform any of the following functions:

a. One or two days before the insertion, LRS teams to be deployed to isolate with the CCT, receive an OPORD, and conduct mission planning.

b. Perform static line or HALO parachute operations to insert into the objective area.

c. Conduct surveillance operations on assigned NAI-for example, road intersections, bridges, main supply route in the objective area, enemy C^2 nodes, helicopter LZs. The main assault force DZ will be treated as a named area of interest.

d. Conduct surveillance of enemy high-value targets.

e. Conduct forward area limited observation program to provide limited weather and terrain information to the commander.

f. Establish communications with friendly forces in the objective area with the TF commander at the home station. For each mission, the LRS team can establish any or all of the following communications nets:

(1) *URC-101 tactical satellite communications.* Used to report to the TF commander en route to the objective area.

(2) *PSC-3 data burst high-frequency transmission device.* Used to send LRS SPOTREPs to the home station from the objective area.

(3) *PRC-104 long-range high frequency.* Used by the teams to report back to the base station in the objective area.

(4) *PRC-77/126 FM radios.* Used for communications within the team and with other agencies in the objective area.

g. Other potential missions as directed by the commander to include:

(1) Conduct radiological/chemical surveys of the objective area before the main body deploys.

(2) Emplace remote sensors, guidance beacons, or jamming equipment.

(3) Direct-fire missions for artillery and NGF.

(4) Conduct pathfinder operations as necessary to support airborne/air assault operations.

(5) Conduct damage assessment and NBC-1 report in the AO.

(6) Conduct linkup operations with conventional and unconventional friendly forces in the objective area.

(7) Assess indigenous communications systems for possible future friendly use.

(8) Collect information through eavesdropping and wiretapping.

A-8. ARMY LONG-RANGE SURVEILLANCE TEAM ORGANIZATION

The LRSU in the airborne division consists of six teams of six men each. The team leader is a SSG; his assistant is a SGT. There are three SP4 scout/observers and one PFC RATELO. All members of the team carry the basic infantry MOS and are required to be parachute qualified. The team leader is coded as an airborne ranger. A TF may employ from one to six LRS teams in the assault with two to three teams being the norm.

Section II. DROP ZONES

The selection and marking of DZs to support the airborne operation is a critical event in the planning stages and supports the ground tactical plan. The DZs must be large enough to accommodate the required number of personnel and equipment to be delivered by airdrop and must be identifiable from the air to prevent a disintegration of the unit as a result of dispersion on the ground.

A-9. DROP ZONE CRITERIA/SELECTION

Drop zone criteria/selection is the joint responsibility of the COMALF and the commander of the forces being supported. In accordance with AF Regulation 3-1, DZs are measured in yards when working with Air Force aircraft. They are measured in meters when working with Army aircraft.

a. **Personnel From Single Aircraft.** The minimum size DZ for one parachutist from a single aircraft is 600 yards wide and 600 yards long. For each added parachutist, 75 yards is added to the length. For example, to find the minimum DZ for a 20-man stick from a single aircraft, the calculation is as follows:

Length for one man = 600 yards

Length for 19 additional men = 19 X 75 = 1,425 yards

Length for 20 men = 600 + 1,425 = 2,025 yards

For unilateral CCT operations or training, the 75-yard increment allowed for each additional parachutist can be computed from the point of impact rather than added to the total length of the minimum size DZ for one man.

b. **Equipment From a Single Aircraft.** The minimum DZ is 600 yards by 1,000 yards for a drop of one heavy equipment platform from a single aircraft. For each other platform, 400 yards is added to the DZ length. (For C-141 aircraft, 500 yards is added to the minimum length for each added platform.)

c. **Multiple Points of Impact.** To meet specific operational requirements, multiple points of impact are authorized if the drop personnel have been properly prebriefed. If the points are placed laterally, the width must be increased accordingly. (This manner of placement reduces the amount of wake turbulence across the DZ.)

d. **HALO/HAHO Personnel.** The size of the DZ varies with the number of personnel to be dropped, their proficiency, the exit altitude, and wind. The CCT leader determines the suitability of a DZ for a HALO/HAHO jump. The CCT leader should be a qualified HALO/HAHO jumpmaster, or a member of the JAAP should be qualified to give advice about the DZ criteria. DZ suitability criteria are identical for HALO and HAHO operations.

e. **Container Delivery System.** The minimum sizes of CDS DZs depend on three factors: the drop altitude, the number of bundles being dropped, and the number and type of aircraft. Tables A-1 provides the minimum DZ sizes consistent with these factors.

f. **AWADS Formation SKE Procedures.** The DZ width is increased by 400 yards.

g. **Limited Visibility and Visual Formation Procedures.** The DZ width is increased by 100 yards (50 yards on each side of the DZ centerline).

h. **Instrument Meteorological Conditions Airdrops.** When airdrops are conducted during instrument conditions, ceiling and visibility minimums must be enforced for Army personnel training drops. A 200-foot AGL minimum ceiling is required. For Air Force training, a 300-foot ceiling and 1/2 mile visibility are required for personnel and equipment. For combat, ceiling and visibility minimums are zero/zero. For joint exercises, AF personnel are authorized to use Army minimums. When the ceiling is less than a 600-foot AGL, all personnel, including CCTs, are cleared from the DZ no later than five minutes before the airdrop TOT. They remain clear until completion of the drop(s).

i. **DZ Selection Criteria.** Some DZs are selected to support highly mobile ground forces, but are not surveyed. Drop zone size is determined by mode of delivery, actual load dispersal statistics, and personal knowledge. Recovery of air items and air load are considered, For example, small trees covering the entire DZ might limit recovery of air items but allow 100 percent recovery of the air loads.

ALTITUDE (FEET AGL)	WIDTH (YARDS)	LENGTH (YARDS)	
		One to eight containers	Nine or more containers
1,500	425	1,050	1,750
2,000	450	1,100	1,800
2,500	475	1,150	1,850
3,000	500	1,200	1,900
4,000	550	1,300	2,000
5,000	600	1,400	2,100
6,000	650	1,500	2,200
7,000	700	1,600	2,300

Table A-1. High-velocity/delayed-opening CDS DZ sizes.

j. **Area DZs.** An area DZ comprises a planned flight track over a series of acceptable drop sites (1/2 nautical mile either side of track). This establishes a line of flight between points A and B. The distance between A and B should not exceed 15 NMs with a change in elevation of no more than 300 feet. The CCT or special operations reception committee is free to receive the drop at any location along the line of flight between points A and B. The selected DZ is marked by a beacon, prebriefed block letter, or GMRS.

k. **Circular/Random Approach DZs.** A circular DZ has multiple run-in headings. The size of the DZ is governed by mission requirements and useable terrain. A verbally-initiated release system can be used with no markings.

A-10. DROP ZONE MARKINGS (DAY)

Drop zones will not normally be marked for combat drops unless the CCT or pathfinder teams have been inserted before H-Hour. Daylight markings must be established and understood by all participants. (Figure A-1, see page A-8.)

a. **Timing Points.** For day VFR airdrop operations, the timing points are not marked. The lead navigator selects the timing point, which is usually a prominent terrain feature. In the absence of such a feature, two timing points can be selected (before employment, if possible) and marked by the CCT. If terrain allows, these points are an equal distance from the extended centerline of the DZ; no more than 1,300 yards before the point of impact, and between 300 and 350 yards on either side of the centerline (350 yards minimum for C-141).

b. **Point of Impact.** For computed air release point drops, except AWADS, the PI is marked with raised-angle markers or colored panels placed flat on the surface. These panels form a block letter a minimum of 35 feet by 35 feet; the only authorized letters are A, C, J, R, and S. (See MAC Regulation 55-130 for suggested circular/random approach DZ markings.) The letters H and O are authorized for circular DZs. Smoke (other than red) can be displayed adjacent to and downwind of the letter identifier to assist in visual acquisition of the DZ and to indicate the surface wind direction. For CDS drops, smoke should be displayed 150 yards before the PI (six o'clock position). The PI is not marked for AWADS drops nor will smoke be displaced other than red smoke.

c. **Trailing Edge.** The trailing edge of the DZ is not marked for daylight operations.

d. **Red Smoke Flare Light.** Red smoke flare lights on the DZ indicate a no-drop.

e. **Signals Other Than Red.** Smoke/flares/lights other than red on the DZ indicate clearance to drop.

f. **No Smoke.** When smoke is not displayed, a prebriefed signal displayed at the PI or a radio call from the CCT (or designated reception party) is clearance to drop.

g. **Emergency Signals.** Communications security permitting, visual signals should be confirmed by radio instructions to the aircrews. Temporary closing of the DZ or temporary postponement of the airdrop is indicated by forming the letter identifier into two parallel bars; they are placed perpendicular to the line of flight. An emergency no-drop or drop cancellation is indicated by red smoke/flares/lights or by forming the letter identifier into the letter X.

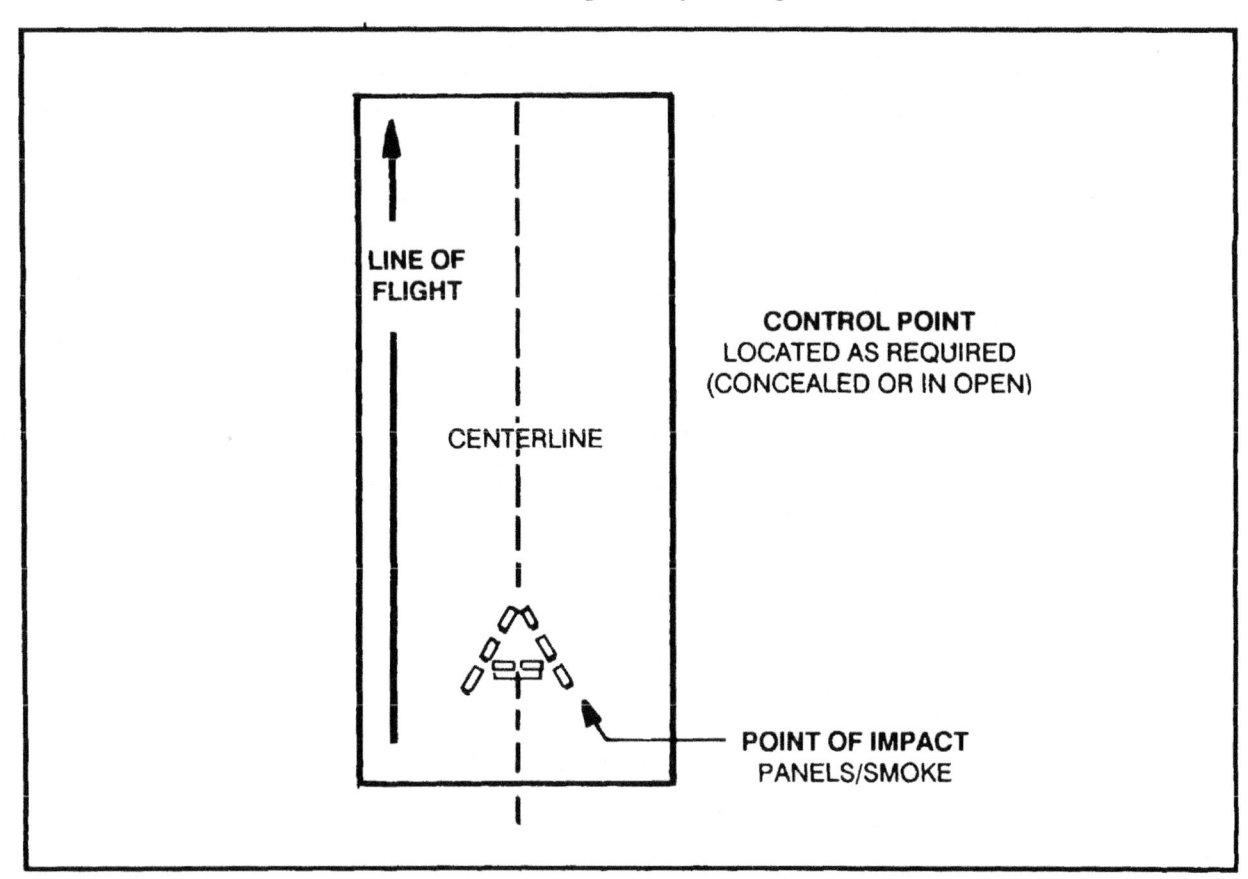

Figure A-1. Drop zone markings (day).

A-11. DROP ZONE MARKINGS (NIGHT)

Assembly of personnel and equipment at night on an unfamiliar and hostile DZ maybe the most difficult task an airborne force must do. The marking of the DZ can be done using the same techniques discussed for daylight DZ marking. However, the uncertainty and confusion that is inherent with a night drop must be considered. (Figure A-2).

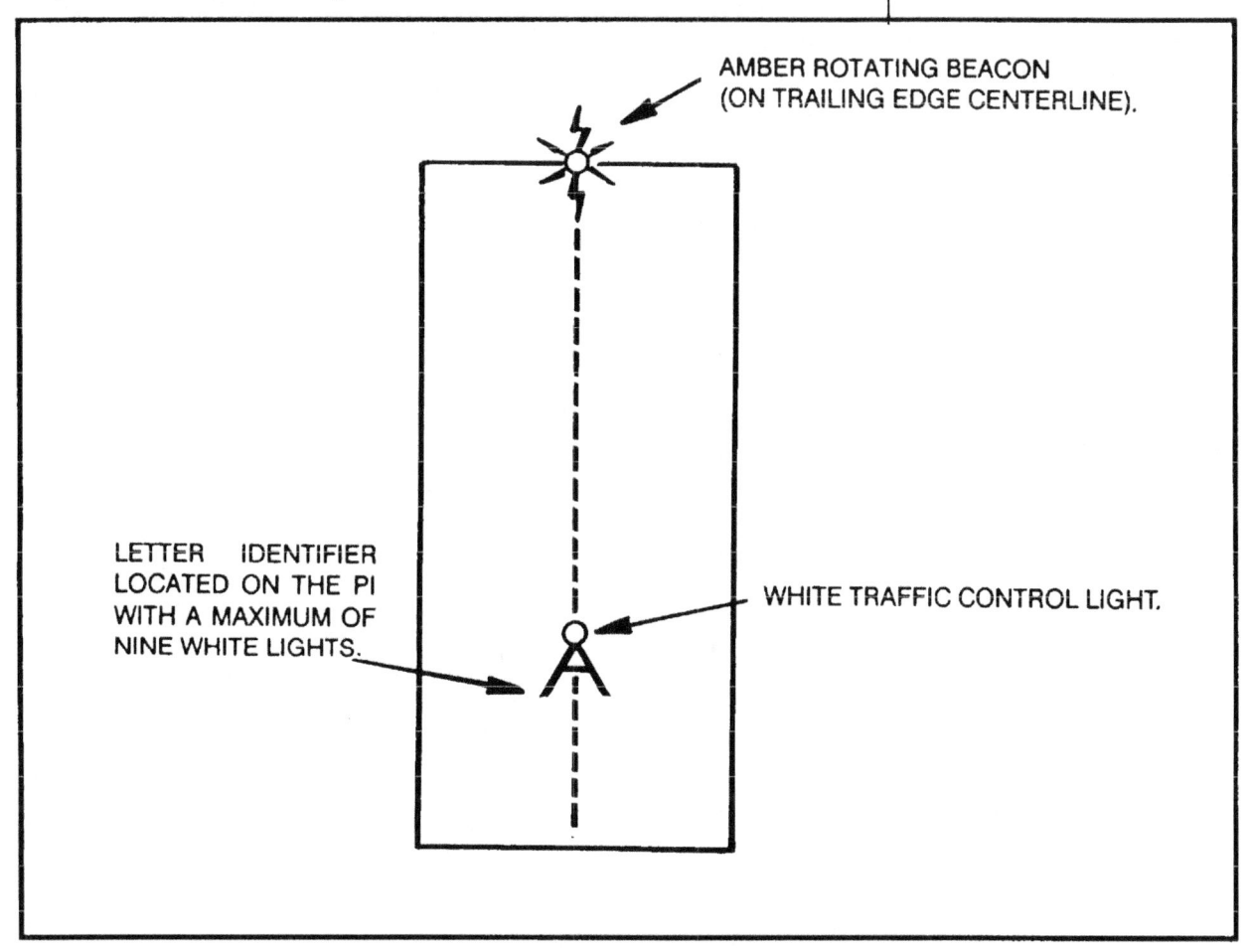

Figure A-2. Drop zone markings (night).

a. **Timing Points.** For night operations, timing points are marked (if the tactical situation permits). If terrain allows, these points should be an equal distance from the extended centerline of the DZ, but not further than 1,300 yards before the point of impact. The timing points should be between 300 yards and 350 yards (minimum 350 yards for C-141) from either side of the centerline. Each timing point is marked with a green rotating beacon.

b. **Point of Impact.** The PI is not marked for AWADS drops. If the hostile environment permits, the PI for VFR airdrops is marked with a minimum of nine white omnidirectional lights placed to form a block letter that is a minimum size of 35 feet by 35 feet. The only authorized letters are A, C, J, R, and S. The letters H and O are authorized for circular DZs. When more than one DZ is in the area, a different letter must be used on each. Besides the block letter, white ATC lights or flares are displayed on the PI. For CDS airdrops, the white ATC lights or flares are displayed 150 yards from the PI at the 6 o'clock position.

c. **Trailing Edge.** An amber rotating beacon is placed on the centerline axis of the DZ at the trailing edge (if the tactical situation allows).

d. **Emergency Signals.** A no-drop condition is indicated by a red beam from the ATC lights and flares. During unilateral training operations, the absence of prebriefed DZ markings indicates a no-drop situation. A cancelled mission is indicated by making the block letter into an X.

Section III. LANDING ZONE OPERATIONS

Airfield criteria to be used in a specific theater of operations are based on local conditions and determined by Army and Air Force staff engineers acting for the joint force commander.

A-12. LANDING ZONE CLASSIFICATION

The following general data are intended to relate the Army airfield classification system to the Air Force classification system. The correlation of these airfields cannot be exact; specifications depend on operating gross loads, use of aircraft arresting equipment, and criteria for the particular instrument approach planned, as well as the model and type of aircraft. Air Force airfields are constructed to standards that indicate the expected life of the airfield. Expedient airfields arc those surfaced with membrane, landing mat, or both. Airfields intended for longer use are of semipermanent construction and conform to the full operational standards of the theater of operations. Pavement standards are usually upgraded by using conventional asphaltic or portland cement concrete. They are constructed to the required thickness for extended use.

a. **Assault Zone.** This is an unsurfaced landing area, usually clay or compacted soil, which meets the following criteria:

(1) It is in uncontrolled airspace with no terminal ATC available,

(2) It is not published in IFR/VFR supplements.

(3) It is 3,500 feet or less in length.

(4) It is surveyed by a CCT.

Requests for CCTs to perform assault zone surveys are evaluated by MAC NAF CCT staff agencies on an individual basis. For example, the zone can be longer than 3,500 feet, paved, and require a CCT survey. Combat control teams are not qualified to perform engineering surveys and, therefore, do not survey sites for anticipated DZ construction.

b. **Expeditionary Zone.** This zone is surfaced with membrane, landing mat, or both. It is usually surveyed by Army or Air Force engineers. Combat control teams can conduct surveys of this type of airfield but require assistance from engineering personnel to determine the weight-bearing capacity of the landing surface

c. **Semipermanent/Permanent Zone.** This is surfaced with asphalt or cement. It is usually surveyed by engineering units but can be surveyed by a CCT. Air Force survey teams may consist of an ALCC/ALCE commander or representative, a flight safety officer, a pavement evaluation engineer, and flight facilities personnel. CCTs can be tasked by the COMALF to conduct reconnaissance reports of captured enemy airfields of this type.

A-13. MARKINGS AND IDENTIFICATION

Specific details concerning the type and location of LZ markings as well as airfield identification procedures are agreed on at joint planning conferences. (Figure A-3, see page A-12.) Existing international agreements are considered. This information is a special subject at the final briefing to ensure all required ground and aircrew members understand the LZ recognition and identification procedures.

a. **Airfield Markings.** Landing zones are designated with conventional markings. The figures in this appendix pertaining to LZs reflect landings in only one direction. When landings can be expected at both ends of the LZ, the first 500 feet at each end are marked as the approach end. The COMALF directs the establishment of required communications and NAVAIDS. These communications and NAVAIDS are usually provided from within CCT resources during transitory operations.

b. **Control Point Location.** The control point should be located so the entire length of the landing, taxiing, and parking areas are in full view of the controllers. It should be upwind of the landing area so the dust and debris that rises from an unimproved landing strip dots not obscure the vision of the controllers.

A-14. DAY OPERATIONS

The usable landing area is marked with vertically mounted VS-17 panels. Orange panels are placed only at the approach end; all other panels arc cerise. The appropriate airlift commander reduces the panel markings to the approach end, touchdown area, and end of runway on well-defined runways during day VMC operations. The taxiways and ramp areas are not marked for daylight operations. For emergency signals, either a red flare or red light beam denotes a go-around. The ATC light gun is aimed directly at the pilot.

> **NOTE:** All marker panels are erected vertically to enable the pilot to readily observe the markings when the aircraft is on the final approach. At the discretion of the mission commander, the panel markers can be erected to provide for landing in the opposite direction by folding the panels in half.

A-15. NIGHT OPERATIONS

The usable landing area must be marked with portable lights (or suitable substitutes). (Figure A-4, see page A-13.) Six green lights are placed at the approach end-three on each side (about 6 feet apart). Four red lights are placed at the departure end of the runway–two on each side (about 6 feet apart). All other runway lights are white. Reflectors can be used to supplement the lights.

FM 90-26

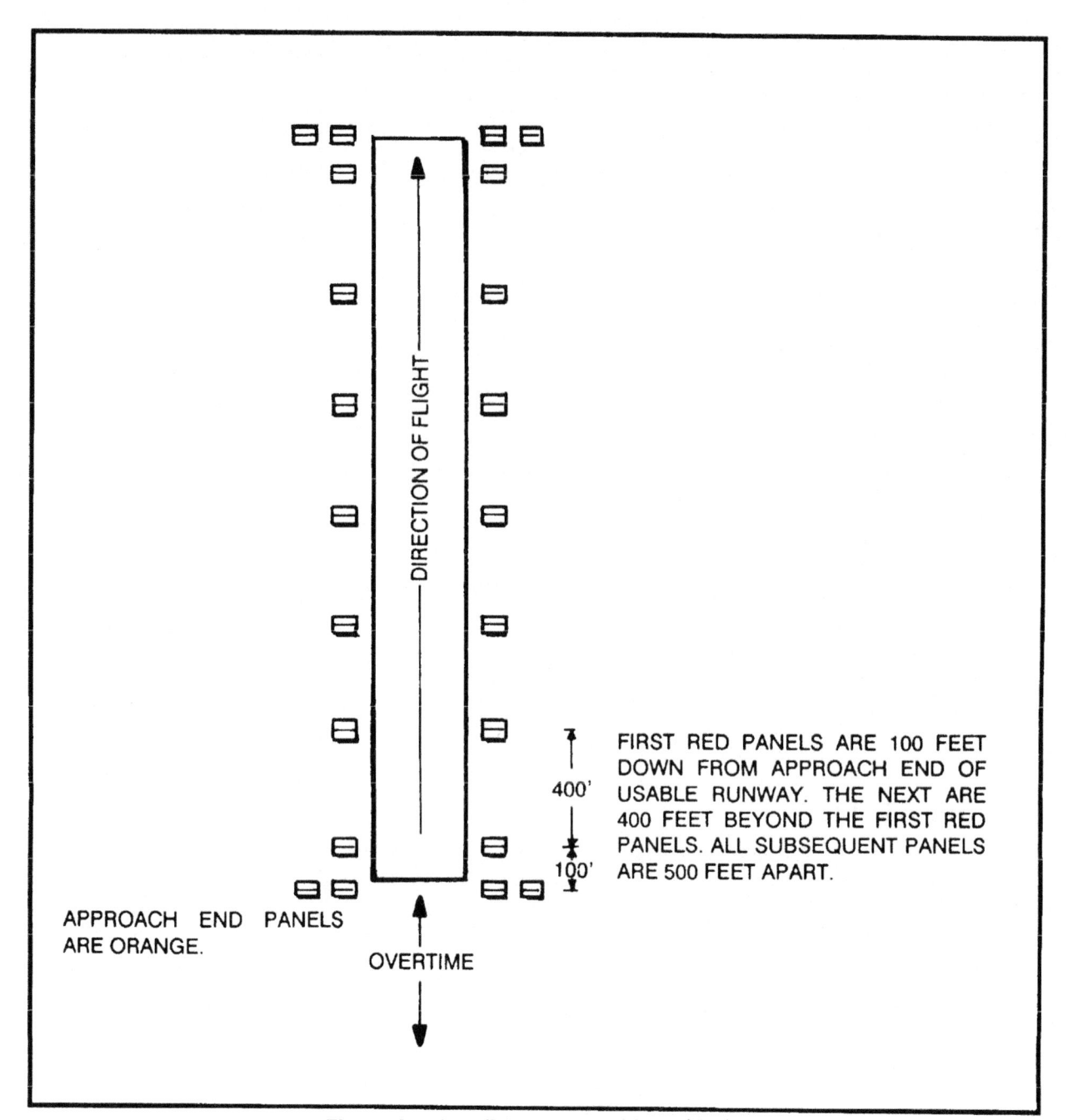

Figure A-3. Landing zone markings (day).

a. **Loading and Taxiing Areas.** Loading and taxiing areas are marked as determined during mission planning. Suitable lights with blue lenses are used; they are placed 500 feet apart on straight parts of the areas. When possible, reflectors are placed halfway between the blue lights. Light spacing can be reduced to 75 feet on curves and at corners or intersections.

b. **Visual Aids.** Visual aids such as strobe lights, rotating beacons, or others may be needed. When strobe lights are used, they are placed 100 feet apart on the extended runway centerline. The light closest to the LZ should be placed at the outer edge of the overrun. The rotating beacon and other visual aids are positioned as determined during mission planning.

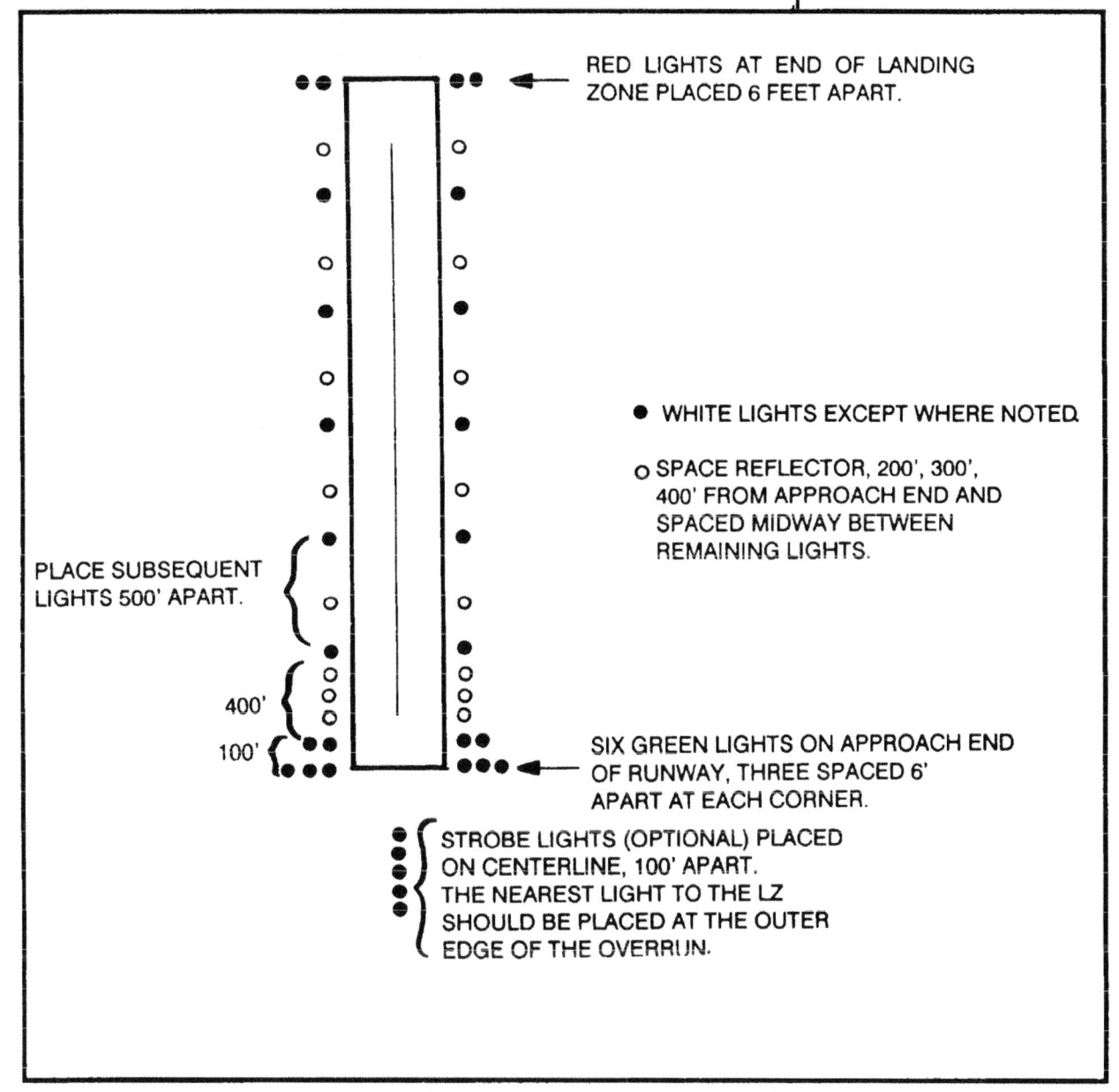

Figure A-4. Minimum landing zone markings (night).

Section IV. LOW-ALTITUDE PARACHUTE EXTRACTION SYSTEM

Sustained ground operations after a successful airborne assault may depend on resupply by means other than airlanding of supplies and follow-on forces. A primary means of resupply is the low altitude parachute extraction system. LAPES is a low-altitude method of aerial delivery. This system employs a 15-foot drogue parachute deployed behind the aircraft and attached to a towplate on the aircraft ramp. At the release point, the parachute forces are transferred from the twoplate to the ring slot main extraction parachute(s), which then extracts single or tandem platforms from the aircraft. Ground friction decelerates the load. The total distance from release to stopping point of the load depends on ground speed, size, number of extractions parachutes, weight of the load(s), and the type of terrain. Using LAPES with tandem platforms, loads up to 37,175 pounds can be delivered into a small EZ. Since proper site selection for the EZ depends on a variety of conditions, specific criteria to ensure safety must be used in physically locating the EZ. (Figure A-5.)

A-16. EXTRACTION ZONE CRITERIA AND MARKINGS FOR LAPES (DAY OPERATIONS)

The impact/slide-out zone should be clear of obstructions and relatively flat, but it can contain grass; dirt; sand; short, light brush; or snow.

a. The approach zone on the leading edge of the impact/slide-out zone should consist of two 400 foot zones (800 feet in total length).

(1) The 400-foot zone nearest the impact/slide-out zone can be a graduated slope. It can slope from a maximum of 1 foot at the leading edge of the impact/slide-out zone to 12 feet at the farthest end from the impact/slide-out zone.

(2) The next 400-foot zone can be a graduated slope from a maximum of 12 feet at the inner edge to a maximum of 50 feet at the farthest end.

(3) The inner portion of the approach zone must be clear enough so the impact panels are visible. Because of the steep aircraft approach, the approach zone slope must not exceed a 15:1 ratio.

b. The clear area can be a maximum of 1 foot high adjacent to the impact/slide-out zone, sloping upward to 2 feet at the outer edge.

c. The lateral safety zone can be a graduated slope with obstacles limited to a maximum of 2 feet at the inner edge to 12 feet at the outer edge.

d. The climb-out zone should contain no obstructions that would prevent a loaded aircraft from maintaining normal obstacle clearance climb rate after an inadvertent touchdown, delivery abort, or extraction malfunction.

A-17. EXTRACTION ZONE CRITERIA AND MARKINGS FOR LAPES (NIGHT OPERATIONS)

The impact/slide-out zone should be clear of obstructions and relatively flat but can contain grass; dirt; sand; short, light brush; or snow. (Figure A-6, see page A-16.)

a. The approach zone on the leading edge of the impact/slide-out zone should consist of two zones: one 600 feet in length and the other 1,000 feet in length (1,600 feet total length).

(1) The 600-foot zone nearest the impact/slide-out zone should be a level area.

(2) The next 1,000-foot zone can be graduated from a maximum of 1 foot at the inner edge to a maximum of 12 feet at the farthest end.

(3) The entire approach zone must be clear so approach zone and impact area lights are visible to the aircraft.

b. The clear area and lateral safety zone are the same as for daylight operations.

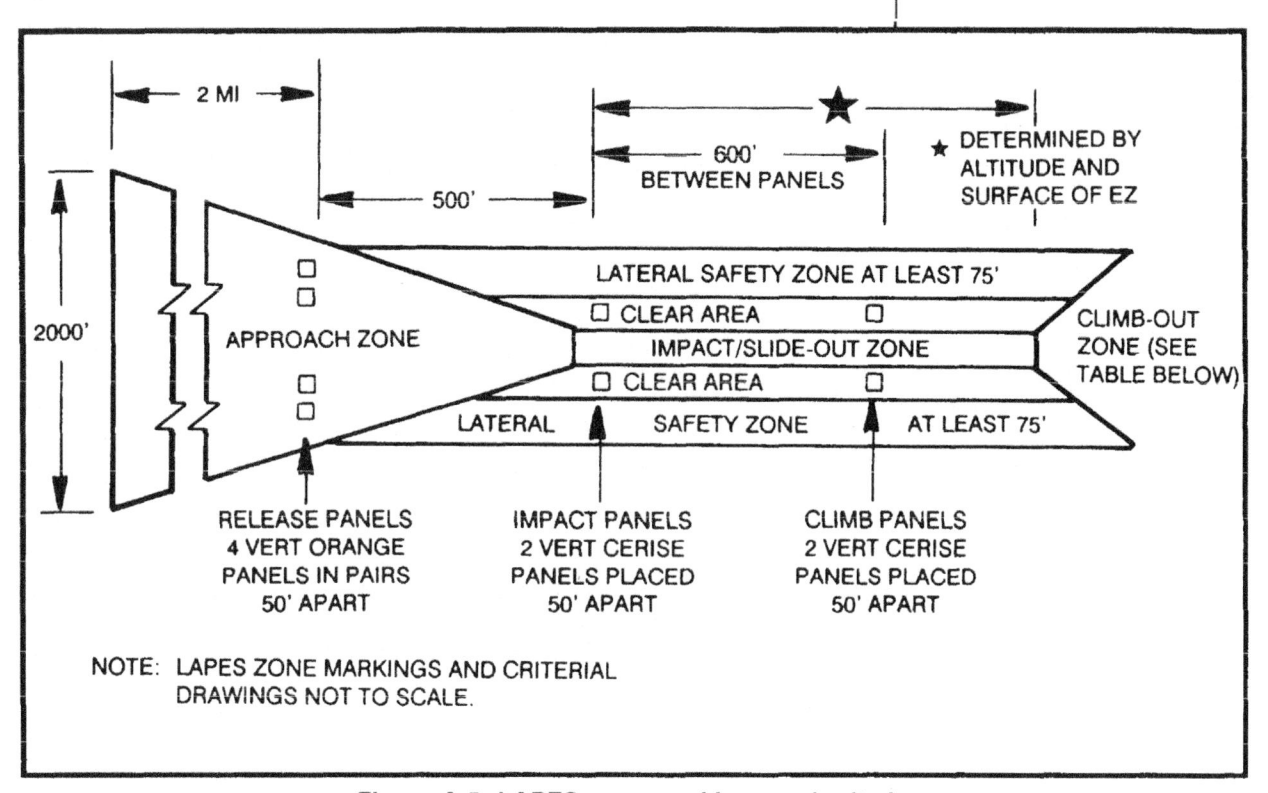

Figure A-5. LAPES zone markings and criteria.

A-18. EXTRACTION ZONE CRITERIA AND MARKINGS FOR LAPES (MULTIPLE OPERATIONS)

Lane dimensions for multiple LAPES operations are the same as for single operations. When establishing two or more lanes, only the right side of the lane is marked. If available, radar reflectors are placed at the trailing edge of the first and last lanes. (Figure A-7, see page A-17.) When possible, additional lanes are staggered 100 feet down from lane one. However, additional lanes can be established side by side beginning at the same parallel starting point. There are always 150 feet between lane centerlines. Extraction lanes are designated in numerical sequence from left to right. The left lane in direction of flight is designated as lane one. The lead aircraft extracts on the downwind lane. Normally, aircraft spacing is either 10 seconds or 1 minute.

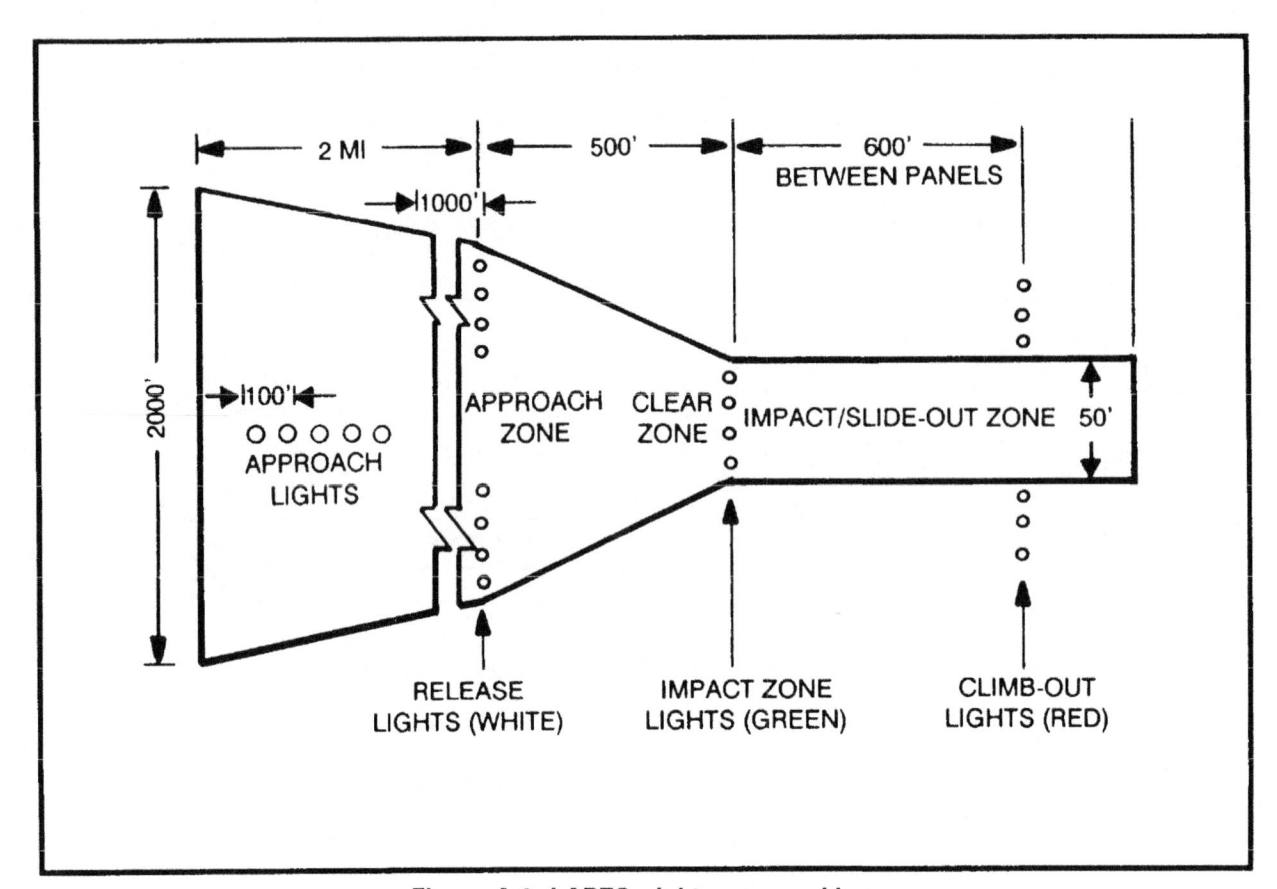

Figure A-6. LAPES night zone marking.

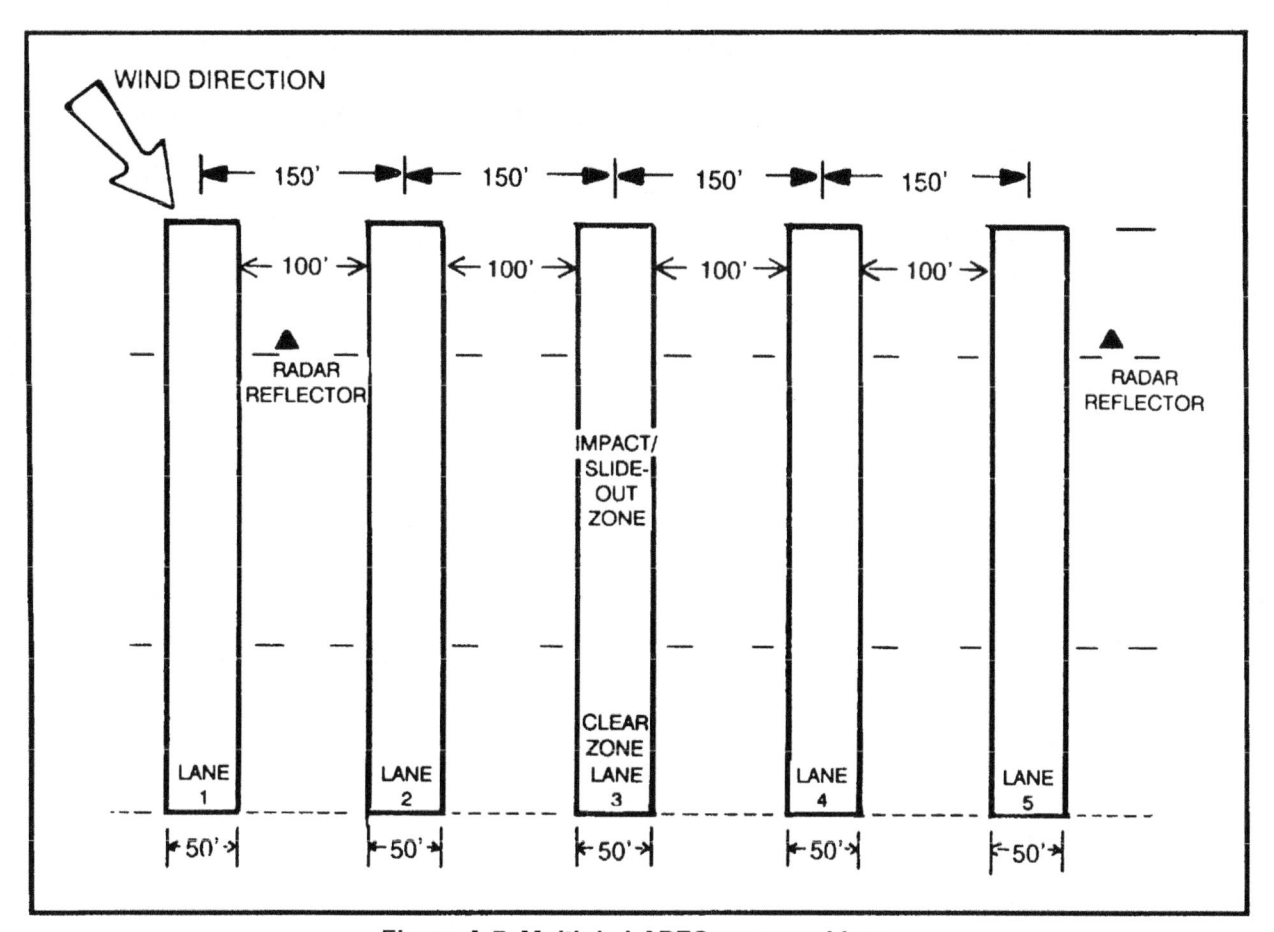

Figure A-7. Multiple LAPES zone markings.

APPENDIX B

DROP ZONE SUPPORT TEAMS

This appendix outlines the requirements for US Army DZ support teams to support tactical airdrop operations. It will be used to develop implementation plans for assuming DZ support responsibilities. US Army DZSTs will support unit airdrops of personnel, equipment, and CDS in single-ship and formation-type airdrops. With some exceptions, these airdrops are limited to day/night visual conditions. MAC Regulation 3-3 governs the operation of Air Force CCT efforts. Many of the requirements of MAC Regulation 3-3 also apply to US Army DZST operations. (When referring to MAC Regulation 3-3, DZSTs must ensure that their copy is current.)

B-1. DROP ZONE SUPPORT TEAM LEADER DUTIES

The DZSTL represents both the airlift commander and the ground forces commander. He has overall responsibility for the conduct of operations on the DZ.

a. Considering flight safety as well as ground safety, the DZSTL coordinates closely with the DZ safety officer to observe and evaluate all factors that could adversely affect the safety of the airdrop operation. If radio contact is possible, the DZSTL will pass surface wind information and limited weather observations to inbound aircraft and C^2 units, as required. When radio contact is not possible, the DZSTL must ensure DZ markings are properly displayed as prebriefed to convey the appropriate message to aircrews. The DZST must have radio contact with the drop aircraft for IMC/AWADS drops.

b. The DZSTL must also evaluate the condition of the DZ before the drop to ensure that it is suitable for a safe personnel landing, as well as to ensure that airdropped equipment can be recovered. The DZSTL places personnel, vehicles, and support equipment so they are not endangered by the airdrop. (Possible parachute malfunction should be considered when determining placement.) He also ensures the DZ is clear of all personnel and equipment not required to support the airdrop no later than 10 minutes before the estimated time over target.

c. The DZSTL is responsible for the operation of all visual acquisition aids and electronic equipment, such as smoke, flares, signal lights, and radios. He ensures that this equipment is not used by untrained personnel.

d. If conditions are not safe for a successful airdrop, the DZSTL uses prebriefed visual signals or radio communications to ensure that the no-drop condition is made known to the incoming aircraft.

B-2. COMPOSITION/QUALIFICATIONS OF DROP ZONE SUPPORT TEAMS

The DZST consists of at least two members. More members maybe required depending on the complexity of the mission. The senior member of the DZST functions as the DZSTL and meets the following requirements:

a. He must be an NCO or officer.

b. He must have completed training as a DZST member and satisfy parent service currency requirements.

c. He must be a qualified and current jumpmaster or an airborne qualified pathfinder for personnel and heavy equipment drops.

B-3. PREMISSION COORDINATION PROCESS

Premission briefings are vital to the successful accomplishment of any operation. When possible, all participating members and agencies should take part in premission coordination and briefing. This allows them to resolve all conflicts and to ensure all agencies are informed of the details of the operation.

a. **Safety Considerations.** The monthly joint airborne/air transportability training, or appropriate joint exercise planning, conference is the source of most taskings for missions. Taskings are coordinated as far out as possible to meet many training requirements.

(1) Add on missions (JA/ATT, special assignment airlift missions, and so on) outside the normal planning cycle may generate additional taskings. Requested add-on missions accepted by a MAC airlift unit must be supported by the requesting unit if a CCT is not available. Add-on mission requirements are fully documented by message traffic to all concerned units.

(2) After the mission is tasked, the receiving unit coordinates as required IAW a checklist. (See Figure B-1 for an example.)

b. **Operational Responsibilities.** Specific responsibilities of the various personnel involved in the establishment of a DZ are as follows:

(1) The senior combat control representative-

(a) Locates in the ALCC or on the AFSOB.

(b) Coordinates with the G3 Air and the TALO.

(c) Ensures that either a CCT element or a DZST is available to operate each drop zone.

DZST/AIRCREW MISSION BRIEFING CHECKLIST

1. Verify DZ name/location and JA/ATT mission sequence number: Friar/AJ04
2. TOT(s) block time (no drop procedures e.g., race track): 091600 Aug 90/ 091500-0
3. Verify current DZ survey (data): YES
4. Type drop (HE, PE, CDS): PE
5. Type release (VIRS, CARP, GMRS, AWADS): CARP
   a. Type parachutes: T-10
   b. Ground quick disconnects: YES
   c. Number of jumpers/bundles: 200/06
6. Number of aircraft: 04
7. DZ information:
   a. Markings/signals:
      (1) Panels/lights: VS-17
      (2) Block letter ID: A
      (3) Smoke, flares: YELLOW
      (4) Emergency no-drop procedures: RED SMOKE
      (5) Mission cancellation indication: RED SIDE VS-17
   b. DZ support capabilities:
      (1) Radios available/frequencies: PRC-77/34.75
      (2) Visual acquisition aids available: SIGNAL MIRROR/SMOKE/SE-11 LIGHT GUN
      (3) NAVAIDS available: YELLOW ROTATING BEACON
      (4) NEW equipment: PILOT BALLOON
      (5) Verify Airspace coordination: YES
8. Aircraft (mission) commander's name, unit of assignment, telephone number:
   DAVIS, ERIC R., 317 TAW, 682-3493
9. DZSTL name, rank, unit of assigment, telephone number:
   ADAMS, DAVID, 03, 1-507, 545-3102
10. Drop score/incident/accident reporting procedure: MAC FORM

Figure B-1. Example of DZST/aircrew mission briefing checklist.

(d) Coordinates airspace.

(e) Resolves conflicts with other missions.

(f) Adjusts DZ dimensions and headings.

(g) Develops aircraft communications and handoff procedures for each mission.

(h) Establishes point-to-point radio communications between the DZST and the ALCC or the AFSOB.

(2) The CCT-

(a) Deploys with the Army airborne and light infantry divisions.

(b) Establishes and operates DZs.

(3) The DZST-

(a) Establishes and operates DZs.

(b) Communicates with the ALCC or the AFSOB.

(c) Maintains the equipment required to operate a DZ.

B-4. EQUIPMENT

The following equipment is required to support DZ operations. It may come with a CCT, but any unit must have-

- Raised angle marker or VS-17 high-visibility signal panels.
- Smoke (red or green, white, or yellow).
- White light (omnidirectional).
- Signal mirror.
- Binoculars.
- Flare device with red and other colored flares (other than pen-type survival flares).
- Surface wind measuring device (anemometer).
- Compass.
- Strobe light.

Normally, rehearsals and exercise drops should have every acquisition aid and safety device available for the airdrop aircraft if the mission scenario permits. Drops should have the benefit of air-to-ground communications, PIBAL mean effective wind measurement, ATC light gun, smoke or flares, and so on, if these items arc available. During contingency or wartime operations, units may not be able to carry as much airdrop support equipment. Therefore, it is vital that premission coordination and briefings thoroughly discuss visual signals (such as drop cancellation, postponement, authentication procedures).

B-5. DROP ZONE OPERATIONS

Drop zone support team leaders must allow enough time to locate the PI, establish a DZ heading, locate the control point, and have the DZ operational at least one hour before the drop. During rehearsals and exercises, the DZSTL maybe required to evaluate the conditions of DZs that have not been used for one year or longer. This should be done before a mission is scheduled to that particular DZ. In such cases, the DZSTL compares data in the DZ survey form with actual conditions in the DZ and surrounding area. He ensures that significant changes are properly annotated and discussed with the aircrew. He also notifies the appropriate MAC NAF of the differences. The DZSTL must be sensitive to the safety requirements of both paratroopers and aircraft.

> **NOTE:** It is common for trees to be within the boundaries of any given DZ. Trees are not always considered DZ obstructions or a hindrance to recovery operations.

a. During combat operations, DZ criteria and selection is the joint responsibility of the airlift commander and the ground forces commander. (For training operations, the minimum DZ sizes are specified in MAC Regulation 3-3.)

b. Normally, the control point is set up at the PI because this location usually offers the best view of the DZ and approaching aircraft. If the tactical condition permits, the DZST may take advantage of this positioning, or he may locate the control point elsewhere.

(1) For CDS operations, locate the control point 150 yards at 6 o'clock in relation to the PI and DZ heading (tactical situation permitting).

(2) For all AWADS and station keeping equipment drops, the control point is off the DZ when the ceiling is less than 600 feet. All personnel are also kept off the DZ.

c. Drop zone markings for computed air release points are discussed in Appendix A.

d. Surface wind limitations for training operations are as follows (unless otherwise established by the airdrop unit's service):

(1) Thirteen knots for personnel drops (including gusts within 10 minutes of drop time).

(2) Thirteen knots for equipment without ground-quick disconnects,

(3) Seventeen knots for equipment with ground-quick disconnects.

(4) Twenty knots for CDS drops using G13/14-type parachutes,

FM 90-26

B-6. PHRASEOLOGY

When radio communication is available to the DZST, it is important for air-to-ground communications to be brief, concise, and clear to reduce cockpit distraction. Aircrew members are extremely busy during run in from the initial point to the DZ and throughout the escape flight path.

> **NOTE:** The DZST must be aware of COMSEC requirements. All air-to-ground signals must be kept to the absolute minimum.

a. For a no-drop situation, the phrase "no drop, no drop, no drop" must be transmitted. The reasons for the no drop should be cited at the first opportunity and the aircraft commander asked what his intentions are. The aircraft commander may elect to airland, or fly a race track and attempt another drop. If the DZSTL notices a factor that could affect the safety of the operation (such as a helicopter transiting low over the DZ while the drop aircraft is on approach), he should notify the aircraft.

b. If the situation requires minimum radio transmissions, a premission coordination or briefing may establish a drop clearance call as the only necessary communication. Few C-130s have FM; however, all are equipped with UHF/AM and VHF/AM capability. Some using units may have UHF/VHF radios. This must be discussed at the premission briefing.

B-7. GROUND MARKED RELEASE SYSTEM

The most common type of GMRS DZ establishment uses the inverted "L" marking system. The ground marked release system places the responsibility for determining the airdrop release point on the ground party. When the DZST is tasked to operate the DZ using the GMRS, several factors must be considered in determining the release point.

a. **Forward Throw.** Basically, this is the distance along the flight path that an object or a paratrooper travels from the time of exit from the jump platform until the parachute canopy fully opens. This allows other natural forces to act on the load and parachute. Different loads have different forward throw values.

b. **Wind Drift.** To determine the distance that an airdropped object travels under canopy as a result of wind action, use the formula: $D = KAV$ (D = distance travelled in yards; K = constant value [4.1 for personnel and 2.5 for equipment]; A = drop altitude in hundreds of feet; and V = wind speed). Mean effective wind speed should be used, if possible.

c. **Panel Placement.** The following procedures are used to establish a GMRS DZ. The placement of the panels is shown in Figure B-2.

(1) Locate the desired PI.

(2) Measure the wind and compute the wind drift using the $D = KAV$ formula.

(3) From the PI, walk the required distance into the direction of the wind.

(4) From this spot, face the direction of the flight path and pace off the distance for the forward throw. This establishes the actual release point overhead.

(5) Turn 90 degrees to the right and pace off 110 yards (100 meters) for the offset. This is done so the aircraft pilot can look out his left cockpit window while abeam the release point and see the panels. The corner panel is placed here. It is best to elevate the panels at a 30- to 45-degree angle for greater visibility from the air.

(6) The other panels are located as shown in Figure B-2.

(7) Night inverted "L" drops are laid out the same way using directional/omnidirectional white lights. Small fires, flares, or flashlights may also be used; however, this should be precoordinated.

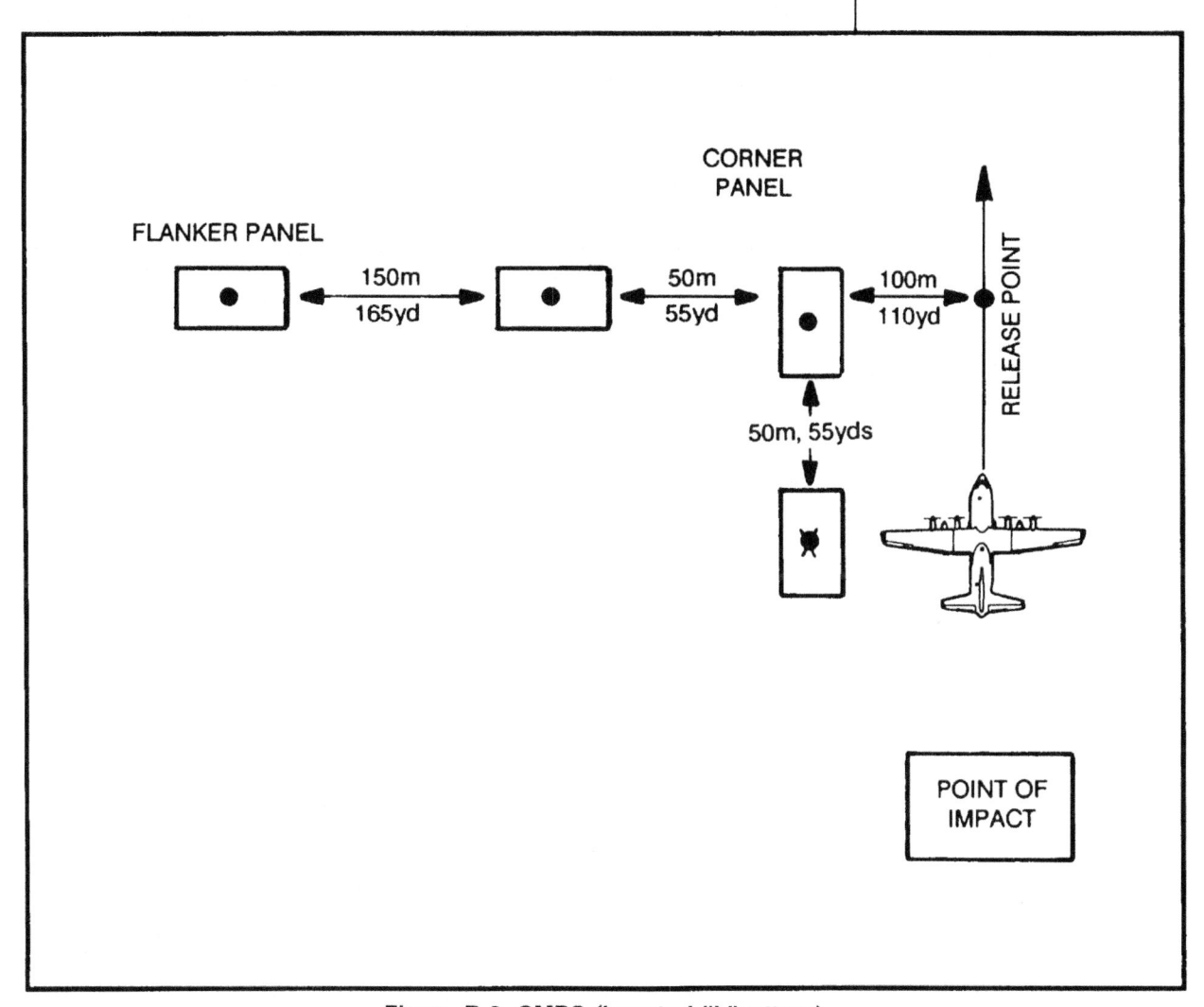

Figure B-2. GMRS (inverted "L" pattern).

B-8. TACTICAL DROP ZONE ASSESSMENTS

During operations, DZSTs are expected to tactically locate and assess a potential DZ for follow-on airdrop resupply/reinforcement.

a. Normally, the Air Force CCT would be tasked to accomplish this reconnaissance-type mission, using the MAC Form 339. When a CCT is unavailable, a tactical DZ assessment may be made using the following checklist guidelines:

- Drop zone name or intended call sign.
- Topographical map series and sheet number.
- Recommended approach axis magnetic course.
- Point of impact location (eight-digit grid coordinates).
- Leading edge centerline coordinates (eight-digit UTM).
- Drop zone size in yards/meters.
- Air traffic restrictions/hazards.
- Name of surveyor and unit assigned.
- Recommendation for approval/disapproval (for disapproval state reason).
- Remarks (include a recommendation for airdrop option CARP, GMRS, VIRS, or blind drop).

b. Airdrop operations on tactically assessed DZs are made only under the following conditions:

(1) During training events, the airdrops will be within a military reservation or on US government leased property.

(2) The supported service accepts responsibility for any damage that occurs as a result of the airdrop activity.

(3) There must be adequate time for safe, effective planning.

B-9. VERBALLY INITIATED RELEASE SYSTEM

A simple, yet accurate means of ground support of an airdrop operation involves guiding the aircraft from the ground to the release point via air-to-ground communications. The DZSTL calculates the release point in the same way as described for GMRS. He places himself on that release point and guides the aircraft to a spot directly overhead and radios the aircraft to release cargo/personnel. The following is a typical scenario:

(Aircraft) L41 - This is Bulldog, over.

(DZST) L41 - authenticate Charlie tango, over.

(Aircraft) L41, Bulldog - Sierra, reporting five minutes, over.

(DZST) Bulldog, L41 - not in sight, continue, over.

After one minute:

(DZST) Bulldog, L41 - In sight, turn left . . . . .

(DZST) (Call sign calls cease) Turn left . . . . .stop turn.

(DZST) Standby (call about five seconds from drop).

(DZST) Execute, execute, execute. L41, out.

> **NOTE:** Direction changes arc given in relation to the direction of flight. Aircraft will drop on the first call of "execute."

This airdrop option is not too difficult, especially after the DZST has the experience of controlling even one drop this way. When executing this option, the DZSTL could conceal himself in bushes, tall grass, or a fighting position at the release point.

APPENDIX C

AIRLIFT PLANNING FACTORS

Air transport resources are seldom sufficient to satisfy all demands, especially in large operations. In planning for airlift, commanders must use the fewest aircraft needed to complete the task in the required time; they decide on the use of airborne combat forces in light of continuous planning at the highest joint headquarters in the field. The allocation of air transport resources to supported services requires detailed staffing. To reduce the time required for staffing, planning staffs must have the following data available:

- The number of aircraft and crews available, by type.
- The payload that the aircraft can carry for the distance that the operation demands.
- The number and weights of soldiers, weapons, vehicles, equipment, and supplies in each unit involved.
- The routine maintenance requirements of the deployed force.
- The availability of materiel-handling equipment.
- Any operational limitations such as the maximum number of aircraft allowed on the ground at any one time (MOG).
- Intelligence on the enemy situation.

Section I. AIRLIFT ESTIMATES

Planning factors presented in this appendix should be used to make rough estimates of airlift capability. Due to the many variables involved in every airlift operation, these factors do not universally apply. Instead, they provide "order of magnitude" estimates. The use of detailed computer simulation models is encouraged for extensive calculations.

C-1. AIRLIFT CATEGORIES

The following paragraphs provide broad airlift planning factors for peacetime and wartime operations. Six airlift mission categories are described, although many airlift aircraft can perform in more than one mission category.

a. **Strategic Airlift.** Aircraft in this category provide continuous air movement from CONUS to or between different overseas areas.

b. **Theater Airlift.** These aircraft provide air movement of personnel, supplies, and equipment on a sustained, selective, or emergency basis to dispersed sites within a theater of operations.

c. **Civil Reserve Air Fleet.** Aircraft in this airlift category provide airlift services during emergencies and contingencies through contractual arrangements with selected US airlines.

d. **Tanker And Cargo Airlift.** Aircraft in this category provide about 8 percent of the wartime cargo airlift capability.

e. **Aeromedical Airlift.** These aircraft move theater casualties to rear area medical facilities during combat. They support the DOD regional health care system in peacetime.

f. **Operational Support Airlift.** Aircraft in this category support the following Air Force requirements:

- Command and staff movements.
- Aircrew repositioning.
- Medical team moves.
- Intelligence.

C-2. PALLET INFORMATION

The standard 463L pallet is 108 inches wide by 88 inches long, weighs 355 pounds with the restraining nets, and uses 2.25 inches of available aircraft height. Unless otherwise noted, a 463L pallet is a Type I as defined by MIL-P-27443 (USAF). After deductions for tie-down equipment, the remaining usable area on the pallet is 104 inches by 84 inches. When one of these pallets is loaded to 8 feet (the height allowance for pallet loads), the space used equals 485 cubic feet. The pallet permits maximum loads, including wheel loads of 250 psi.

C-3. MAXIMUM PAYLOADS

The size, shape, and density of most payloads rarely permit loading to 100 percent of the maximum payload capacity. Maximum payload data should not be used for planning. Using average payload data results in more accurate sorties predictions.

C-4. AVERAGE PAYLOADS

To determine the average payload for bulk cargo, multiply the number of pallets by the average weight of a pallet. Average bulk payloads are calculated using 2.3 short tons for each pallet position, including the weight of the pallet. Oversize and outsize payloads are based on actual loading exercises or output from the load-generator model.

C-5. AIRCRAFT DIMENSIONAL RESTRICTIONS

The following factors are used in determining the longest single item dimensional restrictions.

a. The loading entrance cross-section dimensions usually govern the size of the LSI. (Table C-1.) However, many other factors (such as vehicle ground clearance, ramp incline approach angle, cargo compartment geometry, the three dimensional conditions of the cargo, and floor-loading restrictions) must be considered before conclusive LSI guidance can be provided.

> **WARNING**
> WHEN CARGO CLEARANCE IS WITHIN 6 INCHES OF THE DIMENSIONAL FACTORS GIVEN IN TABLE C-1, DAMAGE TO THE AIRCRAFT COULD OCCUR DURING LOADING.

TYPE AIRCRAFT	CARGO DOOR	HEIGHT
C-5	Front	162
	Rear	150
C-141	Loading	109
	Airdrop	100
C-130	Loading	108
	Airdrop	100
C-23		75
KC-10/DC-10		102
B-747	Side	120-123
	Nose	77-98
B-707		91
DC-8		85

Table C-1. Aircraft cargo door dimensions.

b. Regulations require an aisle of about 14 inches on C-130 aircraft because they do not have catwalks in the cargo compartments. Aircrews use this aisle to inspect loads and systems while in flight.

C-6. FUEL REQUIREMENTS AND CONSUMPTION

When planning an airlift mission, fuel requirements must be considered. Aircraft range and payload are greatly affected by a mission's fuel requirements. As the distance increases, the fuel requirements increase and the allowable load decreases. Payloads shown in various figures of this manual already consider fuel needs. However, these figures usually assume fuel is available at the offload location. Each aircraft requires a specific fuel type and has a unique fuel consumption rate. (Table C-2.) Before using the payload figures in this manual, the planner should ensure that adequate stocks of the correct fuel exist for refueling the aircraft. If refueling is not possible at the offload station, potential payloads could be reduced, or additional en route stops could be required. The payloads generated by figures in this manual are based on zero wind fuel requirements and are suitable for general planning. Actual mission payloads would have to be adjusted to allow for wind factors at the time of the operation.

	C-5A/B	C-130	C-141	C-17A
Fuel Grade	JP4	JP4	JP4	JP4
Type Oil	Syn Jet	Syn Jet	Syn Jet	Syn Jet
Fuel Flow (Lbs/Hr)	20,000	5,000	12,000	N/A

Table C-2. Fuel types and consumption rates.

NOTE: Performance can be affected if alternate grades of fuel are used.

C-7. AIR REFUELING

The mission planner should never consider more than two air refuelings unless unusual circumstances exist. When considering air refueling, the deployment distance divided by three equals the critical leg.

C-8. SPECIAL AIRLIFT DELIVERY MODES

The many variables in determining theater airlift capability make it impractical to show comprehensive planning factors in a tabular form. To correctly estimate the airlift capability for specific missions, headquarters MAC/DOOM can be consulted. Theater airlift missions are developed to support specific exercises and contingency operations in contrast to intertheater airlift missions, which operate over established routes.

C-9. AIRFIELD RESTRICTIONS

Each aircraft has specific requirements and restrictions to ensure efficient operations into diverse airfields worldwide. Airfield size, MOG, weather, ATC, and navigational facilities all influence the selection of alternate airfields. Due to the number of variables involved in determining minimum runway requirements and maximum payloads, an operational decision is made on a case-by-case basis. Headquarters MAC/DOVF, Scott AFB IL 62225-5001, can be contacted to obtain the most current data on suitable worldwide airlift airfields.

C-10. MATERIELS-HANDLING EQUIPMENT

The MHE is a family of forklifts, cargo transport loaders, wide-body loaders, container lift trucks, and associated smaller equipment designed to interface with the rollerized cargo movement systems in air terminals and on military aircraft. They are designed to move palletized cargo on standard 88- by 108-inch pallets between the air terminal and cargo aircraft in support of airlift operations. Materiel-handling equipment is always required at the departure airfield and at the arrival airfield once airland operations begin.

C-11. MISSION SUPPORT REQUIREMENTS

For many airlift missions, MAC support equipment and personnel are necessary to ensure the success of the airlift flow. Depending on the size and specific circumstances of the mission, support can range from small requirements routed through common MAC bases to large requirements routed mainly through undeveloped airfields. These airfields have no capability to receive or process a major airlift flow. While specific planning factors provide a wide range of possibilities, it is important to recognize the likelihood that mission support requirements will increase as the movement requirements increase.

C-12. AEROMEDICAL EVACUATION CAPABILITY

Aeromedical evacuation capability varies significantly by aircraft type. (Table C-3.) The C-141B is the primary strategic aeromedical evacuation aircraft. Although other aircraft can be used on an opportune basis to move patients, the C-130 and C-9A are the primary aircrafts for theater aeromedical evacuation missions.

a. Assigned aeromedical airlift unit equipment is used to determine the mount of retrograde airlift for aeromedical evacuation (retrograde airlift is airlift returning from the area of hostilities).

b. The number of aeromedical evacuation medical crew members required for strategic evacuation operations is computed on the basis of 50 mission hours a month and a crew planning factor of 1:25. (one crew member is planned for each 10 patients. For example, a standard crew complement to support the C-141 planning factor of 65 patients would be three flight nurses and four medical technicians.)

c. The number of aeromedical evacuation medical crew members required for tactical evacuation operations is computed on the basis of 60 mission hours a month and a crew ratio of 1:25. (A standard crew to support C-130 operations would be two flight nurses and three medical technicians.)

d. Airlift requirements for aeromedical evacuation arc determined by dividing the number of patients by the patient load factor. (Table C-3.)

C-13. PLANNING FACTORS

Airlift planning factors can be used as source data in a computer simulation model. They can also be used to estimate how long it would take a given airlift fleet to deliver (close) a force to a specific location. Section II of this appendix gives detailed information on each airlift aircraft.

C-14. ESTIMATION OF PAYLOAD DATA

The average payload of an airlift is a basic factor in converting airlift tonnage requirements into numbers of airlift sorties,

a. Determine the route segment distance.

b. Determine the average payload for each mission. (Table C-4, see page C-7.)

c. Determine the number of missions required using this formula:

$$\frac{\text{Number of Missions Required}}{} = \frac{\text{Move Requirement (tons)}}{\text{Average Payload (tons/mission)}}$$

NOTE: Any fraction of a mission is always rounded up.

	C-9A	C-130 All Models	C-141B W/Comf Pallet	C-141B W/O Comf Pallet
Medical Crew Flight Nurse	2	2	3	3
Med Tech	3	3	4	4
Peacetime Total [1] Litter/Walking	9/30	24/36 [2]	31/78	31/78 [6]
Wartime/Emergency All Litter	40	74 [2]	103	103 161[4]/195 [2,5]
All Walking	40	36/82 [2]	140 [4]/165 [5]	
Surge Litter/Walking	40/0 [1]	30/42 [1,2]	32/79	32/79 40
Floor Loading	Not Available	20	36	
Load Planning Factors	40	50	65	65

[1] Various litter and walking combinations are available at all times.
[2] Side-facing seats are used.
[3] If a full medical crew is on board, only 70 positions are available.
[4] Aft-facing seats are used.
[5] Due to life raft limitations, the number of walking patients may be reduced to 160 on overwater flights.
[6] Peacetime strategic missions normally use a comfort pallet.

Table C-3. Aeromedical airlift capabilities.

C-15. COMPUTATION OF CYCLE TIME

The cycle time of an airlift aircraft can be used to determine the number of tons a single aircraft can deliver a day. Cycle time can be affected by choke points in the airlift system such as diplomatic considerations, airfield availability, weather, and en route support.

a. Determine the block speed for each route segment at peacetime cruise speeds. Average block speed can be calculated using this formula:

Average Block Speed = $\dfrac{\text{Round Trip Distance}}{\text{RTFT}}$

b. Determine the RTFT using this formula:

RTFT = $\dfrac{(\text{Leg 1 distance}) \times 2}{\text{Leg 1 block speed}} + \dfrac{(\text{Leg 2 distance}) \times 2}{\text{Leg 2 block Speed}}$

c. Determine the TGT using this formula: (Table C-5.)

TGT = Onload Time + En Route Time + Offload Time

d. Determine the cycle time using this formula:

Cycle Time = RTFT + TGT

TYPE AIRCRAFT	DISTANCE (NM)	AVERAGE PAYLOAD (TONS) BULK	OVERSIZE	OUTSIZE	MAXIMUM PAYLOAD	PAX CAPABILITY
C-5	2,000	82.8	74.5	101.0	112.7	73
	2,500	82.8	71.9	82.8	99.9	73
	3,000	82.8	69.1	77.7	87.3	73
	3,500	75.7	65.1	66.5	75.7	73
C-130E (H)	Peacetime					
	500	13.8	12.6		22.0 (22.1)	8
	1,000	13.8	12.5		20.5 (20.6)	8
	1,500	13.8	12.1 (12.4)		19.3 (19.5)	8
	2,000	13.8	11.3 (11.4)		15.7 (16.2)	8
	2,500	12.2 (12.8)	10.1 (10.5)		12.2 (12.8)	8
	3,000	8.9 (9.9)	8.0 (8.7)		8.9 (9.9)	8
	3,500	2.7 (5.5)	2.6 (4.8)		2.7 (5.5)	8
	Wartime					
	500	13.8	12.7		24.8	8
	1,000	13.8	12.7		23.3	8
	1,500	13.8	12.6		22.2 (22.3)	8
	2,000	13.8	12.5		20.7 (20.8)	8
C-141	Peacetime					
	2,000	29.9	26.0		34.4	22
	2,500	29.9	25.2		29.9	22
	3,000	25.9	23.9		25.9	22
	3,500	20.3	19.6		20.3	22
	Wartime					
	2,000	29.9	26.5		44.26	
	2,500	29.9	26.5		36.26	
	3,000	29.9	26.4		33.3	26
	3,500	26.6	24.5		26.6	26

Table C-4. General airlift planning factors.

	C-5A/B	**C-130**	**C-141**
Onload Time	3 + 45	1 + 30	2 + 15
En Route Time	2 + 15	1 + 30	2 + 15
Offload Time	3 + 15	1 + 30	2 + 15

NOTE: All times are in hours and minutes.

Table C-5. Average ground times for contingency and exercise planning.

C-16. DETERMINATION OF CLOSURE

Closure is defined as the total elapsed time from takeoff of the first airlift mission at the onload base until the last airlift mission lands at the destination base. The following process provides a closure estimate for moving an airborne division from Tinker AFB to Cairo. Wartime planning factors apply. The aircraft allocation is 20 C-5s and 50 C-141s. This example only covers the cargo requirement; however, the passenger movement could be handled in a similar manner.

a. Determine the Movement Requirements. The Army estimates the Airborne Division, pre-positioned at Tinker AFB, has these characteristics:

Outsize Tons	Oversize Tons	Bulk Tons	Total Tons
500	14,000	500	15,000

Since the movement requirement contains outsize cargo, an outsize capable aircraft must be included in the airlift allocation.

b. Determine the Aircraft Routing. Many common MAC route segment distances are available; however, if a specific route segment is not listed, the planner must use appropriate flight planning documents or compute great circle distances. These figures are available:

Route Segment	Distance (NM)
Tinker - McGuire	1,138
McGuire - Lajes	2,234
Lajes - Cairo	3,154

c. Determine the Average Payload for Each Aircraft Type. The longest route segment is used to determine the average payload; however, operations into a field with a short runway could severely limit the payload. Since over 90 percent of the movement requirement consists of oversize cargo, the "oversize" column should be used to determine average payloads. (Table C-4.) The 3,500 NM row yields:

C-5 average payload = 65.1 tons

C-141 average payload = 19.6 tons

d. Determine the Cycle Time for Each Aircraft Type. To determine the cycle time for each aircraft type, the following formulas are used.

(1) Determine block speeds for each aircraft.

Leg Distance	C-5 Block Speed	C-141 Block Speed
1,138	389	370
2,234	415	394
3,154	427	405

(2) Determine the RTFT for each aircraft type using this formula:

$$RTFT = \frac{\text{distance leg 1} \times 2}{\text{block speed leg 1}} + \frac{\text{distance leg 2} \times 2}{\text{block speed leg 2}} + \frac{\text{distance leg 3} \times 2}{\text{block speed leg 3}}$$

$$RTFT\ C\text{-}5 = \frac{1,138 \times 2}{389} + \frac{2,234 \times 2}{415} + \frac{3,154 \times 2}{427}$$

RTFT C-5 = 5.8 + 10.7 + 14.7 = 31.2 hours.

$$RTFT\ C\text{-}141 = \frac{1,138 \times 2}{370} + \frac{2,234 \times 2}{394} + \frac{3,154 \times 2}{405}$$

RTFT C-141 = 6.0 + 11.0 + 15.2 = 32.2 hours.

(3) Determine the TGT for each aircraft type using this formula (Table C-5):

TGT = Onload Time (Tinker) + En route Time (McGuire) + En route Time (Lajes) + Offload Time (Cairo) + En route Time (Lajes)

TGT (C-5) = (2 + 15) + (2 + 15) + (3 + 15) + (3 + 45)

TGT (C-5) = 13 + 45 = 13.75 hours

TGT (C-141) = (2 + 15) + (2 + 15) + (2 + 15) + (2 + 15) + (2 + 15)

TGT (C-141) = 11 + 15 = 11.25 hours

(4) Determine the cycle time for each aircraft type using this formula:

Cycle Time = RTFT + TGT

Cycle Time (C-5) = 31.2 + 13.75 = 44.95 hours

Cycle Time (C-141) = 32.2 + 11.25 = 43.45 hours

(5) Determine the tons a day, an aircraft type (T/D/AC) using this formula:

$$T/D/AC = \frac{(\text{Average Payload}) \ (24) \ (\text{Number of Aircraft})}{\text{Cycle Time}}$$

$$T/D/AC \ (C\text{-}5) = \frac{(65.1) \ (24) \ (20)}{44.95} = 716.5 \text{ tons}$$

$$T/D/AC \ (C\text{-}141) = \frac{(19.6) \ (24) \ (50)}{43.45} = 654.5 \text{ tons}$$

(6) Determine the total tons delivered a day (TT/D) for the fleet using this formula:

$$TT/D = T/D/AC \ (C\text{-}5) + T/D/AC \ (C\text{-}141)$$

$$TT/D = 716.5 + 654.5 = 1,371.0 \text{ tons/day}$$

(7) Determine the closure using this formula:

$$\text{Closure} = \frac{\text{Movement Requirement}}{TT/D}$$

$$\text{Closure} = \frac{15,000 \text{ tons}}{1,371 \text{ tons/day}} = 10.9 \text{ days}$$

e. **Determine Revised Cycle Time.** This example explains one situation when the cycle time might have to be revised. It involves a large-scale operation where most of the fleet of an aircraft type are scheduled to be used. In this case, the cycle time might have to be adjusted to maintain an objective use rate, The UTE rate is not a limiting factor unless most of the fleet is involved. The example operation involves 210 C-141 aircraft (nearly all of the C-141s) with a cycle time of 32 hours and an RTFT of 22 hours. The fleet must not exceed a UTE rate of 10 hours a day. The planned UTE rate is computed using the following formula:

$$\text{UTE (planned)} = \frac{\text{RTFT} \times 24}{\text{cycle time}} = \frac{22 \times 24}{32} = 16.5 \text{ hours per day}$$

Since the planned UTE rate of 16.5 hours per day exceeds the objective UTE rate of 10 hours per day, a revised cycle time must be computed using this formula:

$$\text{Cycle Time (adjusted)} = \frac{\text{RTFT} \times 24}{\text{Objective UTE}} = \frac{22 \times 24}{10} = 52.8 \text{ hours}$$

The adjusted cycle time should now be used to compute closure.

C-17. PRODUCTIVITY FACTORS

Productivity factors (percentages) are gross measures of an aircraft's ability to move cargo and passengers to a user.

a. On a strategic airlift mission involving an outbound and a return leg, the outbound leg is productive and the return leg is nonproductive. Therefore, the productive factor would be 50 percent. It is assumed that the cargo has already been positioned at the aircraft's departure point. Usually, airlift aircraft must fly one or more positioning legs to an on-load location. Since productive cargo is usually not moved at this time, positioning legs reduce the overall productivity factor to a value less than 50 percent. For example, an aircraft is flying from Charleston AFB to an aerial port of embarkation at Pope AFB (positioning leg). Then to an aerial port of debarkation at Torrejon AB (outbound leg) and back to Charleston AFB (return leg). Although the entire round-trip distance is 7,550 miles, only 3,550 miles (the distance from Pope to Torrejon) is considered productive. Therefore, the productivity factor is 47 percent (3,500 + 7,550).

b. A similar example for theater airlift is not as straightforward. Within a theater, productive cargo is moved on both inbound and outbound legs. However, the overall productivity factor for theater airlift aircraft is lower, because the positioning and repositioning legs compose a greater part of the total distance.

c. Both the strategic and theater productivity factor calculations arc situation specific. To provide productivity factors with broad planning applications, the following average productivity factors are compiled:

Strategic Airlift - 47 percent.
Tactical Airlift - 40 percent.

In this context, strategic airlift refers to any aircraft that is performing an intertheater mission. Theater airlift refers to any aircraft that is operating solely within a theater.

Section II. SPECIFIC AIRCRAFT DATA

This section provides statistical data and comparisons of the characteristics of the major USAF airlift aircraft. (Figure C-1, see page C-16.)

C-18. C-130E/H DATA

a. **Description.**

General	Lockheed, 4 turboprop engines.
Wing span	132 feet, 7 inches.
Overall length	99 feet, 6 inches.
Main gear track	14 feet, 3 inches.
Usable fuel	60,112 pounds.
Mission	Cargo, soldiers, tactical airdrop, and airland.

b. Loading Characteristics.

Rear ramp, ground, or truck bed level, and 463L system.

c. Main Cabin Dimensions.

Length (maximum usable)	470 inches.
Width (maximum usable)	114 inches, 105 inches.
Height (maximum usable)	108 inches.
Usable floor area (fixed and ramp)	370 square feet.
Usable cube (main compartment)	2,818 cubic feet.

d. Door Dimensions.

Width	123 inches.
Height	108 inches.

e. Performance. (H-model characteristics that are different are shown in parentheses.)

Maximum ferry range	3,685 nautical miles. (3,962 nautical miles).
Average cruise speed	280 knots (300 knots).
Takeoff gross weight (emergency or wartime)	173,700 pounds.
Takeoff gross weight (peacetime)	153,700 pounds.
Normal operating altitude	18,000 feet/26,000 feet. (23,500 feet/28,000 feet).

Minimum runway requirements:

Takeoff	2,600 feet (2,300 feet).
Landing	2,700 feet (2,360 feet).
Maximum ACL (floor loaded)	35,000 pounds (35,500 pounds).
Maximum number of 463L pallets	6.

Maximum number of soldiers:

Wartime	91.
Peacetime	74.
Maximum number of paratroopers	64.
Minimum pavement for]N)-degree turn	74 feet.
Minimum runway width	60 feet.

C-19. C-141B DATA

a. Description.

General	Lockheed, 4 turbojet engines.
Wing span	160 feet.
Overall length	168 feet, 4 inches.
Main gear track	21 feet, 7 inches.
Usable fuel	153,352 pounds.
Mission	Cargo, soldiers, tactical airdrop.

b. Loading Characteristics.

Rear ramp, ground, or truck bed level, and 463L system.

c. **Main Cabin Dimensions.**

Length	1,120 inches.
Width	123 inches.
Height	109 inches.
Usable floor area (fixed and ramp)	937 square feet.
Usable cube (main compartment)	7,024 cubic feet.

d. **Main Door Dimensions.**

Width	123 inches.
Heigth	109 inches.

e. **Performance.**

Maximum ferry range	4,531 nautical miles.
Average cruise speed	425 knots.
Takeoff gross weight (emergency or wartime)	343,000 pounds.
Takeoff gross weight (peacetime)	323.000 pounds.
Normal operating altitude	FL 310-410.
Minimum runway requirements:	
Takeoff (wartime weight)	8,420 feet.
Takeoff (peacetime weight)	7,350 feet.
Landing (brakes only)	3,840 feet.
Maximum ACL (floor loaded)	89,000 pounds.
Maximum numbers of 463L pallets	13.
Maximum number of soldiers:	
Wartime	200 (Flying overland).
	153 (Flying over water).
Peacetime	143.
Maximum number of paratroopers	155.
Minimum pavement for 180-degree turn	137 feet.
Minimum runway width	98 feet.

C-20. C-17A DATA

a. **Description.**

General	McDonnell Douglas, 4 turbofan engines.
Wing span	165 feet.
Overall length	175.2 feet.
Mission	Long-range, heavy-lift cargo transport.

b. **Cabin Capacity.**

Length	88 feet.
Width	18 feet.
Height	12.3 feet.
Floor area	1,584 square feet.
Usable cube	20,900 cubic feet.

c. **Main Door Dimensions.**

Width	18 feet.
Length	19 feet, 8 inches.

d. **Performance.**

Maximum ferry range	4,700 nautical miles.
Average cruise speed	460 knots.
Takeoff gross weight	580,000 pounds.
Normal operating altitude	FL 30 to FL 41.
Minimum runway requirements:	
Takeoff	7,600 feet with 167,000-pound payload.
Landing (thrust reversal)	3,000 feet with 167,000-pound payload.
Maximum ACL	172,200 pounds.
Maximum number of 463L pallets	18.
Maximum number of paratroopers	102.
Minimum pavement fo 180-degree turn	90 feet.
Minimum runway width	90 feet.

C-21. C-5A/B DATA

a. **Description.**

General	Lockheed, 4 turbojet engines.
Wing span	222 feet, 8 inches.
Overall length	247 feet, 10 inches.
Main gear track (outside)	37 feet, 6 inches.
Fuel capacity	332,500 pounds.
Mission	Airlift cargo and soldiers.

b. **Loading Characteristics.**

Front and aft ramp, ground, or truck bed level, and 463L system.

c. **Cabin Capacity.**

Length	121 feet, 1 inch.
Width	19 feet, 0 inches.
Height	13 feet, 6 inches.
Usable floor area (fixed and ramp)	2,747 square feet.
Usable cube-main compartment (floor loaded)	18,368 cubic feet.

d. **Door Dimensions.**

Front	228 inches wide, 162 inches high.
Rear:	
Drive in (ramp down) forward or level kneel	228 inches wide, 161 inches high.
Drive in (ramp down) aft kneel	228 inches wide, 153 inches high.
Truck loading (ramp level)	228 inches wide, 114 inches high.

e. **Performance.**

Maximum ferry range	6,238 nautical miles.
Takeoff to block-in speed	436 knots.
Average cruise speed	436 knots.
Maximum takeoff gross weight	769,000 pounds.
Normal operating altitudes	FL310-410.
Minimum runway requirements:	
Takeoff	9,150 feet.
Landing	4,610 feet.
Maximum payload (floor loaded)	291,000 pounds
Maximum number of 463L pallets	36.
Maximum number of soldiers	340 (Airbus configuration; normally 73 soldiers will ride in upstairs troop compartment.)
Minimum pavement for 180-degreee turn	150 feet.
Minimum runway width	150 feet.

FM 90-26

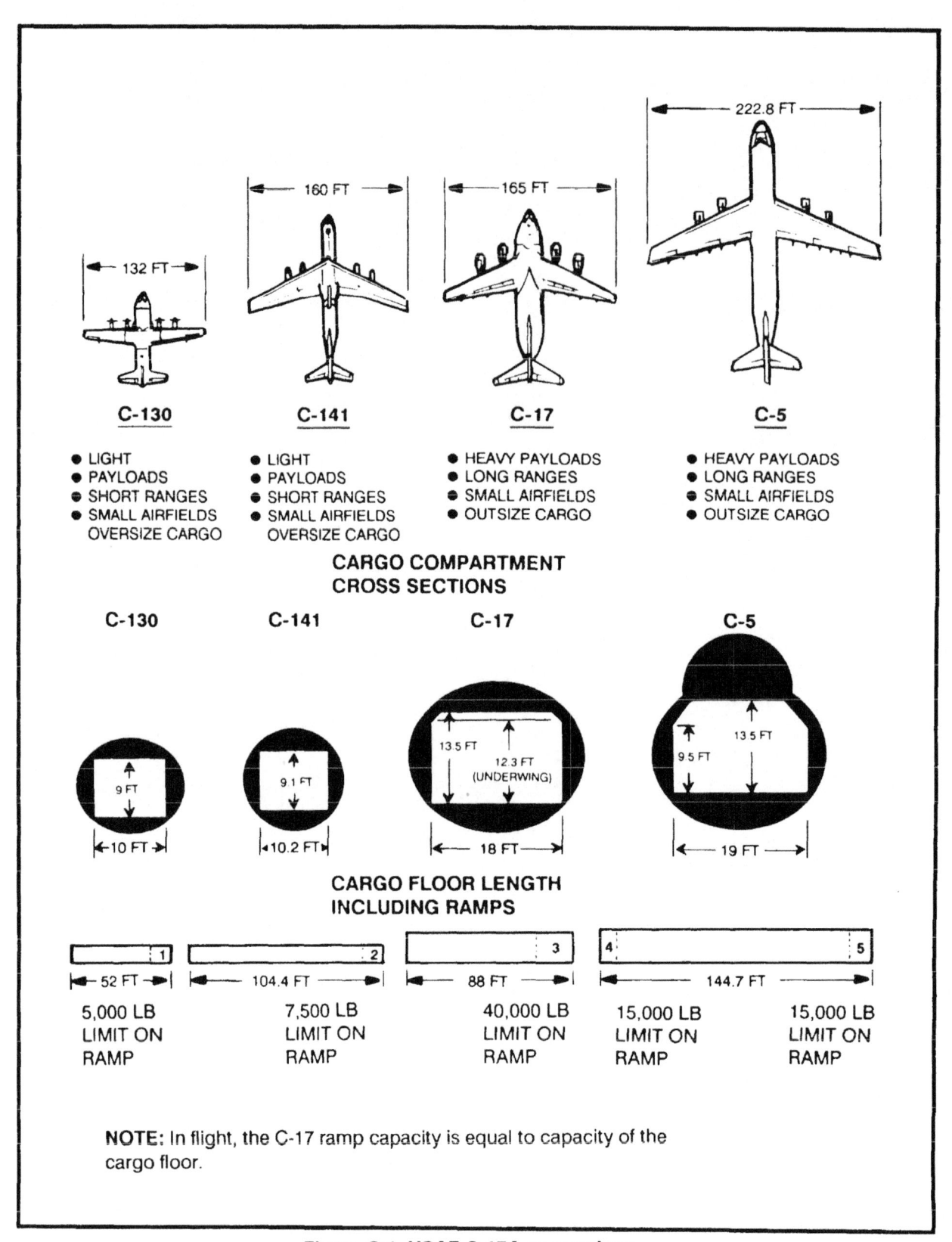

C-130
- LIGHT
- PAYLOADS
- SHORT RANGES
- SMALL AIRFIELDS
  OVERSIZE CARGO

132 FT

C-141
- LIGHT
- PAYLOADS
- SHORT RANGES
- SMALL AIRFIELDS
  OVERSIZE CARGO

160 FT

C-17
- HEAVY PAYLOADS
- LONG RANGES
- SMALL AIRFIELDS
- OUTSIZE CARGO

165 FT

C-5
- HEAVY PAYLOADS
- LONG RANGES
- SMALL AIRFIELDS
- OUTSIZE CARGO

222.8 FT

CARGO COMPARTMENT CROSS SECTIONS

C-130: 9 FT × 10 FT

C-141: 9.1 FT × 10.2 FT

C-17: 13.5 FT, 12.3 FT (UNDERWING) × 18 FT

C-5: 13.5 FT, 9.5 FT × 19 FT

CARGO FLOOR LENGTH INCLUDING RAMPS

C-130	C-141	C-17	C-5
52 FT	104.4 FT	88 FT	144.7 FT
5,000 LB LIMIT ON RAMP	7,500 LB LIMIT ON RAMP	40,000 LB LIMIT ON RAMP	15,000 LB / 15,000 LB LIMIT ON RAMP

NOTE: In flight, the C-17 ramp capacity is equal to capacity of the cargo floor.

Figure C-1. USAF C-17A comparison.

APPENDIX D

AIRBORNE ELEMENTS OF THE TACTICAL AIR CONTROL SYSTEM

Airborne operations require extensive coordination between the US Air Force, US Army, and often other services. The airborne element of the tactical air control system, consisting of the AWACS and the ABCCC, augment and even replace the ground-based elements of TACS when response time is critical.

D-1. AIRBORNE WARNING AND CONTROL SYSTEM

The AWACS (designated by the Air Force as the E-3 radar) is a modified Boeing 707 that houses a radar subsystem and vast communications equipment. It is under OPCON of the TACC. The AWACS radar system can compensate for the major limitations of ground-based radar systems such as their inability to detect low-flying aircraft due to line-of-sight restrictions. Other limitations of ground-based radar systems include their susceptibility to ECM and their vulnerability to attack.

a. **Communications.** To complement its flexible receiving ability, the AWACS can communicate with a wide range of systems. It has extensive HF, VHF, and UHF radios that can be used to communicate with ground controllers, airborne forces, and ground forces.

b. **Missions.** The three major missions the E-3 radar can support are tactical, air defense, and humanitarian.

(1) *Tactical.* In a conventional warfare environment, AWACS serves as an airspace control element. From this vantage point behind the front lines, the tactical commander monitors the allied and enemy forces. He makes the decisions needed to conduct the battle. The E-3's radar flexibility in the tactical environment is one of its major assets.

(2) *Air defense.* The E-3's radar flexibility allows it to support tactical missions, defensive missions, or both at the same time. The aircraft can be used for weapons control or as a surveillance platform. In an air defense role, the E-3 radar provides weapons control and surveillance capabilities. It also provides C^2 for weapons and control for air defense regions during stages of increased alerts.

(3) *Humanitarian.* The E-3 radar can fly into a natural disaster area and can provide an airborne CP to monitor the situation. It can also provide the needed communications and control during large-scale disasters.

D-2. AIRBORNE BATTLEFIELD COMMAND AND CONTROL CENTER

The mission of the ABCCC is to provide a worldwide capability for control of air operations during contingencies; in the absence of or in concert with the ground TACS; and in the forward battle areas beyond the range of ground-based TACS elements. The ABCCC can act as an extension of a TACC combat operation, as an interim TACC combat operation, or as an alternate ASOC. It can also coordinate electronic combat, serve as a joint rescue coordination center, and provide tactical threat warning.

a. **Airborne Battle Staff Composition and Duties.** The ABCCC battle staff is divided into four functional areas: command, operations, intelligence, and communications.

b. **Communications Capability.** The ABCCC was designed to support the air-to-ground war. As such, each capsule has 20 radios for the battle staff to use. They include four VHF/AM, four VHF/FM, four HF, and eight UHF. Six of the eight UHF radios are equipped with HAVE QUICK (antijam). This mix of radios allows the ABCCC to work with all elements of the TACS and the forces employed.

c. **Missions.** The ABCCC has five missions:

(1) *Airborne ASOC.* The ABCCC can fulfill a limited ASOC role or can ensure proper communications between the ASOC and TACPs or between fighters and FACs. ABCCC is often the only agency that can fulfill the ASOC role at the onset of hostilities.

(2) *TACC combat operations.* In the role of combat operations center, the ABCCC maintains ground alert and airborne asset status. The real time compilation of intelligence and operations information allows for flexibility in performing current operations. In the first stages of conflict, ABCCC allows appropriate TAF operations to be conducted in the absence of the traditional ground-based TACS.

(3) *Electronic combat.* With its unique communications ability, the ABCCC can maintain radio contact for coordination with all electronic combat assets (ESM and ECM) available to the tactical commander. The combination of intelligence and operations information within ABCCC allows the situational awareness required to perform the function. Electronic combat coordination is a growing role for the ABCCC.

(4) *Joint rescue coordination center.* As a JRCC, the ABCCC can track aircraft; maintain the status of SAR forces; coordinate with other services' SAR forces; scramble assets; and marshal, coordinate, and control SARs. These SAR operations can be conducted in peacetime or war.

(5) *Crisis management.* The ABCCC can provide on-the-scene C^2 during crisis situations. Tasks are much the same as for TACC/ASOC missions but are accomplished on a time-compressed schedule. (See TAC Regulation 55-130 for more information about employment of ABCCC.)

APPENDIX E

BRIEFINGS, INSPECTIONS, AND REHEARSALS

Preparation for combat includes briefings and briefbacks, inspections, and rehearsals.

Section I. BRIEFINGS

All commanders must closely supervise briefings. Soldiers should receive enough information about the weather, terrain, and enemy in the objective area to perform their duties intelligently. To allow for contingencies, each person should also know the overall plan.

E-1. BRIEFING PLAN

A tentative plan for briefings in the marshaling area is prepared before marshaling.

a. Each of the higher units prepares a briefing plan that includes the following:

- Time and place for each briefing.
- Briefing facilities available.
- Personnel involved in each briefing.
- Details to be covered in each briefing.
- Security measures during each briefing.

b. The briefing schedule is coordinated with airlift units so that the crews of assault aircraft and other selected airlift personnel can attend briefings with the soldiers they transport.

c. The briefing schedule must allow for briefback of all aspects of the plan at each level. This requires flexibility in the plan.

E-2. BRIEFING FACILITIES

On arriving at the marshaling area, units establish briefing rooms in buildings, huts, or tents within the sealed area. Briefing rooms should contain the best possible briefing aids. The rooms should be big enough to hold the platoon, the aircraft load, or the largest group to be briefed at one time. Some platoon and squad briefings take place outside regular briefing rooms with simple aids like maps, photos, and sketches.

a. Each brigade and battalion establishes at least one briefing room. When possible, each company establishes its own. Otherwise, the battalion provides one or more briefing rooms for its companies to use. Platoons (or aircraft loads) are rotated through the assigned briefing rooms according to the briefing schedule. Individual squads can also be rotated through briefing rooms.

b. On the departure airfield, briefing facilities are established in the joint CP for joint briefings of the senior airborne and airlift commanders and their staffs.

c. The briefing facilities used by the assault units are kept for use by buildup units. Advanced landing fields, AAs, and routes in the airhead can be shown to interested personnel, and the current situation reviewed on the basis of situation reports.

E-3. BRIEFING RESPONSIBILITIES

The S3 prepares the briefing schedule in coordination with the S2 for inclusion in the marshaling plan. Briefings are critical and are conducted down to the lowest level of command. Except for key commanders and staff officers, information about the operation is on a strict need-to-know basis before marshaling, so marshaling area briefings must be detailed. Each soldier must know exactly the part he plays in the operation. He must also know the plans of his unit and of adjacent units. Contingency actions for individuals and units must also be included in these briefings. The S2 should ensure that the necessary briefing aids are available before soldiers enter the marshaling areas. An annotated low-altitude air photo of the landing area, explained by photo-interpreter personnel, is the most effective briefing aid. Accurate terrain models and sand tables of the airhead are effective. Large-scale maps with defenses and obstacles overprinted from the latest air photos are valuable as well.

E-4. JOINT BRIEFINGS

For coordination and understanding, a series of joint briefings is conducted during marshaling for selected airborne and airlift personnel. At these briefings, information and instructions are given on all matters that are of joint interest in the air movement and ground assault plans. The schedule and scope of joint briefings are determined at the joint commanders' conference. Airborne and airlift commanders and selected staff officers attend the command briefings conducted as part of their conferences. (FM 100-27 provides a recommended format for joint briefings.)

a. **Airlift Crew Attendance at Airborne Unit Briefings.** The crews of aircraft should attend the briefings of the airborne unit they are transporting; the aircraft crew and the airborne unit land are a team in the objective area.

b. **Ground Unit Attendance at Airlift Briefings.** Ground units send representatives to airlift unit briefings to learn all they can about Air Force plans, especially air movement plans. Although airlift units are responsible for the air movement, airborne units are interested in–

(1) Takeoff arrangements, including marshaling of aircraft on the ground and assembly in the air.

(2) Routes to the objective, including alternate routes.

(3) Final approach to the objective, including direction of flight, checkpoints on the ground, altitude, and aircraft formation.

(4) Details of fighter cover and friendly air defense units.

(5) Intelligence estimates on expected enemy air and antiaircraft opposition.

(6) Evasion and escape procedures.

(7) Ditching procedures.

(8) Anticipated weather, including the direction and velocity of the wind at the object ive.

(9) Communications, including signals for the parachute exit.

(10) Use of alternate DZs/LZs.

c. **Final Briefing.** All aircraft commanders attend the final aircrew briefing, if possible, It is conducted by the airlift commander or representative just before takeoff. It includes all last-minute information and instructions for the air movement.

E-5. MISSION BRIEFING

The mission briefing is presented by the Air Force for the commanders of the various dispersed airfields, and for required crew members, plus representatives from other organizations or services as appropriate. When the dispersed concept is employed, each commander at the dispersed airfields conducts mission briefings for the crew members at their respective locations. Joint representation provides a basis for mutual understanding before the mission and is encouraged at all briefings. This briefing is a comprehensive coverage of all the mission's phases.

a. **Scope.** Since the scope of the mission briefing varies with the nature and complexity of the mission to be performed, it is not possible to outline all detailed matters to be covered. Handouts can be used for certain subjects such as navigation, operations, and others at the discretion of the commander. The briefing order is as follows (although the briefing includes only the items that fit the mission):

- Opening statement by the unit or mission commander.
- Intelligence.

- Operations (first of two sections).
- Navigation.
- Weather.
- Communications.
- Flight surgeon.
- Operations (second section).
- Commander.
- Chaplain.

b. **Content.** The following items are discussed in the mission briefing. Special briefings for more detail are the option of the commander.

(1) *Opening by the unit or mission commander.* This includes–

(a) A brief description of the overall operation.

(b) The purpose of the operation.

(c) The role of the unit.

(d) Participation of other organizations.

(2) *Intelligence.* This includes–

(a) The general situation, enemy, and friendly forces.

(b) Enemy capabilities.

(c) Friendly air and ground activity, including rescue.

(d) Priority intelligence requirements.

(e) Evasion and escape.

(f) Conduct if captured.

(g) Security.

(h) Reports.

(i) Debriefing, as required.

(3) *Operations.* This includes–

(a) Execution of the marshaling plan and trip numbers (including designation of spares).

(b) Loading of emergency equipment needed for the mission.

(c) Inspection of aircraft.

(d) Loading of aircraft, including liaison with unit being transported.

(e) Inspection of personal equipment and crew.

(f) Completion of forms (including clearance, weight and balance, and manifests) and collection of them before takeoff.

(g) Times for stations, engines, taxiing, check-in, and takeoff.

(h) Taxi and runup procedures.

(i) Aborts during runup or takeoff, or while in flight.

(j) Takeoff.

(k) Route and return.

(1) Route, DZ/LZ, and return (including aeromedical evacuation or diversionary routes, if applicable).

(m) Use of CCTs/LRSU.

(n) Coordination of the crew over the DZ.

(o) Landing and taxiing procedures.

(p) Emergency procedures (other than SOP).

(4) *Navigation.* This includes–

(a) Airspace restrictions.

(b) Navigational aids.

(c) Emergency airfields.

(d) Coverage of DZ/LZ and salvo area(s) with photos, maps, or other aids. (This should be covered in a separate briefing after the mission briefing.)

(e) Time hack.

(5) *Weather.* This includes–

(a) Existing and forecast weather at departure time, on the airfield, en route, and in the objective area.

(b) Winds at the departure airfield, en route, and at the objective area (including drop altitude where applicable).

(c) Weather outlook, if the operation is to take place more than 24 hours after the general mission briefing.

(d) Time and location of the final weather briefing (if applicable).

(6) *Communications.* This includes–

(a) Call signs.

(b) Frequencies.

- Check-in.
- Taxi.
- Takeoff.
- En route (including special reporting procedures).
- Objective area.
- Landing.
- Emergency.
- Rescue.

(c) IFF use.

(d) Communications security, authentication, and radio silence.

(7) *Flight surgeon.* This includes–

(a) Health service support missions and type of units involved in the operation.

(b) Required immunizations.

(c) Use of water purification tablets.

(d) Waste disposal.

(e) Endemic and epidemic diseases in the AO.

(8) *Operations (second section).* This includes–

(a) Schedule for further briefings.

(b) Critique.

(c) Messing and transportation.

(d) Flying safety.

(e) Mission reports and other forms.

(f) Maintenance support.

(9) *Commander.* This includes–

(a) Special command instructions.

(b) Designation of time and place for final briefings on topics such as weather decisions.

E-6. COMMAND AND STAFF BRIEFINGS

Although special emphasis is placed on briefing soldiers in the marshaling area, operational briefings for unit commanders and staff officers continue, regardless of the amount and scope of briefings received earlier. Any details of the operation previously withheld for security reasons are divulged. New intelligence and changes in plans are promptly disseminated. Information and instructions previously issued are reviewed. A common briefing on all battalion missions should be given to all regimental/brigade and battalion commanders. If this is done, battalion missions can be shifted with little delay in case of inaccurate landings. Company commanders in a battalion should be given a common briefing so that company missions can be changed if an unexpected event occurs after landing.

E-7. BRIEFBACKS

Briefbacks and rehearsals are not the same. Briefbacks are related to the planning process; rehearsals are related to execution. Briefbacks to the commander of operational concepts should be required from all subordinate commanders and leaders for missions tasked in OPLANs, OPORDs, or FRAGOs. Briefback times and locations are normally specified in the coordinating instructions paragraph of the OPORD/OPLAN. The scope and detail required depends on the mission and time available. It may range from an oral review using operational graphics to an in-depth explanation using terrain models, visual aids, and other devices. The commander should conduct at least two briefbacks with subordinate commanders. When possible, briefbacks should be conducted collectively at a meeting of the order group. The first briefback occurs immediately after the OPORD has been issued to ensure subordinates understand their mission. The second briefback occurs after subordinates have prepared their own concepts of the operation. However, before subordinates issue their OPORDs, the commander may recommend changes. In quickly developing situations, an abbreviated version may be required. The format of the briefback is a matter of unit SOP but should include the following information:

- Division/brigade commander's intent and mission statement.
- Intelligence overview.
- Specified, implied, and mission-essential tasks.
- Constraints and limitations.
- Unit mission statement.
- Unit commander's intent.
- Task organization.

- Concept of the operation (maneuver, fire support, engineering, air defense).
- Coordination.
- Combat service support.
- Command and control.
- Time schedule.
- Rules of engagement (if applicable).
- Minimum force requirements (if applicable).
- Other operational considerations (deception plan, safety guidance, and so on).

E-8. SPECIALIZED BRIEFINGS

Specialized briefings are held to present detailed instructions not required for everyone at the mission briefing. Therefore, the mission briefing requires less time and detail.

a. **Attendance.** Specialized briefings can be held for the following personnel:

(1) Aircraft commanders.

(2) Navigators (for the purpose of studying DZ overlays and timing points, and for comparing routes, checkpoints, and so on).

(3) Radio operators (to detail special communications procedures, use of IFF, strike reports, and so on).

(4) Loadmasters/jumpmasters (including coordination of loading, unloading, or aerial release procedures).

(5) Aeromedical (for air evacuation flights only.)

(6) Combat control team/Army assault team.

(7) Others as required.

b. **S3 Air Brief to Jumpmasters.** As soon as ground tactical and air movement planning is complete and jumpmasters are selected, the S3 Air conducts a jumpmaster briefing. This briefing should include all primary jumpmasters and can include assistant jumpmasters, safety personnel, and leaders of airland chalks in the assault echelon. At this briefing, the S3 Air gives out a jumpmaster packet for each aircraft. The packet and briefing should provide the following:

(1) Mission and ground tactical plan.

(2) Air movement plan.

(3) Names of assistant jumpmasters and safeties; time and place to brief them (if they are not present).

(4) Time and location for initial and final manifest call, prejump training, and uniform and equipment inspections.

(5) Transportation arrangements for moving to the marshaling area or departure airfield.

(6) Time and place for parachute issue and the type of main parachute to be used.

(7) Time a weather decision will be made.

(8) Time and location for briefing.

(9) Aircraft tail numbers, chalk numbers, and parking spots.

(10) Loading time.

(11) Time and location for aircrew and jumpmaster briefing.

(12) Station time.

(13) Takeoff time.

(14) Flight plan (formation, route, checkpoints, direction of flight over the DZ, emergency radio frequencies, and call signs).

(15) Drop time.

(16) Medical support plan.

(17) Landing plan with emphasis on assembly aids and procedures.

(18) Communications procedures on the DZ.

c. **Jumpmaster Briefing to Assistants and Safeties.** Time must be allowed for the primary jumpmaster to brief his assistants and safety personnel before he briefs the jumpers. He provides the information given to him in the S3 Air briefing, assigns duties to all personnel, and gives his concept of actions in the aircraft. He reviews SOP items and addresses possible contingencies. The following are some other items to discuss in this briefing:

(1) Door assignments.

(2) Inspection procedures.

(3) Rigging station assignments.

(4) Exit procedures (including the location in the stick where the jumpmaster exits and the name of the person who assumes his responsibilities after he exits).

(5) Actions of jumpmaster personnel in emergency situations such as emergency bailout, hung parachutist, and so on.

(6) Procedures for handling door bundles.

(7) Briefing duties.

(8) Abort procedures and bump plan.

d. **Jumpmaster/Troop Briefing.** As soon as practical after the first manifest call, the jumpmaster briefs personnel on the details of the operation. Items discussed include the following:

(1) The DZ and alternates.

(2) Type of aircraft.

(3) Chalk number.

(4) Type of parachute.

(5) Briefing on serials, the CDS, heavy drop, and type of aircraft, if part of a larger airborne operation.

(6) Time a weather decision will be made.

(7) Type of individual and separate equipment that soldiers will jump with.

(8) Time and place of parachute issue.

(9) Station time.

(10) Takeoff time.

(11) Length of flight.

(12) Actions in the aircraft.

(13) In-flight emergencies.

(14) Direction of flight over the DZ.

(15) Drop altitude.

(16) Predicted wind speed and direction on the DZ.

(17) Route checkpoints.

(18) Search and rescue procedures.

(19) Landing and assembly plan.

(20) Parachute turn-in points.

(21) Time and place of final manifest call.

(22) Medical support plan.

(23) Obstacles on or near the DZ.

(24) Time and location of any aircraft-related rehearsals.

e. **Aircrew and Jumpmaster Soldier Briefing.** This briefing is given before or after loading the aircraft.

(1) *Preflight.* Items discussed concerning preflight procedures include the following

- Takeoff time.
- Air Force CCT or DZSO contact time (when the jumpmaster will be informed by radio of DZ conditions).
- Drop time.

(2) *In-flight.* Items discussed concerning in-flight procedures include the following

- Movement in the aircraft.
- Smoking restrictions.
- Airsickness.
- Latrine.
- Lighting.
- Flight altitude.
- Formation and interval.

(3) *Approach to the DZ.* Items discussed concerning procedures during the approach to the DZ include the following

- Checkpoint warning.
- Time warning.
- Visual and oral signals.
- "No drop" signal.
- Jump door restrictions.
- Drop zone identification (jumpmaster must be briefed on what marking features, or both to look for).
- Drop altitude.
- Drop speed.
- Drop heading.

- Number of passes.
- Turnoff direction.

(4) *Emergency procedures.* Items discussed concerning emergency procedures include the following:

- Jettisoning of load.
- Fuselage fire.
- Abandonment of aircraft.
- Emergency bailout.
- Crash landing.
- Ditching.
- Rapid depressurization.
- Malfunctions.
- Towed parachutist.
- Teatment of casualties in the aircraft before the drop.

(5) *Other details.* The briefing official should–

(a) State which jump door affords the best view of the DZ for a safety check.

(b) Name the key people on board who must be advised of a ground abort.

(c) Inform the loadmaster who will command the soldiers on board in an emergency if the jumpmaster is not the last parachutist.

(d) Coordinate receipt of information on the direction and velocity of DZ winds (before the one-minute time warning).

(e) Emphasize to the aircrew the importance of receiving accurate time warnings.

(f) Ensure the loadmaster understands that the soldiers should raise and fasten seats.

f. **Cross-Service Representation.** Because of the close coordination required in airborne operations, each unit should be represented at unilateral briefings given by the other. This pertains mostly to the mission briefings that cover the entire air movement phase. The security requirements of airborne operations dictate that such cross-service representation be limited to supervisory staff and liaison personnel on a need-to-know basis.

E-9. BRIEFING AIDS

Thorough briefing of each person taking part in an airborne operation is essential to the success of the operation. The preassault briefing is conducted in detail, and ground reconnaissance by the airborne unit is impractical. Therefore, the procurement and preparation of briefing aids is vital. Each soldier should enter the target area with enough knowledge to independently perform his duties.

a. All units arrange for briefing aids before entering the marshaling area. Divisional units survey the marshaling camp to find what briefing facilities are provided. Other facilities and aids are procured by divisional units, as needed.

(1) Briefing aids (such as maps, air photos, slide projectors, kits for making terrain models, movie projectors, and screens) can be obtained from higher headquarters.

(2) Briefing aids such as charts, sketches, diagrams, terrain models, and sand tables are made.

(3) Low-altitude air photos of the landing area (from intelligence channels), on which photo interpreters mark terrain features and the size and shape of the landing area, are also useful.

(4) Large-scale maps with antiairborne obstacles and defenses overprinted on them are very useful. Accurate sand table models and terrain models can be made from these maps.

b. Requirements for briefing aids vary with the operation, the construction facilities available, and supply of materials and equipment. No standard set of briefings aids is prescribed.

Section II. INSPECTIONS

Unit commanders, leaders, and other selected personnel (jumpmasters, riggers, and so on) conduct inspections to prepare the unit for operations. Several types of inspections are conducted during the marshaling process.

E-10. INITIAL INSPECTION

The initial inspection is performed after the first manifest call. Each parachutist is checked for proper uniform (including ID card and tags), for the condition of his parachutist helmet and air items, and for properly rigged equipment.

E-11. DEPARTURE AIRFIELD LAYOUT INSPECTION

Rigged equipment is checked at the departure airfield to ensure that items such as rucksacks, weapons, and bundles are properly rigged. This can save the time it would take a parachutist to rerig his equipment. The equipment is quickly checked during parachute issue.

E-12. JUMPMASTER PERSONNEL INSPECTION

The jumpmaster personnel inspection is held while parachutists rig. Because individual rigging is completed at different times, care must be taken to maintain the exit sequence. If this is not done, cross loading and unit assembly plans might be affected. (See FM 57-220 for more detailed information.)

E-13. JUMPMASTER INSPECTION OF THE AIRCRAFT

The jumpmaster, accompanied by the USAF loadmaster, inspects the aircraft and coordinates any activities peculiar to the airborne operation. He checks the inside and outside of the aircraft. (See FM 57-220 for more detailed information.)

a. In parachute aircraft, airborne representatives check–

- Coverings on protruding objects that might be dangerous to parachutists.
- Aerial delivery system, including the release mechanism.
- Anchor line cable.
- Static line retrieval system.
- Parachute doors.
- Air deflector/air spoiler.
- Jump platforms.
- Warning and jump signals.
- Seats and safety belts.
- Locations and number of auxiliary exits, first-aid kits, air sickness bags, and ear plugs.
- Stowage of loose equipment in the cargo compartment.
- Ditching equipment and emergency bell.
- Location and condition of latrines.

b. In airlanding aircraft, airborne soldiers check items listed for parachute aircraft and inspect–

- The cargo tie-down system.
- Floors for strength, load spreaders, and treadways.
- Loading ramps.
- Cargo doors for their locations, size, and operation.

c. The pilot and the airborne representative jointly inspect after the equipment and supplies are loaded. The aerial delivery system on parachute aircraft is checked for proper rigging. Weight and balance figures are rechecked for safety. The cargo tie-down system and the ACL are also checked.

d. Just before the soldiers enplane, a final joint check is made to ensure that the aircraft is properly loaded and ready for takeoff.

E-14. INSPECTION OF EQUIPMENT AND AIRDROP LOADS

The marshaling plan should call for detailed inspections of equipment aided by maintenance personnel from the supporting MACG. This ensures that all items of equipment are in the best possible condition before rigging or loading. All rigged loads, low velocity or LAPES, must be inspected to ensure that they, and the equipment used on them, are assembled and installed to meet the criteria outlined in the rigging manuals. The types of inspections are discussed herein.

a. **First Inspection.** This type of inspection must be performed on a rigged load before it leaves the rigging site. It must be conducted by a qualified parachute rigger supervisor other than the one supervising the installation of parachutes and extraction systems.

b. **Before-Loading Inspection.** This type of inspection must be performed on a rigged load before it is loaded into the aircraft. It must be held jointly by school-certified inspectors from the unit supplying the equipment to be dropped, the aerial port loading the equipment, and the aircrew loadmaster dropping the equipment.

> **NOTES:** 1. School-certified inspectors must have successfully completed the Airdrop Load Inspector Certification Course of the US Army Quartermaster School.
>
> 2. DD Forms 1748 or 1748-1 is used to perform and record the before- and after-loading inspections according to AR 59-4/AFR 55-40/OPNAVIST 4630.24B/MCO 13480.1B.

c. **After-Loading Inspection.** This type of inspection must be performed on a load after it has been loaded and rigged in the aircraft. It must be held jointly by school-certified inspectors from the unit supplying the equipment being dropped, the aerial port loading the equipment, and the aircrew loadmaster dropping the equipment. This inspection is not done by inspectors that performed the before-loading inspection.

Section III. SPECIAL TRAINING AND REHEARSALS

Rehearsals are always conducted and are vital to mission accomplishment. Specialized training of ground forces and aircrews is required for some missions.

E-15. PREMISSION TRAINING

As soon as an airborne unit receives a planning directive for an assault landing, all unit training is aimed at preparing the soldiers for that operation.

a. **Analysis of Mission, Enemy, and Terrain.** An analysis of the unit mission, the enemy situation, and the terrain in the objective area reveal the problems that will confront the unit after it lands.

b. **Review of Training Program.** A review of the training program will show what specific operational training the unit needs to improve its combat efficiency for the operation. To add realism, training areas are selected that resemble the objective area. Mock-ups are made of the installations, obstacles, landmarks, and enemy defenses in the objective area.

c. **Specialized Training.** All units, including platoons and squads, receive specialized combat training for the type of fighting and equipment their mission requires, and training on enemy vehicles and equipment, For example, when the unit must capture a town or village, it receives intensive training in house-to-house and street fighting for a night operation, the unit receives night training. Techniques of air movement, landing and reorganization are also trained after landing. As the detailed plan develops, however, specialized or refresher training is given on the methods or techniques to be used in the coming operation. This training includes the following:

(1) Packing of equipment containers.

(2) Loading of personnel and equipment into aircraft, especially when previous training has not included that type of aircraft.

(3) Parachute drops and assault transport landings under the expected combat conditions.

(4) Use of assembly aids.

(5) Prejump training for parachutists.

E-16. SPECIAL TRAINING IN USE OF AIRCRAFT

Before marshaling, units are trained to use the aircraft that will transport them, including loading and ditching techniques and flight safety rules. If training in loading and air movement techniques has not been completed, units will receive more training during marshaling. Sometimes, an unfamiliar type of aircraft will be used, or a known type of airlift aircraft will have new or modified equipment. This could include tie-down devices, loading ramps, cargo doors, light and bell signals, ditching gear, or aerial delivery systems. Units may have to marshal for an airborne assault without recent training in airborne techniques. When airborne soldiers need special training in loading and air movement, the airborne and airlift commanders at the departure airfield prepare a training program together.

E-17. MISSION REHEARSALS

Because speed and precision are important in airborne operations, every detail of the OPLAN should be rehearsed, especially for night operations. Lack of equipment or training can limit the scale of the rehearsal or create artificial conditions. Rehearsals should be like the operation. They are held from squad to the highest level allowed by time and facilities. Because rehearsals may cause a breach of security, division and higher commanders control the conditions under which they are held.

a. The complex nature of airborne operations requires cooperation, coordination, and rehearsals between the participating services. Early planning ensures that the following are available:

- Airlift aircraft.
- Suitable training areas.

- Critical items of equipment to replace those damaged or lost.
- Replacements for casualties sustained during rehearsals.

b. Problems (inherent to airborne operations) that can be rehearsed are listed by priority, not by sequence. During these rehearsals, airborne forces should combine into combat teams exactly as they will in the ground operation. These rehearsals can include the following

(1) Execution of the tactical plan.

(2) Communications procedures for the ground attack and en route.

(3) Assembly and reorganization after landing. (This can be rehearsed by "tailgating" ground transportation.)

(4) Loading of aircraft IAW Air Force balancing procedures and requirements.

(5) Landing and unloading procedures for airland assault aircraft, including actions of the AACG.

(6) Supply and casualty evacuation after landing.

(7) Marshaling procedures.

c. If it is not possible to stage operational rehearsals, a thorough CPX should be held under field conditions similar to those in the projected combat area. Few, if any, restrictions apply for the holding of a CPX on the highest level. Command post exercises should be conducted for all echelons, including airlift forces.

d. A joint critique should be held after battalion and larger-scale airborne rehearsals. Lower echelons should be rated even if time prohibits the joint critique.

E-18. REHEARSAL OF AIRLIFT FORCES

The following are included in rehearsals of airlift forces.

- Inspection, maintenance, and servicing of all aircraft.
- Takeoff and assembly procedures.
- Close formation and low-level flying in both daylight and darkness.
- Use of instruments and navigational aids, including ways to employ the JAAP.
- Assembly of aircraft at departure bases IAW the aircraft parking plan.

APPENDIX F

INTELLIGENCE PREPARATION OF THE BATTLEFIELD

The IPB process is that portion of the intelligence cycle that integrates enemy doctrine with the weather and terrain and relates these factors to the mission and specific battlefield situation. It provides a basis for determining and evaluating enemy capabilities, vulnerabilities, and probable courses of action. It also serves as the planning basis for the formulation of the unit's concept of the operation and for the allocation of combat power as reflected in the unit's organization for combat. The process is especially critical to the commander, the intelligence officer, the operations officer, the battlefield deception element, and the field artillery intelligence officer. The brigade or battalion S2 relies on the higher staff headquarters to provide detailed information to conduct the informal IPB at their level. The formal IPB process is performed at division, corps, and higher levels.

F-1. THE PROCESS

As with the intelligence cycle, the IPB process is cyclic in nature. All IPB functions are performed continuously and concurrently. (Figure F-1.) The IPB provides situation and target information with which to compare friendly and enemy courses of action. This information is used to predict target activity and to produce event-related forecasts of battlefield operations.

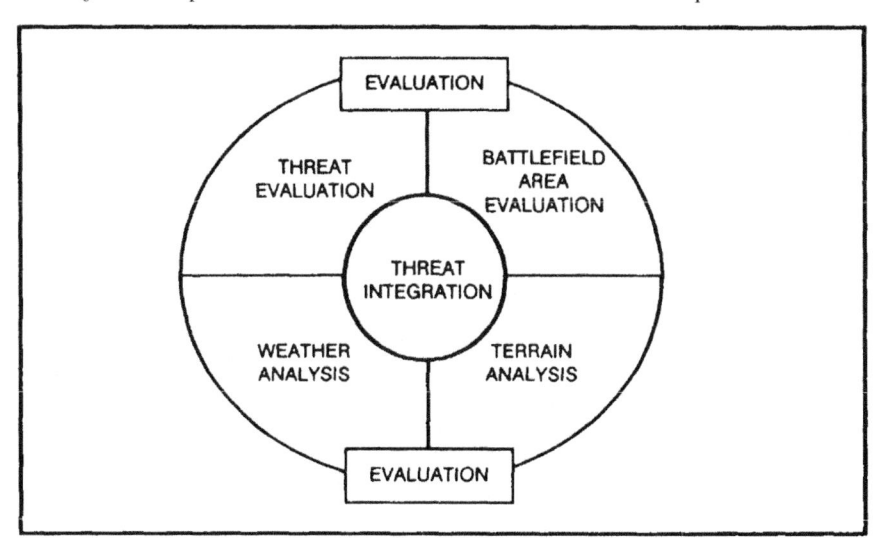

Figure F-1. The IPB process.

a. Information required to develop the IPB is received from all available sources. These include current intelligence holdings, information from higher headquarters, and information from national intelligence agencies.

b. Airborne IPB must combine both ground IPB and air IPB. Airborne operations are offensive in nature and require certain aspects of terrain to be analyzed for success. Landing, drop, and extraction zones are crucial for delivery of the airborne force to the objective area. Requirements for airfields for follow-on forces compel consideration of the MOUT aspects of terrain since airfields are usually located near built-up areas.

F-2. BATTLEFIELD AREA EVALUATION

Battlefield area evaluation involves assessing the battle area with regard to the overall nature of the friendly and enemy forces and the operating environment. The terrain and weather are evaluated to determine how they affect operations. Enemy forces (including, ground, air, and when appropriate, naval forces), which are expected to operate within the battle area, are evaluated to determine their capabilities in relation to the weather, terrain, and friendly mission. Battlefield evaluation should call attention to significant areas and features that must be considered during the IPB effort. (Figure F-2.)

a. The battlefield consists of the following:

(1) The area of operations is the geographical area where the commander has been assigned the responsibility and authority to conduct military operations. The assigned AO is based on METT-T factors and planning considerations beyond the FLOT.

(2) The air area of operation is similar to the ground AO in that air bases, refueling points, LZs, DZs, and air defense weapons and radars operate within the commander's boundaries. The major difference between air and ground operations is the height or operating ceiling within which fixed- and rotary-wing aircraft operate and air defense weapons can fire.

(3) The area of interest is based on METT-T and the commander's concept of the operation. It includes all enemy activities which might affect the friendly force during the operation. The G2 or S2 recommends the AI to the commander based on IPB. The commander approves the AI, and it is forwarded to the next higher echelon by the intelligence officer where it serves as a base for supporting intelligence requirements.

(4) The air AI is normally much larger than the ground AI because of the vast distances they can cover and the speed with which they can influence operations. The air AI extends upward to the maximum ceiling of enemy aircraft and to the maximum effective altitudes of friendly and enemy air defense systems. (Figure F-2 shows the relationship between these elements.)

b. The intelligence officer must fully understand these relationships to assist the commander in planning a successful airborne operation. (See FM 34-130 for a complete and detailed discussion of all aspects of the preparation and use of the IPB.)

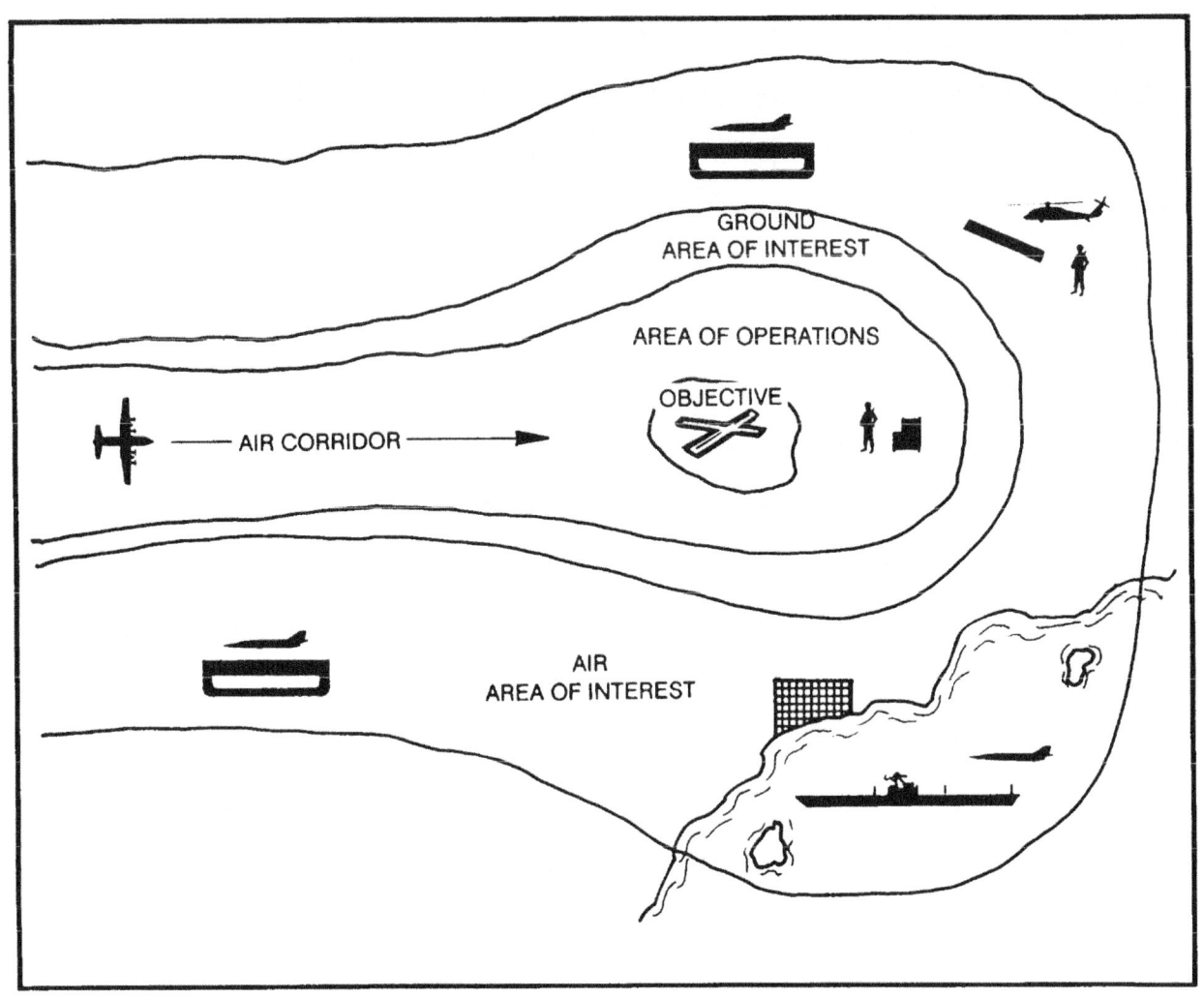

F-2. Ground and air area of operations and interest.

APPENDIX G

N-HOUR DEPLOYMENT SEQUENCE

The N-hour deployment sequence is developed and followed to ensure all reports, actions, and outload processes are accomplished at the proper time during marshaling.

G-1. PREDEPLOYMENT PLANNING AND PREPARATION

Units must prepare internal deployment standing operating procedures and continually update and rehearse them. These SOPS should include actions that are common to all deployments, to include airland as well as parachute assault.

- Conduct no-notice emergency deployment readiness exercise.
- Prepare personnel for overseas deployment.
- Update and review all vehicle load plans.
- Validate and update movement plans with next higher headquarters.
- Update access and recall rosters.
- Review family support group rosters and rear detachment responsibilities.
- Ensure special team personnel are identified and trained (air movement/planning, NBC, outload, ammunition handling, and so on).

G-2. EXAMPLE OF N-HOUR SEQUENCE

The following example N-hour sequence aids a unit in developing their own deployment schedule based on their needs. (Table G-1, page G-2.) It is flexible to allow for modifications based on the mission and the unit commander's concept of the operation.

FM 90-26

N-HOUR SEQUENCE - BRIGADE				
	BDE HQ	**1st BN**	**2d BN**	**3d BN**
N-Hour	**SDO:** Immediately call the EOC to confirm the message and hand carry the message to all units not receiving the FAX. Verify recall of schools and SD personnel.	**SDO:** Execute internal alert and assembly.	**SDO:** Execute internal alert and assembly.	**SDO:** Execute internal alert and assembly.
N+1	**SIGO:** Div command net open. **S3:** Pick up FRAGO at div. **ALL:** Personnel draw weapons, masks, special equipment. Commence property storage plan and securing POVs. **S2, S3, SIGO:** Set up room as OPs center with div cmd net and an STU III.	**S1/S4:** Commence POV and personal property security plan. **S2:** Unit area secured (coord in person, FM, messenger, or landline). **KEY PAX:** List questions for N+2 meeting.		
N+1:30	**S3:** Commence establishment of S3 planning cell. **OPNs SGT:** Make 30 copies of FRAGO for attachments and DRF 1. Open Log. Five drivers from DRF 9 report. Three to DRF 1 and two to DRB 1. **STAFF/LOs:** Meeting in OPs center. Issue FRAGO. **ALL:** POV storage begins.			
N+2	**S1:** Report assembly to EOC; 50 percent assembly required. **KEY PAX:** N+2 brief (seating predesignated). **S2:** Brief HHC bde guard detail.	**ALL:** One hundred percent assembled. Squad-level protective mask inspection. **S3 AIR:** Request through bde the use of scales (if necessary).	**S3 AIR:** Request through bde the use of scales (if necessary).	**S3 AIR:** Request through bde the use of scales (if necessary).

Table G-1. Example brigade alert sequence checklist.

	BDE HQ	1st BN	2d BN	3d BN
N+2 (cont.)	**DRIVERS:** Report to vehicle holding area w/equipment. **COMMO:** Cut phones (cdr, S3); issue contingency LOIs, bde FM net up. **S4:** Prioritize the sequence of basic load ammo from ASP for separate bn DRF slices at N+2 brief.	**DRIVERS:** Report to vehicle holding area w/equipment. **KEY PAX:** N+2 brief. **FIRST 29,** Ready to roll.		
N+2:30	**DRIVERS:** Inspect vehicles; verify load cards. **COMMO:** RATELOs report to SIGO. **AIR REP:** To heavy drop rigging site. **DRIVERS:** Depart vehicle holding area.	**S4:** Ballast ammo departs ASP. **DRIVERS:** Inspect vehicles; verify load cards and depart vehicle holding area. **S3 AIR NCO:** First 29 must depart; dispatch PVL to HDRS and ULACC. Send keys for IRC cage to HDRS.		
N+3	**S3:** Provide LO to EOC. **S4:** Coordinate with DTO for comfort pallets and in-flight rations. Request Class IV from G4 SGM. Coordinate for marshaling area occupation. **COMMO:** Provide SECOMP requirement to ADSO. **S3 AIR:** PVL to DMCC.			

Table G-1. Example brigade alert sequence checklist (continued).

	BDE HQ	1st BN	2d BN	3d BN
N+3 (cont.)	**OPNs SGT:** Break down div OPORD to LOs; issue warning order; establish time schedule.			
N+3:15	**XO, S1, S4:** Meet cdr and S3 at div HQ to provide concept update (NLT N+3:15).	**S4:** Ballast ammo arrives at HDRS. Sign for ballast ammo (after loaded on vehicles) and release of PRVEP.		
N+3:30	**XO and S4:** Attend N+3:30 meeting at N+2 room. **S4:** Update request for contingency items and Class IV with G4. **CHEMO:** Coordinate with div for NBC equipment for entire DRB 1 and attachments.	**XO and S4:** Attend N+3:30 meeting at N+2 room. **S4:** Sign for ballast rations at HDRS. **S3 AIR NCO:** Remaining vehicles report to HDRS/CLACC. **S3 AIR:** Finalize PVL.	**XO and S4:** Attend N+3:30 meeting at N+2 room.	
N+3:45	**S3 AIR NCO:** ADP cards to bn air NCO for assault CP.	**S3 AIR:** update DMMC and HDRS OIC of PVL changes. Link up w/DRF 9, S3 AIR. **ALL:** Load 80 pax (if moving to PHA).		
N+4	Report DRF 2 assembly (85 percent required). **S3:** Complete preformatted OPORD. Prepare charts. **OPNs SGT:** Copy and collate bde OPORD, as required.	**S3:** Provide LO between HDRS and DMMC (Air NCO). **S1:** Coordinate with 82d PSC for POR.	**S1:** Report assembly to bde (85 percent required). Vehicle preparation begins.	

Table G-1. Example brigade alert sequence checklist (continued).

	BDE HQ	1st BN	2d BN	3d BN
N+4:30	**STAFF:** Issue bde OPORD. **S4:** PRVEP derigged if airland option. **S3 AIR:** HD rigging must begin; inform EOC.	**S3 AIR:** HD rigging must begin. Finalize airdrop landing plan. **PA:** Pick up narcotics.		
N+5	**S3 AIR:** N+5 brief at DMMC.	**KEY PAX:** Warning order. **S3 AIR:** Initial pax manifest (paper). N+5 brief at DMMC.		
N+5:30	**S3 AIR:** Organize airland chalks at central area control center. **S3 SECTION:** Move to PHA.	**S3 AIR NCO:** Div assault CP vehicles arrive at HDRS. Organize airland chalks.		
N+5:45	**S4:** Receive door bundle/air item requirement.	**S3 AIR:** Initial JM brief. **S4:** Submit door bundle air item requirements.		
N+6	**S1:** Submit personnel strength report to G1. Provide finance a list of personnel requiring emergency-type financial service. **S4:** Update MMEE shortage with G4. Forward DA Form 3953.	**S4:** MMEE transfer completed. Deliver basic issue worksheet for IIA and ESIP at PHA. Coordinate with OIC ESIP. Forward request for Class A agent fund.	**DRIVERS:** Complete admin procedures and begin moving radios, weapons, and sensitive items.	**ALL:** Eighty five percent completed.

Table G-1. Example brigade alert sequence checklist (continued).

	BDE HQ	1st BN	2d BN	3d BN
N+6 (cont.)	**S3 AIR:** Twenty percent load packets to ADACG. Coordinate with GLO for AMC. Initial HD or A/L chalks move to ramp area. **SIGO:** Confirm number of SECOMPS and chalks w/ADSO.	**S3 AIR:** Twenty percent load packets to ADACG. Hot A Meal.		
N+6:30		**KEY PAX:** OPORD. Run trial manifest.		
N+7	**S4:** Final coordination on w/ESIP OIC; coordinate for parachute issue: 463L pallets, nets, and plastic arrive at PHA (double check). Plan for 1.5 pallets for each company.	**S4:** Final coordination w/ESIP OIC; coordinate for parachute issue: 463L pallets, nets, and plastic arrive at PHA (I.5 pallets for each company). Sign for individual issue rations. **S3 AIR:** ADP cards to ADACG (NLT N+7). **CHEMO:** Hood and filter inspection/change.		
N+8	**S4:** Commence ESIP; coordinate w/DCC to move pallets to ramp area. **SIGO:** Commex.	**S4:** Commence ESIP; rig pallets; mark pallets rigged with chemical defense equipment. **SIGO:** Commex. **S3 AIR/S4:** Rig door bundles.		
N+8:30				**S3 AIR NCO:** Complete vehicle inspection.

Table G-1. Example brigade alert sequence checklist (continued).

	BDE HQ	1st BN	2d BN	3d BN
N+9	**S3 AIR:** One hundred percent load packets to ADACG.	**S3 AIR:** One hundred percent load packets to ADACG; complete rigging door bundles.	**KEY PAX:** Warning order. **S3 AIR:** PVL finalized.	
N+9:15		**PLT LDRs:** Issue OPORD.	**S4:** Sign for ballast ammo at HDRS.	
N+9:45			**S4:** Pax load 7 x 80 pax. **S3 AIR:** To DCC w/load plans, etc., and tentative air movement plan.	
N+10		**S1:** Funding team arrives to fund Class A agents.	**SELECT ELEMENTS:** Arrive PHA. **S3 AIR:** Run manifest.	**ALL:** Continue personnel and admin preparation. **S3 AIR:** ULACC opened; vehicle preparation begins; driver's equipment moved.
N+10:15	**ALL:** Initial manifest call.	**ALL:** Initial manifest call.	**CHEMO:** Squad leader mask inspection.	
N+10:30	**S4:** Submit door bundle/air item requirement for DRF 2.	**JMs:** Latest time to conduct prejump.	**S4:** Submit door bundle/air item requirement.	
N+10:45			**S3 AIR:** Initial JM brief. **S3 AIR NCO:** Vehicles depart ULACC.	
N+11			**S4:** Sign for ballast rations at HDRS. **PA:** Pick up narcotics.	
N+11:30	**SIGO:** RATELO rig inspection.			

Table G-1. Example brigade alert sequence checklist (continued).

FM 90-26

	BDE HQ	1st BN	2d BN	3d BN
N + 12	**S4:** Notify DMMC and EOC of pickup point for DRF 3. **S3:** Div staff brief covering changes (optional). **S3 AIR:** Coordinate for AMB. **TAC CP:** Assembly/mission rehearsal.	**LEADERS:** Assembly/mission rehearsals. **S4:** Sign for in-flight rations; direct position of parachutes and air items.	**S4:** Coordinate w/ESIP OIC for N + 14 issue requirements. **S3 AIR:** Heavy drop rigging begins.	
N + 12:30			**KEY PAX:** OPORD.	
N + 13	**S4:** Final coordination for DRF 2 ESIP. **ALL:** Final manifest.	**ALL:** Final manifest. **S3 AIR:** Brief drivers on HE recovery, chalks for airland.	**S4:** Door bundle air items, 463L pallets, nets, and plastic arrive at PHA. **S3 AIR:** Determine type parachute issue.	**KEY PAX:** Warning order.
N + 13:15	**SIGO:** SECOMPS commo check.			
N + 13:30			**S3 AIR:** Final JM brief. **S3:** Sand table brief.	
N + 13:45				**S4:** Sign for ballast ammo at HDRS.
N + 14	**S3 AIR:** HD rigging for DRF 1 complete. **S1:** Submit strength report for DRF 3.	**S3 AIR:** HD rigging complete.	**S4:** Commence ESIP; rig pallets (mark those w/chemical equipment). **JMs:** Rig door bundles.	**S4:** Move pax to PHA w/7 x 80 pax.
N + 14:30	**ALL:** Move to ramp area.	**S4:** Move to ramp area.		**KEY PAX:** OPORD.
N + 15		**JMs:** Mock door training.	**S3 AIR:** Twenty percent load packet to ADACG.	**S3 AIR:** Run initial pax manifest. **PA:** Pick up Mark I injectors and narcotics.

Table G-1. Example brigade alert sequence checklist (continued).

	BDE HQ	1st BN	2d BN	3d BN
N + 15:30	**KEY LEADERS:** Final update/change brief on the ramp.	**KEY LEADERS:** Final update/change brief on the ramp.		
N + 15:45				**S3 AIR:** Initial JM brief. **S4:** Provide door bundle/air item request.
N + 16	**ALL:** Parachute issue. **S1:** DRB deployment roster and PERSTAT to G1.	**ALL:** Parachute issue. **ALL:** Move to ramp area if in-flight rig.		
N + 16:30	**S4:** Provide supplemental meal, if desired.			
N + 17				**S4:** Final coordination w/OIC ESIP. **S3 AIR:** Determine type parachute issue.
N + 17:15	**ALL:** Load time.	**ALL:** Load time.		
N + 17:30	**ALL:** Station time.	**ALL:** Station time.		Sand table briefings.
N + 18:00	WHEELS UP FIRST AIRCRAFT. **NOTES**	WHEELS UP FIRST AIRCRAFT.	**LEADERS:** Rehearsals. **S3 AIR:** One hundred percent load packets to ADACG.	**S4:** Commence ESIP, rigging 463L pallets. **JMs.:** Rig door bundles. **S3 AIR NCO:** Vehicles move from ULACC.

Table G-1. Example brigade alert sequence checklist (continued).

GLOSSARY

AA	assembly area
AAA	air avenues of approach
AACG	arrival airfield control group
AALPS	automated air loading planning system
AATCC	Army air traffic control center
AB	air base
ABCCC	airborne battlefield command and control center
abn	airborne
ACC	air control center
ACL	allowable cargo load
ACP	assembly control post
ADA	air defense artillery
ADACG	arrival/departure airfield control group
ADP	automatic data processing
ADSO	assistant division signal officer
AECC	aeromedical evacuation control center
AF	Air Force
AFB	Air Force base
AFM	Air Force manual
AFR	Air Force regulation
AFSOB	Air Force special operations base
AFSOP	Air Force standing operating procedure
AG	Adjutant General
AGL	above ground level
AH	attack helicopter
AI	air interdiction
A/L	air land
ALACC	aircraft landing area control center
ALCC	airlift control center
ALCE	airlift control element

ALFT	airlift
ALO	air liaison officer
ALPS	automated load planning system
AM	amplitude modulation
AMB	air mission brief
AMC	air mission commander
ammo	ammunition
AMO	air movement officer
ANGLICO	air and naval gunfire liaison company
AO	area of operations
APO	Army Post Office
AR	Army regulation
ARFOR	Army forces
ARNG	Army National Guard
ASAP	as soon as possible
asbly	assembly
A S K	Army Standardization Coordinating Committee
ASL	authorized stockage list
ASOC	air support operations center
ASP	ammunition supply point
AT	antitank
ATC	air traffic control
atch	attachment
ATO	aircraft transfer order
ATT	air transportability training
A^2C^2	Army airspace command and control
avg	average
AWACS	airborne warning and control system
AWADS	adverse weather aerial delivery system
BAI	battlefield air interdiction
BCC	battlefield coordination center
bde	brigade
bn	battalion

BOS	battlefield operating systems
BSA	brigade support area
C^2	command and control
C^3	command, control, and communications
camo	camouflage
CARP	computed air release point
CAS	close air support
cbt	combat
CCT	combat control team
cdr	commander
CDS	container delivery system
CESO	communications-electronics staff officer
cfm	cubic feet per minute
chemlite	chemical light
chemo	chemical officer
CI	counterintelligence
CIF	Central Issue Facility
CINC	Commander in Chief
CLACC	central loading area control center
clas	classified
cmd	command
c o	commanding officer
COMALF	Commander of Airlift Forces
COMDTINST	commandant's instruction
comf	comfort
commex	communications exercise
commo	communications
COMSEC	communications security
CONPLAN	contingency plan
const	construction
CONUS	continental United States
coord	coordinate; coordination
COSCOM	Corps Support Command

CP	command post
CPX	command post exercise
CRC	command and reporting center
CRP	control and reporting post
CS	combat support
CSF	casualty staging facility
CSS	combat service support
CTA	common table of allowances
CUCV	commercial utility cargo vehicles
CWIE	container, weapon, and individual equipment
DA	Department of the Army
DACG	departure airfield control group
DACO	departure airfield control officer
DCA	Defense Communications Agency
DCC	DISCOM control center
DCS	Defense Communications System
DF	direction finding
DISCOM	Division Support Command
div	division
DLIC	detachment left in contact
DMCC	division movement control center
DMDG	digital message device group
DMJP	Dragon missile jump pack
DMMC	division materiel management center
DOD	Department of Defense
DRB	division ready brigade
DRF	division ready force
DS	direct support
DSA	division support area
DSC	division support communications
DST	decision support templating
DTO	division transportation officer
DZ	drop zone

DZST	drop zone support team
DZSTL	drop zone support team leader
EAC	echelon above corps
E&E	escape and evasion
ech	echelon
ECM	electronic countermeasures
EDRE	emergency deployment readiness exercise
EEFI	essential elements of friendly information
e.g.	for example
elev	elevation
enl	enlisted
EOC	Emergency Operations Center
EPW	enemy prisoner of war
equip	equipment
ESIP	equipment supply issue point
ESM	electronic warfare support measures
etc.	et cetera
EW	electronic warfare
EZ	extraction zones
F	Fahrenheit
FA	field artillery
FAAR	forward area alerting radar
FAC	forward air controller
FACE	forward aviation combat engineering
FACP	forward air control post
FARP	forward area resupply point
FASCAM	family of scatterable mines
FASCO	forward area support coordinator
FAST	forward area support team
fax	fascimille
FCT	firepower control teams
FDC	fire direction center

FEBA	forward edge of the battle area
1SG	first sergeant
FIST	fire support team
fl	flight
fld	field
FLOT	forward line of own troops
FLS	field landing site
FM	field manual; frequency modulated
FMSC	Federal Manual for Supply Cataloging
FO	forward observer
FOB	forward operating base
FORSCOM	United States Army Forces Command
frag	fragmentary
FRAGO	fragmentary order
FSA	fire support area
FSB	forward support base
FSE	fire support clement
FSMC	forward support medical company
FSO	fire support officer
FSS	fire support station
ft	foot
G1	Assistant Chief of Staff (Personnel)
G2	Assistant Chief of Staff (Intelligence)
G3	Assistant Chief of Staff (Operations and Plans)
G4	Assistant Chief of Staff (Logistics)
G5	Assistant Chief of Staff (Civil Affairs)
gal	gallon
GAR-I	ground to air responder–interrogator
GLO	ground liaison officer
GMRS	ground marked relief system
gren	grenade
GRREG	graves registration
GS	general support

GSR	ground surveillance radar
GTP	ground tactical plan
HAHO	high altitude, high opening
HALO	high altitude, low opening
HD	heavy drop
HDRS	heavy drop rigging site
HE	heavy equipment
HEPI	heavy equipment point of impact
HF	high frequency
HHC	headquarters and headquarters command
HMMWV	high-mobility, multipurpose wheeled vehicle
HQ	headquarters
hr	hour
HUMINT	human intelligence
hwy	highway
IAW	in accordance with
ID	identification
IEW	intelligence and electronic warfare
IFF	identification, friend or foe (radar)
IHF	improved high frequency
IMC	instrument meteorological conditions
inc	included
IOM	install, operate, and maintain
IP	initial point
IPB	intelligence preparation of the battlefield
IPW	prisoner of war interrogation
IR	infrared
IRC	initial ready company
ISB	intermediate staging base
JA	joint airborne
JAAP	joint airborne advance party
JACC	joint airborne communication center

JAG	Judge Advocate General
JCS	Joint Chiefs of Staff
JCSE	joint communications support element
JFC	joint force commander
JM	jumpmaster
JOC	joint operation center
JRCC	joint rescue coordination center
JSEAD	joint suppression of enemy air defenses
JSOF	joint special operation force
JTF	joint task force
KIA	killed in action
KIAS	knots indicated air speed
KTAS	knots true air speed
LACC	loading area control center
LAPES	low-altitude parachute extraction system
LAW	light antitank weapon
LBE	load-bearing equipment
lbs	pounds
LC	line of contact
LD	line of departure
ldr	leader
LIC	low-intensity conflict
LMF	Light Marine Force
LO	liaison officer
LOB	line of bearing
LOC	lines of communication
LOI	letter of instruction
LOS	line of sight
LRS	long-range surveillance
LRSU	long-range surveillance unit
LSA	logistics support area
LSI	largest single item

LZ	landing zone
m	meters
MAC	Military Airlift Command
MACG	marshaling area control group
MACR	Military Airlift Command regulation
maint	maintenance
MASF	mobile aeromedical staging facility
max	maximum
MBA	main battle area
MC	mobility corridors
MCO	movement control officer
mech	mechanized
med	medical
MEDEVAC	medical evacuation
METT-T	mission, enemy, terrain, troops and time available
MHE	materiels-handling equipment
MHz	megahertz
mi	miles
MI	military intelligence
mil	military
min	minute
mm	millimeter
MMC	Materiel Management Center
MMEE	minimum mission-essential equipment
MOC^2	mission-oriented command and control
MOG	maximum-on-ground
MOPP	mission-oriented protective posture
mort	mortar
MOS	military occupational speciality
MOUT	military operations on urbanized terrain
MP	military police
mph	miles per hour
MRE	meal–ready to eat

MRO	materiel release order
msn	mission
MTP	mission training plan
MVR	maneuver
NAF	Naval Air Forces
NAI	named areas of interest
NATO	North Atlantic Treaty Organization
NAVAIDS	navigational aids
NBC	nuclear, biological, chemical
NCO	noncommissioned officer
NCOIC	noncommissioned officer in charge
NCS	net control station
NEO	noncombatant evacuation operation
NGF	naval gunfire
NM	nautical miles
No.	number
NOD	night observation device
NWP	Naval Warfare publication
obj	objective
OEG	operational exposure guide
off	officer
OIC	officer in charge
OP	observation post
OPCON	operational control
OPLAN	operation plan
OPNAVINST	operational naval instruction
opns	operations
OPORD	operation order
OPSEC	operations security
opt	optional
ORF	operational readiness float
OVM	on-vehicle materiel

PA	physician's assistant; public address (system)
PAM	pamphlet
PAO	Public Affairs Office(r)
pax	passenger(s)
PDF	Panamanian Defense Force
PE	priority equipment
PERSTAT	personnel status
PHA	personnel holding area
PI	point of impact
PIBAL	pilot balloon (observation)
PIR	priority intelligence requirements
PLL	prescribed load list
plt	platoon
POL	petroleum, oil, and lubricants
POM	preparation of oversea movement of units
POR	preparation of replacement for overseas movement
POV	privately owned vehicle(s)
PP	passage point
PPI	personnel point of impact
prep	prepare; preparation
PRVEP	prerigged vehicles/equipment package
PSC	personnel service company
PSG	platoon sergeant
psi	pounds per square inch
PSYOP	psychological operation
PT	(aircraft)
PVL	priority vehicle list
PW	prisoner of war
R&S	reconnaissance and surveillance
RATELO	radiotelephone operator
RATT	radio teletypewriter
RB	radar beacon

RCT	regimental combat team
recon	reconnaissance; reconnoiter
ref	reference(s)
REMAB	remote marshaling base
REMBASS	remotely monitored battlefield sensor system
rep	representative
reqd	required
retrans	retransmission
ROE	rules of engagement
RP	release point
RSL	remote spring launch
RSTA	reconnaissance, surveillance, and target acquisition
RTFT	round-trip flying time
Rv	radius of Vulnerability
S1	Adjutant
S2	Intelligence Officer
S3	Operations and Training Officer
S4	Supply Officer
S5	Civil Affairs Officer
SACR	Strategic Air Command regulation
SALT	supporting arms liaison team
S&T	supply and transport (unit)
SAR	search and rescue
SATCOM	satellite communication(s)
Scty	security
SD	special duty
SDO	staff duty officer
SEAD	suppression of enemy air defense
SECOMP	secure en route communications package
SERE	survival, evasion, resistance and escape
SCM	sergeant major
SGT	sergeant
SHF	super high frequency

SHORAD	short-range air defense
SIGINT	signal intelligence
SIGO	signal officer
SKE	station keeping equipment
SKE/ZM	station keeping equipment/zone marker
SO	safety officer
SOCCE	special operations command and control element
SOF	special operations force
SOI	signal operation instructions
SOP	standing operating procedure
spt	support
sq	square
SSAN	Social Security Account number
SSB	single side band
sta	station
STANAG	Standardization Agreement
STOL	short takeoff and landing
STU III	(a secure telephone)
syn	synthetic
sys	system
t	ton
TAACOM	Theater Army Area Command
TAC	Tactical Air Command
TACAIR	tactical air
TACC	tactical airlift control center
TACP	tactical air control party
TACS	tactical air control system
TACSAT	tactical satellite
TAES	tactical aeromedical evacuation system
TAP	Tactical Air Force
TAI	target areas of interest
TALO	tactical air liaison officer
TAW	tactical air wing

TB	technical bulletin
TBP	to be published
T/D/AC	tons per day per aircraft
TDAR	tactical defense alert radar
tech	technician
TEMIG	tactical electronic magnetic ignition generator
TF	task force
tgt	target
TGT	total ground time
TLP	troop-leading procedure
tm	team
TM	technical manual
TO	takeoff
TOC	tactical operations center
TOE	table(s) of organization and equipment
TOT	time over target
TOW	tube-launched, optically tracked, wire-guided (missile)
TPL	time phase line
TRADOC	Training and Doctrine Command
trns	trains
TSR	tactical surveillance and reconnaissance
TT/D	total tons per day
UAV	unmanned aerial vehicle
UHF	ultra high frequency
ULACC	unit loading area control center
US	United States
USAF	United States Air Force
USAR	United States Army Reserve
USMC	United States Marine Corp
USNG	United States National Guard
UTE	utilization time
UTM	universal transverse mercator (grid)
veh	vehicle

vert	vertical
VFR	visual flight rules
VHF	very high frequency
VIRS	verbally initiated release system
VMC	visual meteorological conditions
VTOL	vertical take-off/landing
w	with
w/o	without
WO	warning order
WOC	wing operations center
wpns	weapons
wt	weight
xmtr	transmitter
XO	executive officer
yds	yards

REFERENCES

DOCUMENTS NEEDED

These documents must be available to the intended users of this publication.

*CTA 50-909.	Field and Garrison Furnishings and Equipment. 1989.
*FM 1-100.	Doctrinal Principles for Army Aviation in Combat Operations. 28 February 1989.
*FM 57-220.	Basic Parachuting Techniques and Training. 31 December 1984.
*FM 57-230.	Advanced Parachuting Techniques and Training. 13 September 1989.
*FM 100-27.	US Army/US Air Force Doctrine for Joint Airborne and Tactical Airlift Operations (AFM 2-50). 31 January 1985.
*FM 100-28.	Doctrine and Procedures for Airspace Control in the Combat Zone (AF Manual 1-3; NWP 17, LMF 04). 1 December 1975.
*FM 100-42.	US Air Force/US Army Airspace Management in an Area of Operations. 1 November 1976.
*FM 100-103.	Army Airspace Command and Control in a Combat Zone. 7 October 1987.
*TM 38-250.	Packaging of Materials Handling: Preparing of Hazardous Material for Military Air Shipments. 15 January 1988.

READINGS RECOMMENDED

These readings contain relevant supplemental information

AR 59-4.	Joint Airdrop Inspection Records, Malfunction Investigation and Activity Reporting (AFR 55-40; OPNAVINST 4630.24B; MCO 13480.1B). 27 November 1984.
AR 210-1.	Private Organizations on Department of the Army Installations. 15 July 1981.
AR 210-10.	Administration. 12 September 1977.
AR 220-10.	Preparation of Oversea Movement of Units (POM). 15 June 1973.

*This source was also used to develop this publication.

FM 90-26

AR 350-30.	Code of Conduct/Survival, Evasion, Resistance and Escape (SERE) Training. 10 December 1985.
AR 750-1.	Army Materiel Maintenance Policy and Retail Maintenance Operations. 31 October 1989.
FM 3-5.	NBC Decontamination. 24 June 1985.
FM 5-101.	Mobility. 23 January 1985.
FM 6-20-30.	Tactics, Techniques, and Procedures for Fire Support for Corps and Division Operations. 18 October 1989.
FM 7-8 (HTF).	The Infantry Platoon and Squad (Infantry, Airborne, Air Assault, Ranger), How to Fight. 31 December 1980.
FM 7-20.	The Infantry Battalion (Infantry, Airborne and Air Assault). 28 December 1984.
FM 7-30(HTF).	Infantry, Airborne and Air Assault Brigade Operations, How to Fight. 24 April 1981.
FM 7-85.	Ranger Unit Operations. 9 June 1987.
FM 8-55.	Planning for Health Service Support. 15 February 1985.
FM 10-20.	Organizational Maintenance of Military Petroleum Pipelines, Tanks and Related Equipment. 20 February 1984.
FM 10-30.	Central Issue Facility. 14 November 1985.
FM 10-400.	Quartermaster Airdrop and Airdrop Equipment Support Units. 2 November 1984,
FM 12-6.	Personnel Doctrine. 23 August 1989.
FM 14-7.	Finance Operations. 9 October 1989.
FM 16-1.	Religious Support Doctrine: The Chaplain and Chaplain Assistant, 27 November 1989.
FM 20-150.	National Search and Rescue Manual. (NWP-19; AFM 64-2; COMDTINST M16130.2). 1 November 1986.
FM 21-76.	Survival. 26 March 1988.
FM 22-100.	Military Leadership. 31 October 1983.
FM 24-1.	Combat Communications. 11 September 1985.

Reference-2

FM 25-100.	Leadership Counseling. 3 June 1985.
FM 25-101.	Battle Focused Training: Battalion Level and Lower. TBP.
FM 34-25.	Corps Intelligence and Electronic Warfare Operations. 30 September 1987.
FM 34-60.	Counterintelligence. 14 August 1985.
FM 34-80.	Brigade and Battalion Intelligence and Electronic Warfare Operations. 15 April 1986.
FM 34-130.	Intelligence Preparation of the Battlefield. 23 May 1989.
FM 41-10.	Civil Affairs Operations. 17 December 1985.
FM 43-5.	Unit Maintenance Operations. 28 September 1985.
FM 55-9.	Unit Air Movement Planning. 31 August 1981.
FM 63-20.	Forward Support Battalion. 17 May 1985.
FM 90-10-1 (HTF).	An Infantryman's Guide to Urban Combat (How to Fight). 30 September 1982.
FM 100-10.	Combat Service Support. 15 February 1988.
FM 101-5.	Staff Organization and Operations. 25 May 1984.
FM 101-5-1.	Operational Terms and Symbols. 21 October 1985
FM 101-10-1/2.	Staff Officers Field Manual-Organizational Technical, and Logistical Data, Planning Factors (Volume 2). 7 October 1987.
MAC Regulation 3-3.	Combat Control Team Operations and Procedures. 12 April 1983.
MAC Regulation 55-130.	Loadmaster Abbreviated Checklist. October 1987.
STANAG 3466/ ASCC 44/18C.	Responsibilities of Air Transport Units and User Units in the Loading and Unloading of Transport Aircraft in Tactical Air Transport Operations, Edition 2. 5 June 1975.
STANAG 3570/ ASCC 44/13G.	Drop Zones and Extraction Zones–Criteria and Markings, Edition 3. 26 March 1975.
TAC Regulation 55-130.	EC-130 Aircrew Operational Procedures. September 1988.
TM 5-330.	Planning and Design of Roads, Airbases, and Heliports in the Theater of Operations. 6 September 1968.

TM 5-337.   Paving and Surfacing Operations. 21 February 1966.

TRADOC Pam 34-4.   AWACS–Army Contingency Voice Operating Procedures: (ATDO). 4 March 1986.

INDEX

A

aeromedical evacuation, C-5 to C-6 (illus)

airborne battlefield command and control center (ABCCC)
    communications capability, D-2
    duties, D-2
    missions, D-2

aircraft specific data and comparisons, C-11 to C-16

air defense
    early warning, 8-15
    elements, 8-14 to 8-15

airdrop. See combat service support.

Air Force support
    air traffic control, 8-12
    command and air control, 8-11 to 8-12
    missions, 8-9 to 8-10
    tactical support, 8-10 to 8-11

airhead
    assault objective, 3-4 to 3-6
    early warning capability, 8-15
    line, 3-4 to 3-6
    occupation, 3-14
    organization, 3-14
    size, 3-14

airland
    advantages, 4-9
    disadvantages, 4-9
    organization, 4-9 to 4-10

airlift
    aeromedical, C-2, C-5
    civil reserves, C-2
    commanders
        airborne, 2-2
        airlift, 2-2
        joint responsibilities, 2-2
    cycle time, C-6 to C-7
    factors, C-1

    operational support, C-2
    resources, C-1
    strategic, C-1
    support requirements, C-5
    tanks and cargo, C-2
    theater, C-2

air movement plan
    administative movement, 5-2
    aircraft loads, 5-10 to 5-11
    air movement table, 5-12 to 5-13
    considerations, 5-3 to 5-5
    joint planning, 5-1
    manifests, 5-13
    requirements, 5-2 to 5-3
    tactical movement, 5-2
    vehicle load planning, 5-6 to 5-7

ANGLICO forces, 8-7 to 8-8

Army aviation
    deployment, 8-13 to 8-14
    helicopter, 8-12 to 8-13

Army warning and control system (AWACS), D-1

assault
    buildup, 3-14 to 3-16
    combat power, 3-14 to 3-16
    conduct of, 3-12 to 3-14
    development, 3-14
    echelon 2-8, 3-11
    follow-on echelon, 2-8, 3-11
    objectives, 3-4 to 3-6
    organization,
        assault echelon, 2-8, 3-11
        rear echelon, 2-8, 3-11
    reorganization, 4-27

assembly
    equipment, 4-19
    security, 4-26 to 4-27

B

battlefield operating systems (BOS), 1-7

briefbacks, 2-9, E-7 to E-8
    planning, E-1

briefing
    aids, E-12 to E-13
    command and staff, E-7
    facilities, E-1 to E-2
    joint, E-2 to E-3
    jumpmaster, E-8 to E-1 2
    mission, E-3
    responsibilities, E-2
    scope, E-3 to E-7
    specialized, E-8
    troop, 4-22

C

combat control team (CCT)
    deployment, A-1 to A-2
    employment, A-1
    functions, A-2 to A-4
    mission, A-2
    organization, A-4

combat service support
    airdrop, 9-9
    considerations, 9-3 to 9-5
    field services, 9-12 to 9-13
    logistical structure, 9-1 to 9-2
    maintenance, 9-9 to 9-12
    responsibilities, 9-2 to 9-3
    resupply, 9-9 to 9-10
    supplies, 9-5 to 9-9
    transportation, 9-12

combat support
    aspects, 8-2 to 8-3
    elements, 8-1
    execution, 8-4 to 8-5
    liaison, 8-4
    planning, 8-5 to 8-6

command and control, 1-10

communications
    aircraft, 8-26 to 8-28
    command and control nets, 10-6 to 10-16
    considerations, 10-3 to 10-4
    controlling airspace, 10-18
    electronic warfare assets, 10-18 to 10-19
    plans, 10-4 to 10-6
    signal facilities, 10-2 to 10-3
    techniques, 10-17 to 10-18

container delivery system, 4-6, A-6, A-7 (illus)

countermobility, 1-9 to 1-10

D

decision-making process, 2-3, 2-4 (illus)

drop zones
    assembly aids, 4-19
        aircraft, 4-21
        audible, 4-20
        clock system, 4-18
        electronic, 4-20 to 4-21
        equipment, 4-19 to 4-21
        field expedient, 4-21
        line-of-flight, 4-18
        Stiner, 4-19 to 4-20 (illus)
        visual, 4-19
    assembly and reorganization
        cross loading, 4-15 to 4-16
        heavy-drop loads, 4-16
        individual equipment and weapons, 4-16
        personnel, 4-16
    assessments, B-8
    configuration
        capacity, 4-12
        shape, 4-11
        size, 4-11 to 4-12
    construction, 4-11
    cover and concealment, 4-11
    criteria/selection, A-5 to A-7
    day markings, A-7 to A-8
    factors affecting assembly
        dispersion, 4-23
        state of training, 4-23
        visibility, 4-23
    identification, 4-10
    key terrain, 4-11
    natural, 4-19
    night markings, A-9 to A-10
    operations, B-5
    orientation, 4-12 to 4-13
    out of range, 4-10
    selection of, 4-10
    straight-line approach, 4-10
    support team leader
        duties, B-1 to B-2
        qualifications, B-2
        responsibilities, B-2, B-4
    unit assembly, 4-22 to 4-24
    visibility, 4-23
    weather and terrain, 4-10 to 4-11

E

early warning capability, 8-15

echelonment, 2-8

equipment delivery
    airland 4-9 to 4-10
    container delivery system, 4-6
    door bundles, 4-7
    free drop, 4-6
    heavy drop, 4-7
    high altitude, low opening (HALO), 4-7
    high velocity, 4-6
    low-altitude parachute extraction system (LAPES), 4-8
    low velocity, 4-7
    sequence of delivery, 4-4
    supply airdrop
        advantages, 4-5
        disadvantages, 4-5
    wedges, 4-7

engineers
    countermobility, 1-9 to 1-10
    FACE missions, 8-17 to 8-18
    mobility, 1-9 to 1-10
    survivability, 1-9 to 1-10

exfiltration, 7-8 to 7-9

extraction zones, 4-10

F

fire support, 1-9, 8-2

follow-on echelon, 2-8, 3-11

forms (examples)
    air movement planning worksheet, 5-8 (illus)
    basic planning guide, 5-8 to 5-9 (illus), 5-10
    drop zone support team/aircrew mission briefing checklist, B-3 (illus)
    vehicle load card, 5-6 to 5-7 (illus)

forward area combat engineering (FACE) missions. See engineers

forward operating base (FOB), 7-19

G

ground marked release system, B-6 to B-7

ground tactical plan, 3-1

H

helicopter missions, 8-12 to 8-13 (illus)

high altitude, low opening (HALO)/high altitude, high opening (HAHO), A-6

I

identification markings
    assault aircraft, 4-21
    equipment, 4-21, B-4
    personnel, 4-21

inspections, E-13 to E-15

intelligence, 1-8 to 1-9
    assets, 8-22
    evaluation, F-2 to F-3 (illus)
    support 8-22 to 8-23

intelligence preparation of the battlefield (IPB)
    area evaluation, F-2 to F-3
    process, F-1

intermediate staging base (ISB), 7-18 to 7-19

J

joint airborne advance party (JAAP), 4-18, A-1

joint responsibilities. See airlift.

L

landing plan
    area study, 4-3
    commander's priorities, 4-2 to 4-3
    considerations, 4-3 to 4-4
    methods of landing, 4-4
    priorities, 4-4
    requirements, 4-2 to 4-3

subunit plans, 4-3
tactics, 4-3
time-space factors, 4-4

landing zone
    assault zone, A-10
    construction, 4-11
    day and night operations, A-11 to A-13
    expeditionary zone, A-10
    markings, A-11
    visual aids, A-12 to A-13

limitations of forces, 1-6

long-range surveillance (LRS) team
    functions, A-4 to A-5
    mission, A-4
    organization, A-5

low-altitude parachute extraction system (LAPES), 4-8
    day operations, A-14
    multiple operations, A-15
    night operations, A-14

M

maneuver, 1-8 to 1-9

manifests
    flight, 5-13

marshaling
    camps, 6-4 to 6-5
    dispersal, 6-3
    movement, 6-2 to 6-3
    N-hour, 6-1
    passive defense during, 6-3
    plans, 2-6, 6-1
    preparation before, 6-1 to 6-2
    rehearsals, 6-1
    requirements, 6-5 to 6-9
    responsibilities, 6-10 to 6-12

materiels-handling equipment, C-4

military police support, 8-32 to 8-33

missions
    operational, 1-4
    strategic, 1-4
    tactical, 1-4 to 1-5

mobility, 1-9 to 1-10

multiple-lateral impact points, 4-24 to 4-25

N

naval gunfire (NGF), 8-7 to 8-9

NBC
    MOPP levels, 8-36 to 8-39
    planning, 8-33
    protective measures, 8-34 to 8-36
    responsibilities, 8-33 to 8-34

N-hour
    example brigade checklist, G-2 to G-9
    sequence, G-1
    standing operating procedure, G-1

noncombatant evacuation operations (NEO), 7-14 to 7-16

O

outload, 6-12

P

parachute(s)
    areas, 6-8 to 6-9
    issue, 6-2 to 6-3
    rigging, 6-7 to 6-9

payloads
    average, C-2
    maximum, C-2
    restrictions, C-2 to C-3

personnel
    casualty reports, 9-14
    replacement, 9-13 to 9-14
    responsibilities, 2-2
    strength accounting, 9-13

phases of airborne operations
    air movement, 1-7
    ground tactical, 1-7, 3-1
    landing, 1-7
    marshaling, 1-6 to 1-7

planning
    assets, 2-6 to 2-7
    considerations, 2-7 to 2-11
    responsibilities, 2-1

prisoners of war, 9-17 to 9-18

R

rapid assembly
    activities, 4-25

rear echelon, 2-8, 3-11

reconnaissance and security forces, 3-7

rehearsals, 2-9, 6-1 to 6-2, E-16 to E-17

remote marshaling base, 7-17 to 7-18

reserves, 3-11
    battalion, 3-12
    brigade, 3-12
    division, 3-11

reverse planning
    air movement plan, 2-5 to 2-6
    assets, 2-6
    considerations, 2-7 to 2-11
    ground tactical plan, 2-3
    landing plan 2-5
    marshaling plan, 2-6

S

security
    force operations, 7-14
    measures, 4-26 to 4-27

special operations force (SOF), 2-10 to 2-11

specific missions
    operational, 1-4
    strategic, 1-4
    tactical, 1-4 to 1-5
survivabiilty, 1-9 to 1-10

T

tactical operations, 7-1
    airfield seizure, 7-10
    breakout from encirclement, 7-9
    exfiltration, 7-8 to 7-9
    raids, 7-1 to 7-4
    recovery, 7-4 to 7-5
    relief, 7-10
    supporting 7-16
    survival, 7-9
    withdrawal, 7-3

training
    premission, E-15 to E-16
    program, 1-3
    specialized, E-16
    unit, 1-3
    use of aircraft, E-16

U

unit withdrawal/evacuation
    factors, 7-6
    responsibilities, 7-6 to 7-7
    sequence, 7-6

W

warning and control systems, D-1

FM 90-26
18 DECEMBER 1990

By Order of the Secretary of the Army:

CARL E. VUONO
General, United States Army
Chief of Staff

Official:

JOHN A. FULMER
Colonel, United States Army
Acting The Adjutant General

DISTRIBUTION:

Active Army, USAR, and ARNG: To be distributed in accordance with DA Form 12-11E, requirements for FM 90-26, Airborne Operations (Qty rqr block no. 4655)

☆ U.S. GOVERNMENT PRINTING OFFICE : 1992 O - 324-919 (45107)

Printed in Great Britain
by Amazon